BUILDING TRADES PRINTREADING-Part 3

HEAVY COMMERCIAL CONSTRUCTION

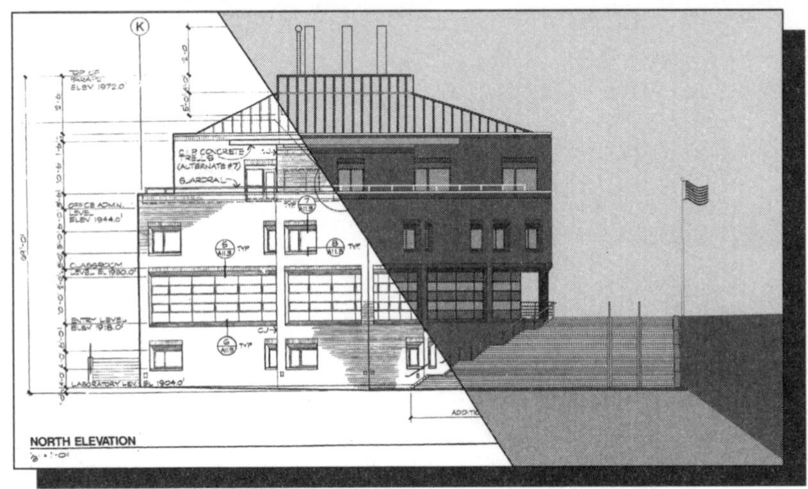

AMERICAN TECHNICAL PUBLISHERS, INC.
HOMEWOOD, ILLINOIS 60430

Leonard P. Toenjes

5
A7.3

Acknowledgments

The author and publisher are grateful to the following companies and organizations for providing technical information and assistance. Companies preceded by an asterisk (*) have provided material that was used on the cover.

BSI Constructors Inc.
The Burke Company
Butler Manufacturing Company, Buildings Division
The Construction Specifications Institute
Dayton Superior Corporation
Elcon Associates
*Fabcon, Inc.
Fred Weber, Inc.
*INTEGRUS Architecture, P. S.
Joint Center for Higher Education
Missouri State Highway Department
MW Consulting Engineers
Nunn's Hauling Co., Inc.
Republic Steel Corporation
Rilco Laminated Products, Incorporated
Riley Engineering, Inc.
RoseWater Engineering, Inc.
Spokane Intercollegiate Research & Technology Institute
Symons Corporation
Tarlton Corporation
Tate Access Floors, Inc.
United States Steel Corporation

© 1996 by American Technical Publishers, Inc.
All rights reserved

1 2 3 4 5 6 7 8 9 – 96 – 9 8 7 6 5 4 3

Printed in the United States of America

ISBN 0-8269-0455-6

ATP made in USA

Contents

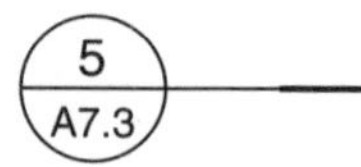

Introduction

Building Trades Printreading - Part 3 is a completely new book designed to provide printreading experience in heavy commercial construction. This text-workbook presents and reinforces concepts regarding elements commonly found on prints of large structures. Included are types of construction, specifications, sitework, structural steel construction, reinforced concrete construction, mechanical and electrical systems, and finish construction. Many of the illustrations were adapted directly from CAD plans of heavy commercial construction projects.

Chapters 1 through 7 conclude with Review Questions designed to test chapter content. Chapters 2 through 7 follow the Review Questions with Trade Competency Tests. Chapter 8 is the Final Test for the book and is based on content throughout the book. Prints of actual construction projects are used to answer Trade Competency Tests and the Final Test. References indicating the particular sheet(s) containing prints for each test are given before the first question. The legend around the borders of the print sheets indicates the print(s) located on both sides of the sheet. The size of each print has been modified and should not be scaled. Space is provided for all answers for Review Questions, Trade Competency Tests, and the Final Exam. Always record answers in these spaces. All answers are given in *Building Trade Printreading - Part 3 Instructor's Guide.*

A comprehensive Appendix contains many useful tables and other reference information. See page 169 for a listing of material in the Appendix. The Glossary contains terms used in *Building Trades Printreading - Part 3* and heavy commercial construction.

The Publisher

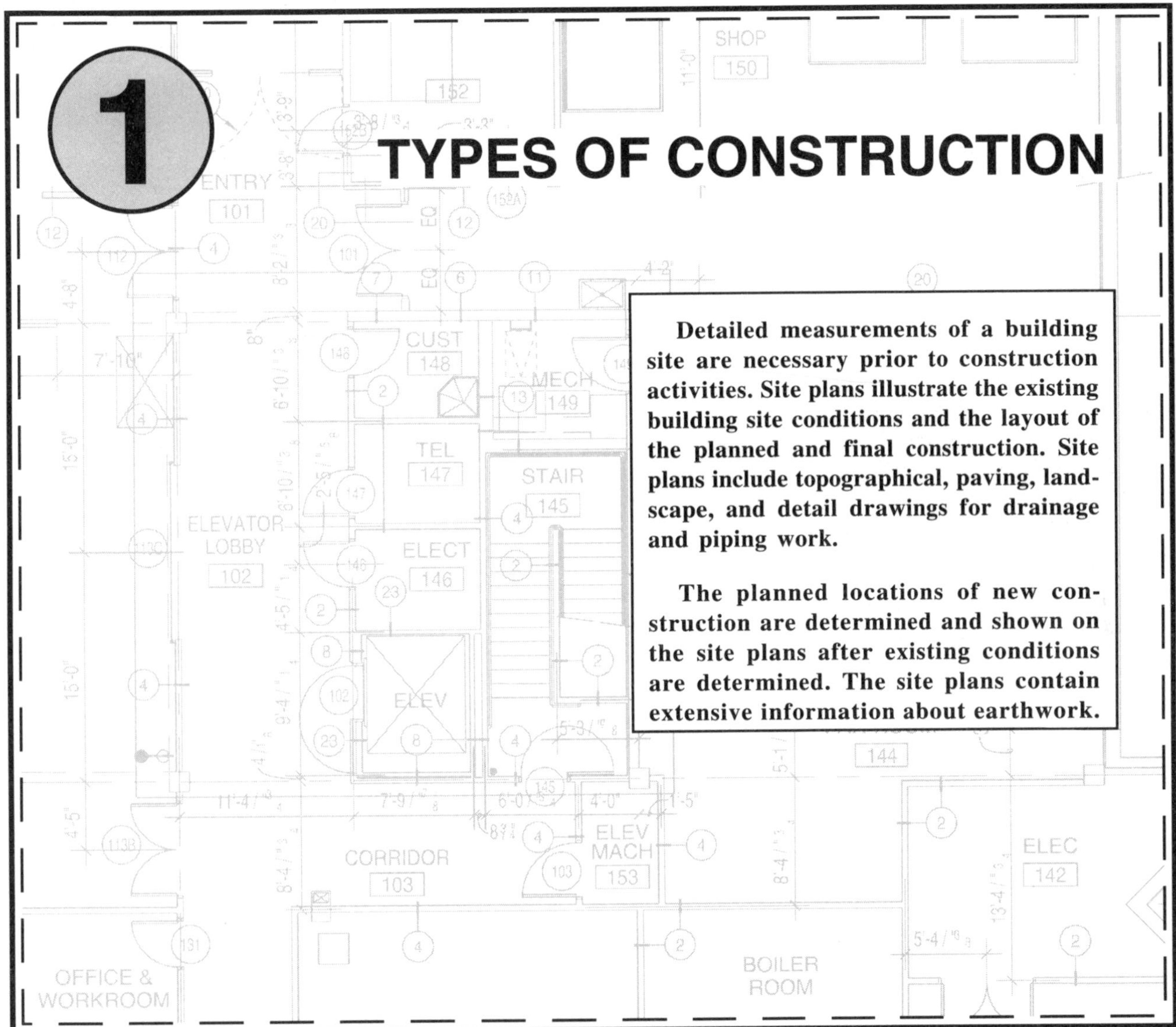

1 TYPES OF CONSTRUCTION

Detailed measurements of a building site are necessary prior to construction activities. Site plans illustrate the existing building site conditions and the layout of the planned and final construction. Site plans include topographical, paving, landscape, and detail drawings for drainage and piping work.

The planned locations of new construction are determined and shown on the site plans after existing conditions are determined. The site plans contain extensive information about earthwork.

BUILDING PLANNING

Buildings are made in a great number of types and styles to serve many functional requirements as well as artistic concepts. Industrial and commercial construction is the business of planning and building many types of structures. These structures include roads, bridges, waterworks, retail establishments, manufacturing plants, office buildings, schools, places of worship, public gathering places, and many other large structures. The accurate interpretation of all components of a large scale set of prints is important for all members of the construction team on any building project. New problems of enclosing space and building engineering structures occur constantly.

Building Process Participants

To properly plan and build complex structures, many individuals must communicate with each other in a clear manner. Owners, architects, engineers, contractors, suppliers, and tradesworkers involved in the building process need printreading skills to agree on the size and scope of the overall building project.

Owners. An individual or organization must fully and accurately communicate its building needs to begin the building process. The needs for a structure which must be considered include location, size, placement, appearance, use, and cost. Owners or their agents can benefit from printreading knowledge, ensuring their building needs are met.

Architects. The architect's primary responsibility is to listen to an owner and accurately interpret their needs and desires into a building plan. The architect must ensure that the owner's final product meets all structural, building code, and final use requirements. Architects meet with owners and develop prints and specifications which guide the construction process. See Figure 1-1. These prints are also used by owners and governmental agencies to obtain financing, competitive bids, and building permits.

Figure 1-1. Architects and owners define the scope of a building project together and communicate their project with prints and specifications.

Engineers. Structural, mechanical, environmental, soil, and electrical engineers assist the architect in the planning process. Engineers provide accurate information concerning the allowable and tolerable stresses which various components of a structure can bear. This includes soil-bearing capacity, the live and dead loads placed on structural members, electrical loads, and the ability of mechanical systems to properly heat, cool, and ventilate an area. See Figure 1-2.

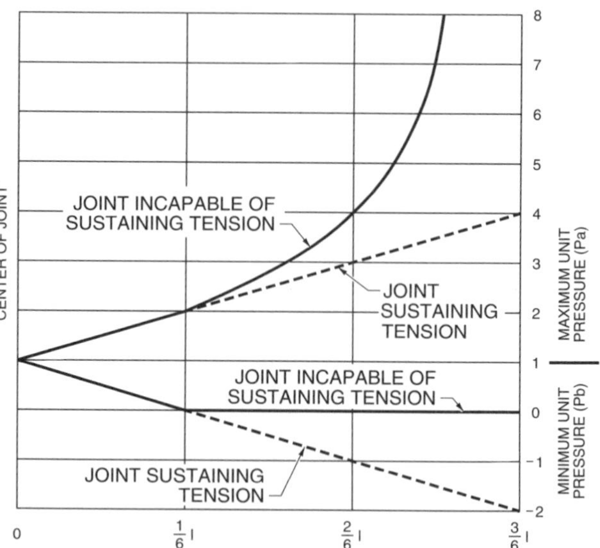

Figure 1-2. Engineering measurements and charts provide the specific scientific information necessary to ensure workability and safety of a structure.

Contractors. General contractors and subcontractors use prints to generate costs for building construction. Estimates for quantities of building materials and labor times are taken from the prints. The prints and specifications are also used along with the labor and material estimates to plan and perform the actual construction when awarded a contract.

Contractors may supply various services to owners and architects. Various arrangements, such as design-build, construction manager, and project manager allow the contractor to combine a broad range of services, including architectural, engineering, oversight of the bidding process, and building services into a single package.

Suppliers. Architects, engineers, and contractors must rely on suppliers for the latest information concerning available materials. Suppliers also rely on other members of the building planning team to use their materials in the construction project. Specifications often mention a specific material or building component by manufacturer's name to ensure a certain level of quality. See Figure 1-3.

Tradesworkers. It is ultimately the responsibility of the superintendents, lead workers, and journey-level workers on the job site to build the structure. Knowledge of printreading, tools available, and proper materials use are all combined to complete the construction project.

MANUFACTURER'S PART NUMBER

```
2.02 Double Check Valve Assembly

     Double Check Valve Assembly shall be a Rainbird Model
     DCA-250, Febco #805Y, or equal.  All check valve internal
     parts shall be easily accessible from the top of the
     device without removing the check valve body from the
     line.
```

Figure 1-3. Certain building products may be mentioned by manufacturer's name and part number to clarify the architect's design specifications.

Competitive Bidding Process

It is in the best interest of the owner and architect to obtain the construction services lowest in price. It is also in their best interests to ensure that the contractor selected to build the project meets certain quality and reliability standards. In some states, contractors must be licensed to perform construction work. In other states, architects and owners must make judgments concerning the skill and integrity of contractors.

For these reasons, many elements must be considered in the competitive bidding process in addition to the lowest bid price. These include bonding capacity, association affiliation, quality of previously completed projects, and references from prior and current customers.

Standard Forms. The American Institute of Architects (AIA) and the Associated General Contractors of America (AGC) are two construction industry groups that have developed standard forms for bidding construction projects. See Figure 1-4.

THE AMERICAN INSTITUTE OF ARCHITECTS

AIA Document A191

Standard Form of Agreement Between Owner and Design/Builder

THIS DOCUMENT HAS IMPORTANT LEGAL CONSEQUENCES; CONSULTATION WITH AN ATTORNEY IS ENCOURAGED.

This Document comprises two separate Agreements: Part 1 Agreement—Preliminary Design and Budgeting and Part 2 Agreement—Final Design and Construction. Hereinafter, the Part 1 Agreement is referred to as Part 1 and the Part 2 Agreement is referred to as Part 2.

PART 2 AGREEMENT—FINAL DESIGN AND CONSTRUCTION

AGREEMENT

made as of the day of in the year of Nineteen Hundred and

BETWEEN the Owner:
(Name and address)

and the Design/Builder:
(Name and address)

(Include Project name, location and detailed description of scope.)

Figure 1-4. Standardized bidding forms provide all participants in the bidding process a common method for communicating bid information.

These forms provide reliable and consistent information for all involved in the bidding process. Governmental agencies also use standardized bidding documents for federal, state, and municipal projects.

Role of Participants. Architects distribute plans and specifications with a closing date for bids to be accepted. Contractors and subcontractors prepare their bids according to the plans and specifications and submit prices for their work. Subcontractors bid their particular component of the project and submit their costs to a general contractor. The general contractor combines the subcontractor bids with the costs for general contracting services. These make up the total project bid cost.

After the bid closing date, the architect, owner, or governmental agency opens the bids and determines if a qualified bid has been received within their projected cost. If not, the project may be modified and rebid. If the bids are satisfactory, a contract is awarded to the lowest qualified bidder and work begins. Permits are obtained, materials ordered, and the project is built.

Figure 1-5. CD-ROM provides up-to-date materials information in a readily accessible format.

Materials and Methods

Many technological developments in construction materials and methods have created the ability to build structures which could not have been built in the past. These developments include newly developed materials and new uses for existing materials, uses for computerized building control systems, and new construction procedures made possible by advances in tools and equipment.

Materials. Engineering developments in the design and properties of new materials create an almost endless variety of alternatives for structural engineers and architects. The exchange of information between engineers, product designers and manufacturers, building owners, and architects is essential to ensure the most appropriate materials become part of the structure. Catalogs and computer media available on CD-ROM provide a wealth of information each year concerning the latest developments in materials. See Figure 1-5. Planners of modern structures determine the proper uses of many different materials, such as concrete, steel, wood, metals of many types, plastics, glass, and fiberglass.

In addition to these materials, computerized building systems require careful planning of the mechanical and electrical equipment systems installed in new structures. Controllers of sophisticated design are installed in buildings to control lighting, landscape watering, heating and cooling, ventilation, communication, and alarm systems. Each of these requires a high level of technical and printreading knowledge to ensure proper installation and operation.

Methods. The development of new construction methods has greatly changed the length of time necessary, the skills required by all involved in the building process, and the procedures for building construction. Automation and prefabrication play an ever increasing role in the building process.

New methods of scheduling and the ability to install large prefabricated units has shortened the time necessary for many construction processes. New tools and procedures have increased the skill levels needed by tradesworkers on a construction site. For example, the use of laser equipment for operations as diverse as surveying and finish ceiling installation requires skills which were not necessary in the past. See Figure 1-6. New procedures, such as the use of tilt-up and precast materials place additional demands on the expertise of all involved in a construction project.

Figure 1-6. Developments in tools and equipment have changed construction methods.

Geographic Requirements

Planners must take a number of regional variations into account in the design and construction of large building projects. Variations in climate, soil conditions, building codes, construction materials, environmental legislation, and construction methods have great impact on the design and entire building process.

Climate. Climactic conditions, such as variations in temperature, rainfall, and snow loads impact the design of structural frames and exterior protective systems against the elements and building mechanical systems. Soil conditions vary from area to area and in many cases can change dramatically on a single construction site. This has an impact on foundation planning, shoring requirements, and drainage structures.

Building Codes/Legislation. Even though some standardized building codes exist, local building and zoning commissions normally make modifications to meet the needs of their residents. See Figure 1-7. Environmental legislation creates a need for careful and thorough planning of any structure. These legal requirements may vary from city to city, state to state, and country to country. Planners and designers must remain up-to-date on the latest legislation and the materials available to meet environmental requirements.

PURPOSE OF SECTION

SECTION 1000.0 GENERAL

1000.1 Scope: The provisions of this article shall control the foundation design and construction of all buildings and structures hereafter erected to insure adequate strength of all parts thereof for the safe support of all superimposed live and special loads, in addition to their own dead load, without exceeding the allowable stresses or design capabilities.

BUILDING PERMIT APPLICATION REQUIREMENTS

SECTION 1001.0 BEARING VALUE OF SOILS

1001.1 Soil analysis: All applications for permits for the construction of new buildings or structures, and for the alteration of permanent structures which require changes in foundation loads and distribution shall be accompanied by a statement describing the soil in the ultimate bearing strata, including sufficient records and data to establish its character, nature and loadbearing capacity. Such records shall be certified by a licensed professional engineer or a licensed architect.

SITE-SPECIFIC ALLOWABLE MATERIALS

1001.2 Satisfactory foundation materials: Satisfactory bearing materials for spread footings shall include ledge rock on its natural bed; natural deposits of sand, gravel or firm clay, or a combination of such materials, provided they do not overlie an appreciable amount of peat, organic silt, soft clay or other objectionable materials.

Figure 1-7. All building projects in a certain geographic location must conform to the building code adopted for that area.

Materials. Availability of building materials is not consistent in all areas of the world. Building design may be dictated to some extent by the materials which are reasonably available at a building site. Structures in remote locations may require special considerations when necessary building materials must be moved over long distances.

Methods. Local construction methods and terminology vary greatly. For example, the term "jack" in one part of the country or one trade may have an entirely different meaning in another location or another trade. Knowledge of local building practices ensures that all members of the construction team are talking the same language.

CONSTRUCTION SYSTEMS

After consideration of all the factors involved, the owner, architect, and engineer must choose the type of construction system which best fits a particular project. These systems include wood or metal framing, masonry, heavy timber, structural steel, and reinforced concrete. Each has specific applications and advantages. Most structures combine several of the systems to achieve their overall design and purpose. Knowledge of printreading for all the various construction systems is necessary to combine them into a single structure.

Framing

The framing construction system is used in all types of buildings, but is primarily used in small structures, such as dwellings and small commercial buildings. The framing construction system is commonly used for interior partitions. A series of smaller components, including studs, plates, runners, braces, trimmers, and cripples are joined together to form a rigid frame structure. See Figure 1-8. Openings between framing members allow for installation of mechanical and electrical systems. After frames are built from wood or metal components and mechanical and electrical systems and insulation installed, they are covered with any number of materials, such as gypsum drywall, masonry veneer, or wood or metal siding. Flexibility of design and economy are gained in using the framing construction system.

Figure 1-8. The framing construction system is commonly used for interior partitions.

Masonry

Brick and block members are available in many sizes and shapes. See Figure 1-9. Brick and block members are made from many different materials, such as clay, concrete, and glass. Stone is also used for structural and decorative applications. Masonry members are joined with mortar which may be reinforced with various steel shapes. Structures of large size and weight-bearing capacity can be built with masonry materials. These materials are highly fire resistant and often used as fire breaks between adjoining areas of a structure. Considerations must be made to provide openings for piping and ductwork for mechanical and electrical systems during masonry installation. Masonry is also commonly used as a veneer material for other types of construction, such as framing, structural steel, and reinforced concrete. When used as a veneer material, ties are used to anchor the masonry veneer to the structure.

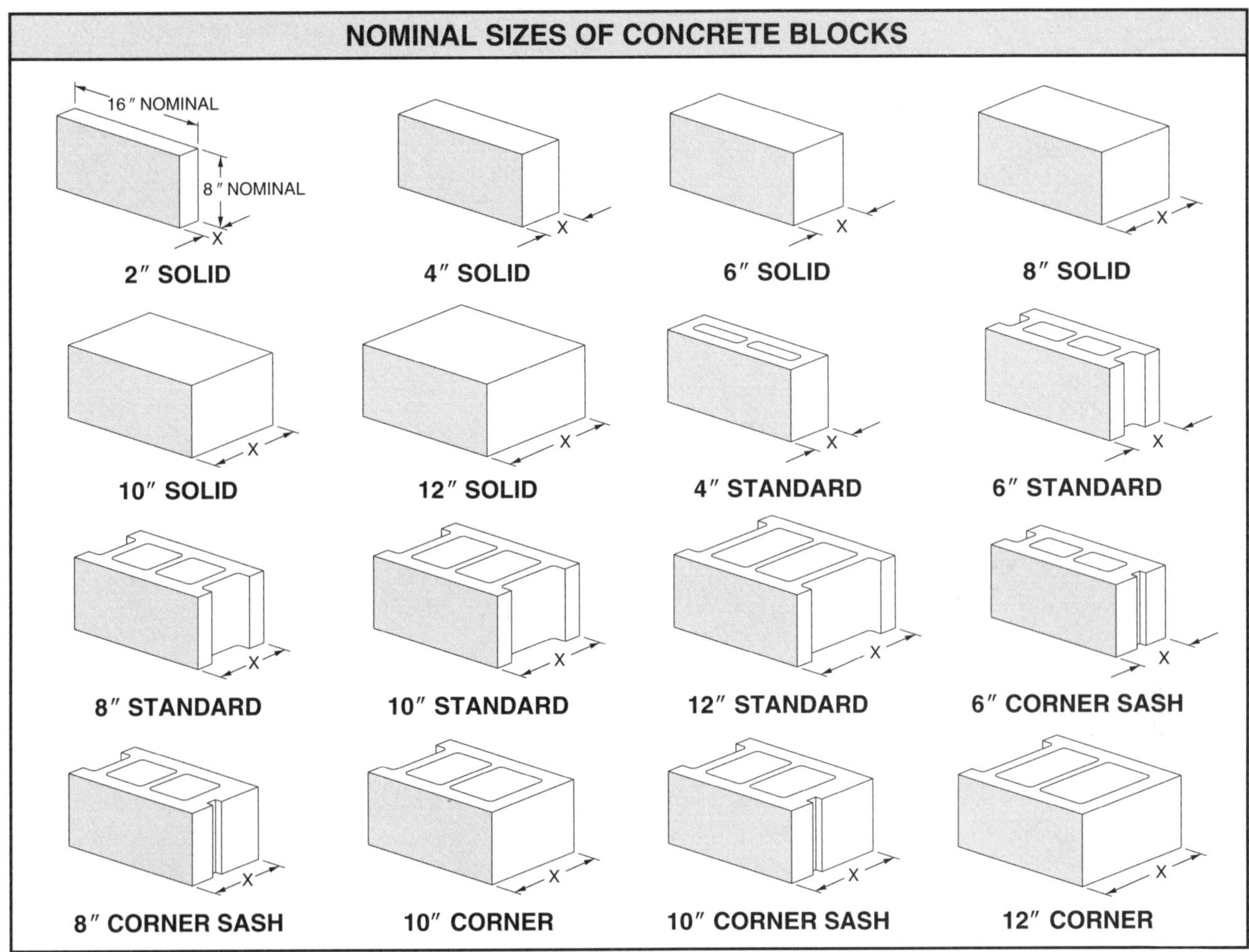

Figure 1-9. Concrete block is a common masonry product which can be obtained in a variety of designs and sizes.

Heavy Timber

In heavy timber construction, large single-piece wood members and glued and laminated members span large, open areas. See Figure 1-10. Exterior and interior applications of heavy wood timbers create open spaces with visual appeal. Either solid timbers or glued and laminated wood members are designated on the prints. The architect designates the sizes and types of wood members to be installed and their properties. This information is provided in the specifications and on the architectural prints.

Solid Timbers. Heavy wood timbers are solid wood members with a minimal nominal thickness of 5″ and a minimal nominal width of 5″. Lengths for these members start at 6′ and increase in increments of 1′ or 2′. Solid wood members are available with rough or smooth surfaces.

Glue-Lam. A series of wood members are joined together to form glued and laminated (glue-lam) wood members. In this method, many smaller and shorter pieces of wood are joined together to span long distances and support heavier loads than could otherwise be carried by single wood members. Use of glue-lam members also allows architects and engineers to create curved wood members which would not be possible with solid timber members. Applications for glue-lam members include floor and roof beams, columns, and trusses of all designs.

Specific types, sizes, and grades of lumber are chosen in engineering glue-lam members. Choices of lumber are based on structural requirements for span and loading and on appearance.

Rilco Laminated Products, Incorporated

Figure 1-10. Heavy timber construction is used by architects to span large, open areas with decorative members.

Engineering of each glue-lam member creates a design which specifies the number of wood plies, the glue to be used, and the overall width, thickness, and length. Wood members are smoothed on the faces to be joined. The individual pieces of lumber are set in their approximate locations relative to each other. Adhesives are applied and the members are clamped together with high-pressure clamping devices. After the adhesives have set, the surfaces of the entire unit are surfaced according to the manufacturing and design specifications.

Structural Steel

Many of the largest buildings in the world are built with the structural steel construction system. Structural steel construction may use lightweight members to build industrial buildings and storage structures or large beam and truss assemblies to build skyscrapers and bridges. A series of horizontal beams and trusses and vertical columns are joined together to create large structures with open areas and great flexibility of design. See Figure 1-11.

Special considerations are given to rigging requirements, working at heights, lifting heavy members into place, and safety for all on the worksite. Structural steel buildings have a number of bracing systems which give this construction system great strength against exterior stresses, such as wind, earthquakes, and other imposed loads. Many different types of cladding can be attached to the exterior of these structures. The cladding materials include glass, metal, masonry, and precast concrete.

Structural steel is a common material for long-span roof truss systems and bridges. Careful engineering and design is performed to ensure that the proper steel shapes, sizes, and connections are used to meet all loading requirements.

Reinforced Concrete

Poured-in-place concrete and precast concrete are two types of reinforced concrete construction systems. Poured-in-place concrete is a system in which wood or metal forming materials are set to a specific shape and act as a mold for the plastic concrete. Reinforcing steel is set in the forms and concrete is placed into the forms around the reinforcing steel. The concrete provides compressive strength and the reinforcing steel provides tensile strength. This mixture of the best qualities of two materials creates a long-lasting structure. See Figure 1-12. The forms are removed after the concrete has reached a specified degree of set.

Figure 1-11. Structural steel construction allows for almost unlimited variations in design and construction.

Figure 1-12. Concrete reinforced with steel creates a building system which has high tensile and compressive strength.

Precast concrete is a system in which concrete components are formed, placed, and cured to a specific strength at a location other than their final installed location. Precast members include beams, pipes, walls, flooring sections, and exterior cladding. Consideration must be given to transporting and lifting the large, heavy members into place. Tilt-up construction is a variation of precast construction in which the concrete for large wall sections is placed on a flat slab with a bond breaker. Reinforcing and lifting hardware is installed in the wall system prior to concrete placement. After the concrete has been placed, finished, and is cured, the walls are tilted up into place.

Road and Bridge Building

Highway, road, and bridge construction requires specialized printreading skills and construction knowledge. Specifications for road and bridge construction may have special requirements for climactic conditions under which paving may be placed. Certain temperature and curing conditions must exist to ensure long life for traffic surfaces. New roads and bridges often require extensive earth moving, grading, and surface preparation. See Figure 1-13. Paving operations begin after the grading and subgrading are completed. For either concrete or asphalt paving, the roadbed subgrade is carefully prepared to ensure proper compaction and the ability to withstand imposed loads. Edge forms and reinforcing steel are set in place for concrete roadways. String lines or targets are set to specific elevations to act as guides for the heavy equipment which place the paving materials.

The placement of concrete or asphalt is done according to the prints in respect to the elevations and slopes shown. Proper surface finishing, scoring, and curing of the paving material are necessary to ensure that proper compressive strength and overall design requirements are achieved. Finish grading, shoulder work, guardrails, signage, and fencing are additional items necessary to complete the construction.

Bridge building relies on either reinforced concrete or structural steel construction. Piers, columns, and abutments are commonly constructed of reinforced concrete. Beams which create a support system for the bridge deck may be formed of precast concrete, structural steel, or poured-in-place concrete.

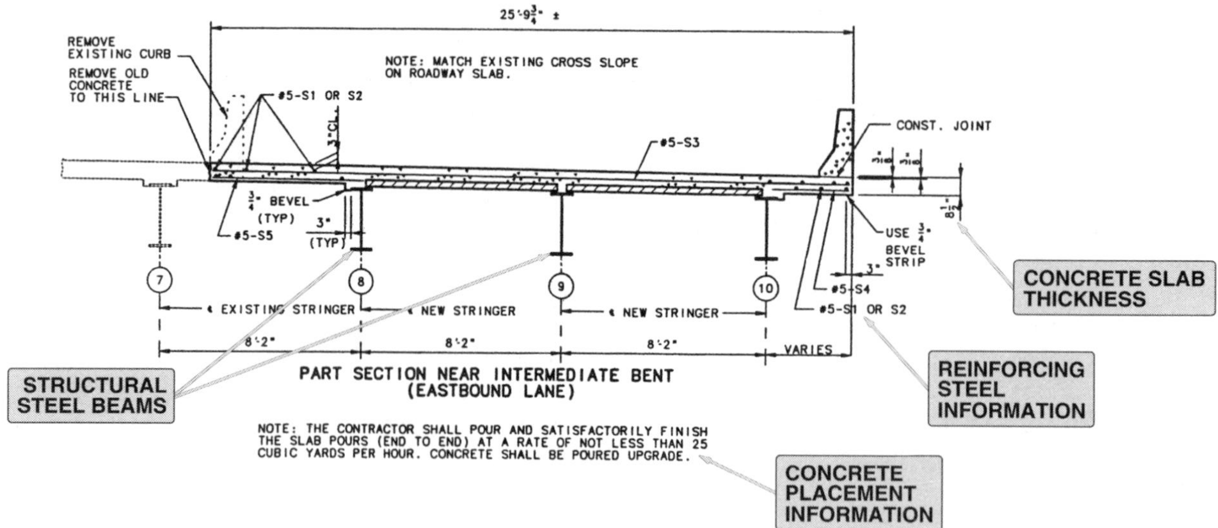

Figure 1-13. Prints for road building include information about all aspects of the building process, including grading, paving, and finishing.

PRINT FORMAT AND READING SKILLS

All individuals involved in the building process require a common source of information which is legally and functionally reliable. All members of the building team must read and interpret prints with skill and accuracy to ensure the final building project is in accordance with building codes, the needs of the owner(s), and the design of the architect(s). The drawings that make up a large set of prints are divided into separate categories to help readily find information. The use of symbols and abbreviations and the ability to interpret portions of the prints across the categories are necessary skills in the building process.

Print Divisions

The prefix of a capital letter denotes the division of prints. Architectural prints are noted by a capital A followed by the page number. In a similar manner, structural prints are denoted by an S, mechanical prints by an M, electrical prints by an E, and civil prints by a C. See Figure 1-14. Architects may use other divisions depending on the nature of the building project. Print numbering begins with the number 1 within each set. For example, the architectural prints may run from page A1 to page A65.

The structural prints begin with page number S1. Subcategories within these prints may be given as S1.1, S1.2, and S1.3 where several pages apply to a similar print division.

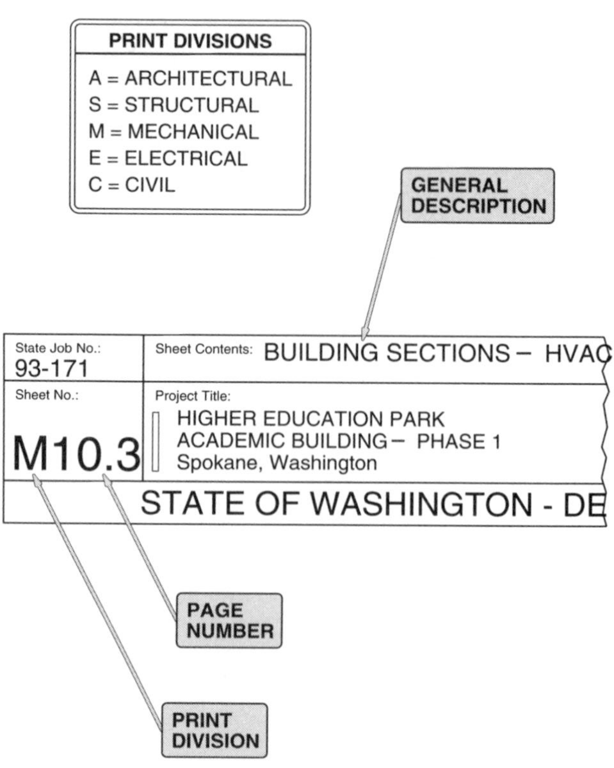

Figure 1-14. Prints are divided into specific sections to allow for faster information retrieval.

Architectural (A). The general building information, floor plans, elevation views, section drawings, and detail drawings make up the architectural prints. This is commonly the largest portion of prints for a construction project.

Structural (S). Structural prints provide information about sizes, styles, and placement for foundations, beams, columns, joists, and other framing and load-bearing members. These may be built of wood, masonry, reinforced concrete, or structural steel.

Mechanical (M). Plumbing, heating, ventilating, and air conditioning information, including ductwork, piping, and equipment placement and sizes is part of the mechanical prints. Information about piping for fire protection systems may also be a part of the mechanical prints or may be provided in a separate section.

Electrical (E). The electrical prints indicate the capacity and placement of power plant systems, lighting, cable trays, conduit and panel schedules, finish fixtures, wiring, switches, and any other electrical installations.

Civil (C). The overall site layout, grading, elevations, and topographical information are located in the section of civil prints. Other information also includes site drainage, paving designs, and parking layout. Landscaping may also be a part of these prints or provided separately.

Specifications

Written specifications for a large building project are divided into sections according to a format developed by the Construction Specifications Institute, commonly referred to as the CSI Format. Various divisions and an established numbering system allow for access to building information in a common method by all users of the specifications. See Figure 1-15.

Symbols

Common symbols are used in architectural prints. These symbols denote materials, building objects, and various dimensions and locations. Architects on large building projects commonly provide their own illustrations for symbols commonly used on a particular project. See Figure 1-16. The illustrations include elements that are repeated often and specialty items for one specific job. The symbols shown on a plan by an architect supersede any other common interpretations for the symbols.

Abbreviations

In a manner similar to symbols, architects commonly include a listing of abbreviations for a set of prints. The list is not a complete list, but a partial list of common terms and specific specialty terms. *Note:* Periods are commonly used with abbreviations to avoid confusion when the abbreviation spells a word. See Figure 1-17.

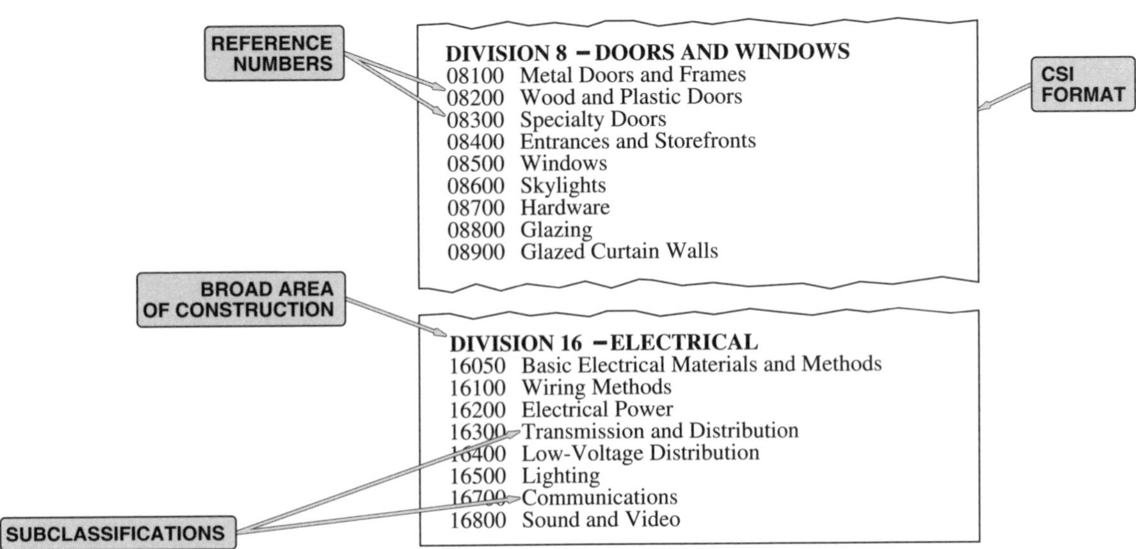

Figure 1-15. The CSI Format presents specification information using a standardized system.

MATERIAL SYMBOLS

EARTH	PLANTING SOIL
GRAVEL	LIMESTONE
CONCRETE	METAL FRAME WALL
BRICK	CONCRETE MASONRY UNITS
METAL	SMALL SCALE METAL
ROOFING INSULATION	RIGID INSULATION
BLANKET INSULATION	ACOUSTICAL TILE
FINISH WOOD	PLYWOOD
FRAMING LUMBER	BLOCKING OR SHIMS
GYPSUM WALLBOARD	GLASS MESH MORTAR UNITS

Figure 1-16. Architectural symbols are illustrated on a set of prints for large construction projects.

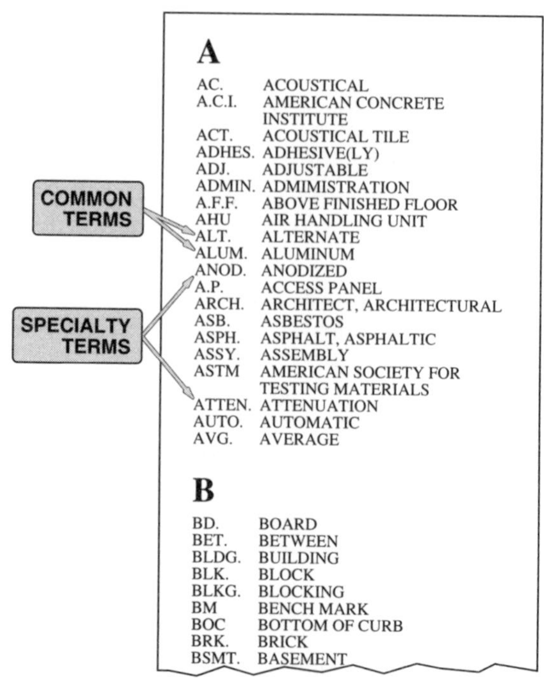

A

AC.	ACOUSTICAL
A.C.I.	AMERICAN CONCRETE INSTITUTE
ACT.	ACOUSTICAL TILE
ADHES.	ADHESIVE(LY)
ADJ.	ADJUSTABLE
ADMIN.	ADMIMISTRATION
A.F.F.	ABOVE FINISHED FLOOR
AHU	AIR HANDLING UNIT
ALT.	ALTERNATE
ALUM.	ALUMINUM
ANOD.	ANODIZED
A.P.	ACCESS PANEL
ARCH.	ARCHITECT, ARCHITECTURAL
ASB.	ASBESTOS
ASPH.	ASPHALT, ASPHALTIC
ASSY.	ASSEMBLY
ASTM	AMERICAN SOCIETY FOR TESTING MATERIALS
ATTEN.	ATTENUATION
AUTO.	AUTOMATIC
AVG.	AVERAGE

B

BD.	BOARD
BET.	BETWEEN
BLDG.	BUILDING
BLK.	BLOCK
BLKG.	BLOCKING
BM	BENCH MARK
BOC	BOTTOM OF CURB
BRK.	BRICK
BSMT.	BASEMENT

Figure 1-17. Common terms and abbreviations are listed at the beginning of large sets of prints.

Interpretations

One of the most necessary and difficult skills to develop in reading large sets of prints is the ability to visualize an entire project and the relationship of all components from a set of prints and specifications. In addition to an overall view, it is often necessary to obtain information from several different print pages and the specifications to fully understand a single building element. The ability to pull information from a variety of sources and combine this information into a common understanding is the biggest challenge in reading prints for a large building project.

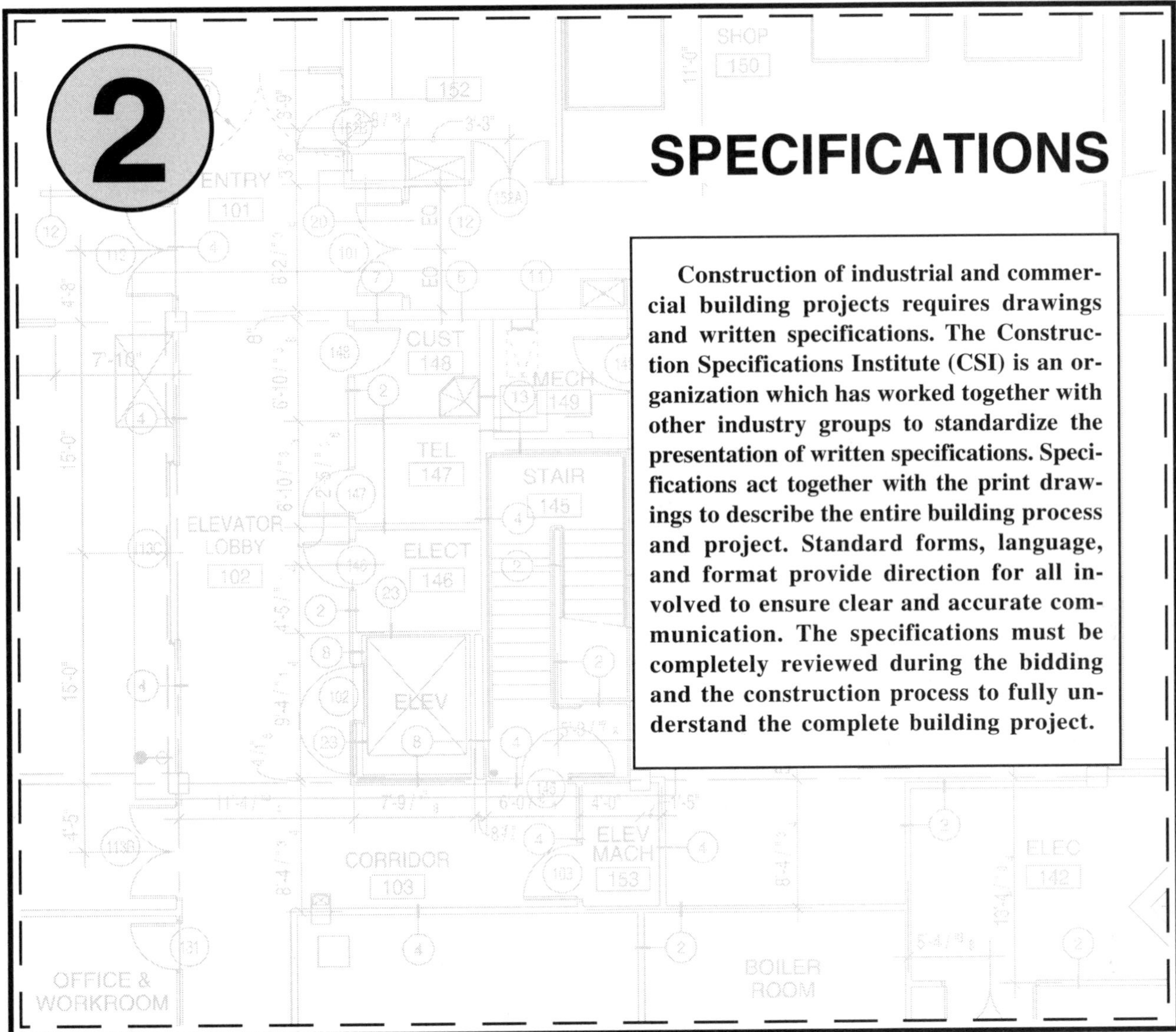

SPECIFICATIONS

Construction of industrial and commercial building projects requires drawings and written specifications. Specifications act together with the print drawings to describe the entire building process and project. Specifications contain information related to the legal, building materials, construction procedures, and quality control issues of building construction. The organized presentations of bidding information, contract requirements, and all phases of the construction operation are done in the written specifications. Standard forms, language, and format provide direction for all involved to ensure clear and accurate communication.

Different construction projects and architects use the specifications in different manners. The specifications must be completely reviewed during the bidding and construction process to fully understand the complete building project.

CSI FORMAT

The Construction Specifications Institute (CSI) is an organization which has worked together with other industry groups to standardize the presentation of written specifications. The CSI, in cooperation with the American Institute of Architects (AIA), the Associated General Contractors of America (AGC), the Council of Mechanical Specialties Contracting Industries Inc., and other industry groups developed the CSI Format for Construction Specifications and The Uniform System for Construction Specifications, Data Filing, and Cost Accounting. The CSI continues to promote and update the CSI Format.

Purpose

There are 16 divisions in the CSI Format which define the broad areas of construction. See Figure 2-1. See Appendix. The 16 divisions are numbered 1 through 16. Each division is designed to give complete written information about individual construction requirements for building and materials needs. Each of these broad areas is further divided into subclassifications. For example, Division 16–Electrical has subclassifications, such as Electrical Power, Lighting, and Communications. Each subclassification has a reference number for ease of identification. For example, the reference number for Electrical Power is 16200.

Groupings

A large portion of the work on any large construction project takes place before the first shovel of soil is turned. This includes the entire process of bidding, bonding, and signing of contracts. Groupings prefacing the CSI format divisions primarily pertain to the legal aspects of a building project. The groupings give all the information necessary to ensure that all members of the building team understand the legal steps which must be complete before project construction.

Bidding Information. An advertisement for bids gives general and bidding information. The legal name of the project, the owner, the bid range, accepting time and date, and opening time and date are all listed in the advertisement for bids. See Figure 2-2. In many instances, a pre-bid meeting is held. The pre-bid meeting allows all interested parties to meet with the architect to discuss the building project. Attendees may include general contractors, subcontractors, building trades union officials, government officials, and community representatives. Plans and specifications may be available for review or purchase at a number of locations. Any registrations, bonds, and guarantees required of bidders are explained in the pre-bid meeting information.

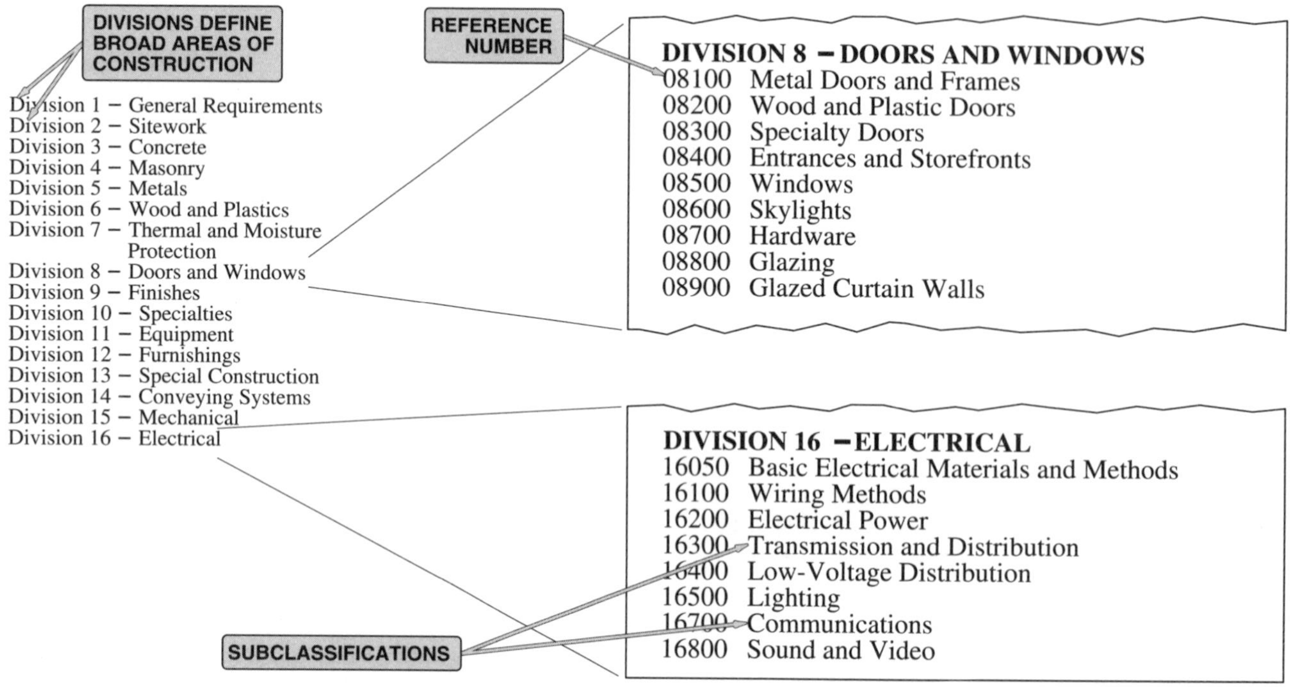

Figure 2-1. The Construction Specifications Institute Format has 16 divisions and is the most comprehensive and widely used construction specifications format.

SECTION 00020

ADVERTISEMENT FOR BIDS

LEGAL NAME OF PROJECT

A. GENERAL INFORMATION

1. Project Name: Phase I - Classroom Building
Spokane, Washington

OWNER

2. Owner: Joint Center for Higher Education (JCHE)
Spokane, Washington

3. State Project Number: 93-171

BID RANGE

4. Estimated Bid Range: $11,400,000 - $12,000,000

5. Pre-Bid Meeting: To be held at 1 p.m. on Tuesday, June 28, in the JCHE Board Conference Room, Suite 245, at the Riverpoint One Office Building, North 501 Riverpoint Blvd., Spokane, WA, for the purpose of answering questions from bidders and interested parties relating to the project.

PRE-BID MEETING INFORMATION

NOTE: **Attendance at the Pre-Bid Meeting is MANDATORY for all General Contractors intending to bid this project. A roster of those attending the Pre-Bid Meeting will be issued to all planholders by addendum following the meeting. Any bid received from any General Contractor whose name does not appear on this roster will be considered nonresponsive and will be rejected.**

6. Architect Contact: INTEGRUS Architecture, P.S.
Gordon E. Ruehl
Gary D. Joralemon

7. JCHE Contact: R.K. "Butch" Slaughter
Physical Plant Manager, JCHE

BID ACCEPTING DATE AND TIME

B. BIDDING

1. Sealed bids for construction of the Phase I - Classroom Building, Spokane, Washington, will be received by the Joint Center for Higher Education, North 501 Riverpoint Blvd., Suite 245, Spokane, WA 99202-1649, on Tuesday, July 12. Part I - Price Proposals must be received on or before 6 p.m. Part II - Price Proposals must be received on or before 7 p.m.

BID OPENING TIME AND DATE

2. All bids received will remain sealed until 7 p.m. on July 12, when they will be opened and read aloud in the JCHE Board Conference Room, Suite 245, North 501 Riverpoint Blvd., Spokane, WA 99202-1649.

3. Proposals received after times and dates set for opening will not be considered.

Figure 2-2. Architects, contractors, and subcontractors use the specifications to define bidding procedures.

Conditions of Construction. Contractor and owner responsibilities and duties are described in the conditions of construction. Contractors who bid on the project accept certain responsibilities in such diverse areas as complete site exploration and disadvantaged business enterprise participation. Other state or local governmental requirements are also listed. Owners and architects commonly list the items for which they are not held responsible and which must be part of the contractor's portion of the construction bid.

Division 1–General Requirements

Division 1 of the specifications includes the forms which must be submitted by contractors for payment and for documentation of various project requirements pertaining to materials, change orders, and substitutions. Health and safety, quality control, and contract closeout are also described.

Procedures and Schedules. The first section of Division 1 gives a description of the overall construction work. This is done with an index of all the plan drawings and several paragraphs giving a general overview of the project. See Figure 2-3. General descriptions of alternates are provided along with the bidding procedures for building projects that have several alternate additional construction items.

Procedures for filing for approval and payment of change orders and unit pricing are listed. Some of the most important procedures given in this section are those which must be followed by the contractor to receive payment. Standardized invoice forms are commonly used for payment requests. See Figure 2-4.

The time in which the construction project must be completed is given in Division 1. Depending on the project, there may be penalties assessed if not completed during a certain time. The format for submission of the construction schedule to the owner and others involved in the building project may be given.

Procedures for completion of the project are listed. These include the final cleaning and preparation of the project, submission of all documents, such as contract drawings, specifications, addenda, change orders, shop drawings, warranties, and operation and maintenance data.

Quality. Regular meetings of the architect, owner, contractor, and major subcontractors help ensure the project is completed correctly and on schedule. Meeting procedures are detailed in this portion of the specifications, including preconstruction conferences and progress meetings.

A variety of industry association and governmental standards exist for construction. Items such as field engineering, construction materials, hazardous material handling, equipment installations, and health and safety should be performed according to any standards listed in the specifications.

The contractor is responsible for employing qualified workers, providing samples and mock-ups, and using approved testing agencies.

Division 2–Site Construction

Division 2 of the specifications includes information concerning the items below ground, such as foundations, tunnels, pipes, and piers, as well as the items on the ground, such as landscaping, fencing, and paving. Contractor's responsibilities for subsurface exploration, excavation, compaction, and disposal of excavated materials are part of Division 2.

1.4 DESCRIPTION OF THE WORK

A. The SIRTI facility is located on property in the Riverpoint area of downtown Spokane, bordered on the north by the Spokane River, south by Riverpoint Boulevard and on the east by Trent Avenue. To the west of the site there is additional undeveloped property.

B. In general, the structure is concrete slab on grade, structural concrete frame, dome pan (waffle slab) floor system, open web steel joists with fluted steel decking, rigid insulation and a single ply roof membrane. The exterior walls are constructed of structural steel studs, sheathing and brick veneer. Mechanical systems include gas-fired boilers; water-cooled screw compressor chillers; centrifugal fan, open evaporative cooling tower; air handling units; VAV terminal boxes; direct digital electronic control system, and automatic fire sprinkler system. Electrical systems include power distribution, interior and exterior lighting, raceways for power, data and communications, and fire alarm system.

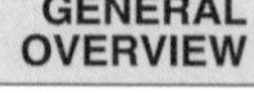

C. Site work includes excavation, soil improvement, on-site drainage, paving, curbs, walks, site lighting, landscaping and irrigation system, as well as coordinated connections to existing sanitary sewer, water, power, gas, and telephone, provided by others.

Figure 2-3. A general statement concerning the size and scope of the building project is included in Division 1 of the specifications.

FORM SF 8254 REV 09

STATE OF WASHINGTON

APPLICATION AND CERTIFICATE FOR PAYMENT ON CONTRACT

CERTIFICATE FOR (Partial/Final) PAYMENT. For period from ________________ to ________________

Contract For:
Location:

Contractor: ________________ Contract No. ________________

Original Contract Amount $

Change Order No.

Adjusted Contract Amount $ ________________

ITEM NO.	DETAIL	ESTIMATED COST	AMOUNT TOTAL EARNED	%	PREVIOUSLY CLAIMED	THIS ESTIMATE
(*) Items Sales Tax Exempt	TOTALS					
	Sales Tax on Applicable Items					
	TOTAL					
	Less Retainage . . . . %	XXXX				
	NET	XXXX				
	Less Previous Payments	XXXX			XXXX	XXXX
	Adjustments (specify)		XXXX		XXXX	
	Amount Due This Estimate	XXXX			XXXX	

This is to certify that, the contractor having complied with the terms of the above mentioned contract there is due and payable from the State of Washington, the amount set after "Amount due this Estimate."

________________ (Contracting firm) ________________ (Supervising Engineers or Architects)

By ________________ By ________________

-GEN-1202- 3

Figure 2-4. The specifications include many standard forms to be used throughout the construction process.

Site Preparation. The CSI specifications detail the contractor's responsibilities for testing and handling of the construction site soils, fill, and backfill materials. Bearing capacities for the subsurface must be achieved and measured according to industry standards, such as the American Society for Testing and Materials (ASTM). Removal and use of surface soils and necessary soil improvements are given. Where surface geomembranes are installed, specific information may be provided concerning their properties. See Figure 2-5. Information in this division is also given for drainage piping, manholes, and inlets.

Paving. Paving materials and standards for their use and installation are described in Division 1. The specifications include the weather conditions under which paving may or may not be installed. Slopes and smoothness requirements are indicated.

SECTION 03200

CONCRETE REINFORCEMENT

1. PART 1 GENERAL

1.1 SECTION INCLUDES

1.3 REFERENCES

A. ACI 301 - Specifications for Structural Concrete for Buildings (latest Edition).

B. ACI SP-66 - American Concrete Institute - Detailing Manual.

C. ACI 315 - Manual of Standard Practice For Detailing Concrete Structures.

D. ANSI/ASTM A82 - Cold Drawn Steel Wire for Concrete Reinforcement.

E. ANSI/ASTM A185 - Welded Steel Wire Fabric for Concrete Reinforcement.

F. ANSI/AWS D1.4 - Structural Welding Code for Reinforcing Steel.

G. ANSI/AWS D12.1 - Reinforcing Steel Welding Code.

H. ASTM A615 - Deformed and Plain Billet Steel Bars for Concrete Reinforcement.

I. CRSI - Concrete Reinforcing Steel Institute Manual of Practice.

INDUSTRY STANDARDS

PROPERTY	TESTING STANDARD	MINIMUM ACCEPTABLE VALUE
Minimum Aperture Area	I.D. caliper	1.7 in^2
Minimum Aperture Dimension	I.D. caliper	1.3 in.
Percent Open Area	COE method	75% (min)
Thickness, joints	ASTM D-1777	0.10 in.(nom)
Thickness, Ribs	ASTM D-1777	0.02 in.(nom)

C. Flexible Geomembrane The flexible geomembrane shall be placed by the Contractor after all surplus ash fill material from the SIRTI site earthwork has been placed and compacted in designated area of the Milwaukee Trench. The membrane shall be fabricated from high density polyethylene (HDPE) and manufactured in a width of not less than 20 ft with no factory seams. The membrane shall be new first quality material manufactured specifically for the purpose of liquid containment. Two types of liners are required for this project: smooth and roughened surface. The membrane shall be manufactured by Gundle Lining Systems, Poly America or approved equivalent. The membranes shall meet or exceed the following specifications:

SOIL AND SLOPE FINISH INFORMATION

Figure 2-5. Various industry standards are referenced throughout the specifications. Soil and slope finish information includes fabrics which may be placed to inhibit erosion.

Landscaping. Soil mixtures, trees and shrubs, grasses, finish grading, fertilizers, and mulches are detailed in the specifications. Installation, protection, and maintenance procedures for plant materials are given. Piping and connection information is included where irrigation systems are installed.

Division 3–Concrete

Division 3 of the CSI Format contains information concerning concrete including procedures for placement, curing, and finishing of concrete, formwork construction, removal, materials, reinforcing methods, and other related information. Precast concrete members are also described in Division 3 of the specifications.

Materials. The primary material described in Division 3 is concrete. Concrete material information includes the cement to be used, the aggregate, all admixtures, and the quality of water. Reinforcing steel is described according to ASTM references concerning strength and shape. Accessories to be placed in concrete pours, such as chairs for supporting reinforcing steel, dowels, and anchors may be described according to a specific manufacturer's name and number. See Figure 2-6. Materials for forms, form release agents, grout, joint fillers, water stops, and curing compounds are also described.

Methods. Proper placement and curing must be done to ensure that the concrete meets final design requirements. For poured-in-place concrete, the specifications describe the methods of erection of formwork, placement of embedded accessories, such as dowels and waterstops, placement of reinforcement, placement of concrete, finishing operations, curing of the concrete, formwork removal, finishing, and patching. Testing methods for concrete strength and slump are noted. The methods of installation are provided for precast members.

Division 4–Masonry

Components of masonry construction include the masonry units, mortars, reinforcement, and accessories. See Figure 2-7. Division 4 of the specifications addresses all these components.

Figure 2-7. Division 4 of the specifications addresses components of masonry construction.

2. PART 2 PRODUCTS

REINFORCING STEEL DESCRIBED ACCORDING TO ASTM REFERENCES

2.1 REINFORCEMENT

A. Reinforcing Steel: As noted on the Structural Drawings. ASTM A615, 60 ksi yield grade; deformed billet steel bars.

B. Welded Steel Wire Fabric: ASTM A185 Plain Type in flat sheets.

2.2 ACCESSORY MATERIALS

A. Tie Wire: Minimum 16 gage annealed type, or patented system as approved.

B. Chairs, Bolsters, Bar Supports, Spacers: Sized and shaped for strength and support of reinforcement during concrete placement conditions including load bearing pad on bottom to prevent vapor barrier puncture at slab on grade.

MANUFACTURER REFERENCES

C. Special Chairs, Bolsters, Bar Supports, Spacers Adjacent to Weather Exposed Concrete Surfaces: Plastic coated steel type; size and shape as required.

D. Dowel Flanged Couplers (DFC): Williams Form Engineering Corp. CD2 couplings with CD2 indicators, Dayton-Superior D-50 DBR, Richmond Screw Anchor Co. Inc. DB-SAE splicer and DB-S indicator, or approved. Provide in size to meet or exceed rebar capacity. System may be used as substitutions for dowel bars.

Figure 2-6. Specifications commonly mention specific manufacturer's names and product codes to define the types and qualities of materials and hardware.

Materials. Different mortars are used in various applications, such as load-bearing masonry walls, non–load-bearing masonry walls, and tuckpointing. Mortar components are detailed, including the cement, aggregates, water, bonding agents, coloring, and admixtures, such as plasticizers and water repellents. See Figure 2-8.

Sizes and colors of face brick and concrete masonry units may be described according to a specific manufacturer. Where stone is supplied, a specific supplier may be named to ensure stone quality and uniformity. Other masonry material information given includes metal ties and anchors, flashing, and control joints.

Methods. In a manner similar to concrete, certain climactic limits of heat and cold exist on masonry construction. Environmental requirements for masonry construction are defined in the specifications. See Figure 2-9.

Other methods of masonry construction described include testing of mortar and grout mixes, the bond used for brick placement, anchor placement, flashing installation, mortar joint style, tolerances for positioning and variations from plumb and level, cleaning and sealing of the finished surface, preparation of surfaces to be patched, vibration of grout materials, and examination of the final masonry installation.

PORTLAND CEMENT/LIME MORTARS			
Type/Description	**Portland Cement**	**Hydrated Lime or Lime Putty**	**Sand**
M–Mortar of high compressive strength (at least 2500 psi) after curing 28 days and with greater durability than some other types. Used for masonry below ground and in contact with the earth, such as foundations, retaining walls, and manholes. This type withstands severe frost action and high lateral loads.	1	1/4	3
S–Mortar with a fairly high compressive strength (at least 1800 psi) after curing 28 days. Used in reinforced masonry and for standard masonry where maximum flexural strength is required. Also used when mortar is the sole bonding agent between facing and backing units.	1	1/2	4 1/4
N–Mortar with a medium compressive strength (at least 750 psi) after curing 28 days. Used for exposed masonry aboveground and where high compressive strength or lateral masonry strengths are required.	1	1	6
O–Mortar with a low compressive strength (at least 350 psi) after curing 28 days. Used for general interior walls. May be used for load-bearing walls of solid masonry if axial compressive stress does not exceed 100 psi and wall is not exposed to weathering or freezing.	1	2	9

Figure 2-8. Mortar components include cement, aggregates, water, bonding agents, coloring, and admixtures.

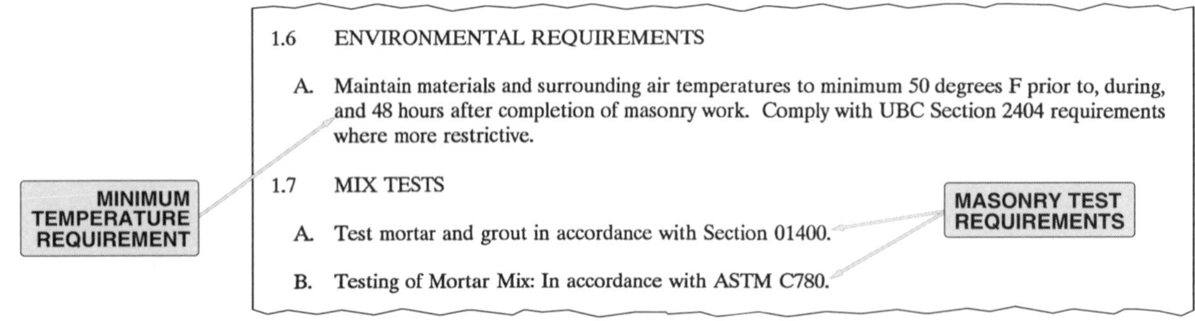
1.6 ENVIRONMENTAL REQUIREMENTS

A. Maintain materials and surrounding air temperatures to minimum 50 degrees F prior to, during, and 48 hours after completion of masonry work. Comply with UBC Section 2404 requirements where more restrictive.

1.7 MIX TESTS

A. Test mortar and grout in accordance with Section 01400.

B. Testing of Mortar Mix: In accordance with ASTM C780.

Figure 2-9. Masonry work may be adversely affected by extremes of cold and heat unless specific precautions are taken.

Division 5–Metals

Division 5 includes metals used on a construction project which include structural steel members, such as columns, beams, and joists; steel decking for floors, walls, and roofs; light gauge metal framing members, metal stairs, and ornamental metals, such as handrails, ladders, and expansion joints. Metal flashings are described in CSI Format Division 7, Section 7600. Metal piping and conduit specifications are described in Divisions 15 and 16.

Materials. Steel material specifications commonly refer to ASTM standards for structural steel shapes, coatings, and connectors, such as bolts, nuts, and washers. See Figure 2-10. The shape, diameter, type of metal, and pipe schedule specifications are given for railings and other ornamental iron.

Methods. The American Welding Society (AWS) Structural Welding Code is the reference which provides information for acceptable methods, certification requirements, and tolerances for welded connections. See Figure 2-11. Metal and steel construction methods described in Division 5 include fabrication procedures, installation tolerances for squareness, plumb and alignment, fastener locations, and finishing processes, such as grinding and paint priming.

Division 6–Wood and Plastics

Division 6 includes rough wood framing, finish woodworking, and plastic materials, such as plastic laminate. In large commercial projects, there is often a limited amount of wood framing. Where heavy timber framing is used, the specifications in Division 6 provide additional information concerning these members.

ASTM STEEL MATERIAL SPECIFICATIONS

1.4 REFERENCES

A. ASTM A36 - Structural Steel.

B. ASTM A53 - Hot-Dipped, Zinc-coated Welded and Seamless Steel Pipe.

C. ASTM A123 - Zinc (Hot-Galvanized) Coatings on Products Fabricated From Rolled, Pressed and Forged Steel Shapes, Plates, Bars, and Strip.

D. ASTM A153 - Zinc Coating (Hot-Dip) on Iron and Steel Hardware.

E. ASTM A283 - Carbon Steel Plates, Shapes, and Bars.

F. ASTM A307 - Carbon Steel Externally Threaded Standard Fasteners.

G. ASTM A325 - High Strength Bolts for Structural Steel Joints.

Figure 2-10. Standardized structural steel coatings and shapes are used by mills and fabricators to ensure consistency and quality.

1.6 QUALIFICATIONS

A. Prepare Shop Drawings under direct supervision of a Professional Structural Engineer experienced in design of this work and licensed in the State of Washington.

B. Welders' Certificates: Submit under provisions of Section 01300, certifying welders employed on the Work, verifying AWS qualification within the previous 12 months.

1.7 FIELD MEASUREMENTS

A. Verify that field measurements are as indicated on Drawings.

Figure 2-11. The American Welding Society (AWS) Structural Welding Code is the reference which provides information for acceptable methods, certification requirements, and tolerances for welded connections.

Materials. As with other materials, various industry group standards are used as references for lumber products. These include the standards of groups, such as the National Forest Products Association (NFPA), the Western Wood Products Association (WWPA), and the American Plywood Association (APA). Finish wood materials are related to standards provided by the Architectural Woodworking Institute (AWI). See Figure 2-12. Wood-related materials described include lumber and lumber treatments, such as fireproofing, softwood and hardwood plywood, finish woods, such as oak or maple, and fasteners, such as nails, bolts, and lag screws. Some finish casework related information provided includes plastic laminate grades and various hardware. The majority of wood casework information is described in Division 12.

Methods. Rough framing methods and requirements are normally defined in the building code and are not part of the specifications. Methods included in Division 6 pertain to items, such as applications for treated lumber, fabrication and finishing of wood casework and finish materials, and installation tolerances for finish woodwork.

Division 7–Thermal and Moisture Protection

Division 7 covers a wide range of different construction products including asphalt roofing, rubberized roofing, mastics, waterproof coatings, vapor barriers, sheet metal flashings, insulation materials, fireproofing materials, and joint sealants. All of these products are used in some manner to stop moisture movement or provide thermal insulation to the structure.

Materials. Due to the specialized nature of many thermal and moisture protection products, this section of the specifications relies heavily on manufacturer's names and product numbers. See Figure 2-13. The specification information is performance based where common materials are used.

For example, specifications for expanded polystyrene insulation board include the required board density, thermal resistance, and compressive strength. Schedules of applications for various materials may be included to assist in locating the placement of each material mentioned in the specifications.

FINISH REQUIREMENTS RELATED TO AWI STANDARDS

JOINT TOLERANCES	PREMIUM GRADE	CUSTOM GRADE	ECONOMY GRADE
Maximum Gap Between Exposed Components	$\frac{1}{64}$″	$\frac{1}{32}$″	$\frac{1}{16}$″
Maximum Length of Gap in Exposed Components	3″	5″	8″
Maximum Gap between Semi-Exposed Components	$\frac{1}{32}$″	$\frac{1}{16}$″	$\frac{1}{8}$″
Maximum Length of Gap in Semi-Exposed Components	6″	8″	12″

NOTE: No gap may occur within 48″ of another gap.

TEST LOCATIONS FOR TYPICAL JOINERY

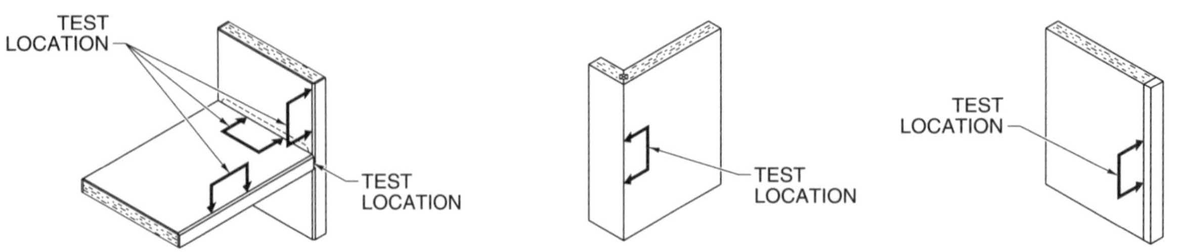

Figure 2-12. Standards from the Architectural Woodworking Institute (AWI) provide references for finished wood products.

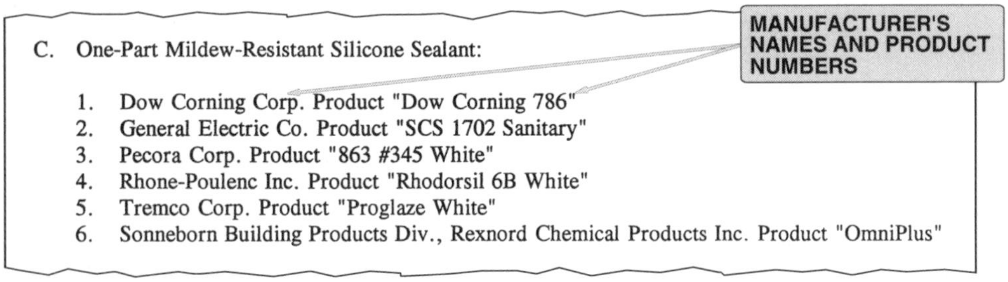

MANUFACTURER'S NAMES AND PRODUCT NUMBERS

C. One-Part Mildew-Resistant Silicone Sealant:

1. Dow Corning Corp. Product "Dow Corning 786"
2. General Electric Co. Product "SCS 1702 Sanitary"
3. Pecora Corp. Product "863 #345 White"
4. Rhone-Poulenc Inc. Product "Rhodorsil 6B White"
5. Tremco Corp. Product "Proglaze White"
6. Sonneborn Building Products Div., Rexnord Chemical Products Inc. Product "OmniPlus"

Figure 2-13. Many manufacturers provide thermal and moisture protection products which are designated in building specifications.

Methods. Proper thermal and waterproofing performances rely heavily on proper initial installation. Division 7 provides information concerning proper surface preparations, seaming and overlap requirements, mastic and fastener applications, the proper number of coatings of a particular product, and final quality inspection. See Figure 2-14.

Figure 2-14. The proper procedures for roofing installation are included in the specifications in Division 7.

Division 8–Doors and Windows

Division 8 contains extensive information concerning swinging metal doors and frames, swinging wood doors and frames, access doors, overhead doors and grilles, glass doors, and sliding doors. Windows of all types are also described, including glass curtain walls. See Figure 2-15. This section also contains schedules for doors, windows, and their necessary hardware.

Figure 2-15. Curtain walls are composed of glass panels set in metal trim frames which are attached to structural members.

Doors. Metal and wood doors are described in terms of their fire rating, core materials, and finishes. Finishes include primer and finish paint coatings for metal doors and veneers and finish materials for wood doors. There is additional information concerning door frames, louvers, glass lights, and astragals in Division 8. A schedule of door information relating each door to a numbered opening on the architectural drawings is included. See Figure 2-16. Tolerances for door warp, bow, and variation from plumb and level are also part of the door specifications.

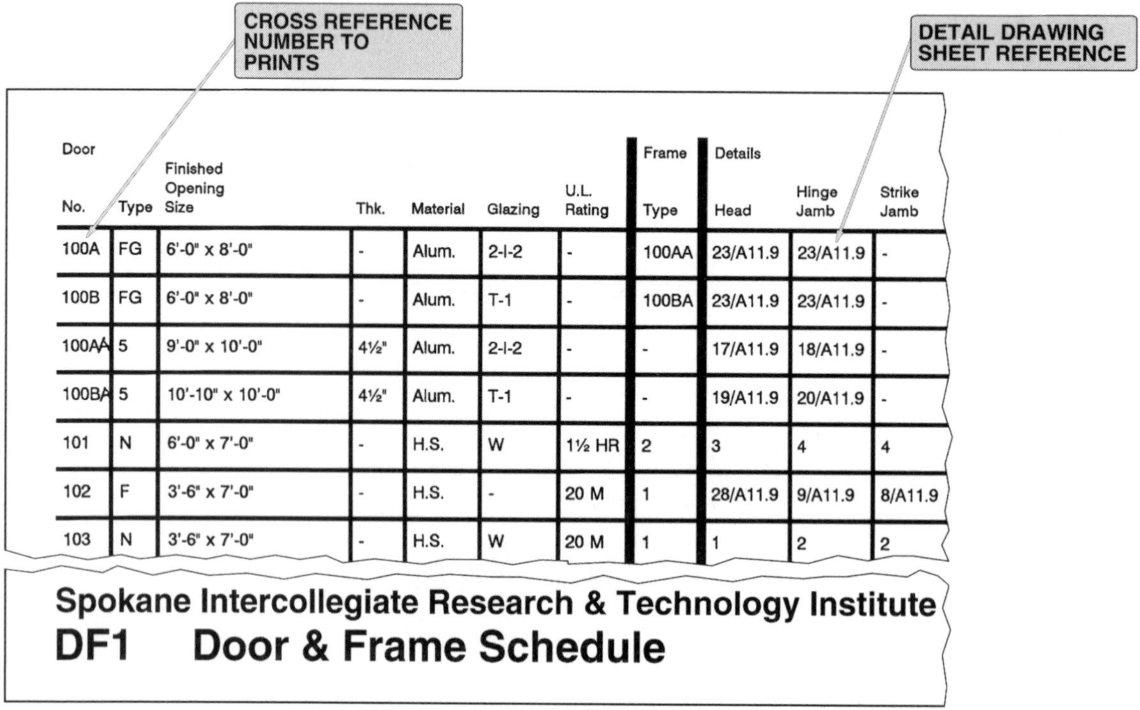

Door No.	Type	Finished Opening Size	Thk.	Material	Glazing	U.L. Rating	Frame Type	Details Head	Hinge Jamb	Strike Jamb
100A	FG	6'-0" x 8'-0"	-	Alum.	2-I-2	-	100AA	23/A11.9	23/A11.9	-
100B	FG	6'-0" x 8'-0"	-	Alum.	T-1	-	100BA	23/A11.9	23/A11.9	-
100AA	5	9'-0" x 10'-0"	4½"	Alum.	2-I-2	-	-	17/A11.9	18/A11.9	-
100BA	5	10'-10" x 10'-0"	4½"	Alum.	T-1	-	-	19/A11.9	20/A11.9	-
101	N	6'-0" x 7'-0"	-	H.S.	W	1½ HR	2	3	4	4
102	F	3'-6" x 7'-0"	-	H.S.	-	20 M	1	28/A11.9	9/A11.9	8/A11.9
103	N	3'-6" x 7'-0"	-	H.S.	W	20 M	1	1	2	2

Spokane Intercollegiate Research & Technology Institute
DF1 Door & Frame Schedule

Figure 2-16. Schedules provide detailed door information in a format which is directly related to door locations on the architectural prints.

Windows. Types and finishes of frames, glazing, and weatherstripping comprise a large portion of the window specifications. Window types may be specified by manufacturer product codes. Other window performance requirements given include ability to withstand wind pressures, deflection, air leakage, thermal performance, and water leakage. Drawings in the specifications may give additional details for large or complicated window installations. See Figure 2-17. The specifications may also include a schedule for placement of various glazing materials, such as glass types and glazing compounds.

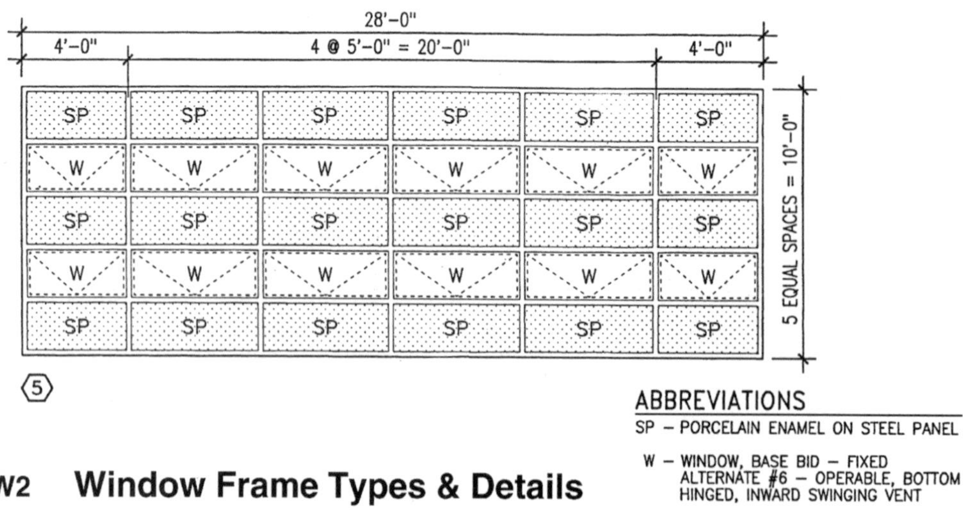

Figure 2-17. Working shop drawings may be included in the specifications to clarify complicated installations.

Hardware. A wide variety of hardware components are described in the specifications with information about the types and locations for installation. Manufacturer names, designs, sizes, types, finishes, and functions are an important part of the hardware specifications in Division 8. The hardware schedule for each door includes hinges, locks, door closers, door pulls, push plates, kick plates, stops, bolts, coordinators, thresholds, weather strips and door seals. See Figure 2-18. Spacing of hinges and locations for locksets are given.

Division 9–Finishes

Large commercial buildings have many different usage areas which each require different floor, wall, and ceiling finishes. Many different tiles, wood products, gypsum products, plasters, cement materials, paints, and special treatments are necessary to meet these varying usage demands. Division 9 of the CSI Format details specific information concerning applications of finish materials in each building area. See Figure 2-19.

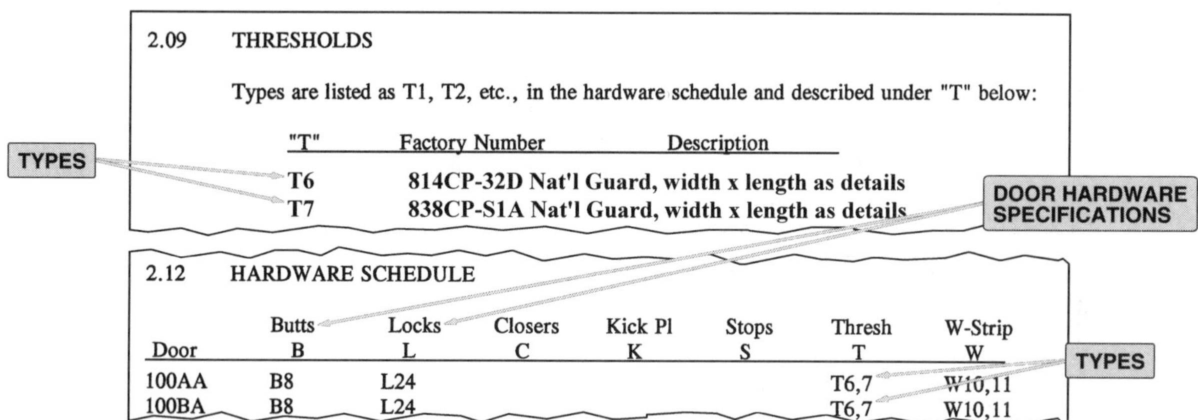

2.09 THRESHOLDS

Types are listed as T1, T2, etc., in the hardware schedule and described under "T" below:

"T"	Factory Number	Description
T6	814CP-32D	Nat'l Guard, width x length as details
T7	838CP-S1A	Nat'l Guard, width x length as details

2.12 HARDWARE SCHEDULE

Door	Butts B	Locks L	Closers C	Kick Pl K	Stops S	Thresh T	W-Strip W
100AA	B8	L24				T6,7	W10,11
100BA	B8	L24				T6,7	W10,11

Figure 2-18. A wide variety of hardware components are described in the specifications with information about the types and locations for installation.

ROOM FINISH SCHEDULE

Room		Floor			Base			Walls North			South			East			West			Ceiling				Notes
No.	Name	Mat.	Fin.	Col.	Mat.	Fin.	Col.	Mat.	Fin.	Col.	Mat.	Fin.	Col.	Mat.	Fin.	Col.	Mat.	Fin.	Col.	Mat.	Fin.	Col.	Ht.	
000	LOBBY	14	F3		21	---		33	F8	P1	33	F8	P1	32	F8	P1	33	F8	P1	41	---		11'-½"	
000A	STAIR 1	10	F1		20 23	F17 F17		33	F8	P2	33	F8	P2	33	F8	P2	33	F8	P2	41	---		11'-½"	
001	CORRIDOR	14	F3		21	---		32	F8	P1	33	F8	P1	32	F8	P1	33	F8	P1	41	---		11'-½"	
009	MEN'S TOILET	13	F2		22	F2		32	F11 F6	P4	32	F11 F6	P4	32	F11 F6	P4	32	F11 F6	P4	42	F8	P4	8'-0"	
009A	VESTIBULE	13	F2		22	F2		32	F8	P4	32	F8		32	F8		32	F8		42	F8	P4	8'-0"	
010	WOMEN'S TOILET	13	F2		22	F2		32	F11 P6	P4	32	F11 F6	P4	32	F11 F6	P4	32	F11 F6	P4	42	F8	P4	8'-0"	

Materials

Floor Materials

10	Concrete (CONC)
11	Slate Pavers (SP)
12	Not Used
13	Ceramic Mosaic Tile (CMT)
14	Vinyl Composition Tile (VCT)

Base Materials

20	Hardwood (Maple)
21	Vinyl Cove
22	Ceramic Mosaic Tile

Wall Materials

31	Concrete
32	Gypsum Wallboard (Single Layer) on Metal Studs
33	Gypsum Wallboard (Single Layer) on Metal Furring

Ceiling Materials

41	Exposed Concrete
42	Gypsum Wallboard

Finish

F1	Concrete Hardener/Sealer
F2	Clean & Seal
F3	Clean, Wax, & Buff
F4	Tackable Wall Covering
F5	Vinyl Fabric Wall Covering
F6	Ceramic Mosaic Tile
F7	Paint - Masonry System
F8	Paint - GWB System
F9	Traffic Membrane
F10	Rubber Treads, Risers, Sheet Rubber Nonslip Tile @ Landing
F11	High Build Glazed Coating

Color

P1	Columbia #5391W
P2	Columbia #5393M
P3	Columbia #5394D
P4	Columbia #5390W

Figure 2-19. A large commercial project has many different floor, wall, and ceiling finishes which are described on the room finish schedule.

Materials. Finish materials for each area of a large building may be denoted on a room finish schedule. The finish materials included in this division of the specifications are metal lath and plaster, gypsum products including drywall materials, metal stud framing and accessories, ceramic floor and wall tile, resilient flooring, carpeting, wood flooring, suspended ceiling systems, special wall and ceiling coverings, and paint materials, including stains, varnishes, and exterior and interior paint. Manufacturers of various finish materials are commonly named.

Methods. To ensure that the proper floor, wall, and ceiling finishes are obtained, the architect may specify the qualifications of the installers, proper material handling prior to installation, environmental requirements, and the sequence of installation. See Figure 2-20. Cleaning of the finished areas and protection of the final product are also noted.

Division 10–Specialties

Division 10 contains a list of items which may or may not be part of any large construction project. See Figure 2-21. Among the more common of these items to be included in most projects are toilet compartments, signage, and fire extinguishers. In a manner similar to other divisions of the specifications, there is extensive reliance on manufacturer names and types.

Tate Access Floors, Inc.

Figure 2-21. Access flooring is one of the many specialized types of construction covered by Division 10 of the CSI Format.

PROCEDURES

B. Erect single layer non-rated gypsum board in most economical direction, with ends and edges occurring over firm bearing.

C. Erect single layer fire rated gypsum board vertically, with edges and ends occurring over firm bearing.

D. Use screws when fastening gypsum board to metal furring or framing.

E. Double Layer Applications: Use gypsum backing board for first layer, placed over framing or furring members. Use fire rated gypsum backing board for 2-hr. fire rated partitions. Place second layer perpendicular to first layer. Offset joints of second layer from joints of first layer.

F. Double Layer Applications: Secure second layer to first in manner required by code for indicated fire rating. Apply adhesive in accordance with manufacturer's instructions.

G. Treat cut edges and holes in moisture resistant gypsum board and glass mesh mortar units with sealant.

H. Place control joints consistent with lines of building spaces.

I. Place corner beads at external corners. Use longest practical length. Place casing beads where gypsum board abuts dissimilar materials.

3.9 JOINT TREATMENT

A. Tape, fill, and sand exposed joints, edges, and corners to produce smooth surface ready to receive finishes.

B. Feather coats onto adjoining surfaces so that camber is maximum 1/32 inch.

Figure 2-20. Architects provide detailed information concerning procedures for finishes to ensure a quality product.

Division 11–Equipment

Various commercial buildings require equipment to be built into the initial project. Projection screens, dishwashers, ovens, water treatment machinery, and a wide variety of industrial equipment may be installed in the structure during construction. The equipment is part of the initial construction bid. The general contractor and subcontractors are responsible for obtaining and installing the specialized equipment prior to completion of the project according to the information provided in Division 11.

Division 12–Furnishings

Division 12 provides information concerning metal and wood cabinetry and countertops. This includes material, finishes, hardware, fabrication, and installation. See Figure 2-22. Other information commonly contained in this section includes installed seating, such as for a theater or classroom, as well as window blinds and curtains.

Division 13–Special Construction

The subclassifications in Division 13 of the CSI Format shows that there are many highly specialized types of construction for various commercial projects. Information from the manufacturer is critical to this division. Several of the more common areas of this division included in specification books are seismic controls and building automation systems which control such items as lighting, fire protection, and heating and cooling systems.

Division 14–Conveying Systems

Machinery for moving people, materials, and equipment are included in most large construction projects. Elevators are essential in large office buildings. Retail stores often rely on elevators and escalators to move customers. In manufacturing plants and power plants, conveyors and monorail systems move materials and products from one area to another. Division 14 describes all of these conveying systems.

Elevators. The most common conveying system in Division 14 is elevators. Elevator specifications include the net capacity, speed, travel distance, number of stops, car size and interior finish, power requirements, and automatic control systems. See Figure 2-23. A variety of industry standards and governmental regulations apply to elevator construction including the American National Standards Institute (ANSI), the Americans with Disabilities Act (ADA), the National Electrical Code® (NEC®), Underwriters' Laboratories, Inc. (UL®), and others.

Material Handling Systems. Material handling systems take many shapes and sizes. Overhead lifts and monorail systems are normally electrically controlled. They are described in the specifications according to their lifting capacity, speed of lift and movement, and height of lift required. Conveying systems move items as varied as cans, coal, and pieces of mail. Conveyor type, speed, and capacity are part of Division 14.

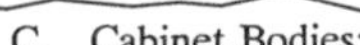

C. Cabinet Bodies:

1. Fabricate, assemble and finish each cabinet as a complete and self-supporting unit. Unless otherwise shown, counter and tall storage units to be 24 inch minimum overall depth.
2. Ship counter tops separate for field installation.
3. Provide backs on all cabinets and boxed into rabbets at all edges.
4. Fabricate bottom and top panels of lock-joint construction, glued and fastened to end panel-simple butted joint not permitted. Top and bottom of cabinets to be 3/4" thickness. Fasten partitions and fixed shelves into tops, bottoms or ends, as applicable; partitions and fixed shelves 3/4" thick except shelves 4'0" or wider to be 1" thick.
5. Unless otherwise shown, provide toe-space on floor-mounted units, 4-1/4" high and 3" deep.
6. Adjustable Metal Feet: Except for open shelving, equip bases of fixed floor-mounted cabinets 24" width and over, with adjustable metal feet at each corner, with adjustment being made with tool after removal of insert cap in cabinet bottom.
7. Adjustable Shelving: Support each shelf with four shelf clips permitting adjustment on 1-inch centers.

Figure 2-22. Manufactured cabinetry and casework are installed which are built according to the project specifications.

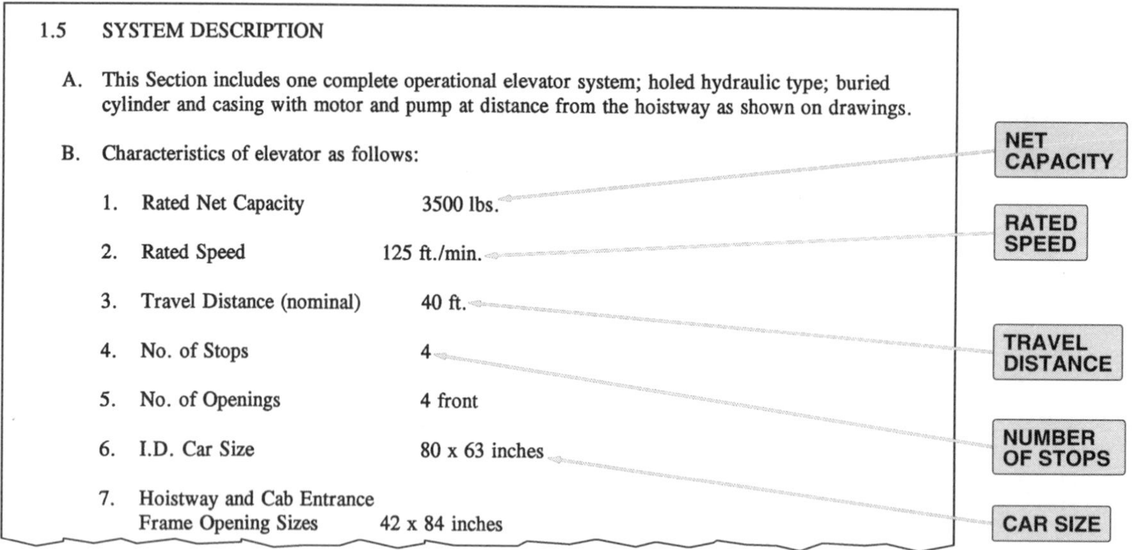
1.5 SYSTEM DESCRIPTION

A. This Section includes one complete operational elevator system; holed hydraulic type; buried cylinder and casing with motor and pump at distance from the hoistway as shown on drawings.

B. Characteristics of elevator as follows:

1.	Rated Net Capacity	3500 lbs.
2.	Rated Speed	125 ft./min.
3.	Travel Distance (nominal)	40 ft.
4.	No. of Stops	4
5.	No. of Openings	4 front
6.	I.D. Car Size	80 x 63 inches
7.	Hoistway and Cab Entrance Frame Opening Sizes	42 x 84 inches

Figure 2-23. Division 14 of the specifications provides information about conveying systems including elevators.

Division 15–Mechanical

Modern mechanical systems for large commercial projects are extremely complex. Architects, mechanical engineers, electrical engineers, and various general contractors and subcontractors must coordinate their work to ensure proper operation of these systems. General conditions of Division 15 include product and equipment warranties, maintenance instructions, and balance and test run reports. Basic materials and methods information, such as pipe types, hangers, and supports, duct and pipe connectors, insulation, gauges, flow control and measurement devices, electric motors and starters, and fuel tanks is given. Many types of control systems are installed on mechanical systems which are defined in Division 15.

Plumbing. Several sections of Division 15 apply to plumbing work. Water supply and treatment information includes connections to available water supplies and fire protection service pipes, valves, meters, and hydrants. Wastewater disposal and treatment information is given for waste piping and fittings and storm water drains. Piping and valves are specified by type of pipe, size, material, and ability to withstand certain pounds per square inch (psi) of pressure. See Figure 2-24. Piping and fittings for natural gas, compressed air systems, and vacuum systems are included in this division of the specifications. Tanks described include water heaters and storage tanks. Plumbing fixture information is given in the specifications for sinks, toilets, drinking fountains, and faucets.

HVAC. Heating, ventilating, and air conditioning systems generate heat from sources such as boilers or natural gas heaters, provide cooling with systems of refrigerants, chillers, and compressors, and distribute air throughout large areas with various air handlers, motors, fans, and duct systems. See Figure 2-25. In hot and cold water systems, specifications are given for piping, circulating pumps, and heat and cooling transfer equipment. Small heating and cooling systems, such as unit heaters and air conditioners for special conditions are specified. Other air handling situations described are the filtering, removal, and exhausting of fumes and smoke.

Fire Protection. Various agencies and codes which regulate fire protection equipment and develop standards are the National Fire Protection Association (NFPA), the Uniform Mechanical Code, the Uniform Building Code (UBC), the Occupational Safety and Health Act (OSHA), and local fire authorities. All fire protection systems are designed and installed in accordance with these agencies and codes. Specifications describe piping, sprinkler heads, check valves, and fire department connections for wet pipe systems. Dry pipe systems include much of this same information in addition to air compressor and air pressure requirements.

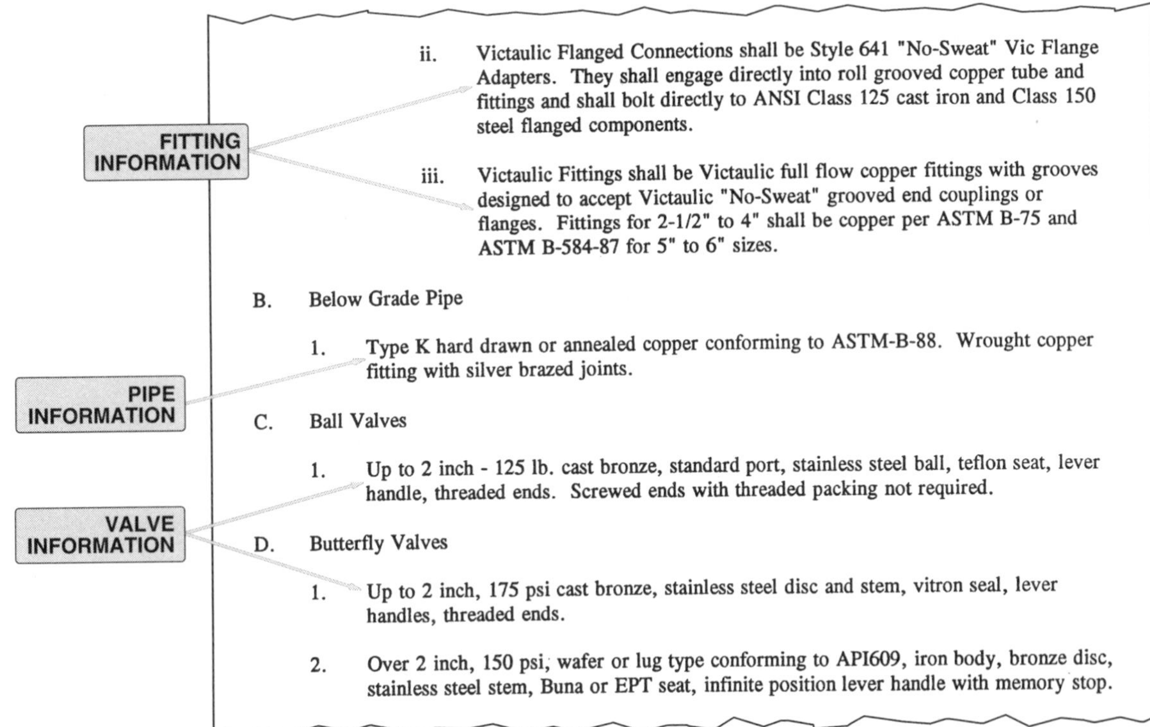

ii. Victaulic Flanged Connections shall be Style 641 "No-Sweat" Vic Flange Adapters. They shall engage directly into roll grooved copper tube and fittings and shall bolt directly to ANSI Class 125 cast iron and Class 150 steel flanged components.

iii. Victaulic Fittings shall be Victaulic full flow copper fittings with grooves designed to accept Victaulic "No-Sweat" grooved end couplings or flanges. Fittings for 2-1/2" to 4" shall be copper per ASTM B-75 and ASTM B-584-87 for 5" to 6" sizes.

B. Below Grade Pipe

1. Type K hard drawn or annealed copper conforming to ASTM-B-88. Wrought copper fitting with silver brazed joints.

C. Ball Valves

1. Up to 2 inch - 125 lb. cast bronze, standard port, stainless steel ball, teflon seat, lever handle, threaded ends. Screwed ends with threaded packing not required.

D. Butterfly Valves

1. Up to 2 inch, 175 psi cast bronze, stainless steel disc and stem, vitron seal, lever handles, threaded ends.

2. Over 2 inch, 150 psi, wafer or lug type conforming to API609, iron body, bronze disc, stainless steel stem, Buna or EPT seat, infinite position lever handle with memory stop.

Figure 2-24. Plumbing specifications give information about all piping components including valves and supports.

Figure 2-25. Ductwork carries heated or cooled air throughout the structure in forced-air installations.

Division 16–Electrical

Division 16 provides wiring, equipment, and finish information for electrical systems. These include written descriptions of electrical sitework, raceways and conduits, panelboards, lighting, communication and telephone systems, and electrical heating and cooling systems. The NEC® is updated every three years and is the model code on which many of the specifications rely. For example, 700-9(c)(1) has been added to the 1996 NEC® for assembly occupancies for greater than 1000 persons or for buildings above 75′ with any of the following occupancies: assembly, educational, residential, detention and correctional, business, or mercantile. Feeder-circuit wiring installed in these locations shall be protected by approved automatic fire suppression systems or by a listed protective system with a 1-hour fire rating. See Figure 2-26.

Wiring Information. Electrical wiring considerations in the specifications include the type and placement of wire and cable raceways, cable trays, conduit, junction boxes, and fittings. Proper procedures for trenching and sitework for placement of wiring and cables are given. Types and sizes of electrical wire and cable are described according to assembly, wire gauge, type of insulation and outer jacketing, and diameter. See Figure 2-27. Procedures for splicing, connecting, and terminations are described.

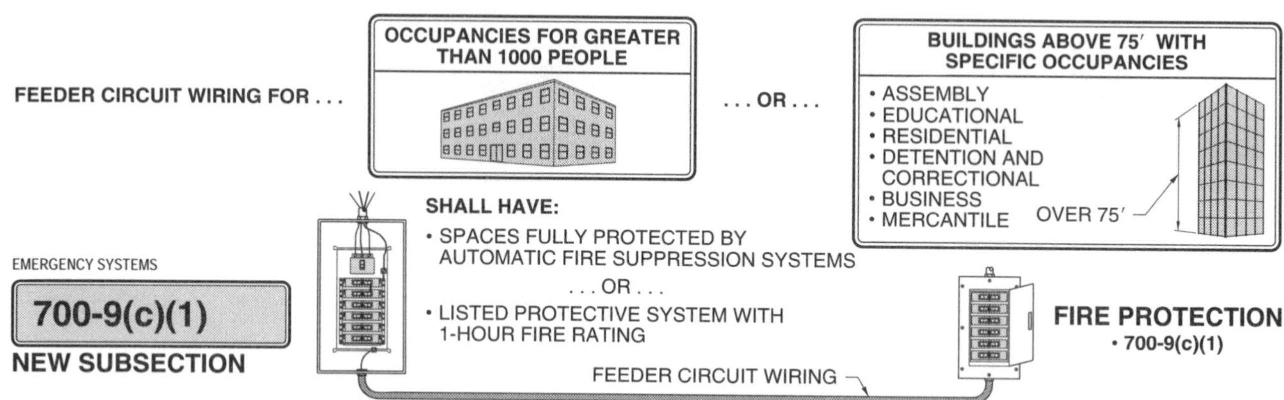

Figure 2-26. Many specifications and local building codes rely on information from the NEC®.

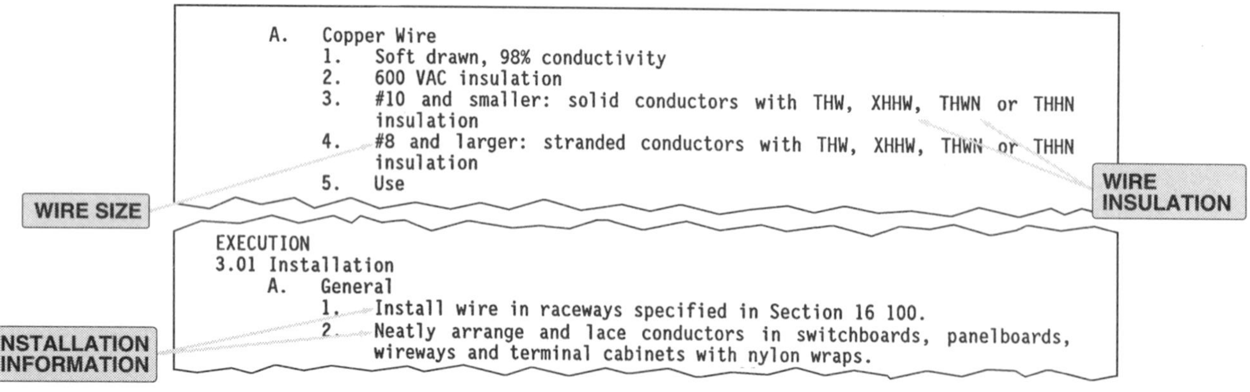

Figure 2-27. Division 16 includes electrical information concerning wires and cables.

Equipment Information. Switches, receptacles, panelboards, circuit breakers, electric heaters, transformers, lighting fixtures, communication systems, and fire and alarm systems are all part of the electrical equipment installed on large commercial construction projects. The specifications contain detailed placement descriptions, quality assurance requirements, acceptable manufacturer names and product numbers, and connection safety requirements for each of these areas. See Figure 2-28.

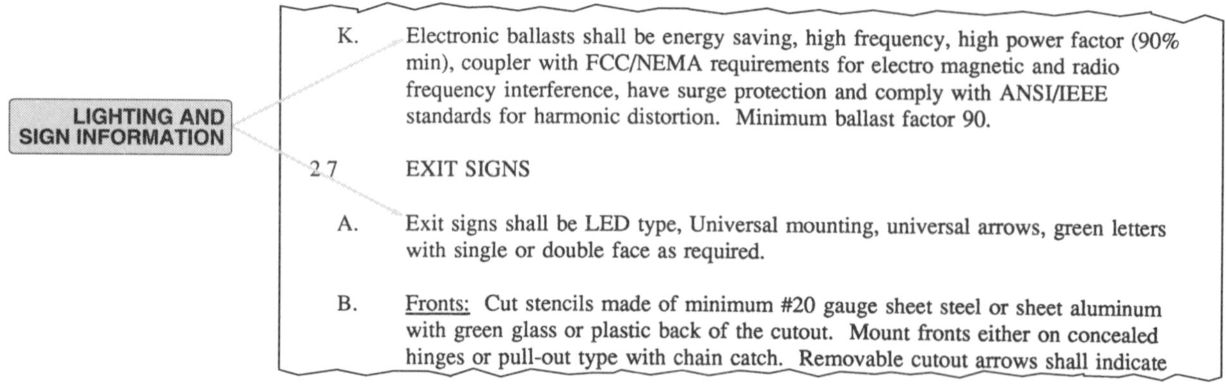

Figure 2-28. Lighting fixture specifications include information on fixture construction, voltage, and applicable industry standards.

Review Questions

Name ______________________ Date ______________

Printreading

T F **1.** The primary purpose of the CSI Format is to standardize the presentation of specifications.

__________ **2.** A chart which provides door, window, and room finish information in the specifications for each opening and room is a(n) ________.

__________ **3.** The NEC® mentioned in Division 16–Electrical of the CSI Format is the ________.

T F **4.** A pre-bid meeting is intended to plan the overall design of the specifications.

T F **5.** Piping specifications include piping requirements for withstanding given amounts of pressure per square inch.

__________ **6.** One of the items contractors may be held responsible for in the specifications is ________.

A. participating in the CSI
B. including disadvantaged business participation
C. providing funding for the project
D. all of the above

T F **7.** The names of the manufacturers and product numbers are commonly used in building construction specifications.

__________ **8.** The primary environmental condition which is given in the specifications concerning masonry and concrete construction is ________.

A. humidity
B. soil moisture content
C. temperature
D. cement content

__________ **9.** The time in which the construction project must be completed is given in Division ________.

__________ **10.** Precast concrete members are described in Division ________ of the specifications.

A. 1
B. 2
C. 3
D. 4

__________ **11.** Metal and steel construction methods described in Division ________ include fabrication procedures, installation tolerances for squareness, plumb and alignment, fastener locations, and finishing processes, such as grinding and paint priming.

A. 0
B. 3
C. 5
D. 7

__________ **12.** Contractor's responsibilities for subsurface exploration, excavation, compaction, and disposal of excavated materials are part of Division ________.

__________ **13.** A large commercial project has many different floor, wall, and ceiling finishes which are described on the ________.

__________ **14.** Paving materials and standards for their use and installation are described in Division ________.

A. 0
B. 1
C. 2
D. 3

__________ **15.** Division ________ provides metal and wood cabinetry and countertop information.

T F **16.** Extensive information concerning swinging metal doors and frames, swinging wood doors and frames, access doors, overhead doors and grilles, glass doors, and sliding doors is contained in Division 10 of the specifications.

__________ **17.** Division ________ provides wiring, equipment, and finish information for electrical systems.

A. 3
B. 10
C. 15
D. 16

T F **18.** Division 14 of the specifications provides information about conveying systems, including elevators.

__________ **19.** Division ________ includes rough wood framing, finish woodworking, and plastic materials, such as plastic laminate.

A. 6
B. 10
C. 14
D. 17

__________ **20.** General conditions of Division ________ include product and equipment warranties, maintenance instructions, and balance and test run reports.

A. 2
B. 5
C. 15
D. 17

__________ **21.** Division ________ of the CSI Format details specific information concerning applications of finish materials in each building area.

__________ **22.** ________ walls are composed of glass panels set in metal trim frames that are attached to structural members.

__________ **23.** Division ________ of the specifications addresses masonry units, mortars, reinforcement, and accessories.

A. 4
B. 5
C. 6
D. 7

__________ **24.** The proper procedures for roofing installation are included in the specifications in Division ________.

A. 2
B. 4
C. 7
D. 10

T F **25.** Division 13 describes elevator specifications such as net capacity, speed, travel distance, number of stops, car size and interior finish, power requirements, and automatic control systems.

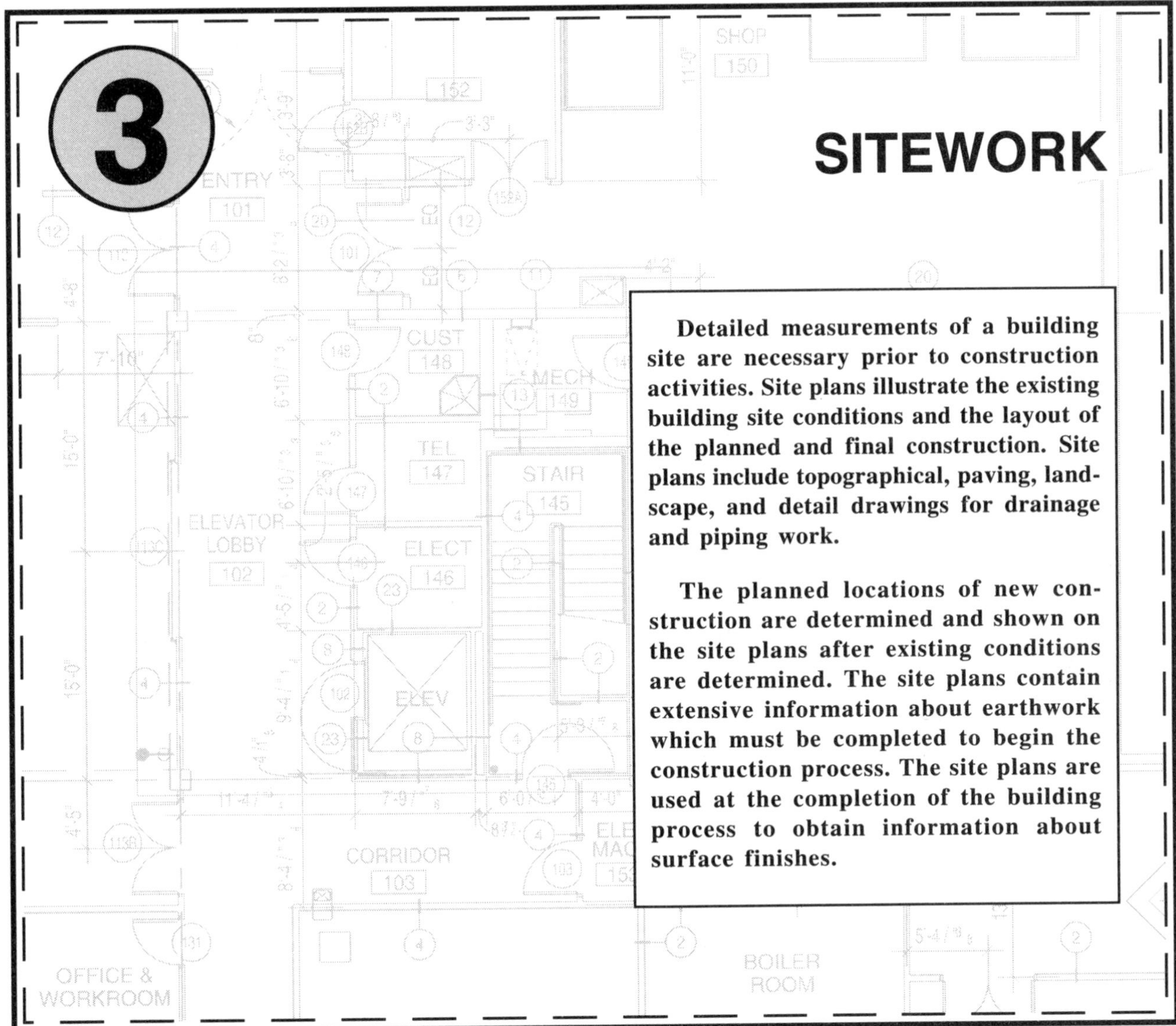

SITEWORK

Site plans illustrate the existing building site conditions and the layout of the planned final construction. Detailed measurements of the building site are necessary prior to construction activities. Horizontal elevations and vertical distances are measured by civil engineers and surveyors to accurately describe the property on which construction is located. The existing surface and subsurface conditions are determined by various methods and communicated on the site plans. The methods include property lines, rock and soil strata, buried items from prior construction, such as foundations, footings, and utilities, existing landscape features, and the possible existence of hazardous materials on the building site.

Site plans are referred to by a variety of names including the site survey, site map, site drawings and civil drawings. Site plans include topographical, paving, landscape, and detail drawings for drainage and piping work. Site plans are commonly noted with the prefix C (civil). For example, drawing sheet C1.1 is the first page of the site plans (civil drawings).

After the existing conditions are determined, the planned locations of new construction are determined and shown on the site plans. The new construction information includes placement of new structures, placements for utilities, surface grading, paving, curbs, walks, and landscaping.

Architects and engineers provide legends on the site plans. These legends describe commonly used lines, symbols, and abbreviations on the site plan. The scale of the site survey is also given. The scale is large enough to allow for large property areas to be shown on a single drawing sheet, such as 1″ = 50′ or larger. An indication of a North direction is also given on the plans. A portion of a city, county, or state map may also be part of the site plans to help locate the building site.

CIVIL ENGINEERING

Civil engineers are trained and licensed to measure and describe property. One of the first steps in any building project is the work of civil engineers. Based on existing elevation and property line information, measurements are taken which verify existing information, establish new points where existing information is inaccurate or incomplete, and provide complete location information for all new construction operations. See Figure 3-1.

Figure 3-1. Surveyors and civil engineers measure the dimensions and elevations of building construction sites.

Legal Information

Land surveyors are licensed by their location of practice. This may be by state, county, or city. A legal system of property description begins with plat plans which are recorded by governmental agencies. These plat plans are recorded with the state, county, or city and provide legal boundaries for property. A *plat* is a drawing of a parcel of land giving its legal description. New surveys rely on these previously recorded surveys as starting points for topographical and property line information. The United States Army Corps of Engineers has established a series of monuments which give clearly defined legal elevations for property description. See Figure 3-2.

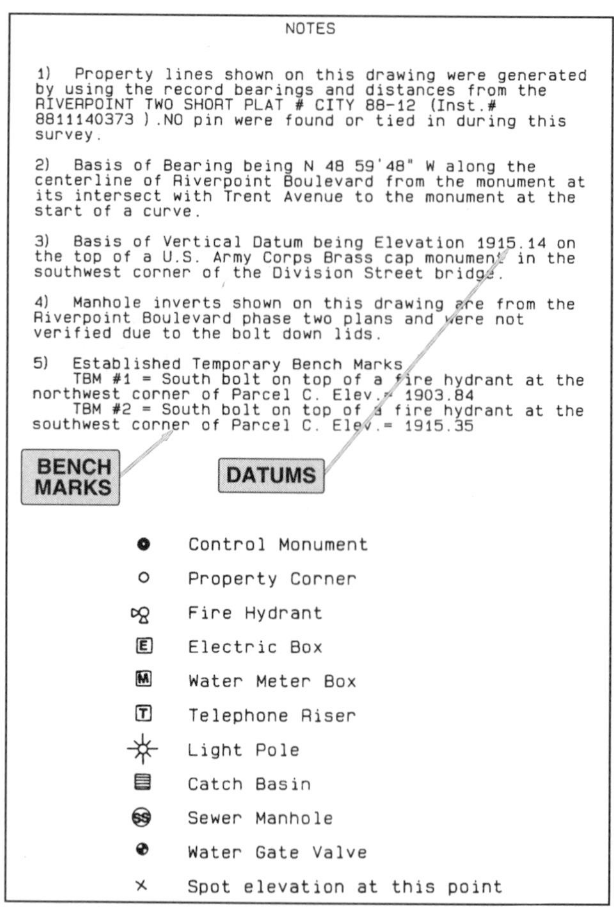

Figure 3-2. Notes on topographical drawings provide information concerning datum points and bench marks.

Property Description. Boundaries for construction projects are measured from street centerlines or from township lines established by the United States Coast and Geodetic Survey. Intersecting points of street centerlines provide surveying stations in metropolitan areas. Township boundaries measured from principal meridians are used where street intersection points are unavailable.

Electronic surveying equipment is available to ensure accuracy when measuring long and irregular shapes. See Figure 3-3. An electronic distance measurement (EDM) device is used with a series of targets to quickly and accurately measure distances. Electronic transits also read and record information from target measurements. In some instances, the information collected by electronic distance measuring and surveying devices can be downloaded directly into a computer which is linked to a computer-aided drafting (CAD) system for the production of the site plans.

Figure 3-3. Electronic surveying equipment helps ensure accuracy when measuring distances and elevations on large construction sites.

Methods are used to describe straight and curved property lines because of the irregular shapes of various pieces of property for commercial construction. Long distances are easily described when divided into smaller segments. For this purpose, a series of stations may be established at regular distances along reference lines.

Straight property reference lines are described by distances and compass directions from recognized points. For example, a centerline or property line may be stated as N 35° 36′ 24″ E 190.52′. This indicates that the centerline or property line between two particular surveying stations is 35 degrees, 36 minutes, and 24 seconds east of a true north/south line and this line continues in this direction for a distance of 190 feet and 52 hundredths of a foot. See Figure 3-4. Compass direction and distance are restated at the next point and between the next two stations.

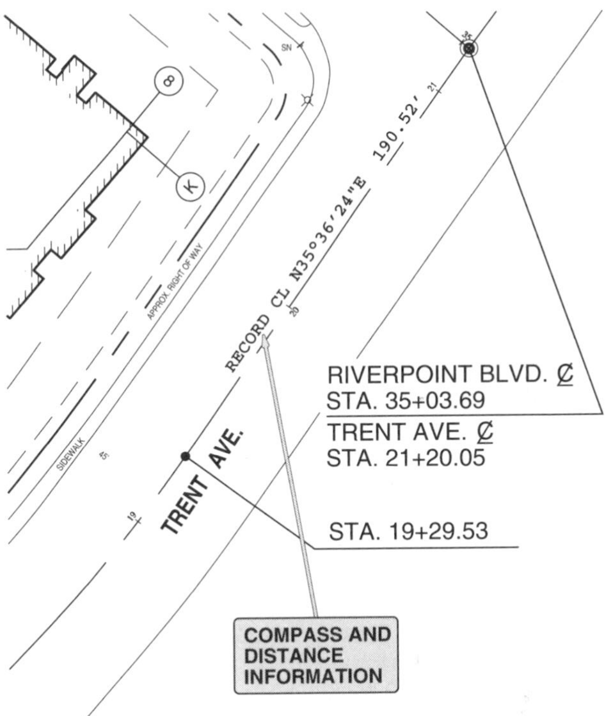

Figure 3-4. Reference and building lines are identified on site plans by a compass reading and a distance dimension.

Curved lines are described in terms of compass direction, the length of the radius for calculating the amount of curve, and the length of the curved segment. For example, a notation of $\Delta = 11° 31' 12''$ R = 605.00′, L = 121.64″ is given on a site plan. The delta sign indicates the change of compass direction, the R indicates the radius of the curve, and the L indicates the length of the arc section. The compass direction changes by 11 degrees, 31 minutes, and 12 seconds. The radius for calculating the amount of the curvature is 605 feet, and the length of the radius segment is 121 feet and 64 hundredths of a foot between two noted points. See Figure 3-5.

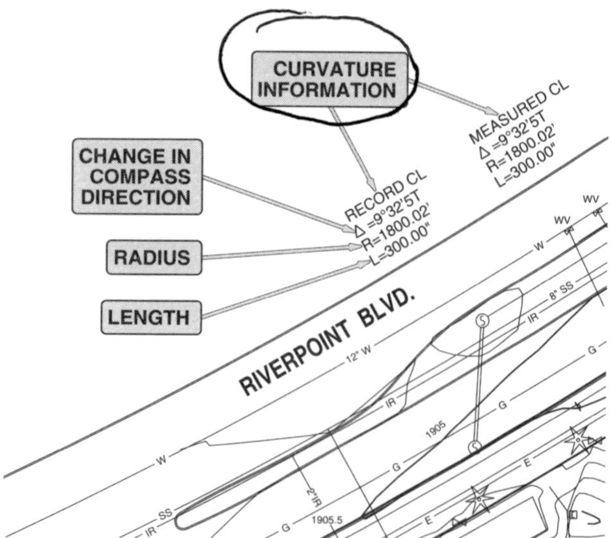

Figure 3-5. Curved property lines or building line segments are noted by a change in compass direction, radius, and length.

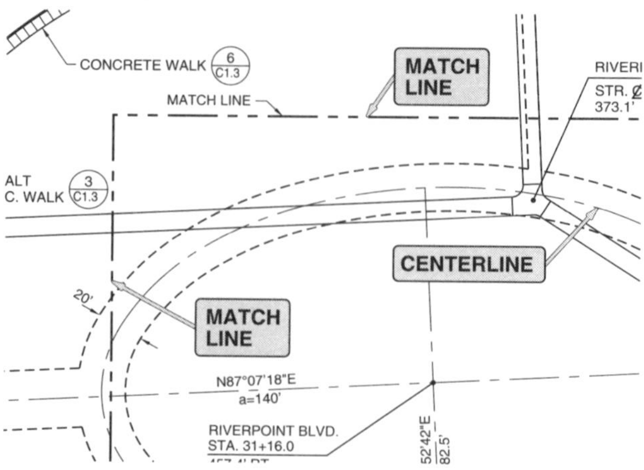

Figure 3-6. Two or more site plans may be easily related to each other with the use of match lines.

Site Layout

Legal boundaries and monuments act as starting points for the remainder of the surveying work. The existing grade of the property is measured. Building and reference lines for new construction are established. Easements and rights-of-way are located and noted on the site plan.

A clear layout of the entire site may not fit on one drawing sheet because of the large size of some commercial construction. A match line is given on the drawings to act as a reference line between individual plan sheets. The match line is used on two or more print sheets and allows for easier understanding of the relationship between drawings. See Figure 3-6.

Topographic Description. Elevations on the property are indicated by a series of contour lines. These lines may be at 1′ or 2′ intervals in elevation, depending on the severity of the slope of the property. Each contour line has a number along its length which indicates the elevation along that line. See Figure 3-7.

Building Lines. Site plans give the dimensions for the location of the new construction on the property. During the surveying process, reference stations are placed on the property from which building layout proceeds. These stations may be in the form of a building reference corner or line which are established by surveyors for use throughout the building project.

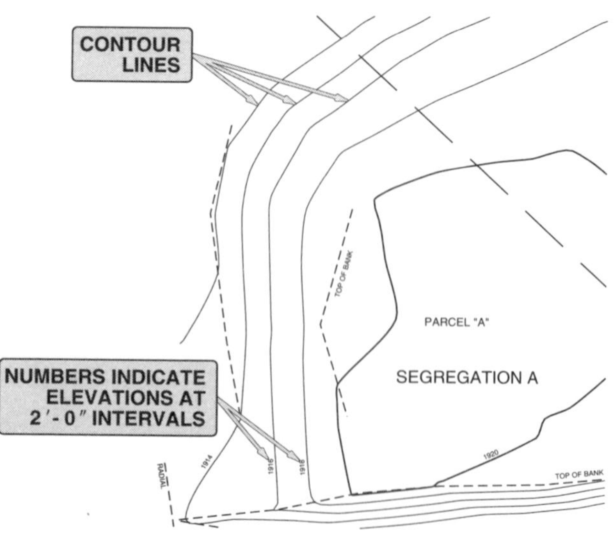

Figure 3-7. Site topographical information is shown with contour lines at regular elevation differentials.

Utilities. Utility information included on site plans includes locations for electrical connections, electrical light standards, natural gas piping, water supply, fire hydrant(s), storm and waste water drainage, and telephone cable. See Figure 3-8. Buried wiring and piping locations are based on prior surveys or information provided by utility companies. They are commonly indicated by a broken line with a letter indicating the utility given by each line. For example, a broken line with a W shows the location of water piping. Familiarity with these locations can avoid accidents involving excavation and severing of existing services. See Appendix.

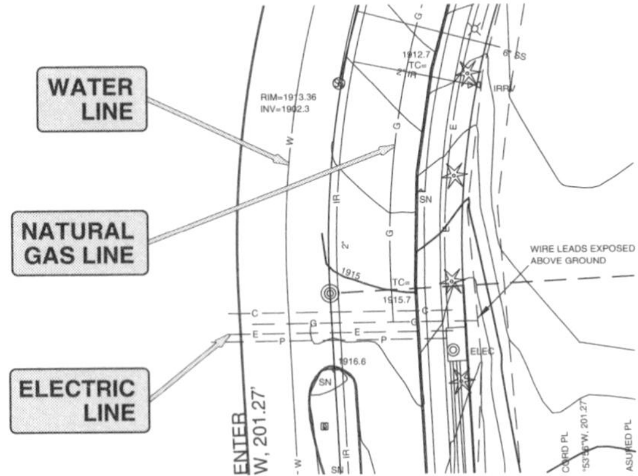

Figure 3-8. Existing utility locations are shown on site plans with broken lines and letters noting the type of utility service.

The width and location of the easements for utilities are also given on the site plans. *Easements* are areas of property set aside for the use of utility companies which allow for placement and maintenance of utility services.

SITE PREPARATION

The site plans contain extensive information about the earthwork which must be completed to begin the construction process. Soil engineers determine the bearing capacities and quality of the strata below the ground level. Operating engineers grade, remove, add, and compact the soil on the site in preparation for new construction. Below-grade and at-grade drainage systems are laid out and installed.

The location for construction equipment and materials is based on the site plan information. Temporary construction trailers are located where they do not interfere with the building process. Staging areas for delivery of materials must be determined. Accessibility of the areas on the building site where poured concrete is to be installed must be planned. Accessibility must be provided for cranes where large members must be lifted into place. Removal of the appropriate trees and shrubs and protection of the trees and shrubs which are to remain must be planned. The general contractor and construction manager use the site plans to lay out the entire construction area.

Soil Engineering

Soil engineers analyze samples taken from the building site. See Figure 3-9. The composition of each sample is determined. A report from the soil engineer to the owner and architect describes the various materials below the surface at specific points on the construction site. Determination of the composition of the subsurface materials provides valuable information for structural engineers when determining the foundation systems. Structural engineers calculate the live and dead loads which the structure places on the bearing strata at the building site. This loading information is compared to the soil engineer samples to determine the steps necessary to ensure that the footings and foundation provide adequate support to bear all imposed loads. Subsurface information is also used by various contractors bidding on drilling or excavation work.

Figure 3-9. Core samples are taken and analyzed to determine the bearing capacities of the building site.

Test Boring. The soil engineer determines a layout for drilling at the building site. A core drill is used to drill holes into the earth at these predetermined points. The various layers of soil, rock, and any other subsurface materials are measured for depth and analyzed for type. These borings are often made to determine the depth at which solid bearing can be reached. The location of the test boring holes may be shown on the site plan or provided on an additional drawing provided by the soil engineering firm. See Figure 3-10.

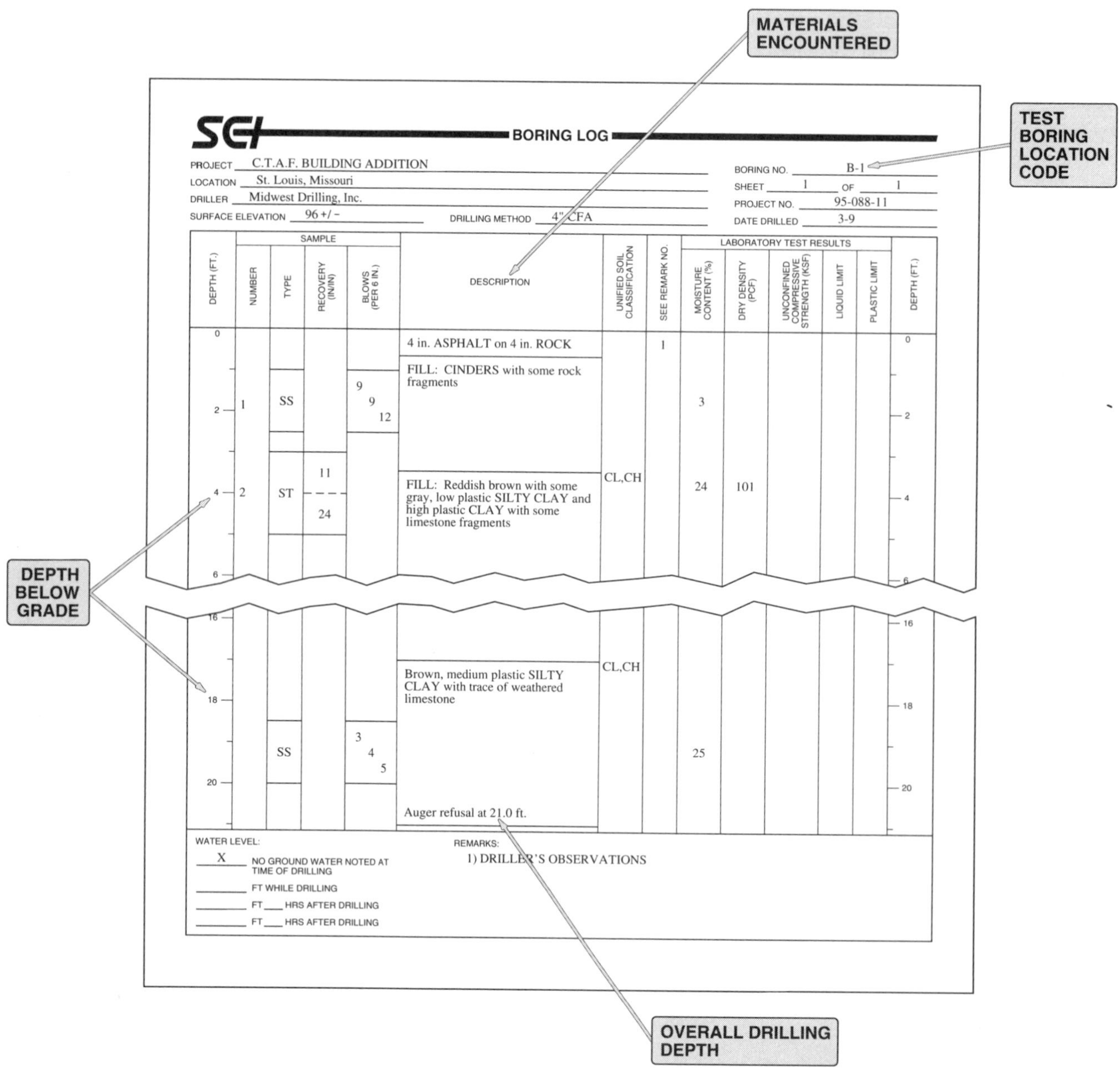

SCI BORING LOG

PROJECT C.T.A.F. BUILDING ADDITION
LOCATION St. Louis, Missouri
DRILLER Midwest Drilling, Inc.
SURFACE ELEVATION 96 +/ –
DRILLING METHOD 4" CFA

BORING NO. B-1
SHEET 1 OF 1
PROJECT NO. 95-088-11
DATE DRILLED 3-9

DEPTH (FT.)	SAMPLE NUMBER	SAMPLE TYPE	SAMPLE RECOVERY (IN/IN)	SAMPLE BLOWS (PER 6 IN.)	DESCRIPTION	UNIFIED SOIL CLASSIFICATION	SEE REMARK NO.	MOISTURE CONTENT (%)	DRY DENSITY (PCF)	UNCONFINED COMPRESSIVE STRENGTH (KSF)	LIQUID LIMIT	PLASTIC LIMIT	DEPTH (FT.)
0					4 in. ASPHALT on 4 in. ROCK		1						0
2	1	SS		9 9 12	FILL: CINDERS with some rock fragments			3					2
4	2	ST	11 / 24		FILL: Reddish brown with some gray, low plastic SILTY CLAY and high plastic CLAY with some limestone fragments	CL,CH		24	101				4
6													6
16													16
18					Brown, medium plastic SILTY CLAY with trace of weathered limestone	CL,CH							18
20		SS		3 4 5				25					20
					Auger refusal at 21.0 ft.								

WATER LEVEL:
X NO GROUND WATER NOTED AT TIME OF DRILLING
____ FT WHILE DRILLING
____ FT __ HRS AFTER DRILLING
____ FT __ HRS AFTER DRILLING

REMARKS:
1) DRILLER'S OBSERVATIONS

Figure 3-10. A careful study of soil test results gives reliable information about subsurface materials.

Subsurface Materials. Many types of materials are found below ground level. These include rock, decayed rock, loose rock, boulders, gravel, sand, clay, silt, and soil. Solid rock is normally considered to provide a stable bearing foundation. Decayed rock may be compact and hard or fully decayed and soft. Loose rock was at one time detached from the rock layer in which it was originally formed.

Boulders are rocks which have been transported by some geological action from their site of formation to their current location. Gravel is composed of pieces of rock smaller than boulders and larger than sand. Sand is classified as fine, medium, or coarse based on grain size. Clay is a mixture of chemicals and water which expands and contracts greatly based on water volume. Soil is measured for its depth at the site and its compaction.

Many other non-geologic materials may be discovered, such as abandoned foundations, wells, caves, and tunnels. Each presents different foundation design requirements for the engineer and architect.

Hazardous Materials. Soil analysis may indicate the existence of hazardous materials on the construction site. Hazardous materials include solid waste, toxic chemicals, and radiation. The Environmental Protection Agency (EPA) has identified specific hazardous waste materials and classified them according to corrosivity, ignitability, reactivity, and toxicity. Special remediation steps must be taken to contain or safely remove hazardous materials when they are found.

Information indicated on the site plan, which relates to hazardous materials, includes the location(s) of contaminated soil areas and locations for installation of geotextiles and groundwater monitoring wells. See Figure 3-11. *Geotextiles* are sheets or rolls of material that stabilize and retain soil or earth in position on slopes or other unstable conditions. Geotextiles divert ground water away from contaminated areas to keep hazardous materials from leeching into drinking water supplies. Groundwater monitoring wells enable regular checks of the subsurface water and ensure lack of contamination.

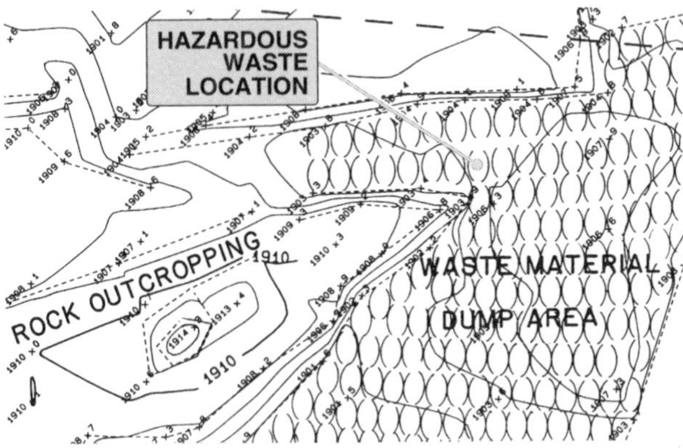

Figure 3-11. Site plans give the location(s) and plans for containment or removal of hazardous materials or contaminants discovered on the building site.

Earthwork

Earthwork is digging and excavating operations. Various plan views and section drawings provide earthwork information. Contour lines indicate the grading necessary for the placement of new construction including buildings, pavement areas, landscaping, and drainage.

Layout. Existing and planned elevations are shown on the site plans. See Figure 3-12. Dashed lines represent existing elevations. Solid lines represent planned elevations. Surveyors lay out and mark elevations at several points on the building site following the elevations and slopes indicated on the site plans. Elevation stakes are marked with elevations and measurements which act as guides to the operators of earth-moving equipment to add and remove earth and rock. Operating engineers refer to the markings on these layout stakes to determine the amount of cut and/or fill necessary. It may be necessary to refer to the architectural and foundation drawings to lay out the depth of excavations for foundations, footings, and piers. Additional layout information for subsurface piping may be found in the mechanical drawings.

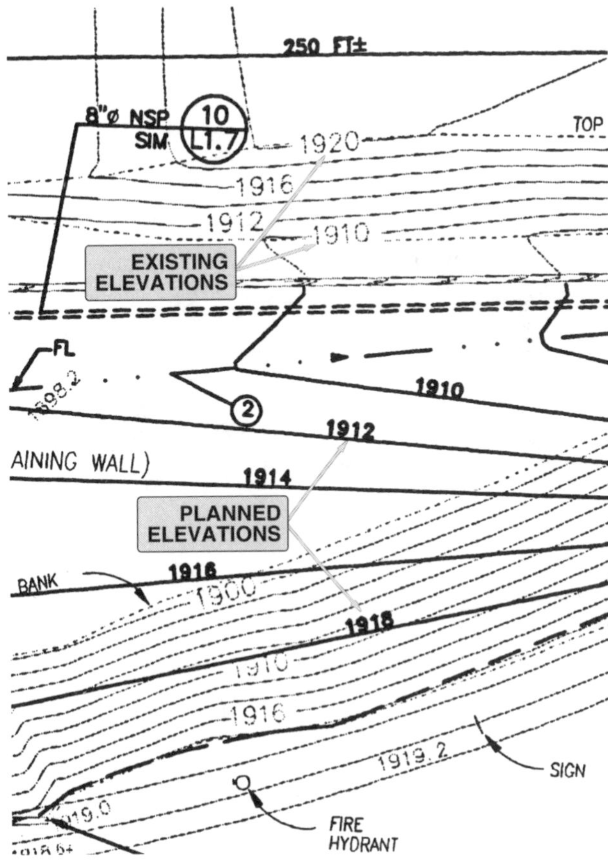

Figure 3-12. Existing and planned elevations are shown on site plans by different types of lines and symbols.

Grading. Many types of drilling machines, backhoes, dozers, and scrapers are necessary to excavate and move site materials. The excavation equipment used depends on the size of the site and the types of earth or rock to be moved. Depending on the soil type and surface conditions, steps may be necessary to control the creation of dust and to minimize soil erosion during the grading process. The proper finish elevations and amount of compaction must be obtained where soil is the primary surface and subsurface material. Failure to fully compact soil may result in settling which changes finish elevations. Use of sheepsfoot compactors and rollers compacts surface and subsurface materials. See Figure 3-13. The slope of the finish grade is often given as a percentage. For example, a 2% grade indicates a change in elevation equivalent to 2′ over a 100′ distance.

Figure 3-13. Proper compaction of layers of subgrade materials is achieved by use of sheepsfoot compactors.

In some instances, it may be necessary to remove rock by blasting. See Figure 3-14. A series of regularly spaced holes are drilled into the rock layers. Explosive charges are carefully placed into these holes. The spacing, number of holes, and amount of explosives in each blasting charge hole is determined by an analysis of the type and strength of the rock to be removed. After blasting, the loose rock is removed by the appropriate excavating equipment.

Figure 3-14. Controlled blasting removes layers of rock by using explosive materials placed below ground level.

Drainage Systems

Methods and materials for the removal of surface and waste water are given on the site plans. These include surface drainage plans, catch basins, trenches, piping, and geomembranes.

Storm Drainage. The flow of surface water into drainage systems is shown on site plans. Finish grade elevations are designed to channel water away from buildings and into surface drains. Catch basins and connecting piping are some of the first construction members installed on the building site. A *catch basin* is an artificial reservoir or tank used to obstruct the flow of objects that would not readily pass through a sewer. Locations and elevations of catch basins are indicated. See Figure 3-15. Catch basin information includes the elevation of the rim of the catch basin, elevation to the bottom of intake pipes, and the slope of intake and outflow pipes. The invert elevation is the elevation to the bottom channel of each connecting pipe. Slopes are commonly given as the percent of grade. Excavation for the installation of catch basins and piping are based on these elevations.

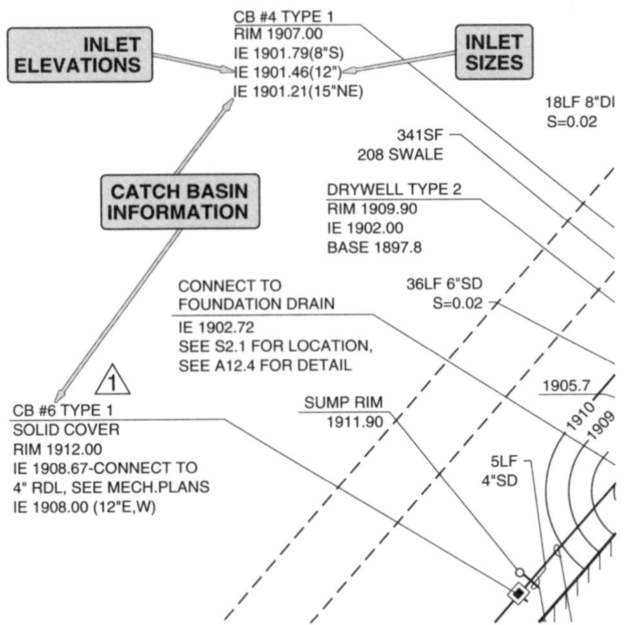

Figure 3-15. Surface water is channeled into catch basins at regular intervals on the building site.

Catch basins and their connecting pipes are commonly made of precast concrete. Detail drawings for catch basins are included which give dimension and material information. Support materials for catch basins include poured concrete and gravel. Proper compaction of subsurface materials is required to maintain catch basins and pipes at their designed elevations. The design and material for surface grates is also part of the detail drawings. See Figure 3-16.

Where roof drains are part of the storm drainage plan, elevations for the connections of the roof drainage piping to underground piping are given. The diameters and type of pipe may also be indicated.

Waste Drainage. A partial site plan may be provided at the beginning of the mechanical drawings. This indicates the location of the connection for the drainage systems to existing storm and waste utility pipes. The remainder of the waste piping for the structure is included in the mechanical drawings.

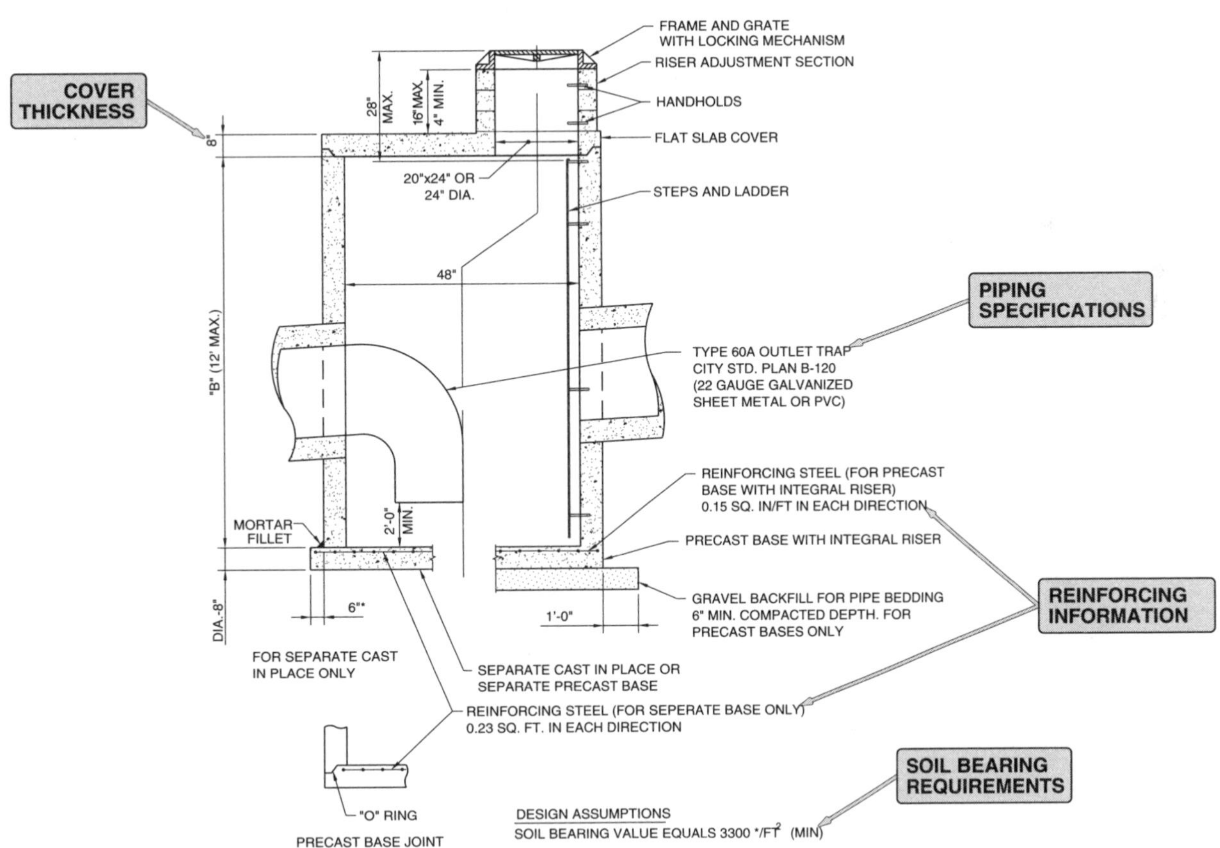

Figure 3-16. Catch basin detail drawings are included as part of the site plans pertaining to site drainage.

FINISH

The site plans are used at the completion of the building process to obtain information about surface finishes. After the majority of the building is constructed, the surrounding areas must be finished to provide the appropriate access and landscape design. Streets, parking lots, walks, and curbs are detailed on the site plans. Landscaping locations and materials may also be part of the site plans.

Drives

Access to the building site is commonly provided by vehicular-access drives. The widths and locations for placement of these drives are given on the site plans. See Figure 3-17.

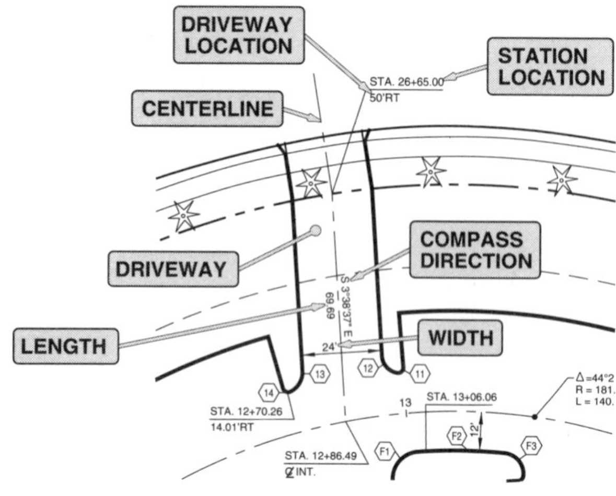

Figure 3-17. Driveway locations on site plans include the compass direction of centerline, station location, length, and width.

Drive Paving. Paving materials for drives include asphalt and concrete. The design of the paving materials depends on the planned usage. Heavier-usage drives are designed to withstand additional loads. Details in the site plans indicate the surface and subsurface paving materials required. Suitable paving performance requires proper compaction of the subgrade, installation and compaction of structural fill materials, and application of surface materials. See Figure 3-18.

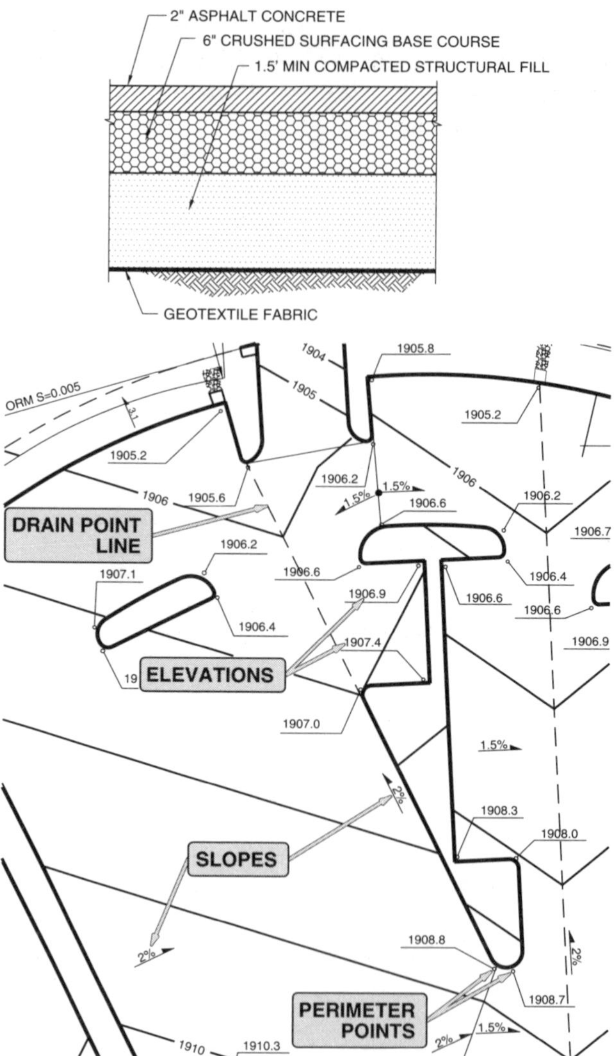

Figure 3-18. Section details of paving provide thicknesses and materials for each paving layer. Parking lot slopes and elevations are given with a series of perimeter points, percentage slopes, and drain point lines.

Slopes, elevations, and dimensions for paving are required to ensure proper drainage and accessibility. Site plans indicate elevations to the top of the edges of paved areas and the percentage of slope. For irregularly shaped paved areas, a schedule of paving designs and curvatures may be given. A parking layout plan indicates the size and number of parking spaces provided in each paved area. Painting and signage in the paved parking areas is shown.

Drive Curbs. Various curb designs are used depending on the possible need to match existing curbs or protect against damage in heavy usage conditions.

Site plans show locations where existing curbs must be removed to provide for new drives. Details in the site plans show the design and materials for new curbing. See Figure 3-19.

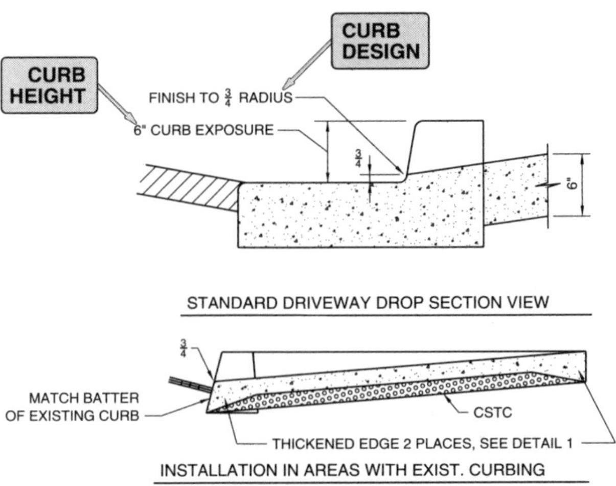

Figure 3-19. The amount of exposure and radius designs for curbing are provided in detail drawings.

Walks

Paved walks are made of many different materials and in many different designs. The proper layout and finishing of walks is given on the site plans. Dimensions include walk finish, width, length, and direction. See Figure 3-20.

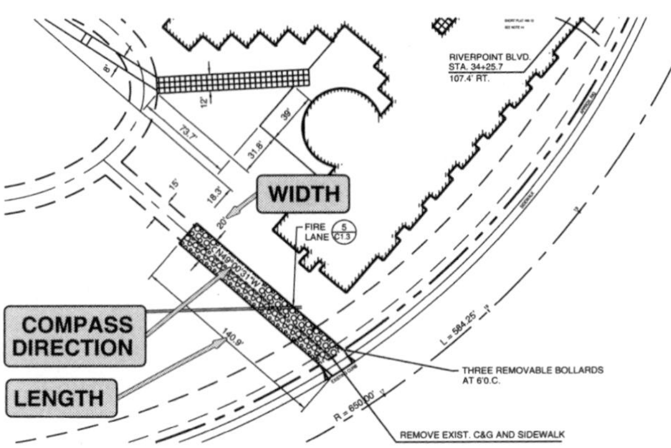

Figure 3-20. Sidewalks are shown on site plans in a manner similar to driveways.

Walk Paving. Finishing of walks must be done in a manner which provides for walkability with a minimum of slippage. Poured concrete, precast concrete, and asphalt are used for walkway materials. In a manner similar to pavement areas, details in the site plans provide subsurface and surface finish information.

Walk Curbs. Where walks and pavements meet, various curb and ramp designs are used to minimize tripping and provide handicapped access. See Figure 3-21. Special curbing around walkways may be necessary around planters or grassy areas.

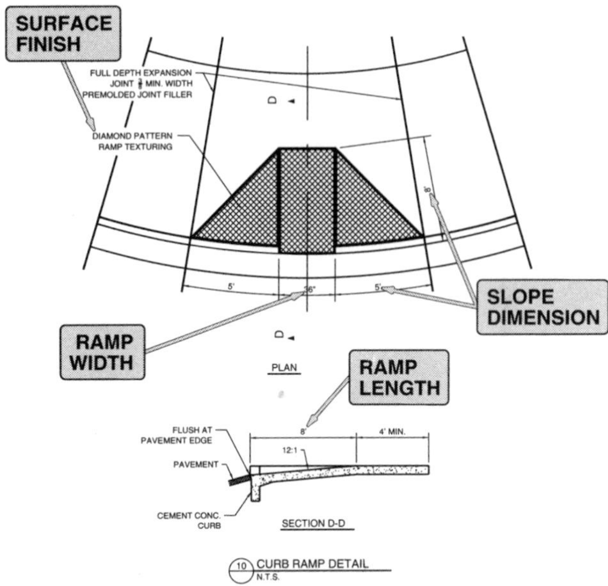

Figure 3-21. Sloping ramps provide safe accessibility and transition from paved driveways to sidewalks.

Landscaping

Many local building codes require a certain amount of landscaping and green space to be provided on new construction projects. The paving portion of the site plans provides the dimensions and locations for planters and open areas. The landscaping plans give information about the types of plant materials, methods for planting, and final surface treatments. If an irrigation system is to be installed, landscape plans indicate the locations and types of sprinkler heads and piping. See Figure 3-22. Detail drawings show piping connections, valve boxes, and sprinkler head details. Locations for exterior signage may also be shown on the detail drawings or on the topographical portion of the site plans.

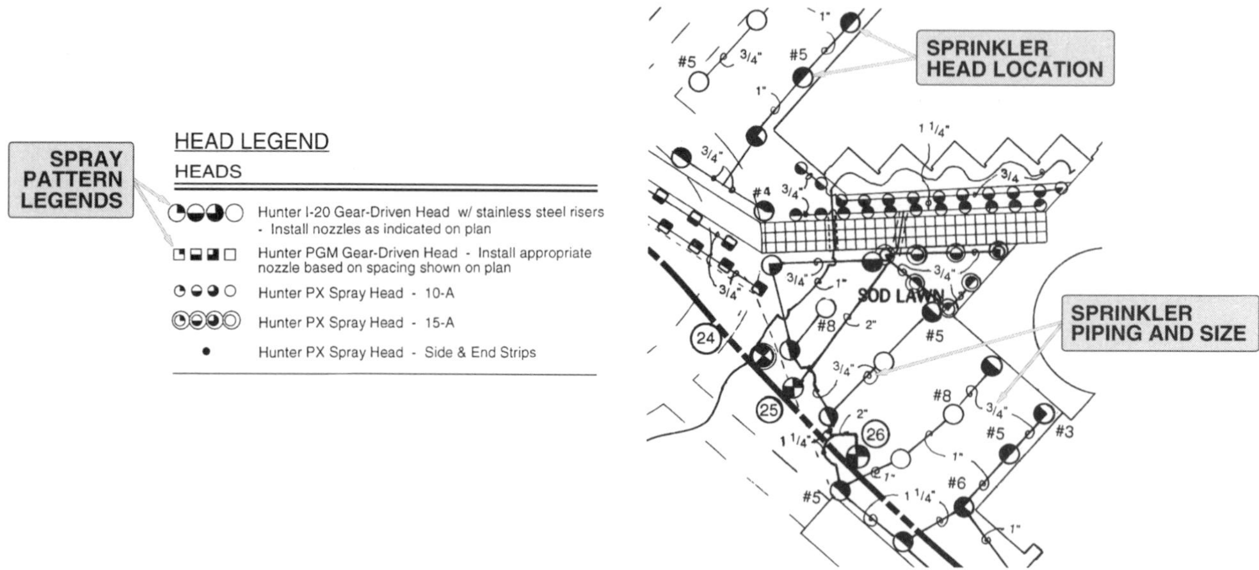

Figure 3-22. The landscape portion of the site plans include a plan view of sprinkler head locations and piping.

Plants. Various types of trees, shrubs, and ground cover are shown on landscape plans. Existing plantings at the building site are noted as to whether they are to remain or be removed. The scientific name, common name, and size of each type of plant is given along with the locations and number of each plant. See Figure 3-23. Detail drawings show the planting methods and materials to be used, including the depth of planting, soil amendments, and mulch.

Open Areas. Unpaved and unlandscaped areas are sodded or seeded for grass or left in their natural state. Treatment of these areas is indicated on landscape plans.

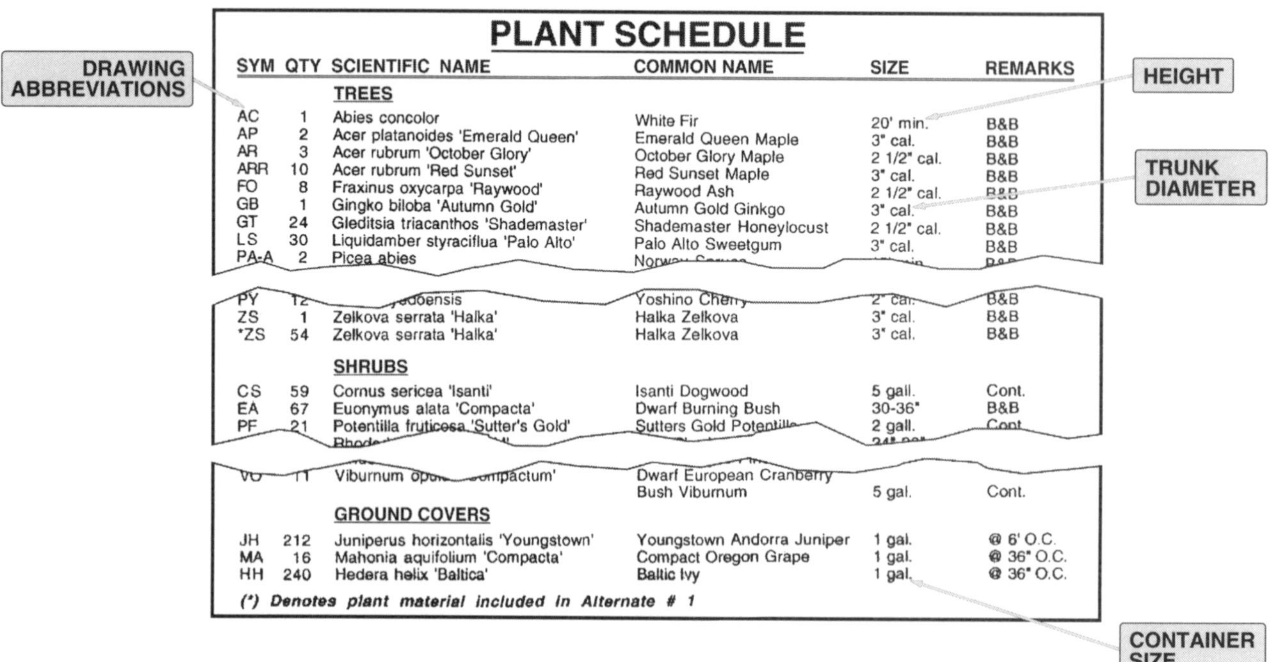

PLANT SCHEDULE

SYM	QTY	SCIENTIFIC NAME	COMMON NAME	SIZE	REMARKS
		TREES			
AC	1	Abies concolor	White Fir	20' min.	B&B
AP	2	Acer platanoides 'Emerald Queen'	Emerald Queen Maple	3" cal.	B&B
AR	3	Acer rubrum 'October Glory'	October Glory Maple	2 1/2" cal.	B&B
ARR	10	Acer rubrum 'Red Sunset'	Red Sunset Maple	3" cal.	B&B
FO	8	Fraxinus oxycarpa 'Raywood'	Raywood Ash	2 1/2" cal.	B&B
GB	1	Gingko biloba 'Autumn Gold'	Autumn Gold Ginkgo	3" cal.	B&B
GT	24	Gleditsia triacanthos 'Shademaster'	Shademaster Honeylocust	2 1/2" cal.	B&B
LS	30	Liquidamber styraciflua 'Palo Alto'	Palo Alto Sweetgum	3" cal.	B&B
PA-A	2	Picea abies			
PY		...yedoensis	Yoshino Cherry		B&B
ZS	1	Zelkova serrata 'Halka'	Halka Zelkova	3" cal.	B&B
*ZS	54	Zelkova serrata 'Halka'	Halka Zelkova	3" cal.	B&B
		SHRUBS			
CS	59	Cornus sericea 'Isanti'	Isanti Dogwood	5 gall.	Cont.
EA	67	Euonymus alata 'Compacta'	Dwarf Burning Bush	30-36"	B&B
PF	21	Potentilla fruticosa 'Sutter's Gold'	Sutters Gold Potentilla	2 gall.	Cont.
		Viburnum ...compactum'	Dwarf European Cranberry Bush Viburnum	5 gal.	Cont.
		GROUND COVERS			
JH	212	Juniperus horizontalis 'Youngstown'	Youngstown Andorra Juniper	1 gal.	@ 6' O.C.
MA	16	Mahonia aquifolium 'Compacta'	Compact Oregon Grape	1 gal.	@ 36" O.C.
HH	240	Hedera helix 'Baltica'	Baltic Ivy	1 gal.	@ 36" O.C.

(*) Denotes plant material included in Alternate # 1

Figure 3-23. A schedule of plant materials indicates abbreviations, types, sizes, and placement of landscaping.

Review Questions

Name ____________________ Date ____________

Printreading

T F 1. Site plans include topographical and paving information.

________ 2. Four pieces of information given for landscape materials, such as trees, are scientific name, common name, size, and ________.

T F 3. Surveyors are commonly licensed to practice land surveying.

T F 4. A match line on site plans pertains to utility connections.

________ 5. A typical scale for site plans is 1″ = ________.

A. 1″
B. 1′
C. 10′
D. 50′

T F 6. Contour lines are commonly placed at 5′ intervals for large commercial building projects.

________ 7. ________ is a material found in the earth which expands and contracts greatly based on water volume.

T F 8. Test borings aid in determining the depth of solid bearing and necessary foundation design.

________ 9. Elevations for the construction of newly paved areas are commonly given ________.

A. around the perimeter
B. at each drive intersection
C. at regular grid intervals
D. by contour lines

T F 10. Operating engineers consult site plans to determine the depth of piping excavations.

________ 11. A notation of a 5% grade over a 50′ distance results in an elevation change equal to ________.

T F 12. Wastewater utility connections are included in the mechanical drawings.

T F 13. Walk placement may be indicated by compass direction.

________ 14. Township boundaries are laid out from ________.

A. street intersections
B. principle meridians
C. property lines
D. centerlines

________ 15. Soil engineers determine ________.

A. elevation readings
B. subsurface conditions
C. landscaping layout
D. overall construction site layout

T F 16. Compaction of soil is relatively unimportant for finish grading operations.

________ 17. For surveying, an EDM is a(n) ________.

_______ **18.** Water quality around hazardous material areas is checked with _______.

A. catch basins
B. monitoring wells
C. geotextiles
D. soil analysis

_______ **19.** An invert elevation applies to _______.

A. finish grading
B. initial surveying readings
C. foundation and footing elevations
D. catch basin piping

T F **20.** A notation of S 32° 24′ 45″ W 50.45′ on a set of site plans is interpreted as a curved line 32° 24′ 45″ west of a north/south line for a distance of 50.45′.

T F **21.** A notation of Δ 12° 45′ 32″, R = 48′, L = 18.25′ is interpreted as a line at 12° 45′ 32″ with a reading of 48′ for a distance of 18.25′.

Contour Lines

_______ **1.** Existing contour line

_______ **2.** Planned contour line

_______ **3.** Existing elevation

_______ **4.** Planned elevation

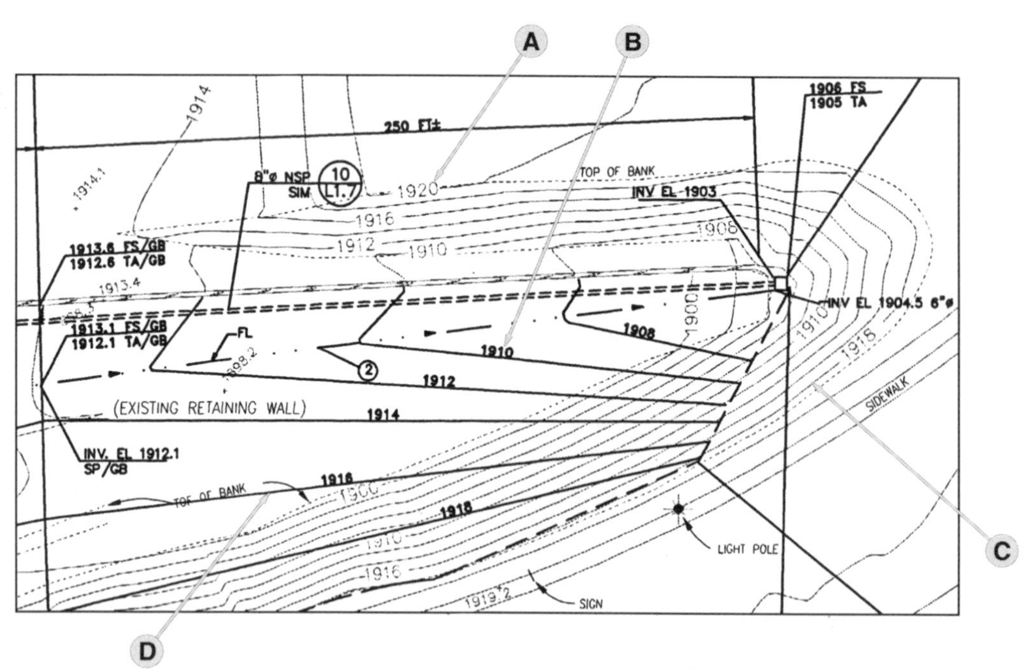

CHAPTER 3

SITEWORK

Trade Competency Test

Name ______________________________ Date ______________

SIRTI

Refer to Sheets 3, 4, 5, 6, 7, and 8.

________ **1.** The thickness of the foundation walls below the outlets is ________″ where catch basins empty into the Spokane River.

T F **2.** The east building line is at compass direction N 41° 0′ 12″ E.

T F **3.** A temporary construction fence is placed around the entire building site.

________ **4.** Catch basin #5 empties into ________.

A. an exposed rock area
B. the river bank
C. catch basin #6
D. the east parking lot

T F **5.** Riverpoint Boulevard is 100′ wide.

T F **6.** There are four surface water drain outlets into the Spokane River.

T F **7.** Most of the detail cuts from sheet L1.1 can be found on landscaping print pages 1.7 and 1.8.

________ **8.** The width of the utility easement is ________′.

T F **9.** A typical parking space size is 8′-0″ × 19′-0″.

T F **10.** Catch basin pipe #1 changes elevation by 1¼″ for each 10″ of lineal length.

T F **11.** The five boxes in the lower left corner of drawing L1.2 show paved areas for river overlooks.

T F **12.** Rock blasting is required approximately halfway between the SIRTI building and the pedestrian bridge to Gonzaga University.

________ **13.** Drain pipes in the three depressed 208 drainage areas along the river are ________.

A. precast concrete
B. 2″ PVC
C. clay tile
D. perforated

T F **14.** Stairs descend from Riverpoint Boulevard to the flagpole on the west side of the SIRTI building.

T F **15.** The controller for the irrigation system is placed near the cooling tower.

________ **16.** The width and length of curb ramps are ________.

A. 3′ × 6′
B. 4′ × 6′
C. 3′ × 8′
D. 4′ × 8′

T F **17.** All of the irrigation system piping is "weathermatic" or approved equal.

T F **18.** The irrigation system is winterized by blowing all water out of the piping.

T F **19.** Structural fill on geotextile fabric is compacted to 100% bearing.

_________ **20.** The typical width of the riverside walk is _________.

A. 10′-5½″ | C. 15′
B. 12′ | D. 20′-11.05″

T F **21.** A concrete curb is placed between the asphalt pavement and soil areas along the river.

_________ **22.** The width of the stone walk in alternate 8 is _________′.

A. 3 | C. 8
B. 4 | D. 11

T F **23.** The geotextile fabric continues horizontally under the footings for a distance of 2′ in contaminated soil areas.

T F **24.** The natural stone paving is made of granite.

T F **25.** All reinforcing steel used in the wing walls for the river catch basin outlets is ⅝″ diameter.

_________ **26.** The number of new fire hydrants to be installed as part of the current construction is _________.

A. none | C. 2
B. 1 | D. 3

_________ **27.** The closest the foundation comes to the building line is _________.

A. 25′ | C. 95′-4″
B. 60′-3″ | D. 100′

_________ **28.** The scale is 1″ = _________′ on the Site Topo map.

A. 30 | C. 50
B. 40 | D. 100

_________ **29.** The diameter of the storm sewer line is _________″.

_________ **30.** The spacing of the contour lines on the Site Topo map is _________.

A. 1′ | C. 3′
B. 2′ | D. there are no contour lines shown

_________ **31.** Irrigation piping through the Riverpoint Boulevard divider strip is _________.

A. polyvinyl chloride | C. copper
B. concrete | D. the material is not shown

T F **32.** The bollards along the river walk improve drainage.

_________ **33.** The top surface of the walkway, which runs the full length of the property along the river, is made of _________.

A. gravel | C. concrete
B. asphalt | D. natural stone

_________ **34.** The primary backfill material in the 208 swale sections along the Spokane River is _________.

_________ **35.** The abbreviation GPM on print drawing L1.4 means _________.

_________ **36.** The dashed lines on sheet L1.2 underneath the southwest walk and driveway indicate _________.

A. electrical lines
B. drain piping for catch basins
C. parking lot striping areas
D. piping for irrigation sleeves

_________ **37.** The planting area at the intersection of Trent Avenue and Riverpoint Boulevard is watered by _________.

A. shrub spray #420
B. lawn spray PK50
C. strip spray #310
D. riser 8024

_________ **38.** The distance from the south SIRTI building line to the northernmost edge of the east parking lot is _________.

_________ **39.** For alternate 8, the irrigation plan changes because the sprinkler heads _________.

A. need to be larger
B. are covered by concrete steps
C. need additional piping
D. are replaced by a different system

_________ **40.** The depth of the structural fill beneath the north SIRTI footing and foundation _________.

A. is 6″ minimum
B. is 12″ minimum
C. is 24″ minimum
D. varies

_________ **41.** The inside horizontal dimension for catch basins is _________.

A. 4′ square
B. 2′ × 4′
C. 4′ diameter
D. 5′ diameter

_________ **42.** The number of monitoring wells on this site is _________.

_________ **43.** Posts supporting the bench on the river walk are _________.

A. painted black steel
B. stainless steel
C. aluminum
D. wood

_________ **44.** The depth of parking lot island planting areas is _________′.

A. 1
B. 2
C. 3
D. 4

_________ **45.** The length of the centerline of Riverpoint Boulevard between point N10000 and N9621.251 is _________′.

_________ **46.** The total number of parking spaces is _________.

A. 75
B. 106
C. 128
D. 220

T F **47.** Both temporary benchmarks are on the south side of the property.

_________ **48.** The elevation of the finish grade surrounding the lowest stair landing nearest the river is _________′.

A. 1902
B. 1904
C. 1906
D. 1908

_________ **49.** The planned I.E. mentioned on the Site Topo map refers to _________.

A. internal electric line
B. interim excavation
C. invert elevation
D. interior elevation

________ **50.** The elevation of the highest point on the property is ________′.

________ **51.** The minimum depth of the irrigation line along Riverpoint Boulevard is ________″.

A. 8
B. 18
C. 24
D. 30

T F **52.** Catch basin #9 is located just east of the cooling tower.

________ **53.** The top of the exposed rock wall at its closest point to Trent Avenue is ________′.

A. 1902.5
B. 1904.5
C. 1908.2
D. 1912.3

________ **54.** The diameter of the irrigation lines in the area of the SIRTI building sign is ________″.

T F **55.** Planting areas require either burlap or geotextile fabric.

________ **56.** The finished typical topsoil thickness at contaminated soil areas is ________″.

A. 8
B. 12
C. 16
D. 24

________ **57.** The primary reference point for elevations and distance on the SIRTI building is in the ________ corner.

A. southeast
B. northeast
C. southwest
D. northwest

________ **58.** The thickness of the gravel base under curb ramps is ________″.

A. 6
B. 12
C. 18
D. 20

________ **59.** There are ________ handicapped accessible parking spots.

A. 2
B. 3
C. 4
D. 5

________ **60.** Catch basin #4 rim elevation is ________ existing grade.

A. approximately 2′-3″ above
B. approximately at
C. approximately 2′-3″ below
D. none of the above

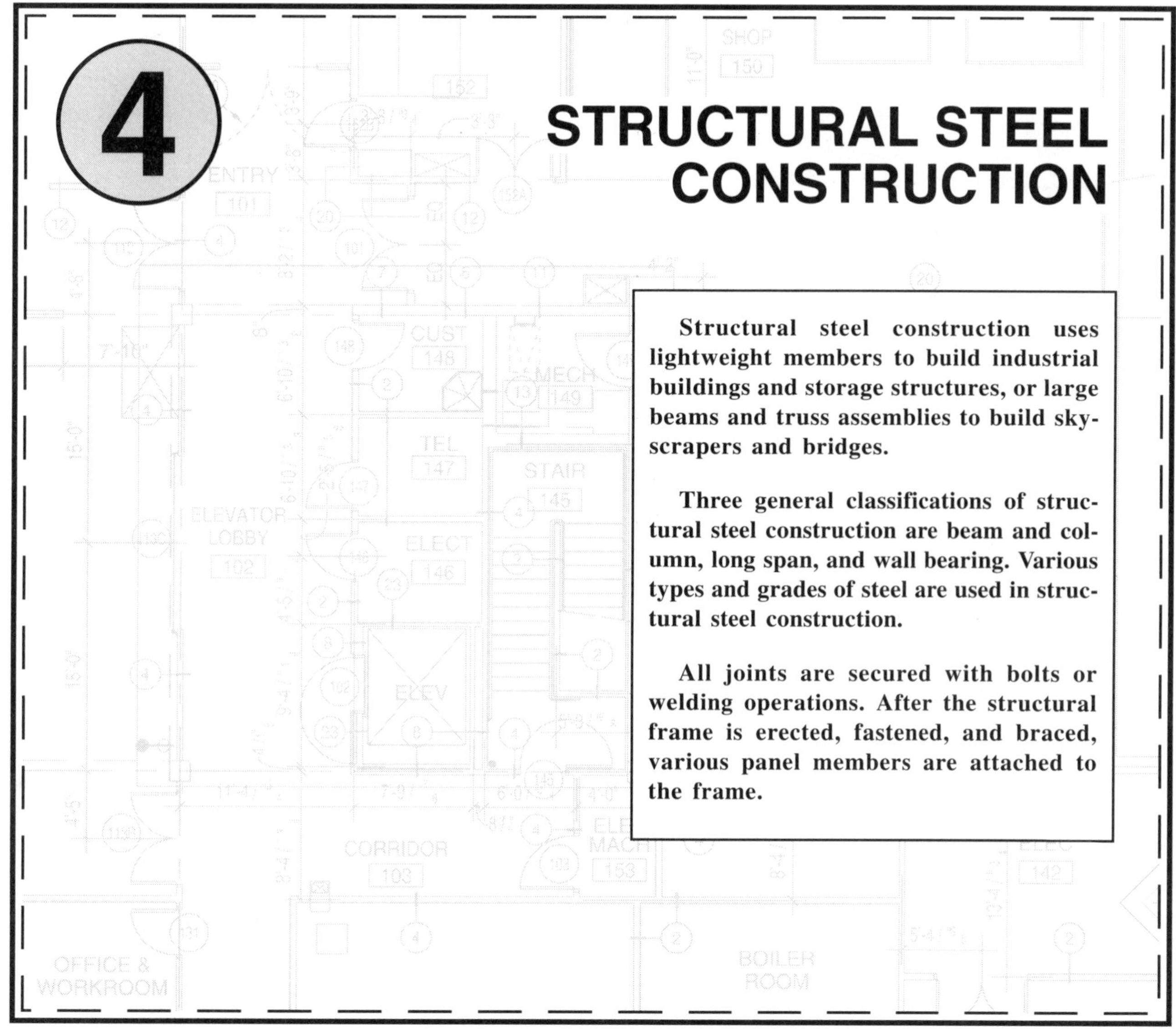

4 STRUCTURAL STEEL CONSTRUCTION

Structural steel construction uses lightweight members to build industrial buildings and storage structures, or large beams and truss assemblies to build skyscrapers and bridges.

Three general classifications of structural steel construction are beam and column, long span, and wall bearing. Various types and grades of steel are used in structural steel construction.

All joints are secured with bolts or welding operations. After the structural frame is erected, fastened, and braced, various panel members are attached to the frame.

STRUCTURAL STEEL CONSTRUCTION

Structural steel construction may use lightweight members to build industrial buildings and storage structures or large beams and truss assemblies to build skyscrapers and bridges. Structural steel may be used as an independent construction method or used with other methods, such as masonry or reinforced concrete. Several common steps are used when building with structural steel.

A structural engineer determines the steel to be used and sizes and shapes of steel members necessary after all loads which are to be placed on the structure have been determined. The various steel members are fabricated at a location away from the building site according to shop drawings. The structural steel components are transported to the job site where the members are unloaded (shaked out). *Shaking out* is the process of unloading steel members in a planned manner to minimize the moving of pieces during the erection process. Structural steel members are lifted into place with various lifting equipment. See Figure 4-1. Structural steel components are erected, braced, and fastened together to create the structural frame. This frame is covered with the materials for floors, walls, and roofing.

United States Steel Corporation

Figure 4-1. Structural steel construction is a system in which steel components are fabricated, transported, lifted, aligned, fastened, and finished into a complete structure.

Republic Steel Corporation

Figure 4-2. In beam and column construction, beams and girders carry horizontal loads onto vertical columns.

STRUCTURAL STEEL CONSTRUCTION METHODS

Varying engineering requirements and construction site conditions create the need for several methods of structural steel construction. Three general classifications of structural steel construction are beam and column, long span, and wall bearing. Erection plans provide information for placement of steel members for each structural steel construction method.

The proper handling, lifting, and placement of steel members is essential in each structural steel construction method. Developments in lifting technology have created the ability to lift extremely heavy loads and large members. Knowledge of safe rigging procedures and crane capacities ensures the erection of steel members is performed quickly and without injury.

Beam and Column

The most common structural steel construction method is beam and column construction. *Beam and column construction* consists of bays of framed structural steel which are repeated to create large structures. See Figure 4-2. A series of footings, foundations, piers, or pilings are constructed. Steel columns are set onto the foundation members and attached with anchor bolts and plates. Horizontal steel beams and girders are attached to the columns.

Angles may be attached to columns to form a seat for the beams or they may be attached to beams that are bolted to columns. Tie rods, channels, and other bracing members are used to enhance stability. Joists and purlins are placed between the columns and beams to finish the structural portion of the construction.

Long Span

Long span construction consists of large horizontal steel members, such as girders and trusses, that are fastened together to create large girders and trusses. Long span construction is used for structures such as bridges and large arenas. In long span construction, a series of built-up girders and trusses is used for spanning large areas without the need for excessive intermediate columns or other supports. See Figure 4-3. This method is commonly used for bridge construction. Large girders and beams span between bridge abutments, piers, and other supports. Decking of concrete or steel is supported by the large structural steel members. Detail drawings and shop drawings show the arrangement of the various angles, channels, and other members used to construct girders and trusses.

Figure 4-3. In long span construction, long distances are spanned with built-up structural steel trusses and girders.

Republic Steel Corporation

Figure 4-4. In wall bearing construction, structural steel beams and joists are used in combination with other supporting wall systems.

Wall Bearing

Wall bearing construction integrates horizontal steel beams and joists into other construction methods such as masonry and reinforced concrete. Steel support members are used to span floors and roofs between masonry or reinforced concrete-constructed walls. Masonry or concrete walls support the vertical loads and structural steel beams and joists carry the horizontal loads. See Figure 4-4. The installation of bearing base plates on the masonry or concrete walls provides proper load distribution at the points where the structural steel members rest on the walls.

Erection Plans

Erection plans include drawings giving information about anchor bolt layout, plan views of the structural steel members at each floor level, sectional views taken from cutting planes, elevation drawings, and detail drawings including steel component information and connection illustrations. See Figure 4-5. The number of drawings required and their complexity depend on the size of the structure and the amount of steel to be placed.

Purposes. Structural steel erection plans are required to ensure that the proper steel members are placed in the correct locations. Structural steel erection plans provide directional information to allow for placement of structural steel members in the proper direction and relation to each other and ensure proper connections are made with other steel members and building components. Connection information includes bolts, welding, or other required fasteners.

Format. Erection plans show the locations of each structural steel member, assembly information, dimensions, the number of steel pieces in a member, and any additional information needed for erection of the steel. Steel members are oriented according to a letter and number grid given in a plan view. See Figure 4-6. The distances between grid lines are given around the building perimeter. Columns, beams, girders, joists, and bracing are coded according to the letter and number grid on the plan views. Grid identifications of letters and numbers on the plan views are related to all other drawings including the elevation drawings, detail drawings, and fabrication shop drawings. Capital letters denote main structural members, such as B for beam or C for column. Small letters denote component parts of a member such as b for a bracket on a beam.

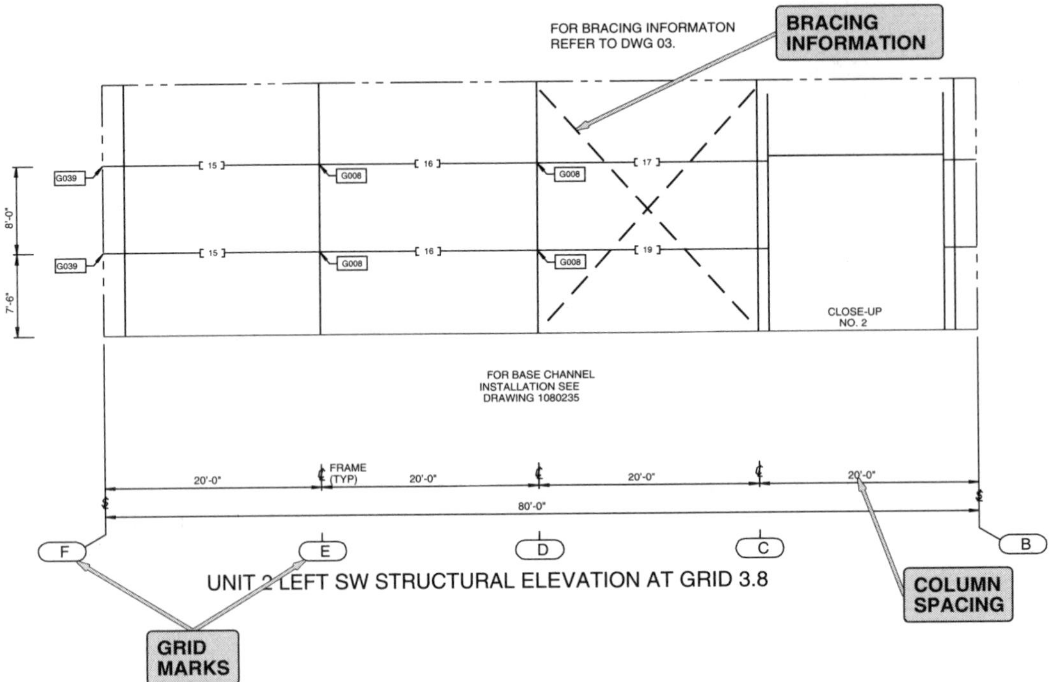

Figure 4-5. Erection plans provide print information specific to structural steel construction.

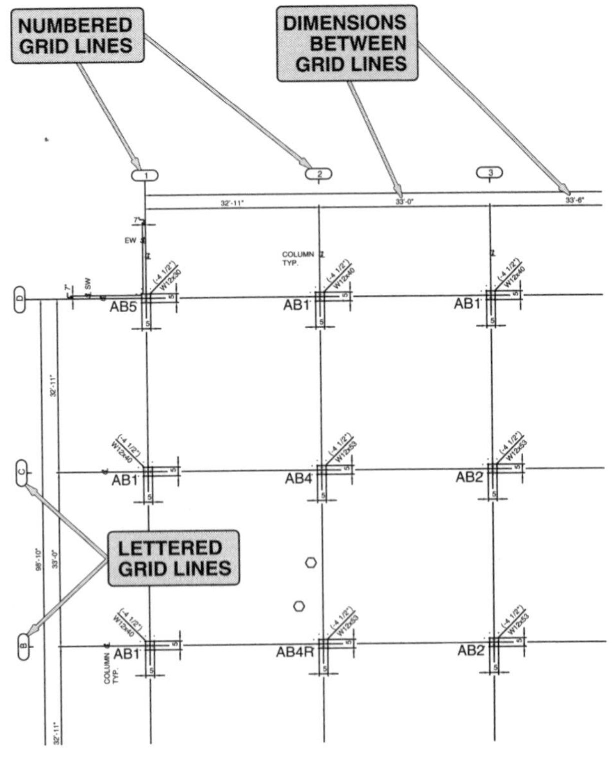

Figure 4-6. A dimensioned grid of letters and numbers provide reference points on erection plans.

A plan view is provided for each level of the structure. For buildings, the lowest level plan view notes anchor bolt information. The next level of plan view shows column and beam placement. Subsequent plan views show floor and roof decking placement. Various elevation views provide information about columns, beams, elevations, and exterior cladding. Various bracing members are also shown. Detail drawings provide connection and fastener information.

STRUCTURAL STEEL MEMBERS

The various types and grades of steel used in structural steel construction include carbon steel, high-strength steel, high-strength low-alloy steel, corrosion-resistant high-strength low-alloy steel, and quenched and tempered alloy steel. See Figure 4-7. The most common type of steel used for structural steel construction is classified by the ASTM as A36 with a pounds per square inch yield strength of 36,000 lb. The uses and applications of the various types of steel depend on the engineering requirements for a particular structure.

STRUCTURAL STEEL				
Steel Type	**ASTM Designation**	**Minimum Yield Stress***	**Form**	**Remarks**
Carbon Steel	A36	36	Plates, shapes, bars, sheets and strips, rivets, bolts, and nuts	For buildings and general structures. Available in high toughness grades
	A529	42	Plates, shapes, bars	For buildings and similar construction
High-Strength	A440	42 to 50	Plates, shapes, bars	Lightweight and superior corrosion resistance
High-Strength Low-Alloy	A441	40 to 50	Plates, shapes, bars	Primarily for lightweight welded building and bridges
	A572	42 to 65	Several types. Some available as shapes, plates, or bars	Lightweight, high toughness for buildings, bridges, and similar structures
Corrosion-Resistant High-Strength Low-Alloy	A242	42 to 50	Plates, shapes, bars	Lightweight and added durability. Weathering grades available
	A588	42 to 50	Plates, shapes, bars	Lightweight, durable in high thicknesses. Weathering grades available
Quenched and Tempered Alloy	A514	90 to 100	Several types. Some available as shapes, others as plates	Strength varies with thickness and type

* KSI (1000 lb)

Figure 4-7. Different types of steel are used for specific purposes in structural steel construction.

Many steel shapes are required for structural steel construction. Common steel shapes include wide flange, beam, lightweight column, channel, angle, tee, bearing pile, zee, plate, flat bar, tie rod, and pipe column. See Figure 4-8. See Appendix. A variety of letters, numbers, and symbols are used to show the different structural steel shapes on print drawings.

A variety of steel designs are manufactured to meet all of the applications and loading requirements for columns, beams, girders, joists, braces, plates, and other building members. Variables in the designs include the steel composition, shape, thickness, weight, and length. Variances in the weight of the steel shape (in lb/ft) creates differences between nominal size classifications and actual sizes of structural steel members. To prevent failure in case of fire, structural steel members are treated with several different spray cement mixtures and may be encased in concrete, masonry, or gypsum.

Columns

Columns are the principle load-carrying vertical member in structural steel construction. Columns are supported by foundations or footings. Columns are normally the first members erected for beam and column construction. Shop detail drawings for columns indicate the overall column height, spacing of holes for the attachment of beams and bracing, base plate information, such as plate thickness and size, locations and angle size, and shear tabs for connections to beams and girders. See Figure 4-9.

Steel columns are commonly made from American Standard beams, commonly referred to as I or S shapes, or wide-flanged shapes classified as W or WF shapes. The size and design of the columns may be provided on a schedule and detail drawings. The loading requirements for the column determine column size and design.

COMMON STEEL SHAPES			
Description	**Pictorial**	**Symbol**	**Use**
WIDE FLANGE	 WEB, FLANGE	WF	24WF76
BEAM		I	15I42.9
LIGHT COLUMN	 NOMINAL DEPTH	M	8 x 8M 34.3
CHANNEL	 DEPTH	⊔	9⊔13.4
ANGLE	 LEGS	L	L 3 x 3 x $\frac{1}{4}$
TEE	 FLANGE, STEM	T	T4 x 3 x 9.2
BEARING PILE		BP	14 BP 73
ZEE		Z	Z6 x 3$\frac{1}{2}$ x 15.7
PLATE	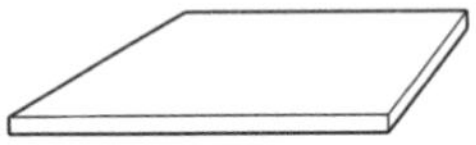	PL	PL18 x$\frac{1}{2}$ x 2′ -6″
FLAT BAR	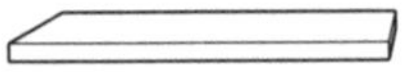	BAR	BAR 2$\frac{1}{2}$ x$\frac{1}{4}$
TIE ROD	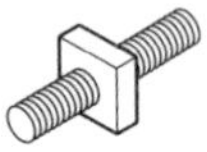	TR	$\frac{3}{4}$ Ø TR
PIPE COLUMN	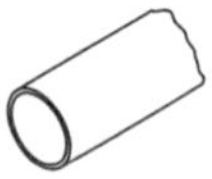	○	○6Ø

Figure 4-8. Common steel shapes, which are manufactured for stand alone use or in the fabrication of large structural units, are identified in standard formats. Manufacturing sizes for structural steel shapes vary from the nominal sizes depending on the weight per foot.

Architects and engineers use standard tables to indicate sizes of structural steel shapes for column applications. Steel columns may also be made from round pipe or square tubing where loads are relatively light. See Figure 4-10.

Installation. Column locations are shown on erection plans according to a grid of letters and numbers. References to the letters and numbers identify each column. For example, a column located at the intersection of grid lines D and 2 is referred to as column D-2.

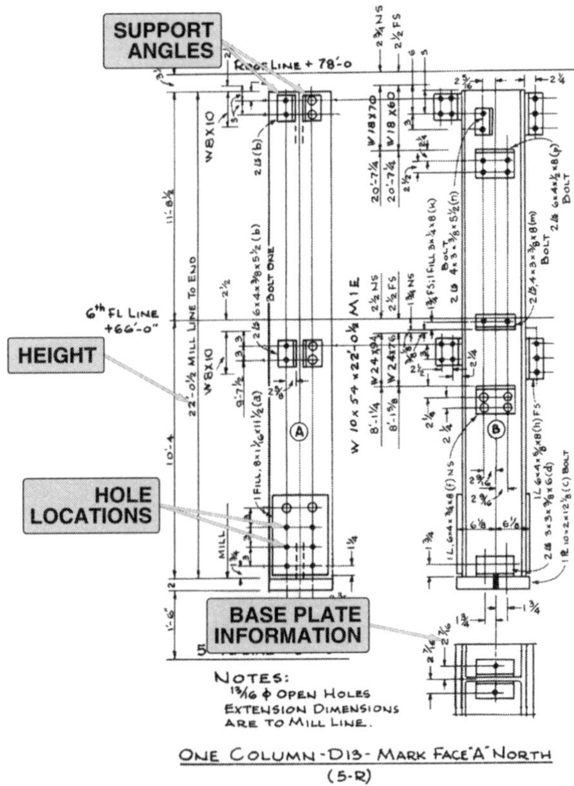

Figure 4-9. Shop detail drawings provide detailed information required for the fabrication of structural steel building components.

W SHAPES

Designation	Depth d*	Flange		Web
		Width b_f*	Thickness t_f*	Thickness t_w*
W18×71	18½	7⅝	13/16	½
×65	18⅜	7⅝	¾	7/16
×60	18¼	7½	11/16	7/16
×55	18⅛	7½	⅝	⅜
×50	18	7½	9/16	⅜
W18×46	18	6	⅝	⅜
×40	17⅞	6	½	5/16
×35	17¾	6	7/16	5/16
W16×100	17	10⅜	1	9/16
×89	16¾	10⅜	⅞	½
×77	16½	10¼	¾	7/16
×67	16⅜	10¼	11/16	⅜
W16×57	16⅜	7⅛	11/16	7/16
×50	16¼	7⅛	⅝	⅜
×45	16⅛	7	9/16	⅜

* in in.

Figure 4-10. Each column size and weight has a specified depth, flange width, flange thickness, and web thickness.

The design, size, and weight of each column may be noted at this intersection. For example, a notation of W12x53 indicates a column made of a wide-flanged shape with a 12″ web weighing 53 lb per lineal foot. See Figure 4-11. A schedule of column information may also be provided to give design, web, and weight information about each column in relation to the plan grid.

The nominal inside diameter and schedule of the pipe is indicated for round pipe columns. For example, a round pipe column shown on prints as 8 Sch. 60 indicates an 8″ diameter pipe column with schedule 60 wall thickness, in this case ½″. The outside dimensions of the tubing are given along with the steel wall thickness for square tubing columns. For example, a print notation of 3x3x¼ indicates a 3″ square tube with ¼″ steel wall thickness.

Anchor bolts and base plates are prepared prior to setting columns in place. When concrete footings and foundations are poured, the anchor bolts for steel columns are set to specific dimensions for spacing and height according to the prints. Templates may be set on the anchor bolts and grouted in place to ensure exact elevations for steel column base plates. Base plates are welded onto small columns at the fabrication shop. Large column base plates are set separately.

When placing columns, the columns must be oriented in the proper direction to ensure beams and girders connect properly. Columns are commonly marked with a directional indication or some other notation to ensure proper placement. For example, an N marked on one side of each column at the fabrication shop gives the directional orientation of North. For multistory buildings, the tier at which the column is to be set may also be noted on the column.

Columns are rigged, lifted, and set onto anchor bolts. A hole may be provided in the web at the top of the column to allow for attachment of lifting hardware. Tall columns may require two or more structural steel members fastened end-to-end, set in place individually, and secured with splice plates. Columns may be temporarily braced in place with guy wires and turnbuckles until beams and girders are secured. Erection plans of elevation drawings give elevation information concerning elevations to tops of columns or to connection points. The time and sequence for completion of connections with bolts or welding is determined by the size and design of the structure.

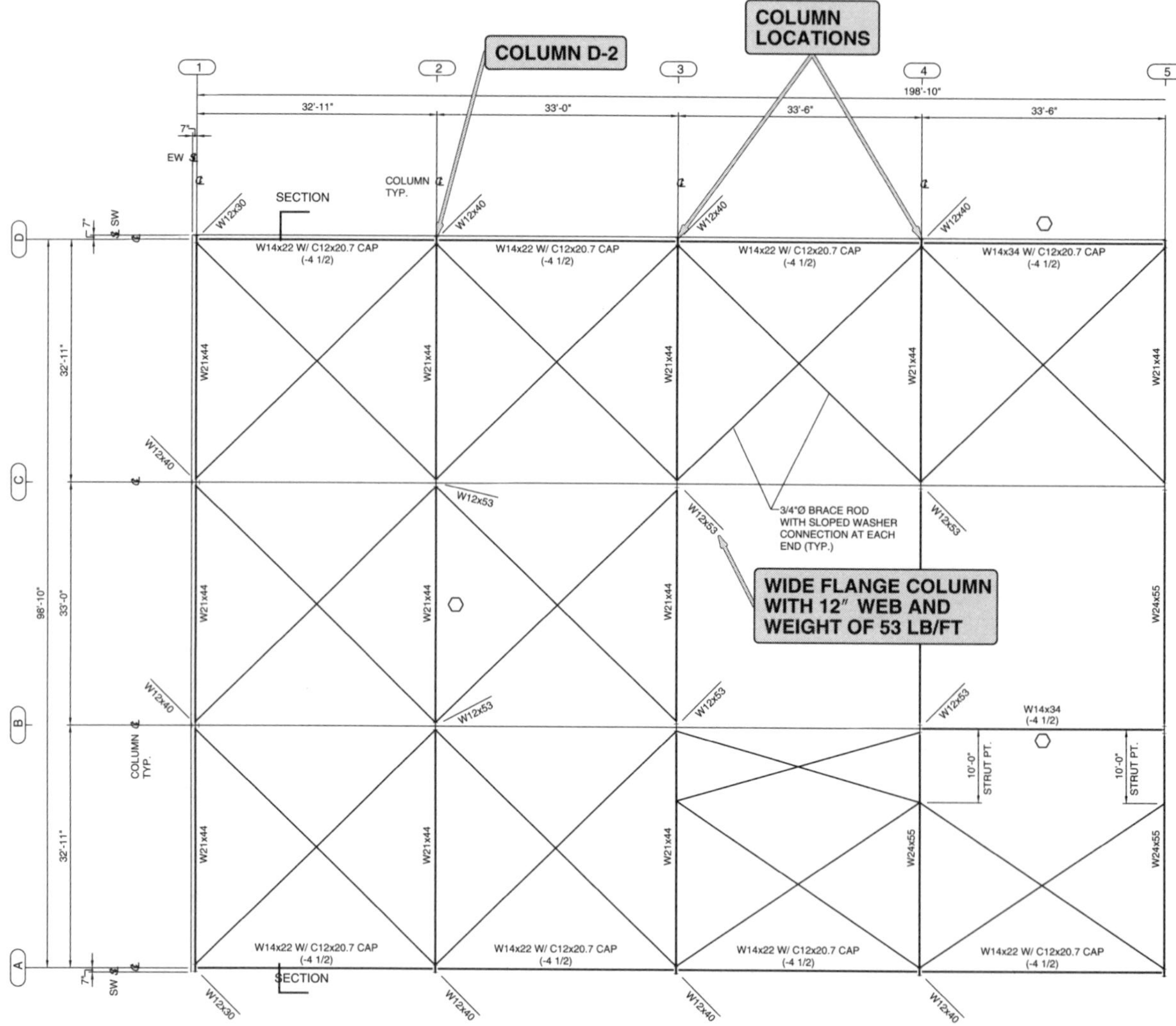

Figure 4-11. Column locations are shown on erection plans with letter and number designations. Specific information about web depth and weight per foot is given at each column location.

Beams and Girders

Steel members are classified as beams and girders where they carry horizontal loads and are spaced greater than 4′ on center. Structural steel beams include wide-flanged beams, American Standard beams, girders, and lightweight beams. Girders carry the horizontal loading of beams and joists. Girders are commonly the heaviest horizontal members in a structure.

Wide-flanged beams are classified as B, CN, CB, or H beams. The notation used on erection plans for wide-flanged beams is W or WF. See Figure 4-12. Wide-flanged beams have a nominal depth and an actual depth which varies depending on the manufacturer and flange and web thicknesses. American Standard beams are commonly referred to as I beams and designated on prints with the letters I or S. Their nominal and actual size are equal. Various types of lightweight beams are shown on erection plans with the letter B or JB for junior beams. Other miscellaneous shaped beams are designated on prints with the letter M.

Information for wide-flanged and I beams is given in a standard format. The sequence of this format is the nominal depth of the web, type of beam, weight per lineal foot, and may include the overall beam length. For example, a beam noted as 12WF29x18′-3 indicates a wide-flanged beam with a nominal web depth of 12″, a weight of 29 lb/ft, and a length of 18′-3″.

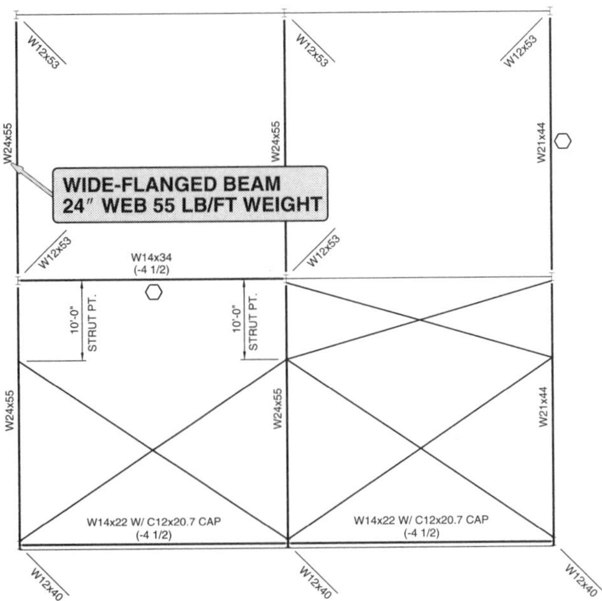

Figure 4-12. Wide-flanged beams are identified on erection plans by the letters W or WF.

A shop drawing for beam fabrication shows the beam type, weight, length, cutouts to allow for intersection with other structural steel members, dimensions for all beam holes, and any required connecting angles. See Figure 4-13. A plan view and elevation view may be necessary to give all required beam fabrication information.

Installation. Beam and girder sizes are given on plan grid and elevation drawings. Sizes are noted along the grid lines on plan drawings. Lengths are obtained from the grid spacing dimensions.

In a manner similar to columns, a letter and number system is commonly used to identify each beam or girder. The letters and numbers are marked on the beam or girder at the fabrication shop and correspond to letter and number notations on the erection plan drawings. A schedule of beam sizes and types may be provided in addition to the drawings.

Beams and girders are rigged and lifted into place before being bolted to columns or other girders. *Spandrel beams* are beams bolted to the columns around the perimeter of a building. Angles attached to the columns or beams enable the fastening of spandrel beams. Care must be taken to turn the beams in the proper direction to ensure each end of the beam is fastened to the proper column.

The initial fastening of columns and beams is commonly performed with bolts and nuts. Seat lugs or shear plates made of angles attached to the columns may be used to support the beam and column connection during erection. For multimember beams, splice plates may be used to hold the end of each beam in place. As construction progresses, guy wires, turnbuckles, sag rods, sway rods, and other cross-bracing members are added to plumb and level all members and hold them at the proper elevations. Pitch information is given as the inches of vertical drop per foot of horizontal run. Bolting or welding of the connections of these members is required to complete the erection.

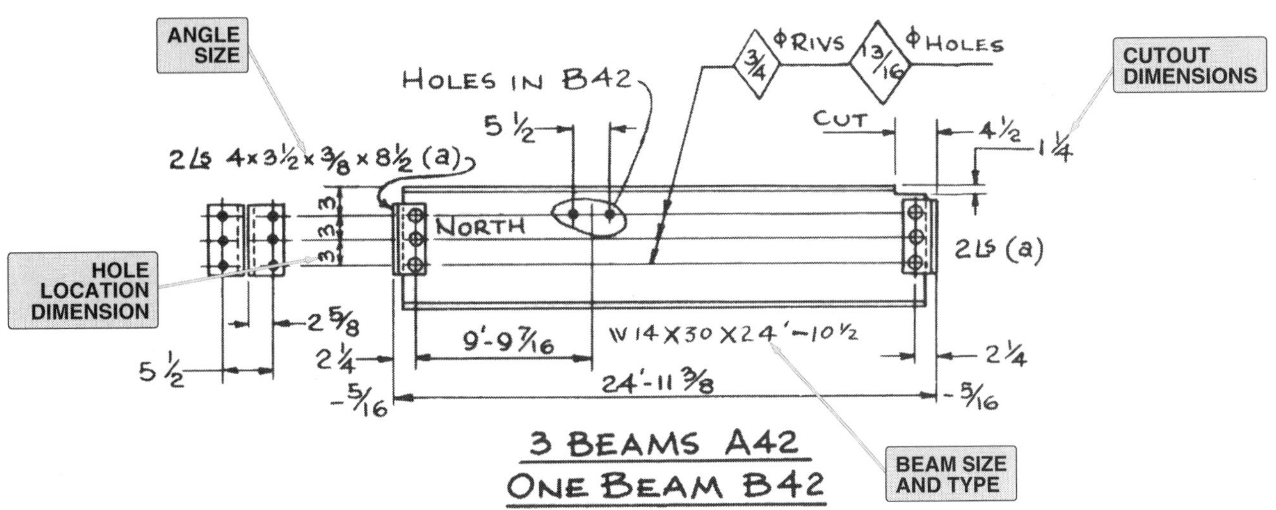

Figure 4-13. Structural steel beams are fabricated based on shop drawings.

Joists and Purlins

Structural steel joists are lightweight beams spaced less than 4′ on center. They are used in all types of steel construction including beam and column, long span, and wall bearing. Purlins are placed to span between beams, columns, or joists to carry intermediate loads, such as roofs or wall panels. Purlins placed horizontally to span between columns to carry wall panels are also referred to as girts.

Joists may be formed of a single structural member or built up as a trussed or open web joist. An open web joist is the most commonly used joist. A *bar joist* is an open web joist with steel angles at the top and bottom of the joist and bars for the intermediate members. See Figure 4-14. Standard designation information for open web joists includes the nominal depth, span classification, type of steel, and size of chord materials. For example, an open web joist with a designation of 28H9 has a nominal depth of 28″, is made of high-strength steel, and has a chord of #9 steel bar with a 1⅛″ diameter.

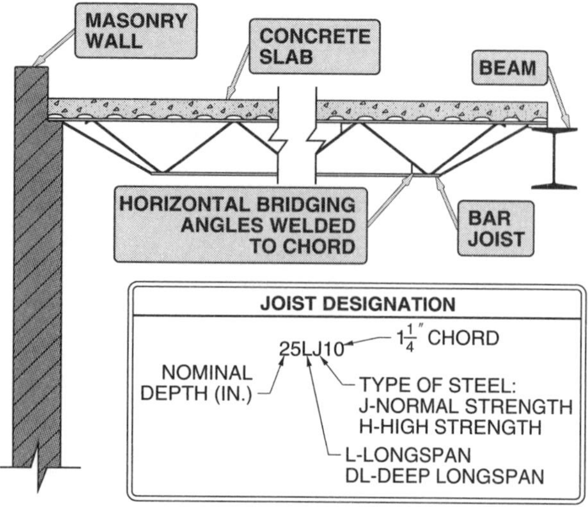

Figure 4-14. Open web bar joists span horizontal distances between beams and girders. A standardized format provides open web bar joist information.

Purlins are formed of a channel or zee. Lightweight channels are referred to as junior channels or C channels. Channels are shown on erection plans with the symbol [. Sizes of channels are given in standard format. Channel width is stated first, followed by the flange width and steel thickness. For example, a notation of [4x2x⅜ describes a channel with a depth of 4″, a flange width of 2″, and a steel thickness of ⅜″.

Light gauge steel framing of C or zee channels are used for purlins and girts. When used to span between columns or roof beams, their dimensions are given on erection plan detail drawings.

Installation. Joists normally are not identified with letters and numbers in the manner of columns and beams. The spacing of joists and the direction for their placement is noted. See Figure 4-15. The type of joist to be installed may also be noted by a manufacturer identification code, standard classification format, or fabrication shop code number. An elevation to the top of the joists may be given on the plan or elevation drawings. Open areas for stairwells or other access between levels of a structure are shown on the joist plan view. Openings are indicated by dashed lines in an x pattern. Solid x lines between joists indicate cross-bracing.

Joists are commonly welded to their supporting members. Detail drawings indicate the manner of joist attachment to the beams and girders. Print information for the installation of purlins and girts includes spacing and direction of placement. C channels or girts are most commonly bolted to their supporting members. Spacing and sizes of bolts are given in detail drawings.

Trusses

For long span structural steel construction, trusses provide maximum strength with minimal weight. Engineers determine all loads and stresses for the truss to withstand. A series of steel members are fastened together to provide structural, compressive, and tensile support. Many different sizes and shapes of structural steel are used to form a truss. Each is noted on the truss drawings. See Figure 4-16.

Many different truss designs are available. The design used depends on the loads to be supported, distance to be spanned, necessary roof and ceiling pitches, and overall allowable height of the truss. Common steel trusses include the Bowstring, Flat, Howe, Pratt, Scissors, and Warren.

Installation. Erection of trusses is accomplished in a manner similar to beams and girders. Steel trusses are normally very large and require great care in rigging, lifting, placement, erection, and final fastening. A series of seat lugs and splice plates may be necessary to ensure proper truss fastening and installation.

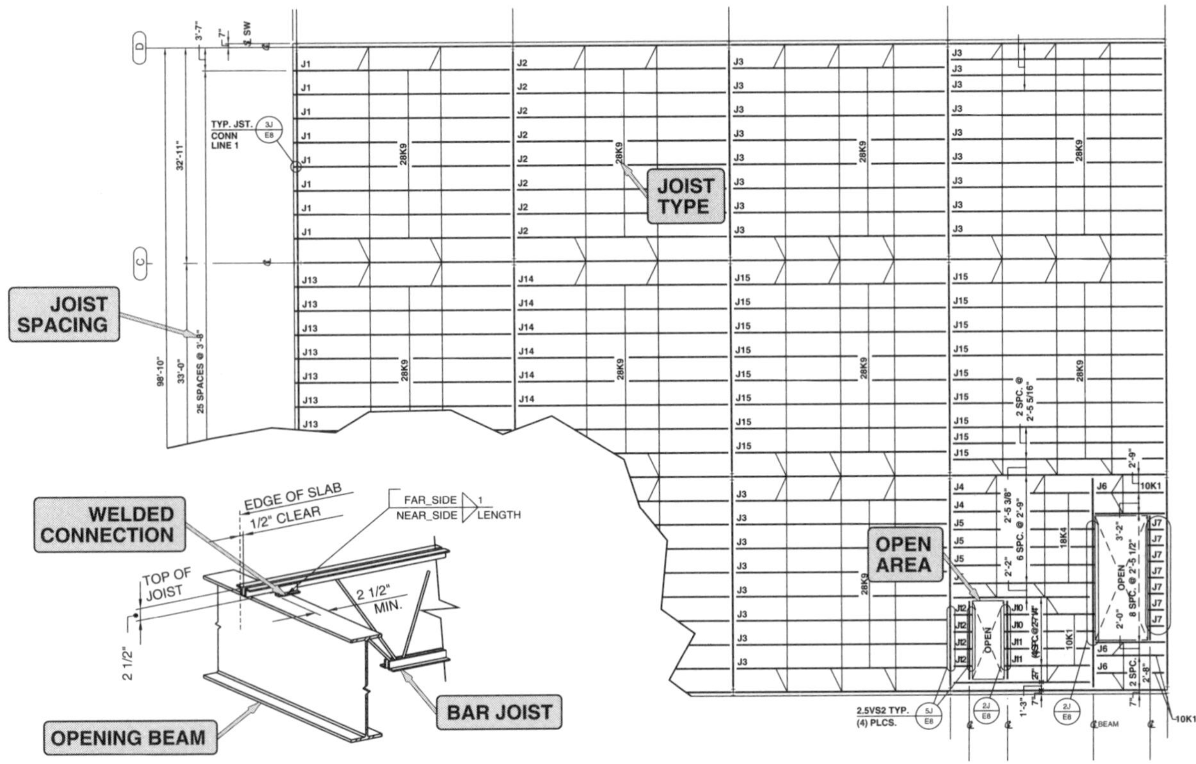

Figure 4-15. Erection plans indicate structural steel joist spacing and installation information. Bar joists are attached to beams and other supporting members with bolts or welding.

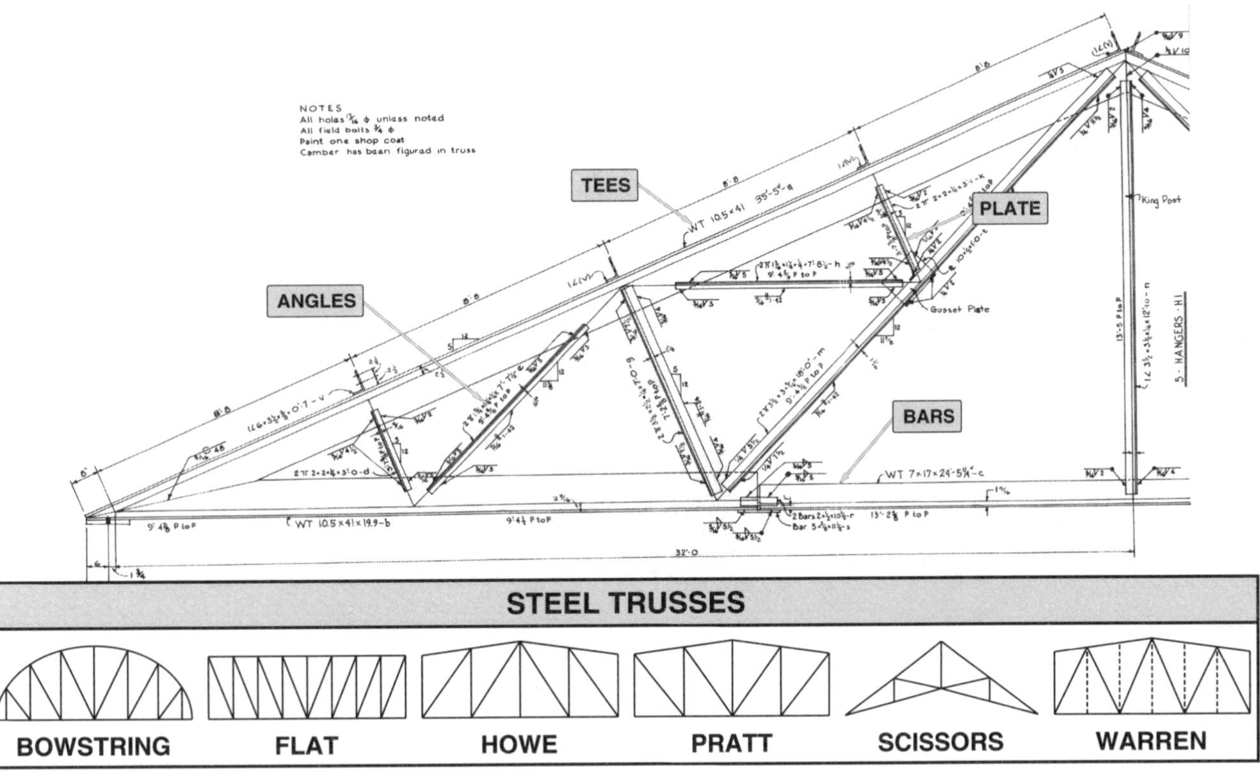

Figure 4-16. A wide variety of structural steel shapes are joined together to form a truss. Common steel trusses include the Bowstring, Flat, Howe, Pratt, Scissors, and Warren.

Bracing

Temporary and final bracing are components of the steel construction process. A variety of temporary braces are used during construction to support initial members until construction is completed. Final cross-bracing of columns, beams, girders, and trusses is performed to prevent sway, sag, and possible collapse of the structural steel supporting members. A series of angular braces is constructed to resist various forces which could cause connections to fail.

Temporary bracing during erection is performed using guy wires of wire rope or rods with attached turnbuckles. These are not indicated on print drawings, but must be installed to hold steel in place during the erection process.

A structure of falsework may be erected for large structural steel projects which require the construction of cantilevered areas or long spans. Towers and other complex shoring falsework are assembled to support girders, beams, and trusses until all supporting components can be erected and fastened to support each other. The design and construction of falsework often requires a separate set of engineering drawings to show the design, construction, and required elevations. The falsework drawings are similar to erection plans.

Final bracing may be done with a variety of structural steel shapes. One of the more common materials used for bracing is steel angle. Angle information is indicated by the angle symbol (L) followed by dimensional information given in a standard format. The format sequence is width of the longer leg, width of the shorter leg, thickness of the steel, and length of the angle. For example, a notation of L5x4x½x 6′-5 denotes an angle with one 5″ leg, one 4″ leg, a steel thickness of ½″, and a length of 6′-5″. Angle bracing may be used as bridging between bar joists and between beams and purlins. See Figure 4-17.

Channel may also be installed as cross- or angular bracing. Cross-bracing is commonly attached to beams and columns with a gusset. A *gusset* is a piece of plate or sheet steel that is welded or bolted to all members at the connecting point. *Plate steel* is flat steel with a thickness of 3⁄16″ or greater. Sheared plate steel is trimmed on all edges during the manufacturing process. Universal plate steel is trimmed only on the ends. Sheet steel has a thickness of ⅛″ or less. Elevation drawings and section drawings provide information on cross-bracing.

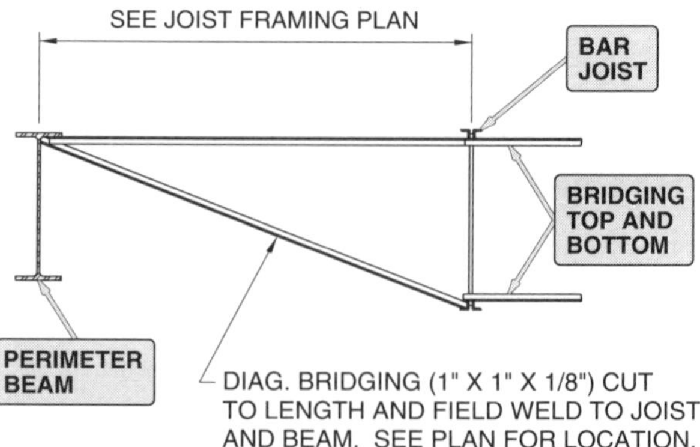

Figure 4-17. Bridging and bracing hold structural steel columns, beams, and joists in alignment and increase the ability of the structure to withstand various loads.

Threaded rods are also used as bracing. Threaded rods are fastened through holes in adjoining members. Beveled washers and nuts are attached to each end of the threaded rods to hold members in place. See Figure 4-18. The size of the rod is given as the diameter of the rod in inches and fractions of an inch.

Other Steel Shapes

Other structural steel shapes used in a variety of applications include tees, bars, and zees. These members are used for bracing and joist and truss construction. Structural tees are commonly made by cutting standard I beams, wide-flanged beams, or smaller beams through the center of their web. This forms two tees.

Notation systems for tees may give the flange width, nominal depth, and pounds per foot or the flange width, nominal depth, and steel thickness. For example, a notation of T4x3x5⁄16 indicates a tee with a flange 4″ wide, a depth of 3″, and made from 5⁄16″ thick steel. Steel bars are shown on prints by their thickness and width dimensions.

Zees are shown on drawings in the standard sequence of depth of the zee, flange width, and weight of steel per foot or steel thickness. For example, a note of Z4x3 1⁄16x3 1⁄16x¼ indicates a Z-shaped steel member with a 4″ height, equal flanges of 3 1⁄16″, and a steel thickness of ¼″.

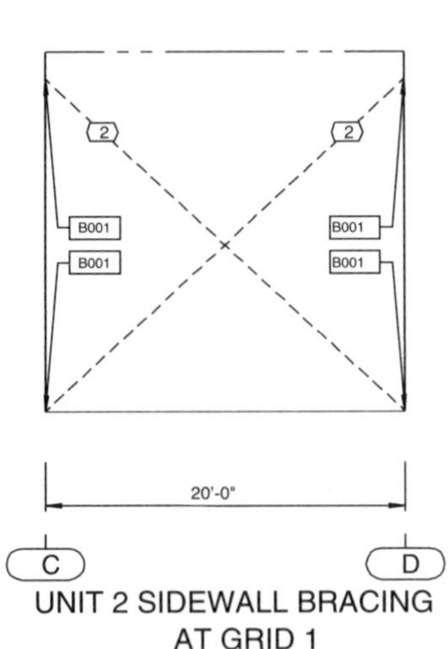

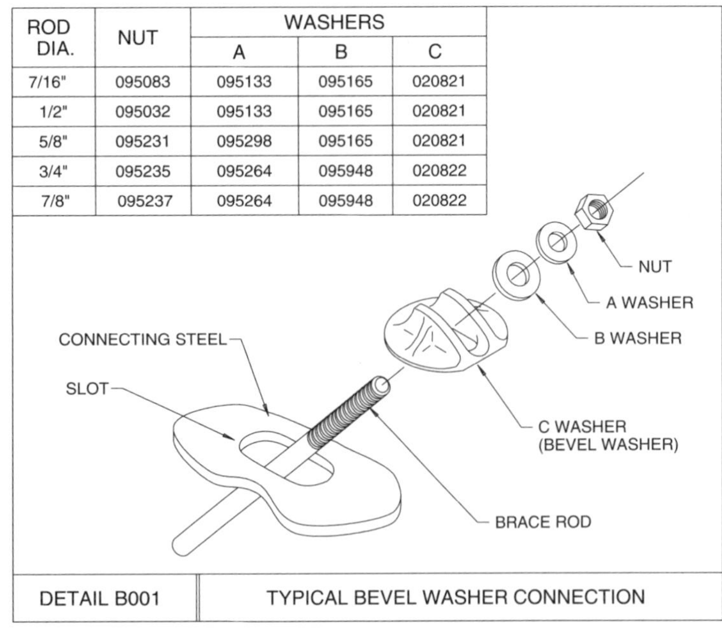

ROD DIA.	NUT	WASHERS		
		A	B	C
7/16"	095083	095133	095165	020821
1/2"	095032	095133	095165	020821
5/8"	095231	095298	095165	020821
3/4"	095235	095264	095948	020822
7/8"	095237	095264	095948	020822

Figure 4-18. Angled, threaded rods are used to brace across longer distances than angles.

FASTENING SYSTEMS

Erection of structural steel is the process of setting the framework in place. Final construction is not complete until all joints are secured with rivets, bolts, or welding operations. Developments in bolt manufacturing and welding technology have made rivets obsolete in modern structural steel construction.

Bolts

Use of the proper bolt, washer, and nut assembly is required in structural steel connections. Variations in bolt design and materials effect the amount of tensile strength the bolted connection can withstand. The process of tightening a bolt and nut provides a frictional connection. Some bolts are used in initial erection, some are designed for light loads only, and some high-strength bolts are designed to withstand tremendous loads.

Structural steel drawings may contain tables concerning the amount of torque to be applied to various types of bolts and the nut rotation for various types of connections. See Figure 4-19. Impact wrenches are used to ensure all connections meet specifications for torque. Detail drawings for bolted connections are a source of information for bolts, washers, and nuts.

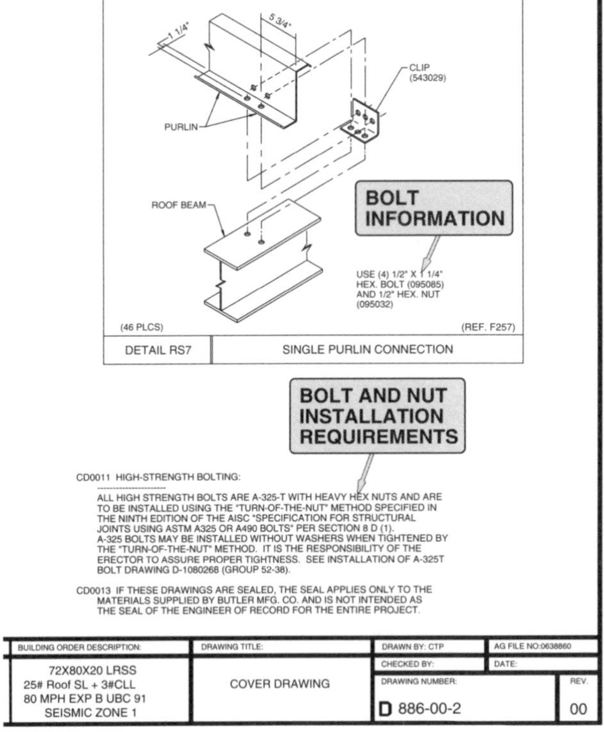

Figure 4-19. Proper bolt and nut installation is essential for proper structural fastener performance. Erection detail drawings are the primary reference for bolted connections.

The length of a bolt or screw is the distance measured from the bearing surface of the bolt head to the end of the bolt. The thread design is stated as the number of threads per inch. Three standard thread designs are coarse (UNC), fine (UNF), and extra fine (UNEF). See Appendix. Coarse threads are the most commonly used thread design in structural steel construction.

Types and Applications. Machine bolts are used for temporary connections and for light stress connections. Machine bolts are referred to as erection bolts when they are used as a temporary connection during the erection process. Erection bolts are removed when the joint is finished by welding or insertion of a high-strength bolt.

Structural ribbed bolts are capable of making high-strength steel connections. See Figure 4-20. Ribbed bolts are driven into holes in adjoining members and tightened to the proper amount of torque. Low-carbon steel bolts are designated as A307 and can be used for light framework and low-stress applications for column splices and beam and girder connections. High-strength bolts are divided into two basic categories by the ASTM. The two categories are A325 and A490. A325 bolts have a lower shear capacity than A490 bolts. These bolts contain a marking on their head with the code A325 or A490. Additional markings include a manufacturer identification symbol. Bolts marked A325 are made by applying a heat treatment process to medium-carbon steel bolts. Bolts marked A490 are made from alloy steel.

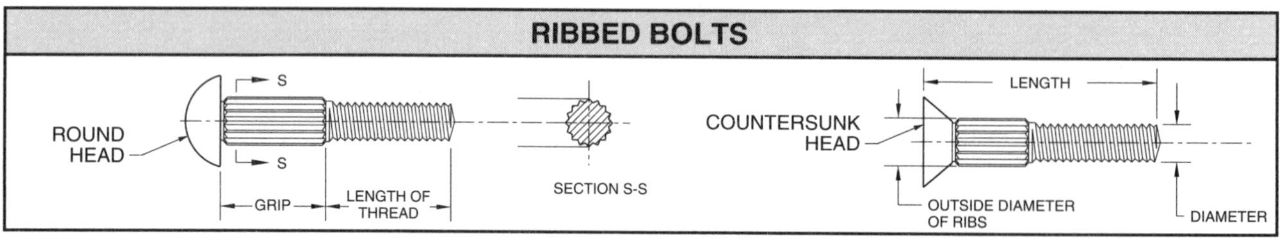

HEAVY HEX BOLT DIMENSIONS*			
Nominal Bolt Size *D*	Width Across Flats *F*	Height *H*	Thread Length
1/2	7/8	5/16	1
5/8	1 1/16	25/64	1 1/4
3/4	1 1/4	15/32	1 3/8
7/8	1 7/16	35/64	1 1/2
1	1 5/8	39/64	1 3/4
1 1/8	1 13/16	11/16	2
1 1/4	2	25/32	2
1 3/8	2 3/16	27/32	2 1/4
1 1/2	2 3/8	15/16	2 1/4

* in in.

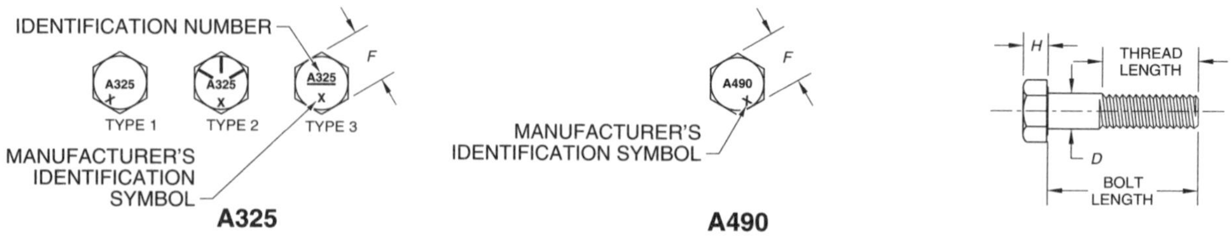

Figure 4-20. Ribbed bolts may be used where steel members are drawn tightly together before fastening. High-strength bolts are identified with markings on the bolt head.

Welding and Cutting

Many structural steel construction job site operations require the use of welding and cutting equipment. Installation of bracing, decking, and final attachment of structural members are several of the processes which require skill in welding and cutting. At the completion of the erection process, many joints between steel members are joined with electric arc welding. Erection plans provide information concerning the type of weld joint, location of weld, welding process, size of weld bead, and surface finish of the weld. See Figure 4-21.

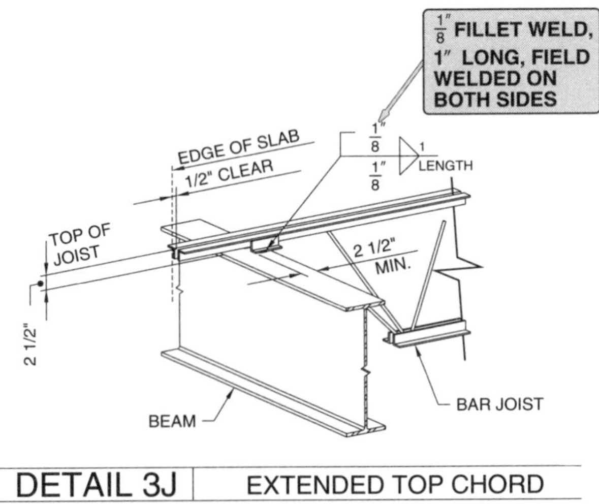

Figure 4-21. Detail drawings give welded connection information.

Welding Types and Applications. The most common type of welding used in structural steel construction is shielded metal-arc welding. Shielded metal-arc welding (SMAW) is an electric-arc welding process in which a coated electrode is used that has a similar metallic composition to the steel to be joined. An electric current flows through a circuit created with the electrode and the steel members. The electric arc melts the base metal and the electrode, joining the steel members. The arcing process is shielded from the atmosphere by a gas created by burning the coating of the electrode.

Gas shielded-arc welding is another electric arc welding process used primarily in industrial applications and fabrication shops. Two types of gas shielded-arc welding are metal inert gas (MIG) and tungsten inert gas (TIG). MIG and TIG refer to the arc shielding method.

The American Welding Society (AWS) has developed standards for materials, testing, and certification for the welding process. In many instances, individuals performing welding operations on a job site must be certified either by the AWS or by a local governmental agency. Print information may specifically note this certification requirement.

Welding Symbols. The most important information obtained by the welder from the erection plans is from the welding symbols. A standard system of welding symbols is used to ensure all welds meet industry standards. See Figure 4-22. See Appendix.

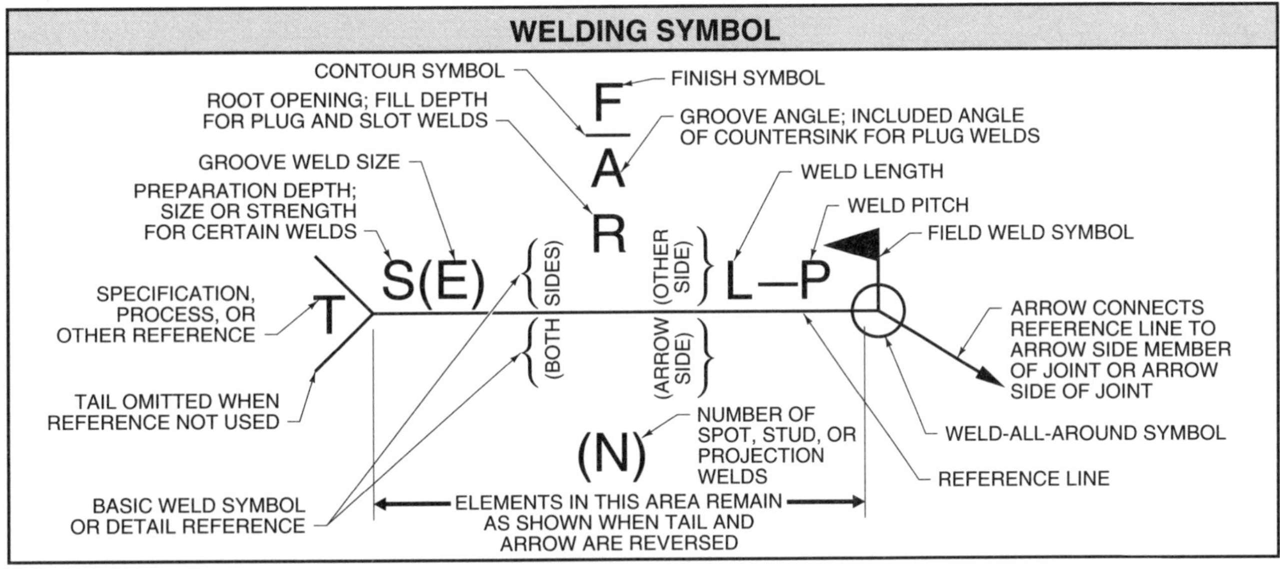

Figure 4-22. A standard format is used for welding symbols to provide location, length, and type of welded joint.

The basic components of a welding symbol include the reference line, the arrow indicating the location of the weld, dimensions for the length of the weld and the depth of penetration, and symbols which describe the type of welding joint. The detail drawings in the erection plans show welding symbols for each welded joint.

Cutting Materials and Equipment. Cutting steel members at the job site requires the use of an oxyacetylene or plasma-arc cutting torch. For oxyacetylene cutting, a mixture of oxygen and acetylene is ignited to create a flame. The flame is used to melt steel for cutting holes or structural members or decking materials to length. See Figure 4-23. While not specified on erection plans, this operation is necessary to create and fabricate members as needed on the job site. Another type of cutting process is the plasma-arc cutter. Gas is heated to an extremely high temperature and forced through a small opening at high velocity. This process provides a cleanly cut edge on many types of metals.

Figure 4-23. Structural steel is cut to length with a cutting torch.

PANEL MEMBERS

After the structural frame is erected, fastened, and braced, various panel members are attached to the frame. For structural steel buildings, the panel members create floors, walls, and roofs on the framework to complete the structure. Erection plans provide information concerning the various panel members.

Decking

The uses of metal floor decking include providing a work platform during construction and a form and reinforcement for concrete slabs. A common method of creating a floor in a structural steel building is by attaching corrugated steel decking to the top of the joists. See Figure 4-24.

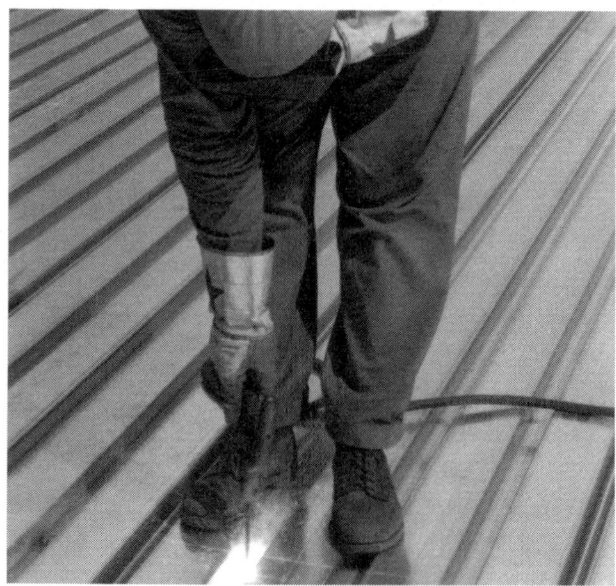

Republic Steel Corporation

CORRUGATED FORMS FOR CONCRETE SLABS-NONCOMPOSITE

FORMS	SPAN*	WIDTH**	MAX LENGTH*
1/2"	1-2	96	2-6
9/16"	1.5-3	30	40
15/16"	3-5	29	40
1"	3-5	28	30-40
9/16"	4-9	27	30-40
2"	7-12	24	30-40

* in ft
** in in.

Figure 4-24. Corrugated steel decking is attached to the top of open web joists to create a floor platform. Steel decking for floors is manufactured in many different designs and dimensions.

The corrugated decking may be fastened to the joists with self-tapping screws or by welding processes. Various types and categories of steel floor decking are available.

A plan view on the erection plans indicates the decking panel layout and opening locations. See Figure 4-25. Detail drawings indicate methods for closing openings and bracing around columns and edge treatments.

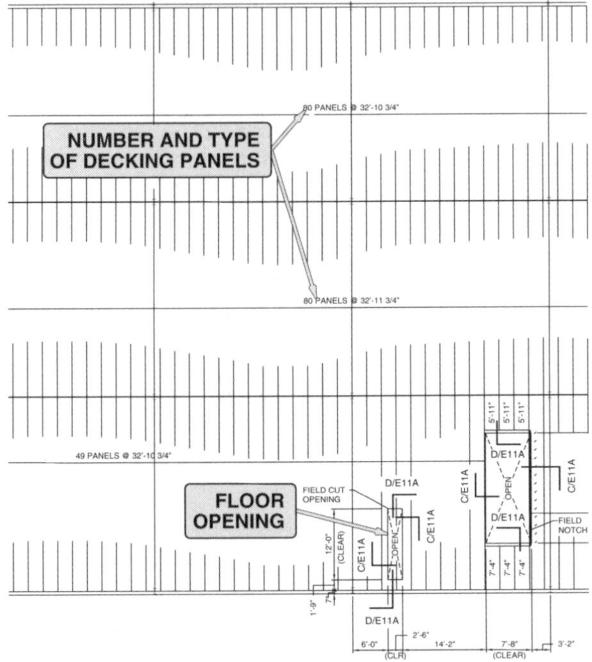

Figure 4-25. Erection plans give the locations for metal decking installation.

Buildings. For building use, corrugated decking is commonly topped with several inches of poured concrete. The depth of the concrete varies depending on the loads to be supported. The thickness of the concrete deck is given on erection plans or detail drawings.

Bridges. For bridge building, the most common decking material is poured-in-place reinforced concrete. Formwork is suspended from the girders and beams. The concrete deck is poured on top of the formwork. After removal of the forms, the steel structural members support the completed concrete deck. In light load applications, some types of steel floor decking may by used for bridge deck slab forms.

Wall Panels

Structural steel framed buildings may be finished with a variety of exterior finishes. A common finish for small metal buildings is the application of corrugated metal sheets. On large commercial buildings, exteriors are covered with glass, stone, precast concrete, or masonry.

Metal Panels. Erection plans and elevation drawings indicate the types and applications for metal exterior panels. See Figure 4-26. Information includes the direction of application, finish trim members at the roof line and corners, and possibly the manufacturer's name and identifying code number(s) and color(s) for the panels. Wall panels are attached to purlins or girts with self-tapping and self-sealing screws. Exterior wall panels may also be used for soffit and canopy coverings as indicated on the drawings.

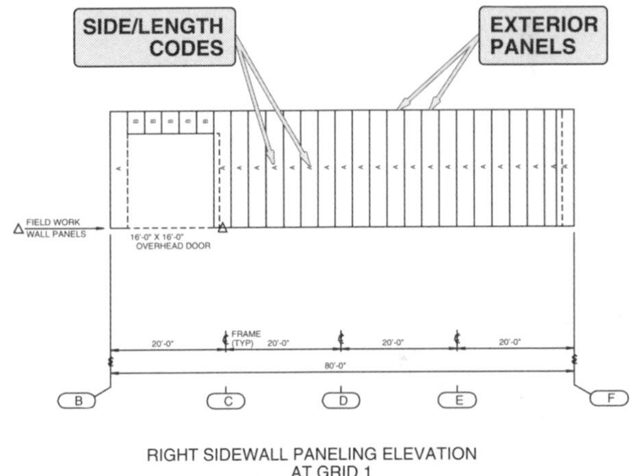

Figure 4-26. Many light gauge metal buildings are covered on the exterior with prefinished metal panels.

Exterior Wall Finishes. Many types of prefabricated panels are attached to the exterior of structural steel buildings. The most common attachment method for prefabricated panels is electric-arc welding. For precast concrete, stone, and masonry, weld plates are cast in or fastened on the panels which allow for welding to columns and spandrel beams. Exterior metal trim members which support glass or other panel materials are attached to structural members with welded clips. Information about these attachments and finishes is found in the architectural detail drawings and elevation drawings.

Roofing. Metal roof decking panels provide a high strength-to-weight ratio which reduces the amount of dead load on structures. Variations in roof decking design include the width and height of the corrugated ribs and the metal finish. Some steel roof decking is designed to create a finished surface with watertight joints between decking pieces. Others are designed to be covered with additional insulation and roofing materials.

A plan view of a steel roof panel application is included in the erection plans. See Figure 4-27. A manufacturer's schedule of the types and sizes of roof panels may be provided to locate all panels correctly. Roof panels are attached to purlins or ceiling joists with self-sealing screws or clips. Elevation drawings and detail drawings indicate any additional roofing materials for waterproofing or insulation.

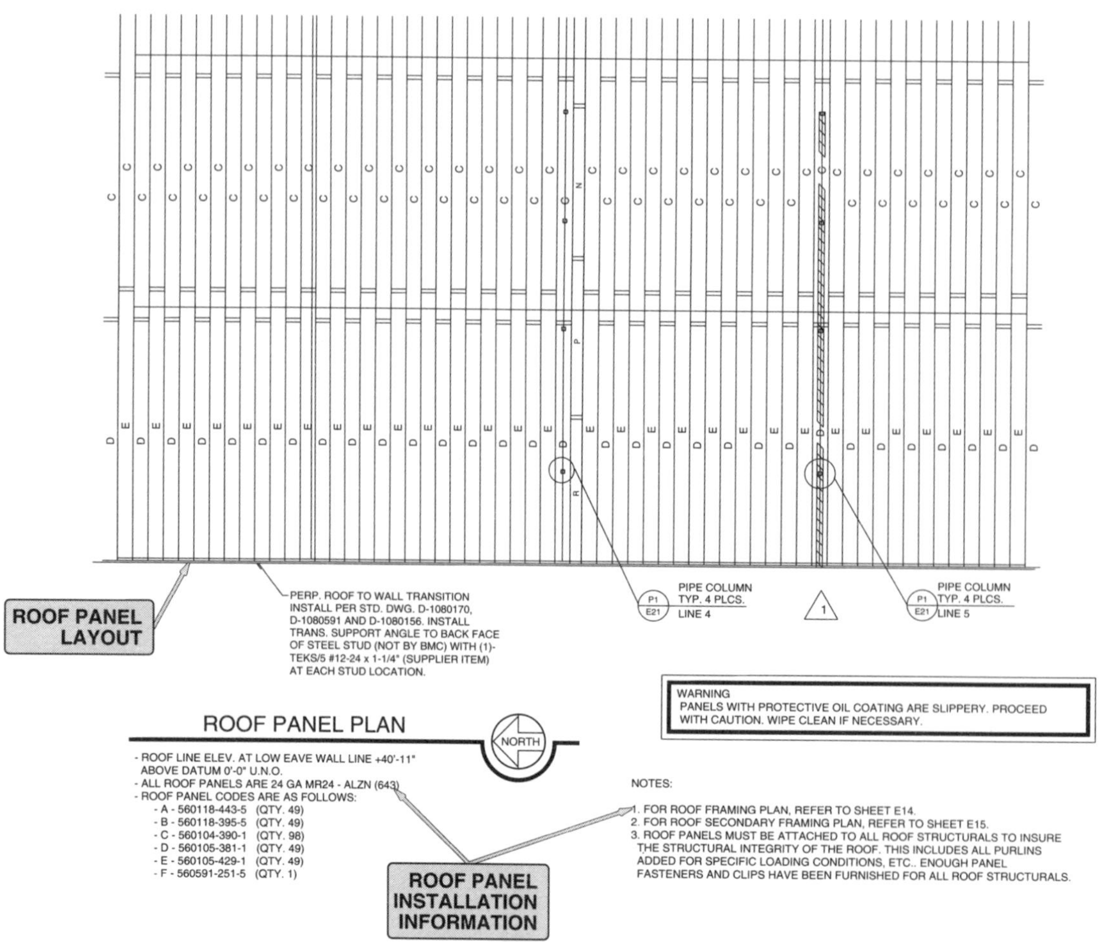

Figure 4-27. Roof decks may be formed of metal decking only or covered with additional waterproof materials and thermal protection.

Review Questions

Name ______________________________ Date ______________

Printreading

T F **1.** Bearing plates on masonry walls distribute loads from structural steel beams and joists.

______ **2.** The weight per foot of a beam noted as W12x14 is ______ lb.

T F **3.** A notation of "N" on one side of a column notes that the column is to be located on grid line N.

______ **4.** On a construction site, the most common on-the-job welding system used is ______.

A. MIG
B. TIG
C. shielded metal-arc
D. plasma

T F **5.** For dimensioning of steel angles, the length of the longer leg is noted first.

______ **6.** The spacing distance which determines the difference between a structural steel being classified as a beam or a joist is ______′.

T F **7.** Corrugated metal sheets are used for concrete floor forms.

______ **8.** The most common type of steel used for structural steel construction is ______.

A. A36
B. A325
C. A490
D. ASTM

______ **9.** The nominal web depth of a column noted as W5x19x8 is ______″.

A. 5
B. 8
C. 19
D. neither A, B, nor C

______ **10.** The general classifications of structural steel construction include ______.

A. beam and column
B. wall bearing
C. long span
D. A, B, and C

______ **11.** The chord diameter of a bar joist noted as 16H6 is ______″.

A. $\frac{1}{6}$
B. $\frac{3}{8}$
C. $\frac{3}{4}$
D. 6

T F **12.** Erection bolts are high-strength bolts.

T F **13.** An A490 bolt has a higher shear capacity than an A325 bolt.

______ **14.** Wire ropes and turnbuckles are used during structural steel erection for ______.

A. welding
B. metal floor decking installation
C. wall bearing construction
D. temporary bracing

__________ **15.** A flat piece of steel which is ½″ thick is referred to as ________ steel.

A. sheet
B. gusset
C. plate
D. S

T F **16.** A steel channel noted on erection drawings as [2x1x3⁄16 has a flange width of 2″.

__________ **17.** Prefinished metal wall panels are attached to girts by ________.

A. self-tapping screws
B. high-strength bolts
C. welding
D. angles and purlins

T F **18.** A spandrel beam is a beam located along an outside wall.

T F **19.** Girts are attached to columns to support metal wall panels.

__________ **20.** The nominal depth of an open web bar joist noted as 18LH05 is ________″.

__________ **21.** The best type of structural steel construction used for a four-story office building is ________.

A. beam and column
B. light steel framing
C. long span
D. open web joists and girders

__________ **22.** A note of F-6 on an erection plan signifies ________.

A. the sixth floor of a building
B. a column at the intersections
C. a 6″ thick firewall
D. a type of metal floor decking

T F **23.** Structural steel construction is a stand-alone method and is not used in conjunction with other construction methods, such as masonry or reinforced concrete.

T F **24.** The most common method of attaching columns to foundations is with anchor bolts through base plates.

__________ **25.** ________ is the process of unloading steel members in a planned manner to minimize the moving of pieces during the erection process.

__________ **26.** ________ construction consists of large horizontal steel members, such as girders and trusses, that are fastened together to create large girders and trusses.

A. Beam and column
B. Long span
C. Wall bearing
D. neither A, B, nor C

T F **27.** American Standard beams are commonly referred to as I beams and designated on prints with the letters I or S.

__________ **28.** A(n) ________ joist is an open web joist with steel angles at the top and bottom of the joist and bars for the intermediate members.

__________ **29.** Common steel trusses include ________.

A. Bowstring
B. Bowe
C. Plat
D. A, B, and C

__________ **30.** ________ construction consists of bays of framed structural steel which are repeated to create large structures.

A. Beam and column
B. Long span
C. Wall bearing
D. neither A, B, nor C

5 REINFORCED CONCRETE CONSTRUCTION

Reinforced concrete is a combination of concrete and reinforcing steel. The best qualities of each material are realized to achieve high overall strength. Reinforced concrete may be poured-in-place or precast concrete.

Poured-in-place concrete uses formwork which allows for the placement of the concrete. Poured-in-place concrete applications require specific print information about dimensions of the finished concrete, reinforcing requirements, inserts, and concrete properties.

Precast concrete may be precast at the job site and lifted into place or formed and poured at a casting yard and then transported to the job site by truck. All precast members require special reinforcing to ensure the meet the stresses of transportation and installation in addition to final structural loads.

REINFORCED CONCRETE CONSTRUCTION

The combination of concrete and reinforcing steel creates an integrated construction system which combines the best qualities of the two materials. Concrete is a material which is high in compressive strength. Reinforcing steel has a great amount of tensile strength. The best qualities of each material are realized to achieve high overall strengths when these materials are properly bonded together.

Reinforced concrete is used in large commercial structures to create foundation systems, floors, columns, beams, roadways, walls, and roof decks. See Figure 5-1.

Figure 5-1. Reinforced concrete is an extremely durable and versatile building material that is used in many construction applications.

Reinforced concrete members may be poured-in-place, precast on the job site, or precast off the job site and used with other construction methods, such as masonry and structural steel.

Specifications give information concerning concrete ingredients, placement, curing, and finishing. Specifications also provide information about reinforcing steel requirements and properties.

Architectural drawings contain most of the print-related information for reinforced concrete construction. The majority of reinforced concrete information is shown on foundation plans, floor plans, structural plans, elevation drawings, and various detail drawings.

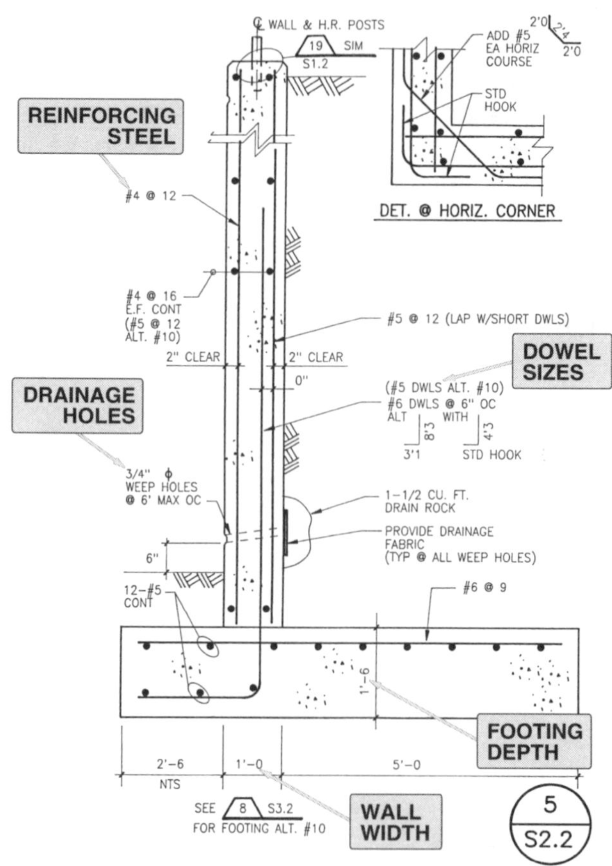

Figure 5-2. Dimensions for all types of reinforced concrete members and their attachments are given on architectural drawings.

POURED-IN-PLACE CONCRETE

Many methods are used to create the formwork which allows for the placement of poured-in-place concrete. The formwork used depends on the overall size of the concrete structure. Forms may be set on or in the ground for pilings, footings, and on-grade slabs. Forms may be set on concrete slabs to support walls, columns, and above-grade slab systems. Each type or application of poured-in-place concrete requires specific print information about dimensions of the finished concrete, reinforcing requirements, inserts, and concrete properties.

Forming

Architectural drawings give the finished dimensions for concrete structures. See Figure 5-2. These dimensions include depth, width, and height for poured-in-place concrete along with information concerning items placed in or through the concrete.

Information concerning the type and design of the forming system is not given on the structural drawings. A separate set of forming plans is provided by the concrete form supplier for many large commercial poured-in-place concrete projects. See Figure 5-3. These drawings are developed by the manufacturer's specialists in form design. Form design is based on concrete dimensions given in the architectural drawings. Form drawings indicate manufacturer form identification numbers and type, placement, form fastening systems, form tie systems, and shoring and bracing information. Concrete form design must take all forces to be placed on the form into account.

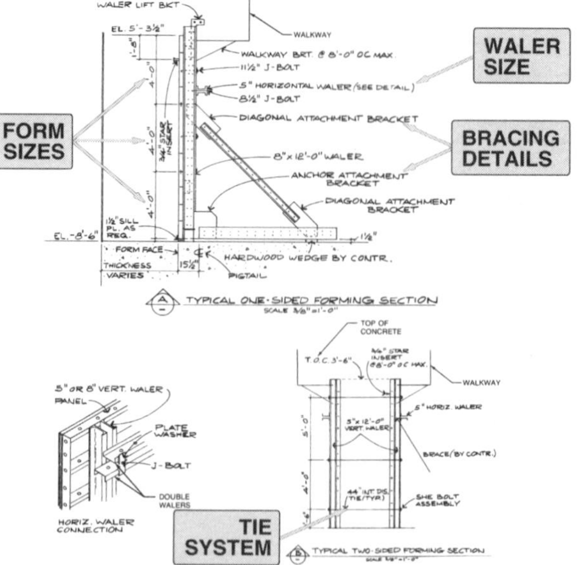

Figure 5-3. A separate set of formwork drawings may be provided by form suppliers and manufacturers to ensure safe and proper concrete forming.

The amount of concrete being placed in a form creates varying load requirements. Hydrostatic pressure within the form creates great pressures which increase as the amount of liquid concrete in the form increases. Form design variables include form width, form height, concrete properties, and the speed of placement of concrete into the form. Plans for form removal at the completion of the concrete placement must also be made.

Piles and Caissons. Piles or caissons may be required for deep foundations where soil bearing is poor. A *pile* is a structural member installed in the ground to provide vertical and/or horizontal support. A *caisson* is a poured-in-place concrete piling of large diameter. A grid of letters and numbers is provided at regular intervals in a plan view. The letter and number grid intersection points provide references for pile placement. Piles are indicated on foundation plans with information including the depth of the lower tip of the pile, the elevation of the top of the pile, and the elevation to the top of the pile cap. See Figure 5-4.

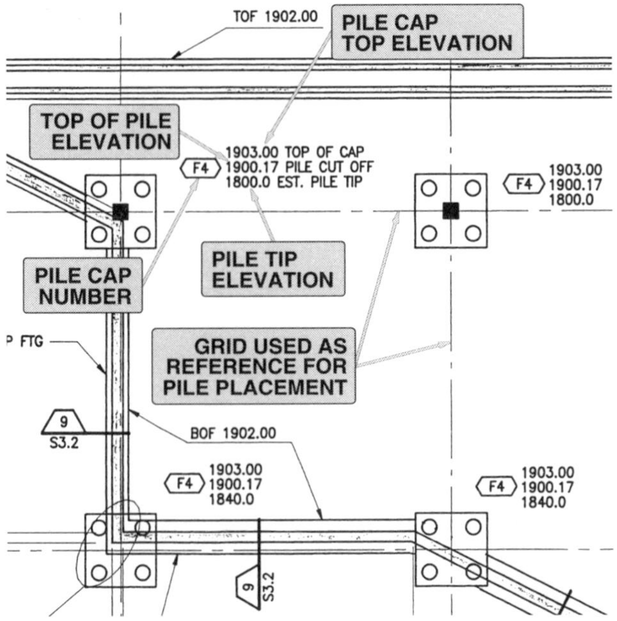

Figure 5-4. Plan views indicate locations, depths, and heights for reinforced concrete piles.

Poured-in-place concrete pile sides are formed by the surrounding soil, a casing which is removed as concrete is placed, or steel pipe. For concrete placed into the surrounding soil, holes are drilled to a specified depth, reinforcing steel is set in place, and the hole is filled with concrete. The bottom of the pile may be belled out to create a larger bearing surface if soil bearing is very poor. A metal sleeve is set into the hole as drilling proceeds in areas where the earthen sides of the drilled hole are not stable enough to remain in place until concrete is placed. Reinforcing steel is set in place. The sleeve is removed immediately after the concrete is placed in the hole. Pipe piles are made of steel pipe which is driven into the ground with a pile-driving hammer. A cap is placed on the tip of the pipe to prevent it from filling with soil during driving. The pipe is filled with concrete after the proper depth is reached. Detail drawings show the diameter of reinforced concrete pile, the steel reinforcing, and the joining of the pile and the pile cap.

Pile Caps and Footings. A *pile cap* is a large unit of concrete placed on top of a pile or group of piles. A pile cap distributes the load of the structure to the pile. Dimensions for pile caps on structural drawings include the width, length, depth, and reinforcing requirements. See Figure 5-5. Pile cap forms may be very large and require many cubic yards of concrete to be placed in a single pour. Proper forming and bracing of the forms is essential to prevent form failure.

Continuous footings are placed on piles, pile caps, or the surface of the ground where there is sufficient bearing. Dimensions on structural foundation plan views provide the footing locations, lengths, widths, and elevations. See Figure 5-6. Extensive section cuts through footings provide specific information. The proper forming for each section of the footing is determined from the section cuts. Section cuts provide additional dimension information, reinforcing steel information, keyways, finishes, and projecting dowels or other inserts necessary for creating a bond between the footing and other poured-in-place concrete members such as slabs or walls.

On-Grade Slabs. Flat or sloping concrete slabs placed on the surface of the ground may be used as a foundation system in light bearing applications. On-grade slabs are also used for basement and ground-level floors and roadways. Prior to placement of concrete, information obtained from the plans includes treatment of the area below the slab, items placed in the slab, and elevations and finishes.

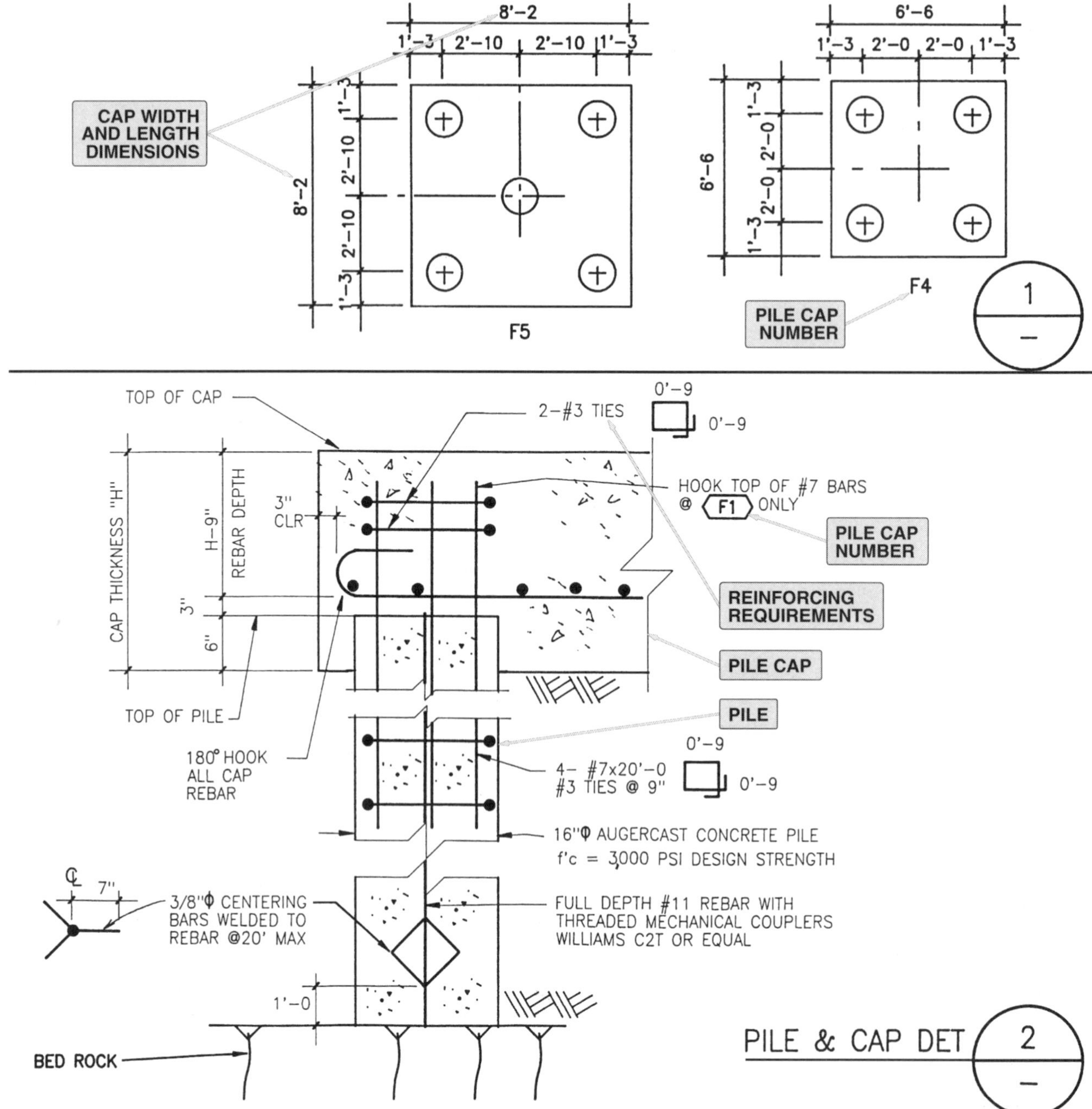

Figure 5-5. A pile cap is a reinforced block of concrete which is poured on a pile to fully distribute structural loads.

A trench may be dug around the perimeter of a floor slab to provide support and protection against movement during freezing and thawing cycles. This trench is shown on architectural drawings. See Figure 5-7. This trench allows the slab to support light to medium weight loads. Spread footings or piles are necessary where heavier load support is required.

Forms may be built for perimeter footings and slabs where they project above the surface of the soil. Other sections of the slab may be thickened to support other loads. Locations for the thickened sections are commonly indicated with dashed lines on plan views and with additional section cut views.

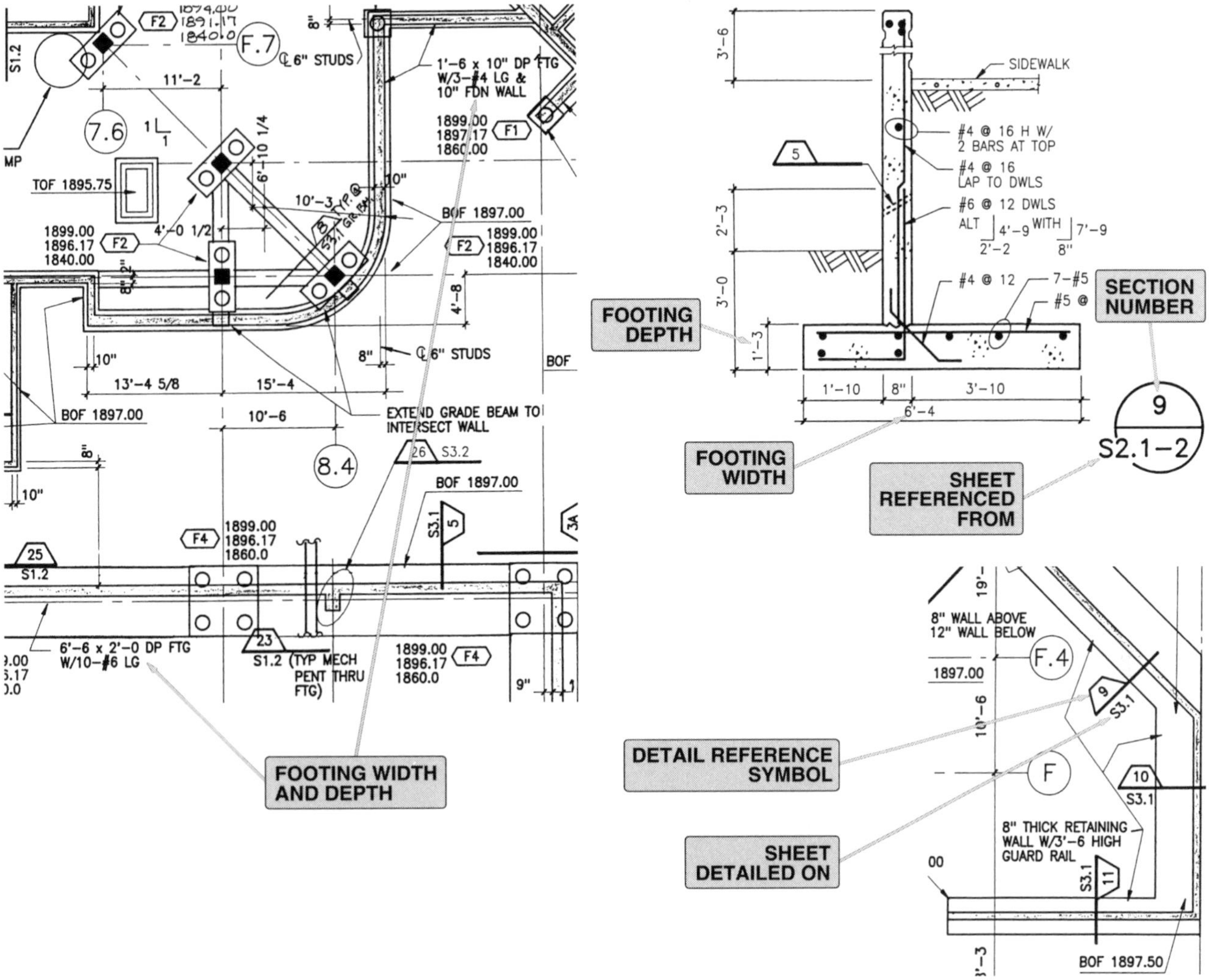

Figure 5-6. Footing dimensions are given on the plan view as width followed by depth. Careful cross-referencing between plan views and section cuts is necessary to ensure proper dimensioning of reinforced concrete footing and foundation walls.

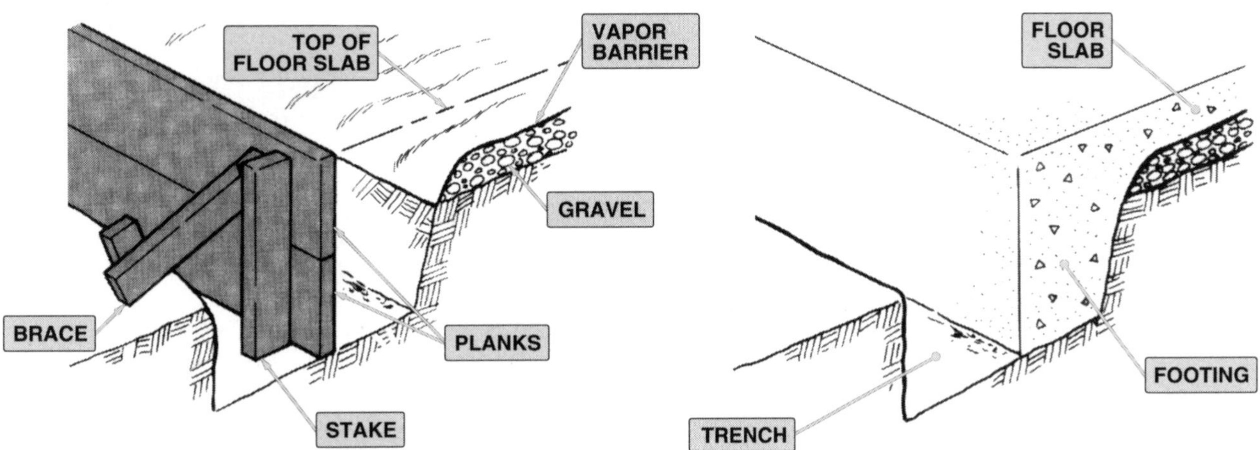

Figure 5-7. Excavation and forming of a shallow wall around the perimeter of an on-grade slab creates a light bearing foundation.

Various methods and materials for moisture protection and insulation may be placed below the slab prior to concrete placement. Section and detail drawings describe any subgrade materials such as gravel, moisture protection such as polyethylene sheets, and insulation such as expanded polystyrene. The compaction requirements and thickness of the subsurface gravel are given.

Architectural plan and detail drawings indicate the thickness of the concrete slab and the method of attachment to or isolation from surrounding members. Forming is not necessary where on-grade slabs are placed between existing walls or other structural members. Isolation joints may be installed at these points to help prevent movement of structural supporting members from creating cracks in the slab. The location and types of these isolation joints are indicated on detail drawings. See Figure 5-8. The edge design of a keyway or dowel is shown if the slab must join to other members. Control joints placed in slabs are also shown on plan and detail drawings. Locations for cutting of the slab are given for roadways.

Electrical conduit is installed in poured concrete floor slabs. Conduit is bent and stubbed out of the slab where electrical service is provided in walls and other locations. The ends of the conduit stubs may be covered with protective tape to prevent concrete from falling into and blocking the conduit.

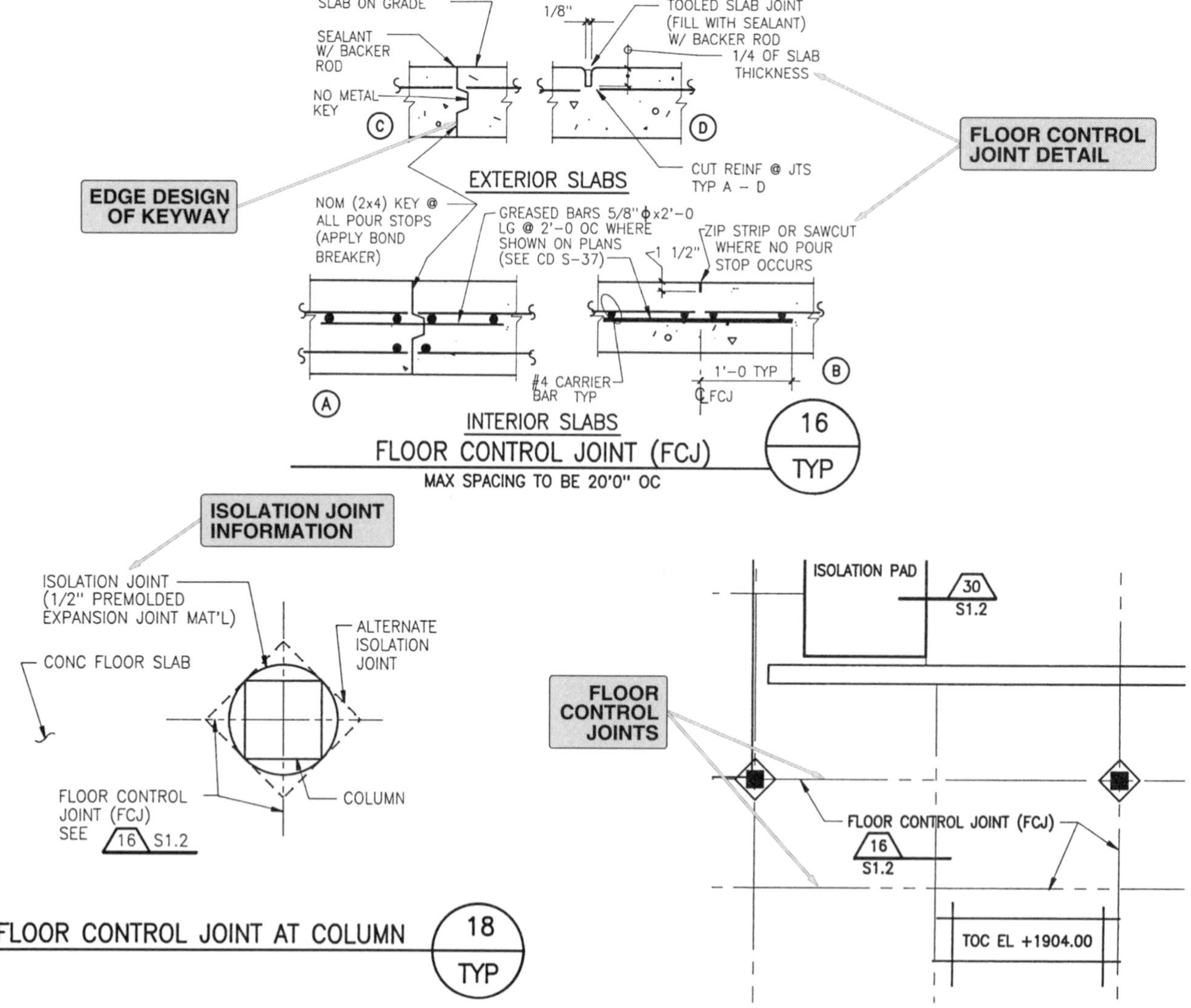

Figure 5-8. Isolation joints around structural members help prevent on-grade slab cracks. Various types of control joints are formed in on-grade slabs for interior and exterior applications.

Conduit sizes and locations are contained in the electrical drawings. Plumbing and other mechanical systems may also be placed in the slab. Mechanical drawings indicate locations for these items in the concrete on-grade slab. It may also be necessary to stub reinforcing steel out of the slab to create attachment points for column and wall reinforcing. Anchor bolts may also be set in the slab for bolting of structural steel columns or mechanical equipment.

Elevations are given to the top of the slab for on-grade and above-grade slabs. These may be given on elevation drawings or indicated as a note on plan views. The amount of slope to be finished into a floor or roadway or built into a ramp is given. A symbol on the plan view drawings indicates the depth or height of the offset in cases where there are many variations in finished slab height for mechanical pits or built-up pads. See Figure 5-9. Additional section cuts provide side wall and other necessary slab offset information. Treatment of the surface of the slab and the type of concrete may be given on cover sheet notes or in the specifications.

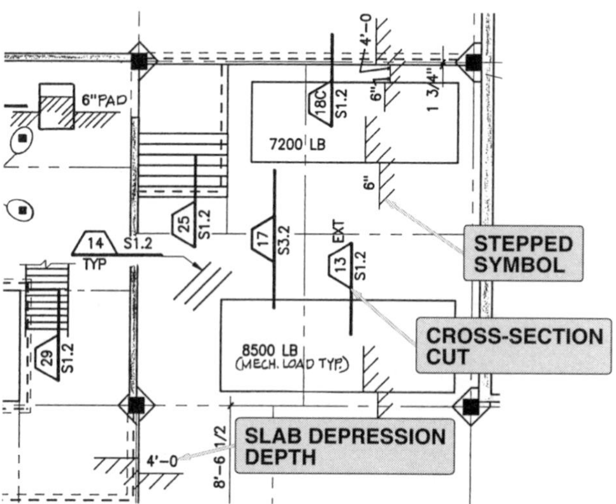

Figure 5-9. Built-up and sunken portions of poured-in-place concrete slabs are indicated with stepped symbols and section cuts.

Columns. Poured-in-place concrete column locations are given on plan views in a manner similar to structural steel columns and concrete piers. A gridwork of letters and numbers intersect at column locations. Each column is identified by letter and number. See Figure 5-10. A schedule that relates to each column's letter and number identification gives column size, shape, height, and steel reinforcement method.

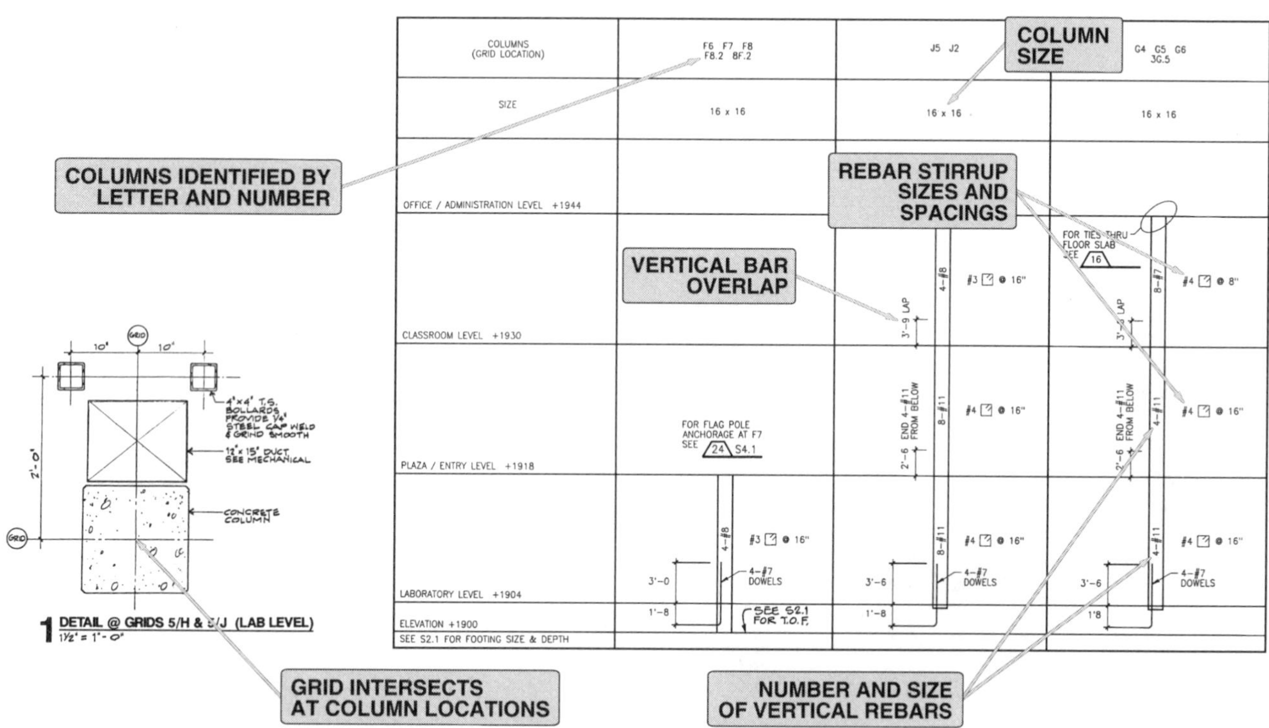

Figure 5-10. Column details are referenced to a gridwork of letters and numbers on plan views. Column schedules provide elevation, dimensions, and reinforcing information referenced to the plan view grid.

Forms and concrete for building columns are commonly placed one level at a time. For example, the columns for the first level of a three story building are formed and poured. The second floor deck is then formed, placed, and finished. The columns between the second and third floor are formed and poured after the second floor deck is completed.

Structural steel columns may be encased in concrete to improve their strength and protect them from fire. Forms are set around the existing structural steel columns and the concrete is placed.

Centerlines for columns are established after slabs, footings, and foundations are completed. Reinforcing steel for columns is set in place. Formwork for columns is built around the steel and braced. Several methods for column forming include fiber forms, wood forms, patented panelized forms, steel forms, and fiberglass spring forms. See Figure 5-11. Concrete is poured with a concrete pump or a concrete bucket attached to a crane when columns are securely braced and plumbed. The forms are removed after the concrete has reached the required strength.

Symons Corporation

Figure 5-11. Fiberglass spring forms are one of the methods for forming poured-in-place concrete columns.

Column Caps. A cap is placed on top of columns that are designed to support loads not directly above the column. Column caps are used primarily in bridge construction. A column cap may be placed on one column or be designed to span between columns and carry beams, girders, and joists. See Figure 5-12. Dimensions for overall width, thickness, and height are given on elevation and plan view drawings.

Column cap forms are most commonly supported by the columns on which they are placed. One forming method uses through bolts which are placed in holes formed in the columns. These bolts support brackets which act as seats for the formwork. Another method uses two-piece friction collars which are bolted around the columns. These collars also have projecting support brackets to hold column cap forms in place.

Walls. Poured-in-place concrete walls are placed on footings or slabs. Length and width dimensions are given on foundation plan views, elevation drawings, and detail section cuts. See Figure 5-13. Poured-in-place concrete wall information includes elevations to the top and bottom of the wall, the thickness of the wall, placement of wall surface features, all embedded items, and reinforcing steel. As with footing forms, there are many section cuts through the concrete wall to show all existing conditions. Solid lines on plan views indicate the locations for changes in wall type between section cuts.

A release agent is applied to the forms prior to their placement. One side of the concrete wall form is set in place and braced. Wall forms may be made of wood or metal faces reinforced with wood or steel frames. Wall forms are held in alignment with walers, strongbacks, and braces. Reinforcing steel, blockouts for doors and windows, bulkheads, and waterstops are set before the opposing side of the wall forms are completed. Many different wall tie systems are used to hold the two wall forms at the proper distance and distribute concrete loads during placement. The type of wall tie system used depends on the width and design of the wall. Some of the different wall ties used include snap ties, wire ties, she bolts, and coil ties. For large commercial jobs with complicated forming requirements, concrete form manufacturers provide detailed drawings of wall form, tie, and bracing placement to ensure proper form construction.

For some applications, only one side of a wall is formed and the opposing side is supported by soil or rock. This may be done for abutment walls, slurry walls, or various retaining walls. Reinforcing is set in place and the forms are set and braced. Additional bracing of one-sided wall forms is necessary to support the hydrostatic pressure which is not offset by another side of a wall as with a conventional wall tie system.

Gang forms may be used for large continuous walls. A series of smaller forms are joined together to create one large form which may be set in place more quickly than many small components. See Figure 5-14. Gang forms are set in place with cranes and may be bolted to existing concrete walls to hold them in place. Concrete is placed after wall forms are set and braced. The forms are stripped when the desired strength is reached.

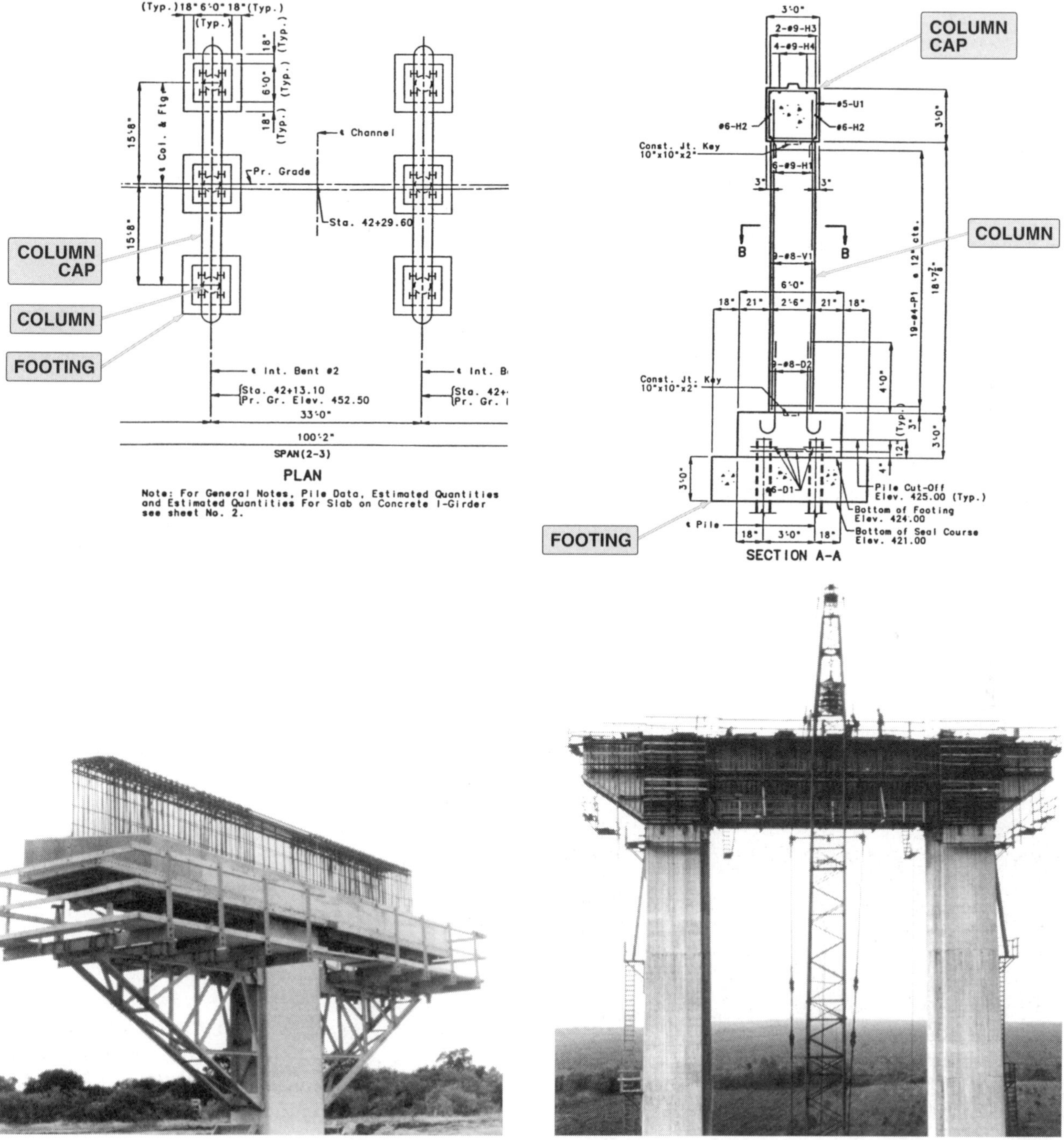

Symons Corporation

Figure 5-12. Column caps are shown in both plan view and section views and are formed by clamping or bolting formwork to supporting columns.

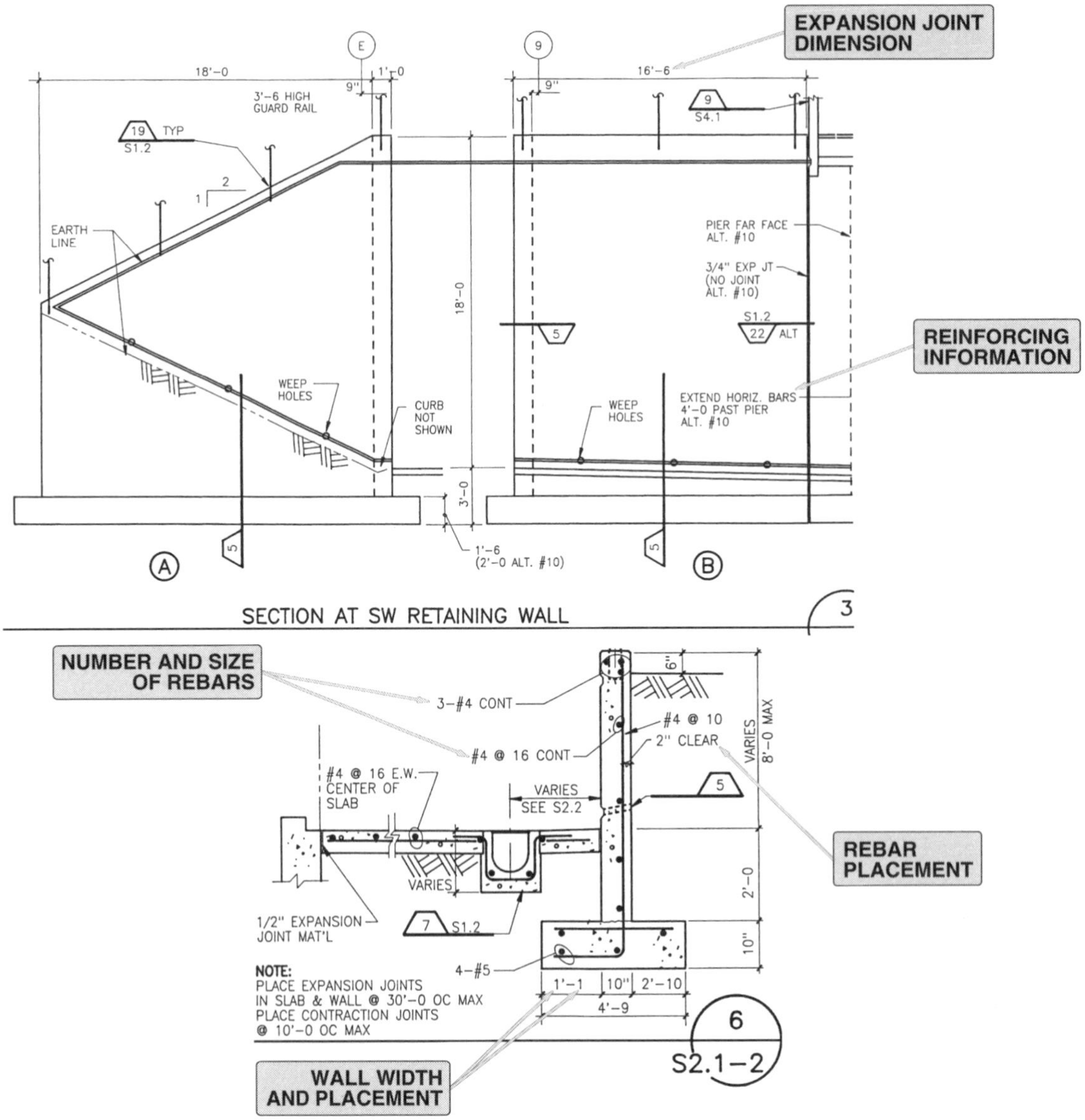

EXPANSION JOINT DIMENSION

REINFORCING INFORMATION

SECTION AT SW RETAINING WALL

NUMBER AND SIZE OF REBARS

REBAR PLACEMENT

WALL WIDTH AND PLACEMENT

NOTE:
PLACE EXPANSION JOINTS IN SLAB & WALL @ 30'–0 OC MAX
PLACE CONTRACTION JOINTS @ 10'–0 OC MAX

Figure 5-13. Section views through poured-in-place concrete foundation walls show surface treatments, reinforcing, and width dimensions.

Figure 5-14. A gang form allows a prefabricated panel of smaller forms to be set in place and braced as a single form unit.

Above-Grade Slabs. Concrete slabs placed above-grade may be built in several different designs. These include a monolithic method with beams and the above-grade slab placed at the same time, supporting the above-grade slab with precast concrete or structural steel beams, or supporting the slab with steel beams and corrugated decking. Openings in an above-grade slab are shown on plan view drawings with two solid diagonal lines forming an × inside a solid shape, such as a square or rectangle. The dimensions of the finished opening in the slab are given. These openings are provided for elevator shafts, stairwells, and mechanical chases.

The two monolithic slab methods include one-way and two-way beam systems. The type of system to be used is indicated on plan view and detail drawings. See Figure 5-15. Dashed lines show beam direction and location. Two-way beam systems are also referred to as waffle beam and slab systems.

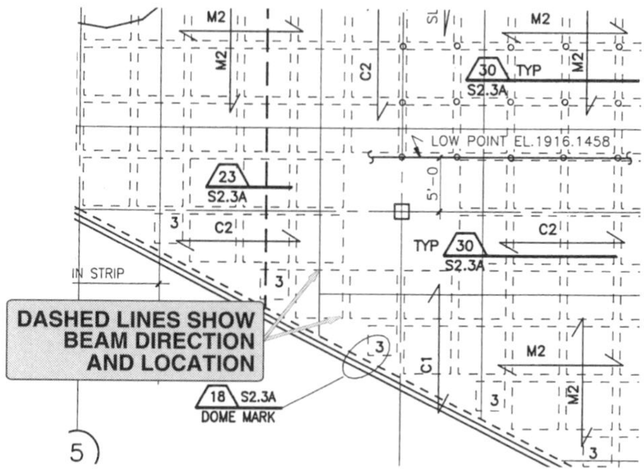

Figure 5-15. Dashed lines on a plan view indicate locations for beams in a two-way poured-in-place concrete monolithic slab and beam floor.

Shoring and decking is used to form a flat surface at the elevation of the bottom of the poured-in-place concrete beams for both systems. Shoring may be made of wood posts, steel pipe shores, or panelized shoring systems. Beams and joists are placed on these shores to support deck forms. The spacing and width of the beams is laid out on the deck. Domes or pans are used to form voids in the concrete slab which create the beams in either one or two directions. See Figure 5-16. Spandrel beams are formed around the outside edge of the deck to provide structural support. Perimeter edge forms are built to hold the concrete in place and keep the top of the slab at the proper elevation.

Reinforcing, electrical, and mechanical installations are made prior to concrete placement. Forming systems are designed by specialists to ensure the proper amount of shoring is in place and the proper amount of camber has been designed into the form. The forms must support the weight of the form itself, the wet concrete, all reinforcing, electrical and mechanical materials, and the workers placing and finishing the concrete. See Figure 5-17. The shoring and formwork are removed after the concrete has been placed, finished, and has reached the proper strength.

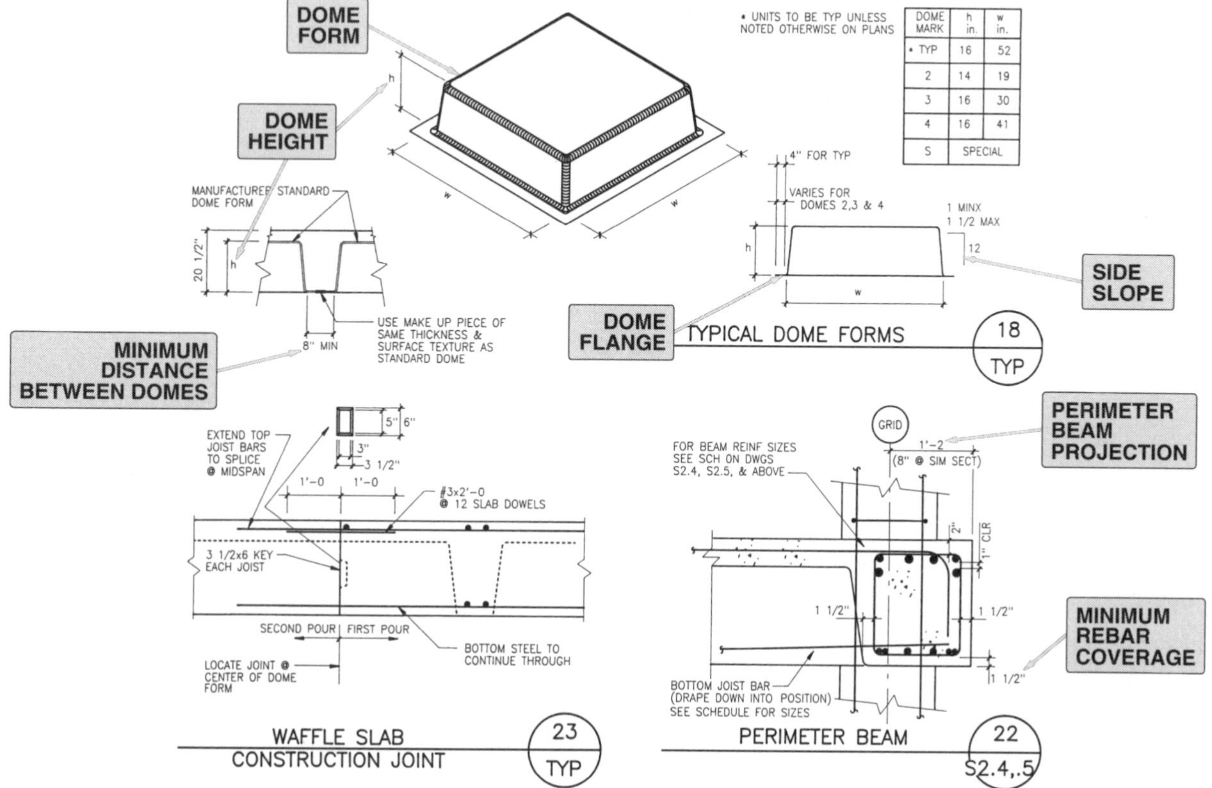

Figure 5-16. Steel domes are manufactured to standard heights and widths to form monolithic beam and slab floor systems. Perimeter beams support the edges of an above-grade slab.

Figure 5-17. Reinforcing is set in place after formwork and domes are in place.

Plans for poured-in-place concrete beams may have a beam schedule. Poured-in-place concrete beams are identified on a plan view with letters and numbers which relate to this schedule. See Figure 5-18. These may be spandrel beams or interior supporting beams between columns.

Precast concrete beams or steel beams may be designed to be placed independently of the above-grade concrete slab. Detail drawings indicate the thickness of the slab and reinforcing placement. Formwork is hung from beams after columns, walls, and beams are in place. Hangers are placed on the beams and allow for temporary joists and bracing brackets to be supported and set to the proper slab height. Threaded rods are lubricated and used to support brackets for joists.

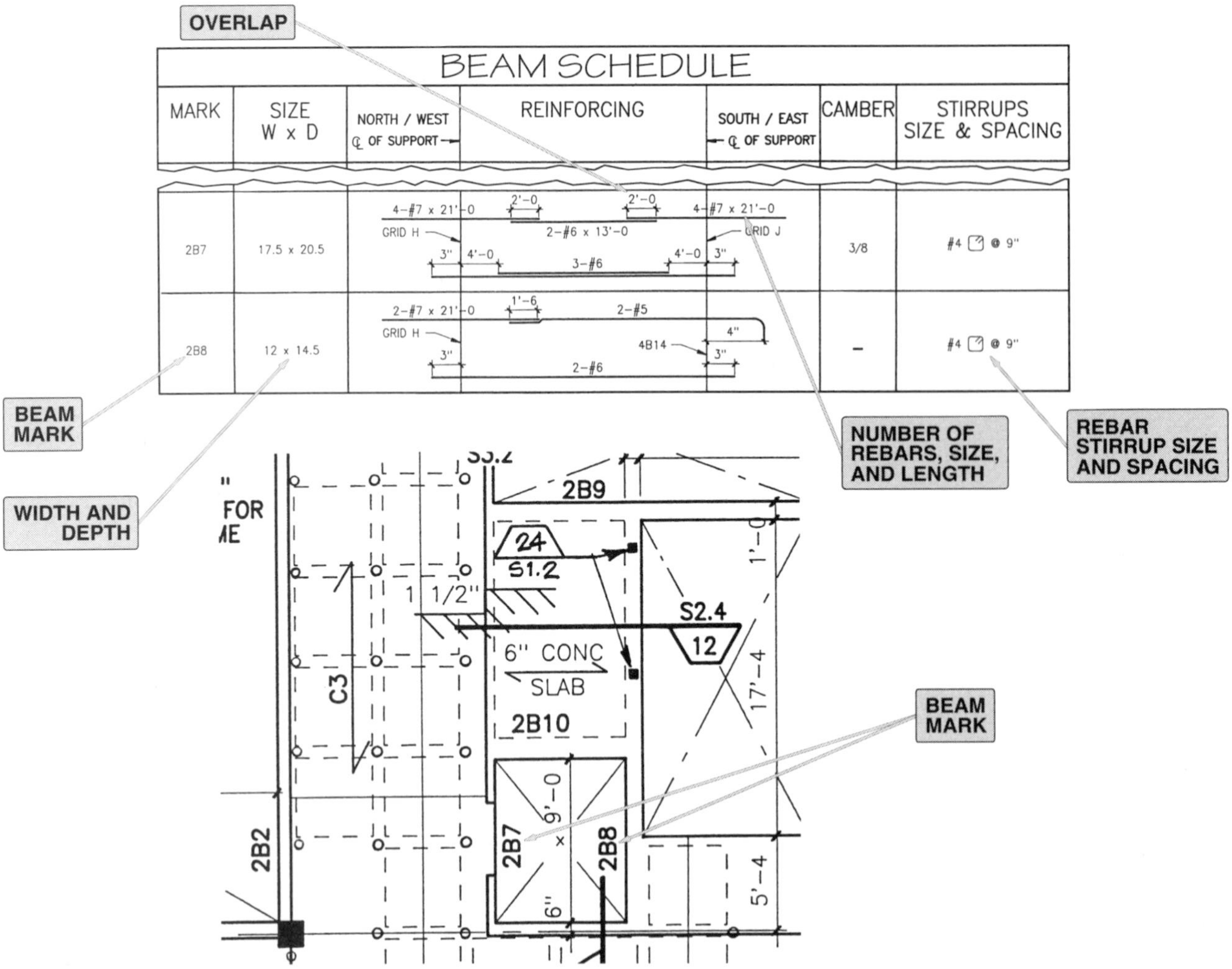

BEAM SCHEDULE

MARK	SIZE W x D	NORTH / WEST ℄ OF SUPPORT →	REINFORCING	SOUTH / EAST ← ℄ OF SUPPORT	CAMBER	STIRRUPS SIZE & SPACING
2B7	17.5 x 20.5	4-#7 x 21'-0 GRID H 3"	2'-0 2'-0 2-#6 x 13'-0 4'-0 3-#6 4'-0	4-#7 x 21'-0 GRID J 3"	3/8	#4 ◳ @ 9"
2B8	12 x 14.5	2-#7 x 21'-0 GRID H 3"	1'-6 2-#5 4B14 2-#6	4" 3"	–	#4 ◳ @ 9"

Figure 5-18. Poured-in-place concrete beam identification codes relate to beam schedule information concerning size and reinforcing.

Form decking is placed on the joists. The slab is tied to the beam by projecting reinforcing steel from a precast concrete beam or welded studs on top of a structural steel beam. An edge form is built around the perimeter of the deck. Electrical piping, mechanical blockouts, and reinforcing are set in place and the concrete is placed and finished. The temporary joists, bracing brackets, and deck forming are removed from below after the concrete has reached its design strength. Threaded lubricated rods are removed and the remainder of the hanging hardware is placed into the concrete deck and remains in place.

Concrete floor slabs are also placed on corrugated decking supported by steel beams or bar joists. See Figure 5-19. A structural steel C channel is welded around the perimeter of the corrugated decking. The top of the channel is set to the top of the slab. Concrete is place directly on the corrugated decking and finished to the proper elevation and slope.

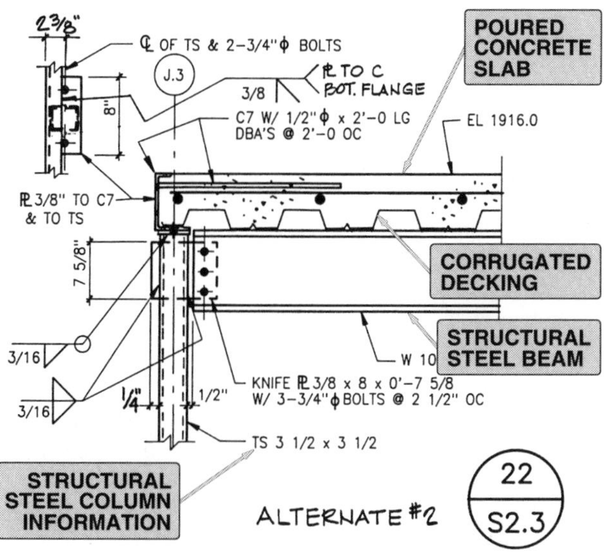

Figure 5-19. Poured-in-place, above-grade concrete slabs may be supported by structural steel and steel decking.

Reinforcing

Poured-in-place concrete is reinforced with various steel materials. These include bars and welded wire fabric. Detail drawings, cover notes, and reinforcing schedules give specific information concerning the type and placement of steel reinforcing. See Figure 5-20.

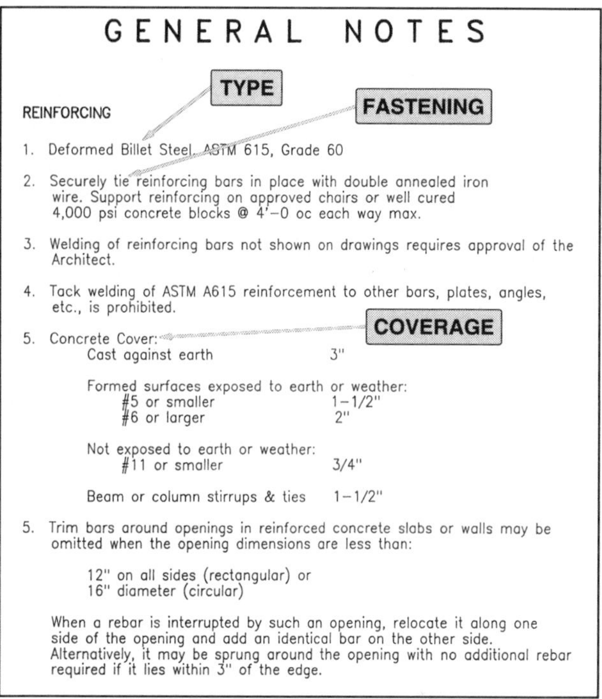

GENERAL NOTES

REINFORCING

1. Deformed Billet Steel, ASTM 615, Grade 60
2. Securely tie reinforcing bars in place with double annealed iron wire. Support reinforcing on approved chairs or well cured 4,000 psi concrete blocks @ 4'-0 oc each way max.
3. Welding of reinforcing bars not shown on drawings requires approval of the Architect.
4. Tack welding of ASTM A615 reinforcement to other bars, plates, angles, etc., is prohibited.
5. Concrete Cover:

Cast against earth	3"
Formed surfaces exposed to earth or weather:	
#5 or smaller	1-1/2"
#6 or larger	2"
Not exposed to earth or weather:	
#11 or smaller	3/4"
Beam or column stirrups & ties	1-1/2"

5. Trim bars around openings in reinforced concrete slabs or walls may be omitted when the opening dimensions are less than:

   12" on all sides (rectangular) or
   16" diameter (circular)

   When a rebar is interrupted by such an opening, relocate it along one side of the opening and add an identical bar on the other side. Alternatively, it may be sprung around the opening with no additional rebar required if it lies within 3" of the edge.

Figure 5-20. General notes on the structural drawings give information about reinforcing steel type, fastening, and coverage.

Materials. The most common method of reinforcing piles, roadways, footings, columns, walls, and beams is with steel bars with deformed surfaces. These bars are tied together in various configurations to reinforce large concrete structures. Ridges are formed into the surface of the bars to improve their adhesion to the surrounding concrete. See Figure 5-21. Reinforcing steel bars are sized in increments of 1/8" diameter. For example, a #4 bar is 4/8" or 1/2" in diameter. Several grades of steel are used for reinforcing bars which vary according to their tensile strength. A grade 40 reinforcing bar has a minimum tensile yielding point of 40,000 psi. Grades 50 and 60 have higher yield strengths. Reinforcing steel bars may be coated with epoxy for exterior applications. Epoxy-coated reinforcing bars are used in road and bridge building to minimize the effects of corrosion on the steel. Reinforcing bars are shown on section views with solid circles for end views and solid lines for edge views.

Welded wire fabric is also used to reinforce concrete slabs. Rolls of the fabric are stretched out and set in place to reinforce lightweight slabs such as sidewalks.

DEFORMED STEEL REINFORCING BARS

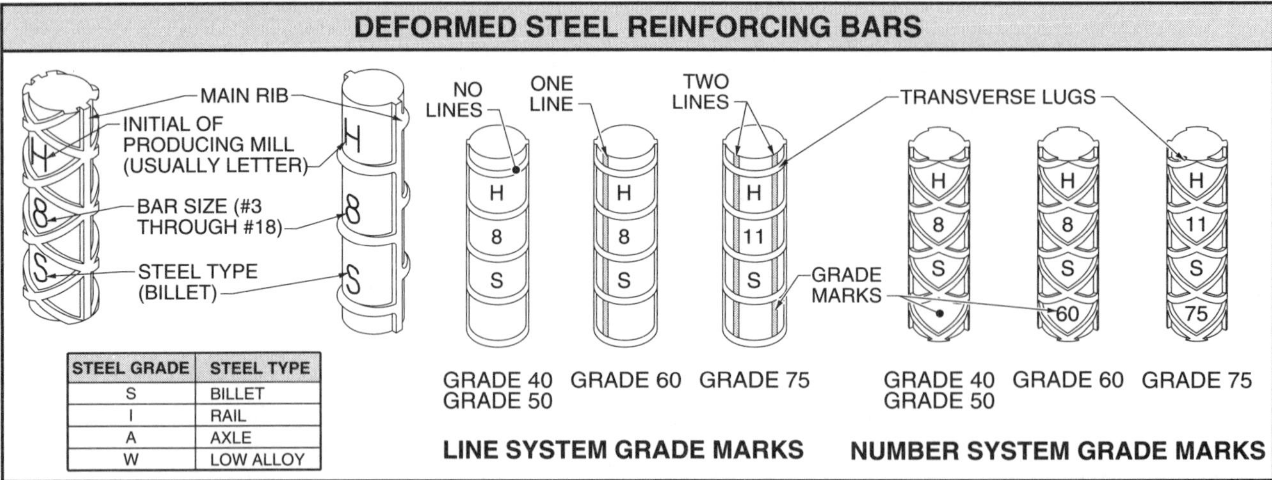

STEEL GRADE	STEEL TYPE
S	BILLET
I	RAIL
A	AXLE
W	LOW ALLOY

STANDARD REBAR SIZES

Bar Size Designation	Weight Per Foot	Diameter	Cross-Sectional Area Squared
	Lb	In.	In.
#3	0.376	0.375	0.11
#4	0.668	0.500	0.20
#5	1.043	0.625	0.31
#6	1.502	0.750	0.44
#7	2.044	0.875	0.60
#8	2.670	1.000	0.79
#9	3.400	1.128	1.00
#10	4.303	1.270	1.27
#11	5.313	1.410	1.56
#14	7.650	1.693	2.25
#18	13.600	2.257	4.00

REINFORCING STEEL STRENGTH AND GRADE

Deformed Billet	Minimum Yield Point or Yield Strength*	Ultimate Strength*
ASTM A-615		
Grade 40	40,000	70,000
Grade 50	50,000	90,000
Rail Steel ASTM A-616		
Grade 50	50,000	80,000
Grade 60	60,000	90,000
Axyl Steel ASTM A-617		
Grade 40	40,000	70,000
Grade 60	50,000	90,000
Deformed Wire ASTM A-496		
Welded fabric	70,000	80,000
Cold Drawn ASTM A-82		
Welded fabric < W1.2	56,000	70,000
Size ≥ W1.2	65,000	75,000

* in psi

Figure 5-21. Deformed steel reinforcing bars are identified by a standardized system. Use of various types of steel results in differing yield strengths.

Sizing of the welded wire fabric is designated by the spacing of the wire and either the cross-sectional area of the wire or the wire gauge. See Figure 5-22. Wires may be either smooth or deformed. Welded wire fabric has yield strengths between 60,000 psi and 70,000 psi. Welded wire fabric is shown on detail drawings as a dashed line with an × at each break in the line.

Installation. Detail drawings for poured-in-place concrete give specific reinforcing installation information. See Figure 5-23. This information includes the size and length of each bar, the location within the finished concrete, and overlap requirements. Manufactured sleeves and fastening devices are available where reinforcing steel is joined end-to-end.

COMMON ROLL STOCK STYLES OF WELDED WIRE FABRIC

New Designation	Old Designation	Steel Area Per Foot		Approx. Wt Per 100 Sq Ft**
Spacing – Cross-sectional Area (in.) – (Sq in./100)	Spacing – Wire Gauge (in.) – (AS & W)	Longitudinal*	Transverse*	
6 × 6 – W1.4 × W1.4	6 × 6 – 10 × 10	0.028	0.028	21
6 × 6 – W2.0 × W2.0	6 × 6 – 8 × 8 (1)	0.040	0.040	29
6 × 6 – W2.9 × W2.9	6 × 6 – 6 × 6	0.058	0.058	42
6 × 6 – W4.0 × W4.0	6 × 6 – 4 × 4	0.080	0.080	58
4 × 4 – W1.4 × W1.4	4 × 4 – 10 × 10	0.042	0.042	31
4 × 4 – W2.0 × W2.0	4 × 4 – 8 × 8 (1)	0.060	0.060	43
4 × 4 – W2.9 × W2.9	4 × 4 – 6 × 6	0.087	0.087	62
4 × 4 – W4.0 × W4.0	4 × 4 – 4 × 4	0.120	0.120	85

* in in. ** in lb

Note: Exact W-number size for 8 gauge and 2 gauge is W2.1 and W5.4.

Figure 5-22. Welded wire fabric is designated by spacing and cross-sectional areas or spacing and wire gauge.

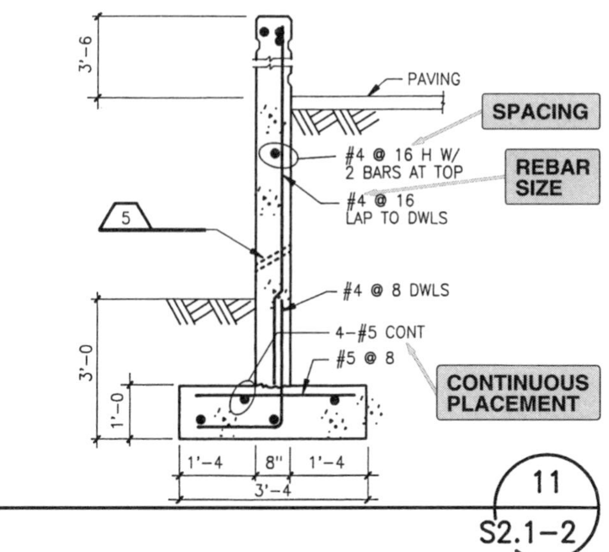

Figure 5-23. Section cuts through poured-in-place concrete foundation walls and footings indicate reinforcing size, type, and placement.

Each portion of the architectural and structural drawings and details for concrete structures provides reinforcing steel information. Cages of upright bars with intermediate stirrup ties are formed for columns. The size of the upright and tying bars for stirrups and the spacing of the bars in both directions are indicated on the column schedule. See Figure 5-24. A variety of different sizes and shapes of bars are required for beams. A schedule for sizes, shapes, and lengths is provided in the beam schedule. The various shapes are obtained by heating and bending the bars at a fabrication shop or on the job site. Schedules for the placement of reinforcing bars in poured-in-place concrete joists and slabs are also included in the structural drawings.

Cages of reinforcing steel for columns and beams and mats for walls and slabs are formed by tying bars together with wire in the configuration given on the print drawings. Where possible and desirable, large cages or mats are tied together and prefabricated at a location which may be more easily accessible than in the concrete forms. See Figure 5-25. These large cages or mats are then lifted into the forms with cranes and set at their final location before concrete placement. The cages or mats are secured and braced to ensure the proper coverage of concrete occurs. Some of the reinforcing bars which make up cages or mats commonly project out of the edges of the forms to create a doweling effect for attachment of adjoining poured-in-place concrete members. The amount of reinforcing steel projection out of the concrete is given on the detail drawings and schedules.

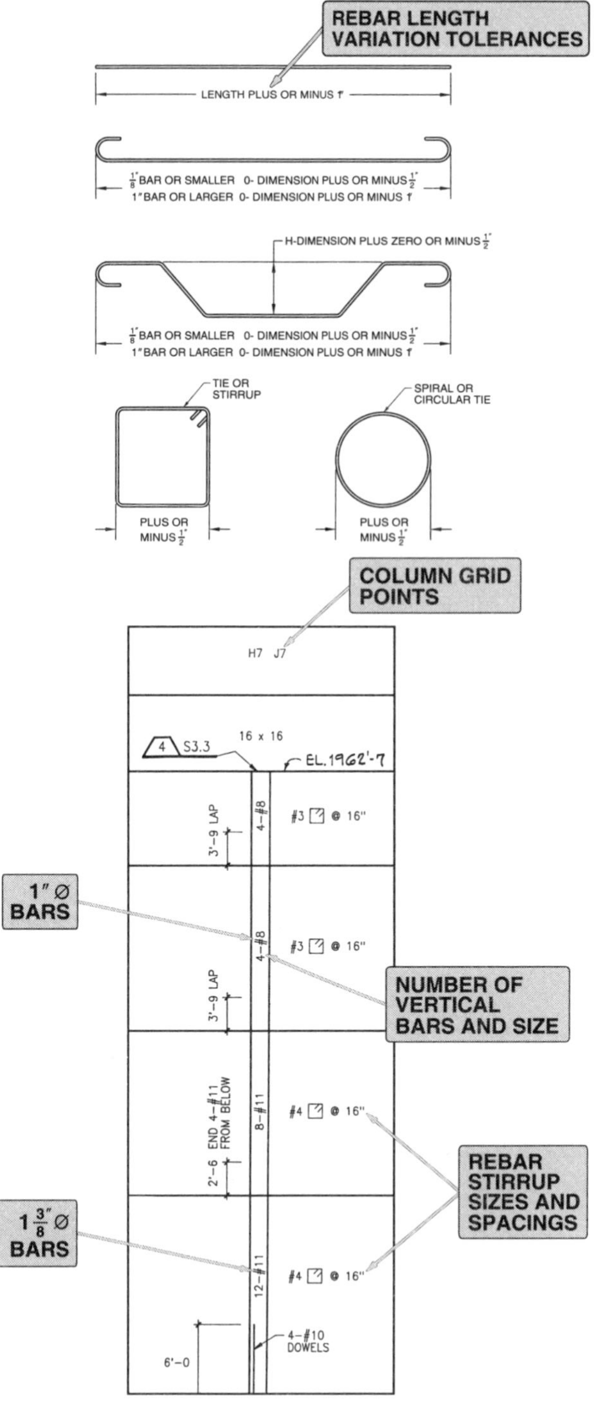

Figure 5-24. Steel reinforcing bars are bent into different shapes/sizes for beam concrete reinforcement. A column schedule indicates sizes and spacing of reinforcing bars and stirrups.

Figure 5-25. A series of individual steel reinforcing bars may be tied together and set in place as a single unit.

For flat slabs and roadways, the mat or welded wire fabric must be supported to a specific distance above the bottom of the slab. Chairs may be used for this purpose. A *chair* is a steel shape formed into a wide variety of shapes to support reinforcing. See Figure 5-26. See Appendix. Chairs are set in place and slab reinforcing is set on top. The reinforcing may rest on the chairs or be tied in place. For welded wire fabric, it may be lifted to the proper location during concrete placement or supported by chairs or some other materials such as concrete bricks or blocks. Chairs and bolsters for reinforcing are also used in other horizontal concrete members such as beams.

Concrete

The primary drawing information concerning concrete has to do with the finished dimensions for shape and location. Information on the architectural and structural drawings concerning the properties and placement of concrete is minimal. Most of the composition, placement, and finishing information is contained in the specifications. There are some notes and information on the drawings which are helpful concerning concrete. Concrete is shown on section cuts as a series of small triangles in a random arrangement.

Properties. The architectural drawings may contain notes concerning specific concrete information. This information includes such items as 28 day strength, aggregate size, slump, water cement ratio, air entrainment, and admixtures. See Figure 5-27.

Overall concrete strength is stated as the pounds per square inch (psi) of pressure which the concrete can withstand after 28 days. A test cylinder mold 6″ in diameter and 12″ long is filled with concrete from the same batch that is placed in the forms. The test cylinder is cured under the same basic conditions as the building concrete. After 28 days, the cylinder is tested at a laboratory to determine the compressive strength. The outer casing is removed, the cylinder is crushed, and the breaking point measured.

CHAIRS

Symbol	Bar Support Illustration	Support	Standard Sizes
SB	5″	Slab Bolster	$\frac{3}{4}$″, 1″, $1\frac{1}{2}$″, and 2″ heights in 5′ and 10′ lengths
CHCM*		Continuous High Chair for Metal Deck	Up to 5″ heights in $\frac{1}{4}$″ increments
JCU**	$\frac{3}{4}$″ MIN; TOP OF SLAB; HEIGHT; #4 or $\frac{1}{2}$″Ø; 14″	Joist Chair Upper	14″ Span. 1″ through 3″ heights in $\frac{1}{4}$″ increments

* Available in Class 3 only, except on special order.
** Available in Class 3 only, with upturned or end bearing legs.

Figure 5-26. Manufacturers provide a variety of shapes and sizes of chairs to support concrete slab or beam reinforcing.

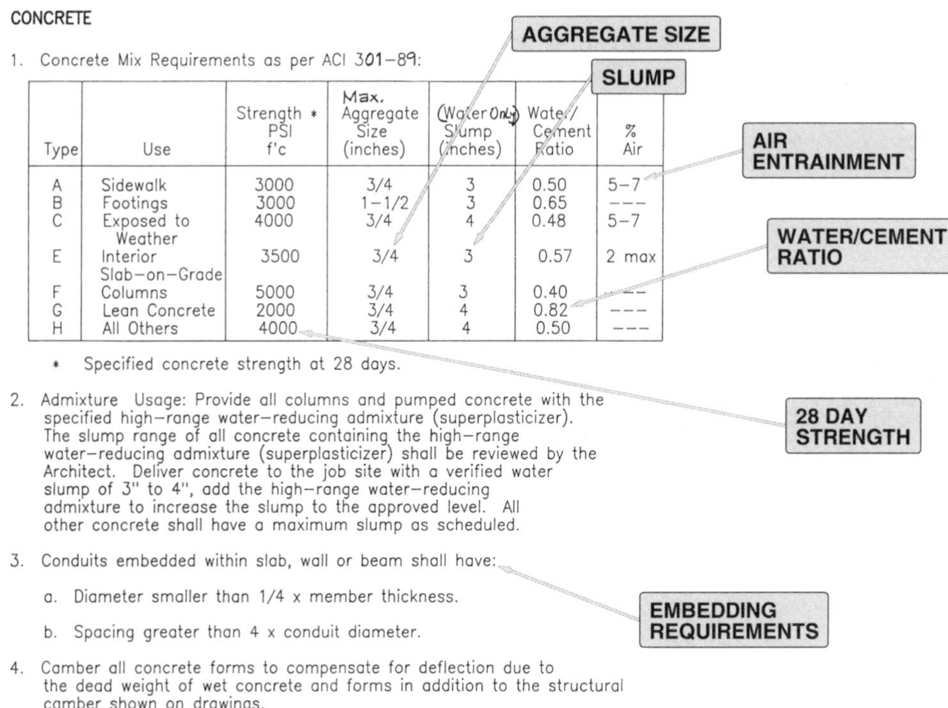

CONCRETE

1. Concrete Mix Requirements as per ACI 301–89:

Type	Use	Strength * PSI f'c	Max. Aggregate Size (inches)	(Water Only) Slump (inches)	Water/Cement Ratio	% Air
A	Sidewalk	3000	3/4	3	0.50	5–7
B	Footings	3000	1–1/2	3	0.65	---
C	Exposed to Weather	4000	3/4	4	0.48	5–7
E	Interior Slab–on–Grade	3500	3/4	3	0.57	2 max
F	Columns	5000	3/4	3	0.40	---
G	Lean Concrete	2000	3/4	4	0.82	---
H	All Others	4000	3/4	4	0.50	---

* Specified concrete strength at 28 days.

2. Admixture Usage: Provide all columns and pumped concrete with the specified high–range water–reducing admixture (superplasticizer). The slump range of all concrete containing the high–range water–reducing admixture (superplasticizer) shall be reviewed by the Architect. Deliver concrete to the job site with a verified water slump of 3" to 4", add the high–range water–reducing admixture to increase the slump to the approved level. All other concrete shall have a maximum slump as scheduled.

3. Conduits embedded within slab, wall or beam shall have:

   a. Diameter smaller than 1/4 x member thickness.

   b. Spacing greater than 4 x conduit diameter.

4. Camber all concrete forms to compensate for deflection due to the dead weight of wet concrete and forms in addition to the structural camber shown on drawings.

5. All exterior slabs shall include polyfiber reinforcing (CFP).

Figure 5-27. Print notes concerning concrete state the mix requirements, usable admixtures, and embedding requirements.

Aggregates represent approximately 70% of the overall volume of concrete. Aggregate information in the general notes greatly affects final concrete strength and finishing properties. General notes may describe the type and maximum size of aggregate used. The slump of concrete measures the consistency of the fresh mix and can be used as a general measure of water content. *Slump* is the amount of sagging which occurs in a 12″ high conical fresh concrete sample.

The amount of water in the concrete mix is crucial to final strength. Enough water is required to fully hydrate with the cement. Too much water weakens the mix. The water/cement ratio is stated in terms of the weight of the water divided by the weight of the cement contained in one cubic yard of concrete. A relatively lower water/cement ratio results in relatively stronger concrete. Air entrainment creates minute air pockets in the concrete which increase workability and resistance to freezing and thawing, and decrease separation of the concrete components. See Figure 5-28. Other admixtures are available to affect such characteristics as flowability and water reduction.

RECOMMENDED AIR CONTENT PERCENTAGE

Nominal Maximum Size of Coarse Aggregate*	Exposure**	
	Mild	Extreme
⅜ (10 mm)	4.5	7.5
½ (13 mm)	4.0	6.0
¾ (19 mm)	3.5	6.0
1 (25 mm)	3.0	6.0
1½ (40 mm)	2.5	5.5
2 (50 mm)	2.0	5.0
3 (75 mm)	1.5	4.5

* in in.
** in percent

Figure 5-28. The desirable percent of air entrainment in concrete varies according to aggregate size and concrete exposure conditions.

Placement. Concrete placement information is contained in the specifications. General rules followed during concrete placement include placing concrete as close as possible to its final location to limit segregation of the mix, placing concrete at a rate that does not place undue stresses on the formwork, avoiding the addition of excessive water at the job site, properly vibrating concrete to ensure consolidation, and properly curing to ensure the concrete meets final strength design requirements.

PRECAST CONCRETE

Developments in concrete design and lifting equipment have led to the widespread use of precast concrete members. Precast concrete members are used for walls, beams, slabs, piling, and a variety of other construction members. Precast concrete members may be precast at the job site and lifted into place or formed and poured at a casting yard and transported to the job site by truck. All precast members require special reinforcing to ensure they meet the stresses of transportation and installation in addition to final structural loads.

Tilt-Up Panels

Tilt-up panels are panels which are precast and lifted into place at the job site. See Figure 5-29. This method of precasting is used for construction of low-rise concrete structures of one to three stories. Print information for tilt-up panels includes wall dimensions, opening dimensions, placement and types of lift anchors and reinforcement, and interior and exterior wall finish.

A planning schedule for casting, lifting, and bracing of tilt-up panels ensures that walls are raised in an orderly manner. A tilt-up panel planning schedule ensures that walls which are cast, raised, and braced first are not in the way of the casting and placement of the walls to follow.

After tilt-up wall panels are in place, floors and roofs are connected to the walls by welded plates, bolted inserts, or supported by ledges formed on the walls. Precast concrete, poured-in-place concrete, or structural steel floors and roofs may be used with tilt-up panels.

Forming. Low forms are set on the slab after placement of the first floor slab. The height of the forms is equal to the thickness of the wall to be precast. The outside perimeter of the forms is set to the dimensions of the wall. Provisions are made around the perimeter of the form to allow for the projection of reinforcing steel as shown on the drawings. A bond breaker is applied to the floor slab to ensure concrete placed for the wall does not adhere to the slab. Blockouts are set in place for door and window openings and beam pockets. Any surface treatment to be provided on the side of the wall which is on the lower side of the form are set in place, such as welding plates for connecting to adjoining panels or form liners to create decorative finishes.

The Burke Company

Figure 5-29. Tilt-up panels are cast on a floor slab and lifted into place after the concrete has reached the desired strength.

Reinforcing. Details for reinforcing steel for precast tilt-up wall panels are similar to those given for poured-in-place concrete. Additional reinforcing may be required to hold the wall rigid during the lifting process. Lift anchors are set in the concrete wall to allow for the attachment of lifting hardware and crane cables. Brace inserts are also set in the concrete wall to allow for attachment of braces. Special symbols on detail drawings and manufacturer's manuals describe the type of lift anchors and brace inserts placed in the concrete. Dimensions on elevation views for tilt-up wall panels show proper locations for lift anchor and brace insert placement. See Figure 5-30. See Appendix.

SYMBOL GUIDE AND INSERT ILLUSTRATIONS

SYMBOL	DESCRIPTION	ILLUSTRATION
	T-41 SL GROUND RELEASE INSERT	
	P-52 SL ANCHOR (EDGE ONLY) Dashed Line indicates special shear bar.	 TYPE SL
	T-6 WALL BRACE ANCHOR (Leg construction may be similar to TYPE T-1.)	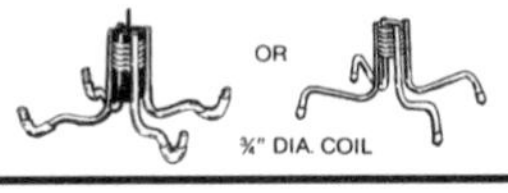 OR ¾" DIA. COIL

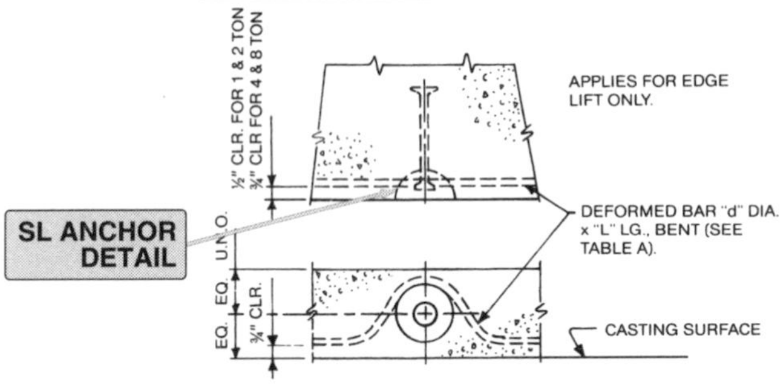

SL ANCHOR DETAIL

½" CLR. FOR 1 & 2 TON
¾" CLR FOR 4 & 8 TON

APPLIES FOR EDGE LIFT ONLY.

DEFORMED BAR "d" DIA. x "L" LG., BENT (SEE TABLE A).

CASTING SURFACE

U.N.O.

EQ. EQ. ¾" CLR.

SL INSERT			MINIMUM	DEFORMED BAR
SIZE	LENGTH	PART NO.	PANEL THK.	SIZE LENGTH
1T x	4¾"	467110	5"	#3 x 1'-6"
2T x	6¾"	467145	6"	#4 x 2'-0"
4T x	9½"	467170	7"	#4 x 2'-6"
8T x	13⅜"	467185	9"	#6 x 3'-0"

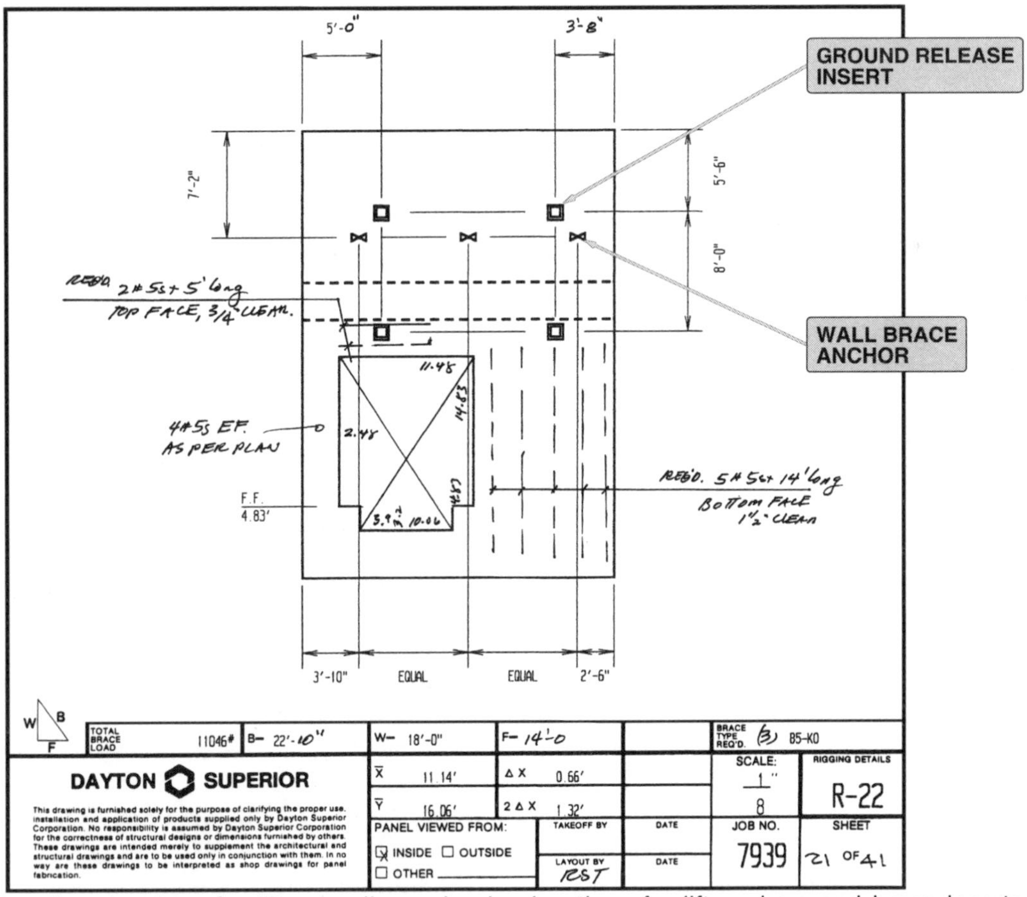

GROUND RELEASE INSERT

WALL BRACE ANCHOR

5'-0" 3'-8" 7'-2" 5'-6" 8'-0"

REQ'D. 2 #5s + 5' long TOP FACE, 3/4" CLEAR.

4 #5s E.F. AS PER PLAN

11.48 14.83 2.48 5.92 10.06

F.F. 4.83'

REQ'D. 5 #5s + 14' long BOTTOM FACE 1½" CLEAR

3'-10" EQUAL EQUAL 2'-6"

TOTAL BRACE LOAD 11046#	B— 22'-10"	W— 18'-0"	F— 14'-0"		BRACE TYPE REQ'D. (3) B5-KO
DAYTON SUPERIOR	X̄ 11.14'	ΔX 0.66'		SCALE: 1"/8	RIGGING DETAILS R-22
	Ȳ 16.06'	2ΔX 1.32'			
	PANEL VIEWED FROM: ☒ INSIDE ☐ OUTSIDE ☐ OTHER	TAKEOFF BY / LAYOUT BY RST	DATE / DATE	JOB NO. 7939	SHEET 21 OF 41

This drawing is furnished solely for the purpose of clarifying the proper use, installation and application of products supplied only by Dayton Superior Corporation. No responsibility is assumed by Dayton Superior Corporation for the correctness of structural designs or dimensions furnished by others. These drawings are intended merely to supplement the architectural and structural drawings and are to be used only in conjunction with them. In no way are these drawings to be interpreted as shop drawings for panel fabrication.

Figure 5-30. Elevation drawings for tilt-up wall panels give locations for lift anchors and brace inserts which are set in place and fastened to the reinforcing steel.

Lift anchors and brace inserts are tied to the reinforcing steel. Proper location of the lift anchors ensures that the wall can be lifted safely and does not break during the lifting operation.

Finishing. Concrete is placed in the forms in a manner which avoids dropping it onto the slab and disturbing the release agent. The surfaces of the wall are in a horizontal position. All surface treatments and finishes are performed at this time, prior to lifting.

Lifting. A crane with a spreader bar to facilitate lifting is used to set the finished tilt-up wall panels in place after the concrete has reached the proper hardness. Some additional surface bracing of tilt-up panels with many voids may be necessary prior to lifting. Cables are fastened to the lift anchors cast in the wall. The wall is lifted and pivoted into final position. Braces are then bolted to the brace inserts cast into the wall. Each wall section is braced for final positioning.

Fastening. Tilt-up wall panels are fastened together by several methods. These methods include flush-poured pilaster, poured column, precast column, steel column, and flush steel plate. See Figure 5-31. Concrete columns may be formed between the sections. The concrete columns are poured-in-place and anchor the tilt-up panels together. Precast concrete columns with steel inserts may be set in place between the tilt-up panels and welded to secure the panels. A structural steel column may be set between adjoining tilt-up panels to allow for the welding of steel angles cast into the edges of the walls. Steel inserts in adjoining tilt-up panels may be welded to a plate which spans between them and joins them together. Detail drawings indicate the type of panel joining system used.

Braces for tilt-up wall sections remain in place until panels are fastened together and floors and roofs are in place. Floors and roofs tie the tilt-up wall sections together and provide stability to the entire structure.

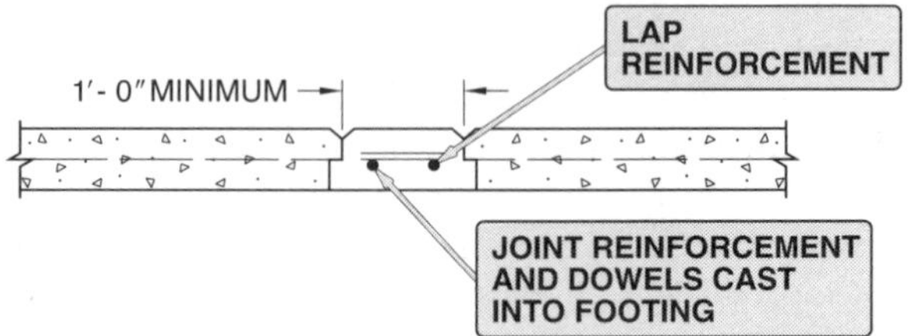

FLUSH-POURED PILASTER

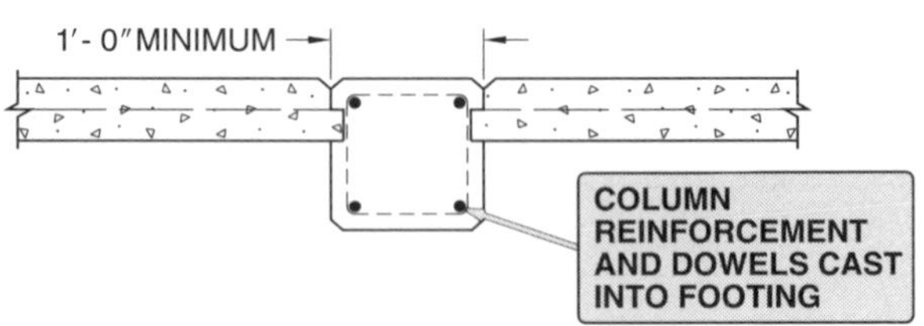

POURED COLUMN

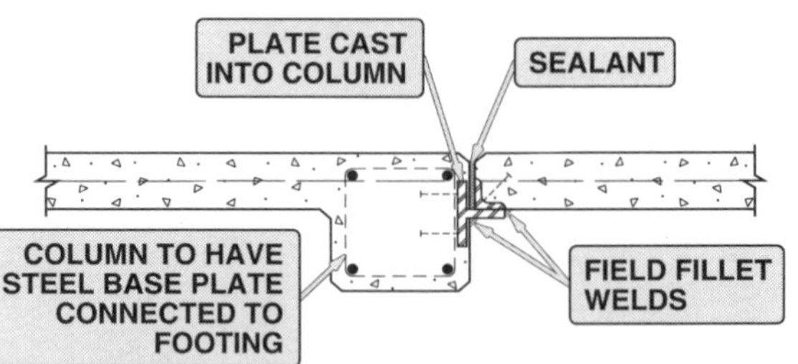

PRECAST COLUMN

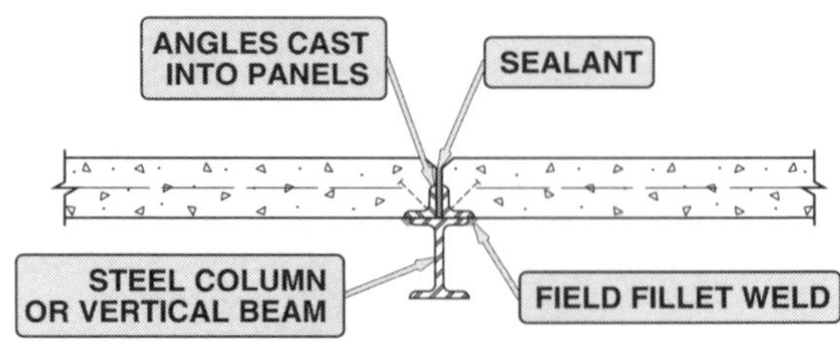

STEEL COLUMN

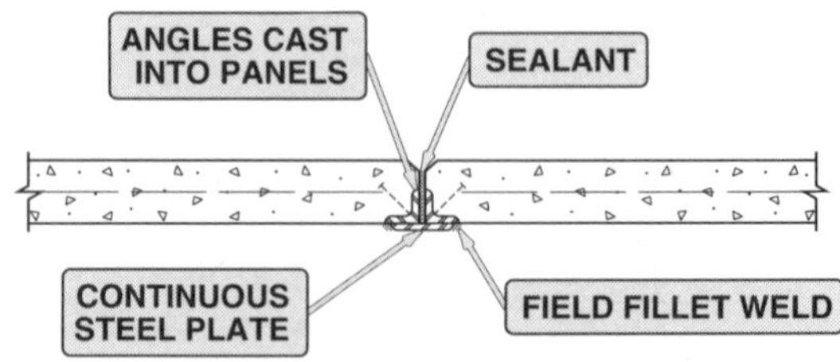

FLUSH STEEL PLATE

Figure 5-31. Plan view detail drawings illustrate fastening methods for adjoining tilt-up wall sections.

Off-Site Precast Members

Concrete members which are precast and transported to the job site include piling, beams, exterior wall finish panels, paving materials, and various piping and masonry units. The primary considerations in construction with large, precast concrete members are proper handling, rigging, and installation to prevent cracking and failure of the units.

Piling. Precast concrete piling is driven in a manner similar to other piling. A pile-driving hammer forces the pile into the ground to a specified depth or resistance. A shoe may be placed on the top of the pile to prevent breakage. Tops of precast concrete piling are cut to the required elevations with a concrete saw. Reinforcing steel is cut with an oxyacetylene torch to allow for the proper amount of projection for attachment of other building members.

Beams and Slabs. Precast concrete beams are used for building and bridge construction. Beams are formed and poured in rectangular, stemmed, L-, or T-shapes according to detail drawings. See Figure 5-32. These drawings provide information for length, height, and width. Structural engineers design the placement for reinforcing steel based on loading to be imposed on the beam. Beams are commonly reinforced by prestressing or post-tensioning. Prestressed beams are cast with steel tendons spanning from end to end of the beam.

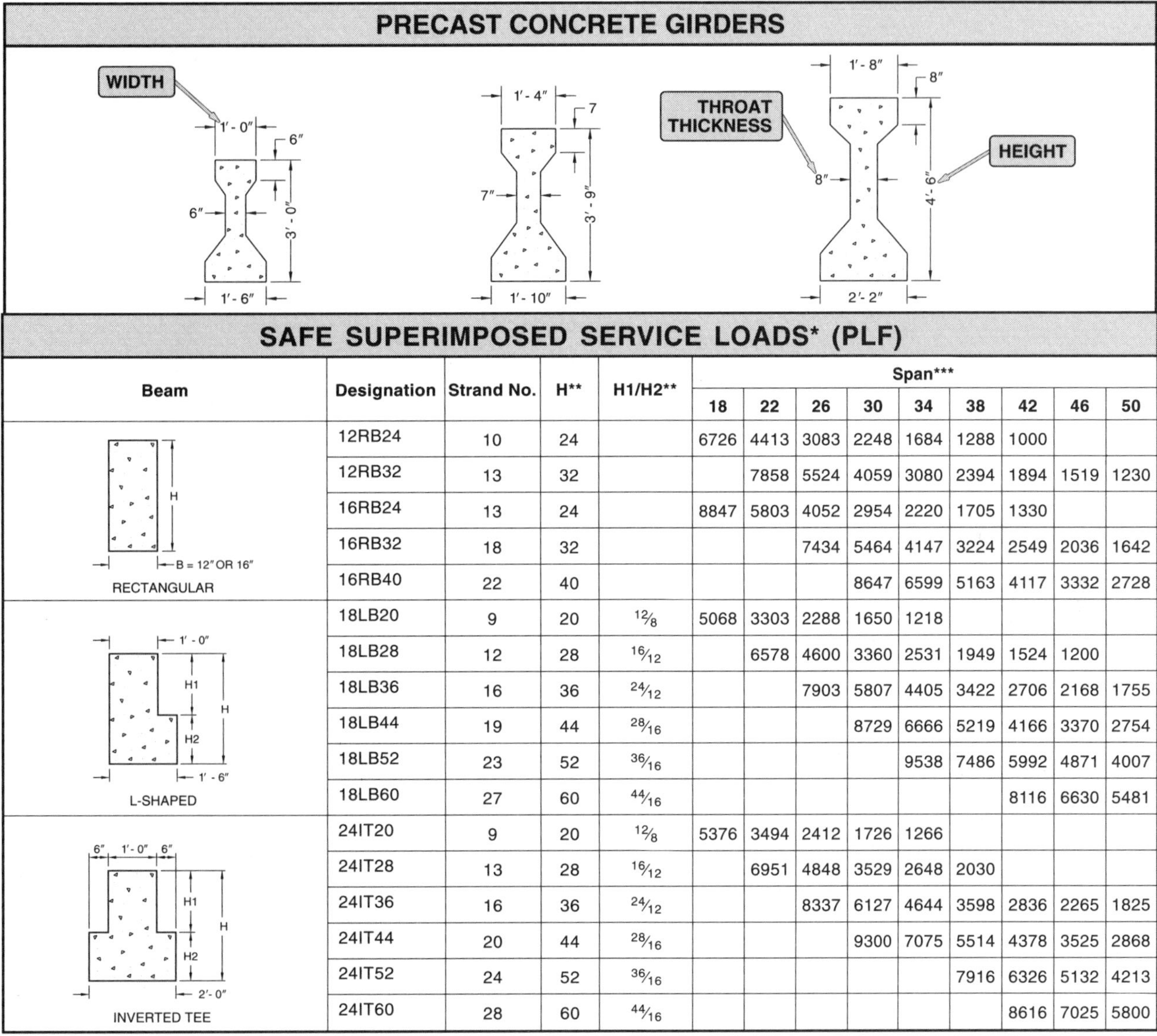

SAFE SUPERIMPOSED SERVICE LOADS* (PLF)

Beam	Designation	Strand No.	H**	H1/H2**	Span***								
					18	22	26	30	34	38	42	46	50
RECTANGULAR	12RB24	10	24		6726	4413	3083	2248	1684	1288	1000		
	12RB32	13	32			7858	5524	4059	3080	2394	1894	1519	1230
	16RB24	13	24		8847	5803	4052	2954	2220	1705	1330		
	16RB32	18	32				7434	5464	4147	3224	2549	2036	1642
	16RB40	22	40					8647	6599	5163	4117	3332	2728
L-SHAPED	18LB20	9	20	12/8	5068	3303	2288	1650	1218				
	18LB28	12	28	16/12		6578	4600	3360	2531	1949	1524	1200	
	18LB36	16	36	24/12			7903	5807	4405	3422	2706	2168	1755
	18LB44	19	44	28/16				8729	6666	5219	4166	3370	2754
	18LB52	23	52	36/16					9538	7486	5992	4871	4007
	18LB60	27	60	44/16							8116	6630	5481
INVERTED TEE	24IT20	9	20	12/8	5376	3494	2412	1726	1266				
	24IT28	13	28	16/12		6951	4848	3529	2648	2030			
	24IT36	16	36	24/12			8337	6127	4644	3598	2836	2265	1825
	24IT44	20	44	28/16				9300	7075	5514	4378	3525	2868
	24IT52	24	52	36/16						7916	6326	5132	4213
	24IT60	28	60	44/16							8616	7025	5800

* safe loads shown indicate 50% dead load and 50% live load; 800 psi top tension has been allowed, therefore additional top reinforcement is required
** in in. *** in ft

Figure 5-32. Precast concrete beams and girders are designed to span long distances.

Tendons are encased in a coating which keeps them from adhering to the concrete. Tendons are stretched to a predetermined amount of tension before concrete is placed. After the concrete is placed and cured, the tension on the tendons is transferred from the tensioning equipment to the beam concrete. Steel plates are cast into the ends of the beam which distribute the tension of the cables to the concrete. The tension on the beam puts the entire member in compression which reduces tension cracking along its length. For post-tensioning, concrete is placed in the forms and reaches a given amount of set. The tendons are then placed in tension and the load transferred to the concrete beam. This method is used where the size of the beam prohibits precasting and transporting to the job site.

T-shapes incorporate beams and slabs into a single unit and are useful for spanning between column caps, beams, or girders in bridge construction. The top section of the T may be from 8′ to 10′ wide. These units may also be formed as a double T with two vertical sections. Precast Ts may be joined side by side to create an integrated unit for bridge beams and road surfaces.

After precast concrete beams are set in place, forms may be set perpendicular between them to provide for placement of poured-in-place concrete. The concrete locks the beams together in a manner similar to bridging. Concrete placed between precast beams prevents tipping and distributes imposed loads. This is commonly placed directly above columns and column caps for bridge construction.

Precast flat floor slabs are available in a variety of thicknesses and designs. See Appendix. They are used for above-grade floor slab systems and for roof panels. The types and sizes of precast slab panels are noted on plan view drawings and elevation drawings. The thickness of the precast slab member is noted in inches. This is followed by FS for flat slab or HC for hollow core. For example, a slab designated as 6FS is a solid flat slab 6″ thick. Identification may also be accomplished with a manufacturer's code number or name. Methods for fastening of the slabs to each other and to supporting members are shown on detail section drawings. Fastening may be accomplished by bolting or welding steel inserts.

Exterior Panels. Many designs of decorative precast concrete panels are used for wall finish and paving. Precast wall finish panels can be cast with various concrete colors, aggregate sizes and types, and surface finishes. Steel angles or plates are cast into these panels which allow them to be welded to other members such as structural steel columns and beams or reinforced concrete members with adjoining steel inserts. Precast wall panels are lifted into place with a crane, braced, and fastened in place. Plan information includes the location of the panels and fastening details.

Precast concrete is also used for coping, window sills, lintels, headers, and other applications on exterior walls of concrete or masonry. See Figure 5-33. Detail drawings provide dimensions and installation information.

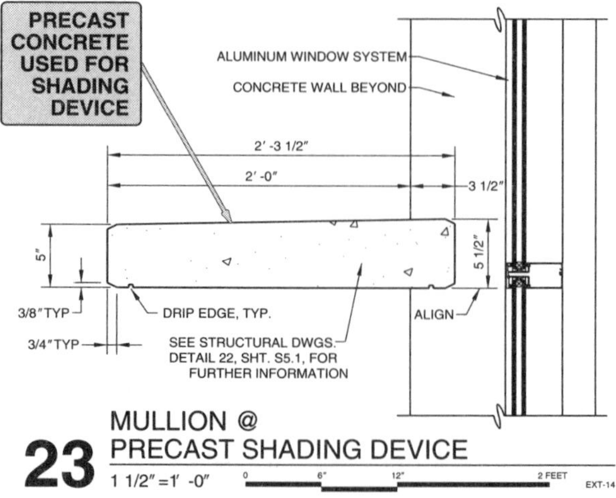

Figure 5-33. Precast concrete is used for non-structural purposes such as sunshades and trim elements.

CHAPTER 5 REINFORCED CONCRETE CONSTRUCTION

Review Questions

Name ______________________________ Date ______________

Printreading

T F **1.** Concrete has high tensile strength.

__________ **2.** A slump test normally measures ________.

A. formwork stability
B. pretensioned concrete beams
C. on-grade slab compaction
D. consistency of fresh concrete

T F **3.** Concrete placed in forms at too fast of a rate increases the hydrostatic pressure.

__________ **4.** A(n) ________ wall is a wall which is precast on a floor slab and set in place with a crane and spreader bar.

T F **5.** Steel pipe is used as a form for poured-in-place concrete piling.

__________ **6.** The water cement ratio which results in the highest concrete strength is ________.

A. .25
B. .50
C. .75
D. 1.0

T F **7.** Additional bracing is normally required for one-sided wall forms.

__________ **8.** A(n) ________ is a series of small wall panels joined together and set in place as one unit.

T F **9.** Domes form voids in concrete decks in a two-way above-grade slab beam system.

__________ **10.** Solid diagonal lines on an above-grade slab plan view indicate ________.

A. cross-bracing
B. a floor opening
C. shoring
D. dome placement

__________ **11.** Above-grade slabs poured on precast concrete beams are ________.

A. formed with joists and hangers
B. supported by a friction collar
C. formed with gang forms
D. set with spreader bars

T F **12.** Reinforcing bars must not project out of the face or edges of reinforced concrete.

T F **13.** Tilt-up walls are commonly used for high-rise structures.

__________ **14.** A(n) ________ is a trench or low wall form placed around the perimeter of an on-grade slab.

T F **15.** Lifting brackets for tilt-up walls are set at 4″ on center.

__________ **16.** Form bracing information for reinforced concrete structures is given on ________.

A. elevation plans
B. section drawings
C. form manufacturer drawings
D. additional architectural plans marked with a prefix of F

T F **17.** T-shaped concrete precast units are used for bridge building.

T F **18.** Precast concrete wall finish panels are fastened to structural steel members with drilled holes and through bolts.

__________ **19.** A pile cap is located _________.

A. below-grade to support pile
B. on top of piling
C. between footings and foundations
D. between columns and column caps

__________ **20.** The column schedule for reinforced concrete columns gives _________.

A. location dimensions
B. form design
C. bracing pattern
D. width dimensions

T F **21.** Aggregates make up approximately 20% of concrete volume.

__________ **22.** The diameter of a #3 reinforcing bar is _________″.

A. 3⁄16
B. 3⁄8
C. 3⁄4
D. 3

T F **23.** Ridges on steel reinforcing bars are designed to inhibit corrosion.

T F **24.** A grade 60 reinforcing rod has greater tensile strength than a grade 40 reinforcing rod.

__________ **25.** The common method of joining reinforcing steel bars for column reinforcing is _________.

A. welding
B. splicing sleeves
C. tying
D. bolting

__________ **26.** Chairs are used to support steel reinforcing for _________.

A. slabs
B. walls
C. columns
D. abutments

T F **27.** Reinforcing steel for columns is set after formwork is in place.

__________ **28.** Pretensioning for reinforcement is used with concrete _________.

A. walls
B. beams
C. on-grade slabs
D. footings

__________ **29.** Friction collars are used to support forms for _________.

T F **30.** Locations for electrical conduit are shown on on-grade slab plan views.

__________ **31.** For an above-grade slab, a perimeter form which is welded to corrugated steel decking is made from _________.

T F **32.** Isolation joints for concrete slabs act to provide thermal insulation.

__________ **33.** Concrete cylinders are tested for compressive strength after _________ days.

T F **34.** Tilt-up wall sections may be joined together after being lifted into place by poured-in-place concrete columns.

CHAPTER 5

REINFORCED CONCRETE CONSTRUCTION

Trade Competency Test

Name ______________________________ Date ______________

Riverpoint

Refer to Sheets 11, 12, 13, 14, 15, and 16.

T F **1.** Openings larger than 1′ in concrete on-grade slabs are reinforced at each corner with three reinforcing bars spaced 1½″ on center.

________ **2.** The abbreviation "CIP" concrete wall means ________.

________ **3.** Utility piping which is 18″ below the bottom of poured concrete footings ________.

A. must be reinforced prior to concrete placement
B. is placed after all footings are in place
C. is encased in lean concrete placed in a trench around the pipe
D. is left undisturbed during footing placement

T F **4.** The floor slab in the bottom of the elevator shaft is 6″ thick.

T F **5.** Where noted on the plans, web shear reinforcing is centered in concrete joists between domes.

________ **6.** The finished floor elevation for the first floor concrete slab is ________.

________ **7.** The elevation to the top of the decking (bottom of the concrete waffle slab) for forming of the second floor above-grade slab is ________.

T F **8.** The 4″ on-grade slabs are placed on a layer of compacted gravel which is 6″ deep.

________ **9.** The largest diameter steel reinforcing used for footing reinforcing according to the footing schedule is ________.

T F **10.** The trench drain on section 2 of print S4.1 is on the east side of the building.

________ **11.** For non-bearing walls, on-grade slabs are thickened ________ deeper than the surrounding slab.

________ **12.** On the first floor framing plan, the width of the openings in the 8″ foundation wall along the north side of the building between grid lines C and E is ________.

A. 3′-4½″
B. 4′-8″
C. 4′-10″
D. 4′-0½″

________ **13.** Designations on the first floor framing plan concerning middle strips and column strips pertain to differences in ________.

A. slab thickness
B. column size
C. slab reinforcing
D. dome placement

__________ **14.** The depth of the floor control joints in the service area is __________″.

T F **15.** Precast concrete is used for window sills on the first floor windows along grid line F between lines 4 and 5.

__________ **16.** Reinforcing stirrups for the shade beams are made of __________″ diameter bars.

T F **17.** Concrete columns are poured continuously without interruption to the roof height with beams and slabs butting against them.

T F **18.** All column reinforcing steel between the basement level and the first floor level is 1⅛″ diameter.

__________ **19.** On the first floor east wall between grid lines 1 and 3, the distance between the outside wall line and the inside of the concrete shade beams is __________.

__________ **20.** The length of the first floor slab reinforcing bars surrounding column G4 is __________.

__________ **21.** Typical floor isolation joints around concrete columns are __________.

A. round
B. square
C. rectangular
D. diamond shaped

__________ **22.** The minimum distance that a 1″ diameter steel reinforcing bar must extend past a wall opening is __________.

__________ **23.** Steel reinforcing bars for an 8″ thick concrete wall are placed __________.

A. on alternating sides
B. toward the outside of the wall
C. toward the inside of the wall
D. in the middle of the wall

__________ **24.** The typical depth of rustication joints is __________″.

A. ½
B. ¾
C. 1
D. 1¼

__________ **25.** The typical amount of concrete coverage for top slab reinforcing bars is __________″.

__________ **26.** The thickness of concrete above a typical dome is __________″.

A. 4½
B. 10
C. 16
D. 20½

T F **27.** Column E.1, 5.5 is outside of the finished building.

T F **28.** The top of the first floor slab elevation is the same at column E2 and column H2.

__________ **29.** The typical center-to-center spacing for dome forms is __________′.

A. 4
B. 5
C. 6
D. 8

__________ **30.** The slab thickness for concrete stair landings is __________″.

A. 4½
B. 5½
C. 8
D. 11

__________ **31.** The inside diameter of formwork for round concrete columns C6 and D6 is __________″.

T F **32.** Section view 25F on the first floor framing plan at grid line H5 refers to a full strength wall.

__________ **33.** The dashed line with a D at each break which is parallel to grid line F indicates __________ on the basement and foundation plan.

A. an auxiliary layout line D
B. a footing drain
C. cutting plane line D
D. dome centerlines

T F **34.** The steel beams at the top of the elevator shaft are installed in a north/south direction.

__________ **35.** The footing width along grid line E between lines 3 and 4 is __________.

A. 8″
B. 12″
C. 1′-2½″
D. 2′

__________ **36.** The distance from grid line 1 to the outside face of the concrete pillars on the north wall is __________.

A. 8′
B. 11′
C. 27′-4″
D. 30′

T F **37.** The east parapet wall is precast and welded in place.

__________ **38.** The four solid circles outside the northwest corner of the elevator shaft on the first floor framing plan indicate __________.

A. column reinforcing steel
B. sleeves through the slab
C. slab anchors
D. slab reinforcing steel

__________ **39.** The typical thickness of the shade beams is __________″.

A. 8
B. 12
C. 16
D. 18

__________ **40.** The unit rise for each step adjacent to column G3 is __________″.

__________ **41.** The diameter of the vertical reinforcing steel in the concrete pillars on the north and east sides of the building is __________″.

A. ½
B. ⅝
C. ¾
D. ⅞

__________ **42.** The width of the concrete basement floor slab between the foundation wall along grid line F and the edge of the lowered pit in the southeast corner is __________.

__________ **43.** A __________ is located at the joining of the footing and foundation wall along grid line F.

A. continuous water drop
B. keyway
C. brick ledge
D. doweled connection

T F **44.** For first floor concrete slab reinforcing, the steel reinforcing bars between columns G4 and G3 are placed before the bars between G4 and H4.

__________ **45.** A formula for reinforcing tie horizontal spacing is __________.

A. height minus 4″ divided by 6
B. height divided by 6
C. the same for exterior and interior columns
D. different for columns with 8 vertical bars and 12 vertical bars

__________ **46.** The minimum allowable height of the concrete forms for the columns between the first and second floors is __________.

__________ **47.** The footing closest to grid line 6 between grid lines H and J has two lines with an S at each end indicates _________.

A. piping sleeves
B. sewers
C. steps in the footing
D. steel reinforcing placement

__________ **48.** For stepped footings on compacted soil, the amount of rise on the bottom sloped grade per one foot of run is _________″.

__________ **49.** The diameter of the steel reinforcing stirrups for spandrel beams is _________″.

__________ **50.** For perimeter beams, the distance between the column centerline and the edge of the nearest dome form is _________″.

__________ **51.** The roof slab is _________.

A. thinner than the third floor slab
B. the same thickness as the third floor slab
C. thicker than third floor slab
D. not formed of poured concrete

__________ **52.** The width of the seismic joint at grid line 5 is _________″.

T F **53.** The brick ledge on the service yard wall is 4″ wide.

__________ **54.** The width of the footing along grid line F is _________.

T F **55.** The driveway opening into the service area is 13′ wide.

T F **56.** The depth of the concrete footing for the service yard which is parallel with grid line J is 12″.

__________ **57.** The width and thickness of the concrete pillars on the north and east walls of the building are _________.

T F **58.** The depth of the slab depression area for tile at grid line G2 is 1½″.

__________ **59.** The spacing for horizontal rustication joints on the north and east wall concrete pillars is _________ on center.

__________ **60.** The elevation of the finished concrete basement floor at column G4 is _________′.

A. 1904.25
B. 1905.25
C. 1906.25
D. 1907.25

__________ **61.** The only square column on the plan is column _________.

T F **62.** An on-grade slab elevation change of 12″ requires wall forming on one side of the offset wall only.

6 MECHANICAL AND ELECTRICAL SYSTEMS

Mechanical systems provide water, gas, heating, cooling, and ventilation for a structure. Mechanical prints include information for plumbing piping and fixtures, heating and cooling equipment, air circulation and ventilation equipment, and ductwork. Plumbing systems include those used for drainage, cold and hot water supply, waste piping, compressed air and gases, and miscellaneous piping for items such as vacuums and irrigation systems. Fire protection systems are designed in accordance with NFPA standards and governmental regulations.

Electrical systems include connections to power supplies, lighting wiring and fixtures, power outlet provisions, electrical equipment attachment and power installation, and wiring and finish details for communications and alarm systems. Electrical prints contain electrical wiring, equipment, and finish material information.

MECHANICAL AND ELECTRICAL SYSTEMS

Mechanical systems provide water, gas, heating, cooling, and ventilation for a structure. Mechanical prints include information for plumbing piping and fixtures, heating and cooling equipment, air circulation and ventilation equipment, and ductwork. Mechanical prints are identified with the prefix M followed by the page number.

Electrical systems include connections to power supplies, wiring and fixtures for lighting, provision of power outlets, installation of all necessary attachments and power for electrical equipment, and wiring and finish for communications and alarm systems. Electrical prints are identified with the prefix E followed by the page number.

Mechanical and electrical prints are used with all other portions of the building prints. Throughout the construction of structural and finish members, allowances for the placement of plumbing piping, mechanical piping and ductwork, and electrical conduit must be made.

Openings in walls, floors, and roofs to allow installation and access for pipes, ductwork, and conduit are required. Anchorage and support allowances are made for mechanical and electrical equipment during structural and finish construction activities. Allowances are made for mechanical equipment, such as furnaces and boilers, and electrical fixtures, such as panelboards, light fixtures, and switches.

Schedules and contents information for mechanical and electrical prints indicate the number of mechanical and electrical sheets and their purposes. Extensive specialized symbols and lines are used on mechanical and electrical prints. These are described on individual cover sheets along with the print schedules and general notes.

PLUMBING

Piping systems included on the plumbing prints are those used for drainage, cold and hot water supply, waste piping, compressed air and gases, and miscellaneous piping for items such as vacuums and irrigation systems. Many types of pipes and pipe fittings are used. Plumbing prints show pipes and fittings with specialized symbols, abbreviations, and lines. See Figure 6-1. Where plumbing systems are complex and need detailed description, portions of the floor plan may be drawn to a larger scale and provided on separate sheets. The larger scale prints allow for clearer viewing of the plumbing systems in a specific portion of the structure.

Drainage and Waste Systems

Surface water is carried to drainage systems from landscaped areas, paved areas, and roofs by a series of catch basins, drains, and piping. Some drainage system information is given on the civil prints. Large pipe placed during excavation of the site and connected to main sewer lines is shown on civil prints. A mechanical site plan may be included in the mechanical prints to show information concerning the location of waste piping and connections to sanitary sewers. See Figure 6-2. Plumbing plan views and detail drawings indicate locations for drain lines in the immediate vicinity of the building and those integrated into the building.

Piping. Waste pipes collect waste water from roof drains, surface drains, floor drains, sinks, lavatories, and toilets and carry the water to sanitary sewers or treatment facilities. Plumbing prints indicate the size, purpose, type, and elevation of each pipe.

PLUMBING/PIPING ABBREVIATIONS AND ANNOTATION

ABBREVIATIONS		ANNOTATION	
AFF	ABOVE FINISH FLOOR	FRWH	FREEZE RESISTANT WALL HYDRANT
AFG	ABOVE FINISH GRADE	NO	NORMALLY OPEN
AH	AIR HANDLING UNIT	OSA	OUTSIDE AIR
AT	ATTENUATOR	PRV	PRESSURE REDUCING VALVE
BLR	BOILER	RA	RETURN AIR
CLG	CEILING	RC	ROOF COWL
CO	CLEAN-OUT	RD	ROOF DRAIN
COIW	CLEAN-OUT IN WALL	TYP	TYPICAL
COTF	CLEAN-OUT TO FLOOR	UH	UNIT HEATER
COTG	CLEAN-OUT TO GRADE	VTR	VENT THRU ROOF
DIV	DIVISION	WHA	WATER HAMMER ARRESTER
DWG	DRAWING	W/	WITH
EF	EXHAUST FAN	@	AT
ET	EXPANSION TANK	Ø	DIAMETER
EXH	EXHAUST	-	FLAT OVAL
FD	FLOOR DRAIN	ARV	ACID RESISTANT VENT
FS	FLOOR SINK	ARW	ACID RESISTANT WASTE
GTV	GAS TANK VENT	ARVTR	ACID RESISTANT VENT THRU ROOF
IE	INVERT ELEVATION	CW	COLD WATER
LAB	LABORATORY	HW	HOT WATER
MFG	MANUFACTURER	HWC	HOT WATER CIRC.
NC	NORMALLY CLOSED	SV	SUMP PUMP VENT
UON	UNLESS OTHERWISE NOTED	AR	ACID RESISTANT
		UON	UNLESS OTHERWISE NOTED

PLUMBING/PIPING SYMBOLS

Figure 6-1. Many different abbreviations and symbols are used on mechanical prints to illustrate plumbing equipment and installations.

This information is shown on plan views and isometric details. Detail section views related to the plan views provide reference points for the isometric piping plans. See Figure 6-3.

Pipe sizes are given in inches which indicate the inside diameter of the pipe. The outside diameter of pipes vary, depending on the material used for the pipe and the schedule of the pipe. Materials and schedules change the pipe wall thickness and the outside diameter.

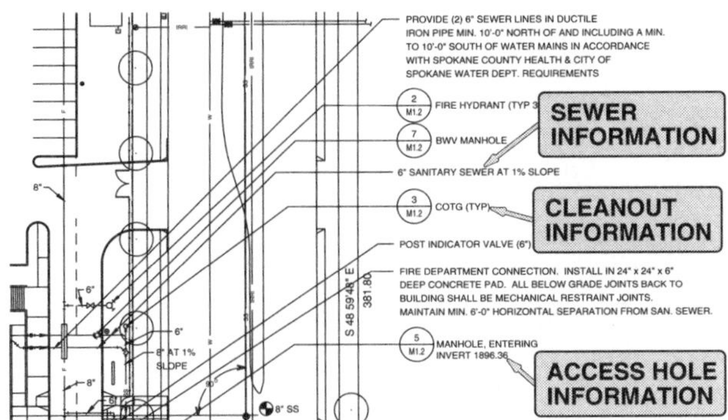

Figure 6-2. Plumbing installations, such as sewers, access holes, and cleanouts are shown on mechanical site plans.

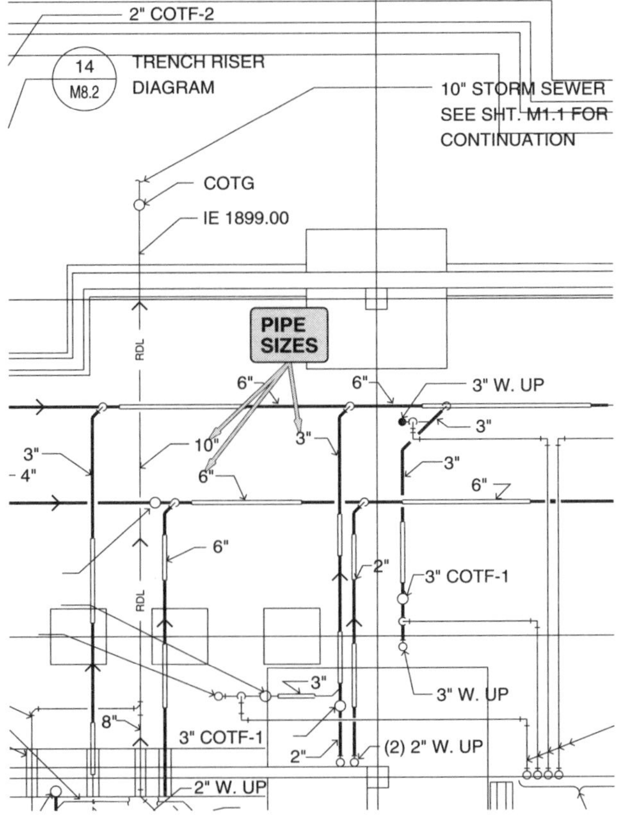

Figure 6-3. Related plumbing plan views give an overall view of plumbing installations and indicate many different size pipe diameters.

The purpose of and materials carried by the pipe are given with abbreviations and symbols. For example, a broken line with an abbreviation of RDL on a plan view indicates a roof drain line. Cross referencing of the plan views with the plumbing abbreviations and symbols describes the use for each pipe.

Materials used for waste piping include cast iron and polyvinyl chloride (PVC) pipe. Specifications contain information concerning the type of pipe used for various applications. General notes on the plumbing portion of the mechanical prints may provide information about the material used for waste pipes.

Elevations for waste pipes are given to the inside elevation at the bottom of the inside flow line of the pipe. See Figure 6-4. Elevations are specific to a location and provide reference points for pipe placement. Elevations for waste piping between these elevation reference points are indicated as a percentage of slope. A slope of 1% is equal to a change in elevation of 1′ over a distance of 100′. For example, a 2% slope on a 10′ length of pipe is calculated by multiplying the length of the pipe by 2%. This equals a slope of 2.4″ (120″ × .02 = 2.4″). On plan views, vertical pipes are indicated with open circles and an architectural note.

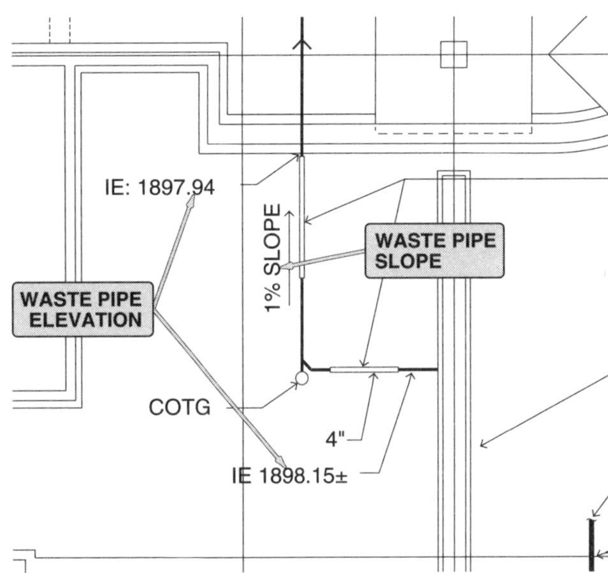

Figure 6-4. Mechanical plumbing prints show waste pipe elevations and slopes.

Exact dimensions for placement of waste pipes are not given on the mechanical prints. Grid lines and some major structural members are shown. Exact dimensional locations are determined by obtaining dimensions from architectural and structural prints. For example, where a waste pipe for a sink is to be placed through an interior wall, the location of that wall is determined from dimensions on the architectural prints.

For poured-in-place concrete floors, walls, and roofs, piping may be set in place prior to placement of the concrete, or chases may be provided for plumbing pipe to pass through the floor, wall, or roof. In cases where this is not done prior to or during concrete placement, a core drill may be used to drill through the concrete and create a hole for pipe placement. Detail drawings for installation of these sleeves are provided in the mechanical prints. See Figure 6-5. Chases and sleeves must be provided in accordance with structural prints. Excessive holes in structural supporting members could create structural failures.

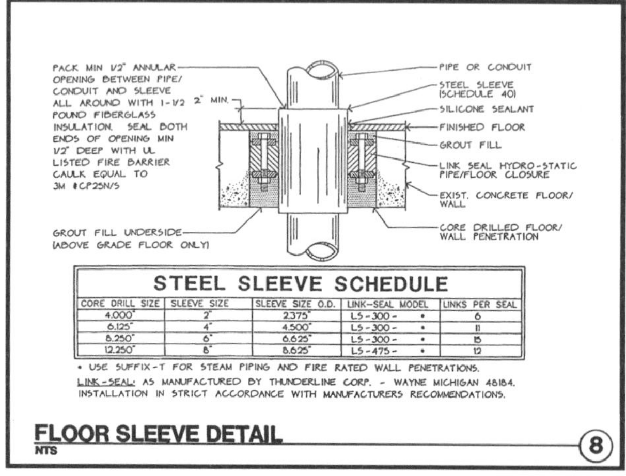

STEEL SLEEVE SCHEDULE

CORE DRILL SIZE	SLEEVE SIZE	SLEEVE SIZE O.D.	LINK-SEAL MODEL	LINKS PER SEAL
4.000"	2"	2.375"	LS-300- •	6
6.125"	4"	4.500"	LS-300- •	11
8.250"	6"	6.625"	LS-300- •	15
12.250"	8"	8.625"	LS-475- •	12

• USE SUFFIX-T FOR STEAM PIPING AND FIRE RATED WALL PENETRATIONS.
LINK-SEAL: AS MANUFACTURED BY THUNDERLINE CORP. - WAYNE MICHIGAN 48184.
INSTALLATION IN STRICT ACCORDANCE WITH MANUFACTURERS RECOMMENDATIONS.

Figure 6-5. Proper pipe and conduit sleeve installation allows for connections between levels of a building without losing structural integrity.

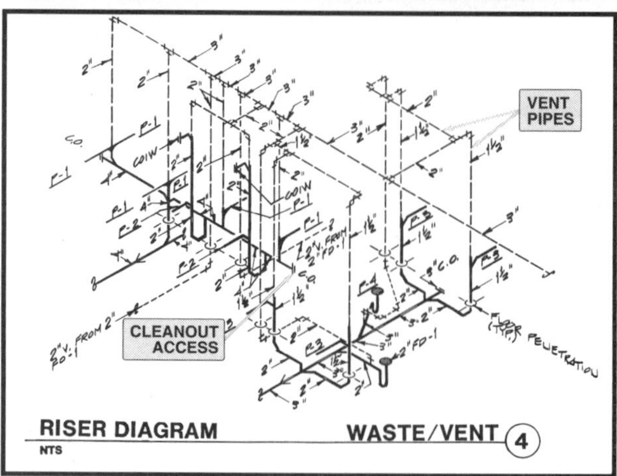

Figure 6-6. Dashed lines on isometric drawings show plumbing vent pipes. Plumbers install waste pipes, fittings, and hangers for waste pipes according to plumbing codes and local building code regulations.

Connections, Vents, and Terminations. Details of the roof and floor drains are given with architectural notes and numbers which refer to a schedule contained in the general notes on mechanical plumbing prints or the written specifications. Diameters for roof and floor drains are given on plan views and isometric drawings.

Odors and gases are removed from the waste piping and exhausted away from inhabited areas by vent pipes. Vent pipes branch off from the liquid-carrying waste pipes and commonly terminate above the roof line. Vent pipes are shown on plan views and isometric drawings in a manner similar to waste pipes. See Figure 6-6. Plumbing prints also indicate locations for placement of cleanout accesses in the waste piping.

Waste and vent pipes and fittings are connected in various methods, depending on the type of pipe used. Cast iron waste pipes and fittings are connected with molten lead or fastened with rubber gaskets. PVC waste pipes are fitted and glued together.

Many different elbows, tees, and unions are available to create plumbing pipe systems according to the mechanical prints. Waste pipes are attached to structural members with hangers and fasteners to support them at the proper elevations. Details of these connections are not included in the plumbing portion of the mechanical prints. A general note concerning connections to structural members may be included in the mechanical notes or the specifications.

Sump pumps are installed where termination points for waste water are below-grade and require pumping to raise wastewater for removal. Detail drawings indicate the sump pump, location, fittings, valves, and piping.

The ends of waste and vent pipes may be stubbed and capped where fixtures are connected after finishes are applied. Waste and vent systems may be subjected to a pressure test in which a certain amount of water pressure is built up inside the piping system for a certain period of time. Leaks can be detected and fixed as required.

Water Supply Systems

Fresh water is supplied at various locations throughout a structure. Common locations for fresh water supplies are in bathroom areas, cooking areas, water fountains, and laboratory areas. Mechanical plumbing prints provide piping, connection, valve, and fixture information.

Piping. Plumbing prints indicate the sizes and locations of pipes for carrying hot and cold water. See Figure 6-7. Pipe diameters are given as the inside diameter of the supply piping. Exact pipe locations are not dimensioned. Dimensions for supply piping are obtained from architectural prints. Pipe information is given on plan views and isometric drawings in a manner similar to waste piping diagrams. Information about the pipe used is provided in the written specifications. The two most common materials for water supply piping are copper and PVC. Copper pipes are connected by solder and fittings. PVC piping and fittings are glued.

Pipes are installed prior to wall, ceiling, and floor finishes. Pipes are stubbed and capped as necessary where plumbing fixtures are to be attached. Fixtures are installed after finishes are applied.

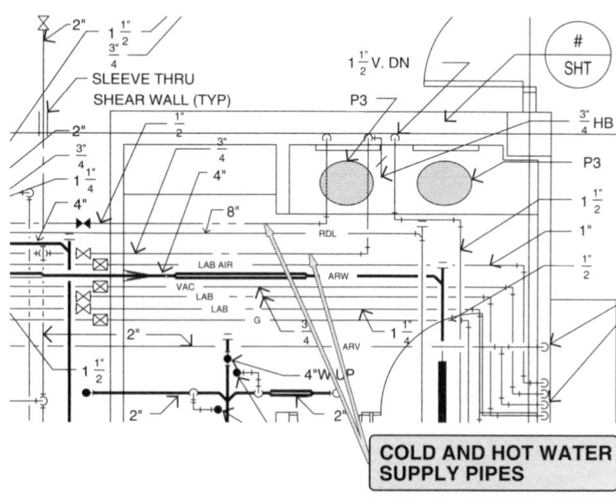

Figure 6-7. Fresh water supply pipes for fixtures such as sinks appear on mechanical plumbing prints.

Valves. Types and locations of valves are shown on plan views and isometric plumbing drawings. Standard symbols indicate the types of valves installed. See Figure 6-8. Gate valves and butterfly valves are used for basic ON and OFF service. Globe valves are used where throttling of flow is required. Check valves are designed to prevent the reversal of flow direction.

Fixtures. A schedule for plumbing fixtures is included in the mechanical prints. Notes on plan views and isometric plumbing drawings relate to the fixture schedule. See Figure 6-9. Schedule information may include the manufacturer's name and product number, sizes, fittings, methods for attachment to the structure, sizes of vent, waste and supply piping, and general notes. Detail drawings for connections to fixtures or equipment, such as hot water tanks, are given where necessary.

Other Piping Systems. Additional piping systems are installed for special applications, such as manufacturing plants or laboratories. These piping systems are used for compressed air, vacuums, gases, or fuels. Pipes of this type are described in the same manner as waste and water supply piping. Special abbreviations and symbols are used on plumbing plan views to describe these pipes. Detail drawings are given where these systems are connected to tanks for fuel supply or vacuums. Plan views and isometric drawings of the piping and valve configurations are also provided. Types of pipe to be installed are given in the general notes or specifications.

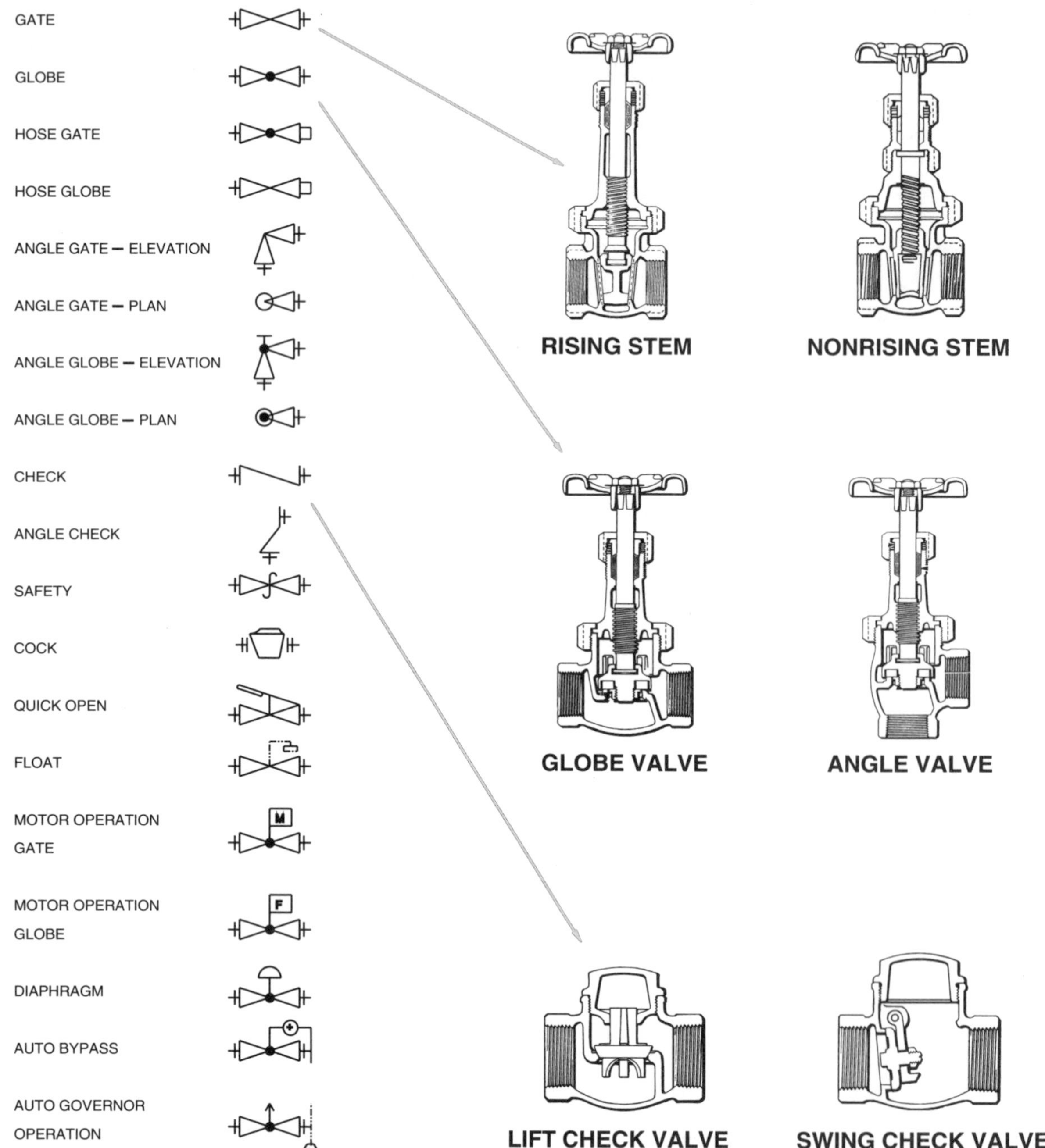

Figure 6-8. Architects use standard symbols for depicting various types of valves in plumbing piping systems.

FIRE PROTECTION

Municipalities and governmental agencies have adopted regulations and requirements for fire protection equipment and systems. The requirements are based on the intended use of the structure and the number of occupants who may be in the structure. The National Fire Protection Association (NFPA) has developed standards to assist local governments in developing local building code fire protection requirements. Mechanical prints for fire protection systems are designed in accordance with these standards and governmental regulations.

PLUMBING FIXTURE SCHEDULE													
Symbol	**Fixture**	**Mfr.**	**Model No.**	**Mounting**	**Type**	**Material**	**Size**	**Drain**	**Trap**	**W**	**V**	**HW**	**CW**
P1	Water closet	American Standard "Afwall"	2477.016	Wall	Siphon jet	White vitreous china	Elongated bowl	—	—	4″	2″	—	1″
P2	Urinal	American Standard "Jetbrook"	6570.022	Wall	Blowout	White vitreous china	21″×14½″×15⅛″	—	—	2″	2″	—	1″
P3	Lavatory	American Standard "Aqualyn"	0476.028	Counter	Self-rimming	White vitreous china	Oval 20″ × 17″	American Standard #7723.018	1½″ × 17 GA	1½″	1½″	⅜″	⅜″

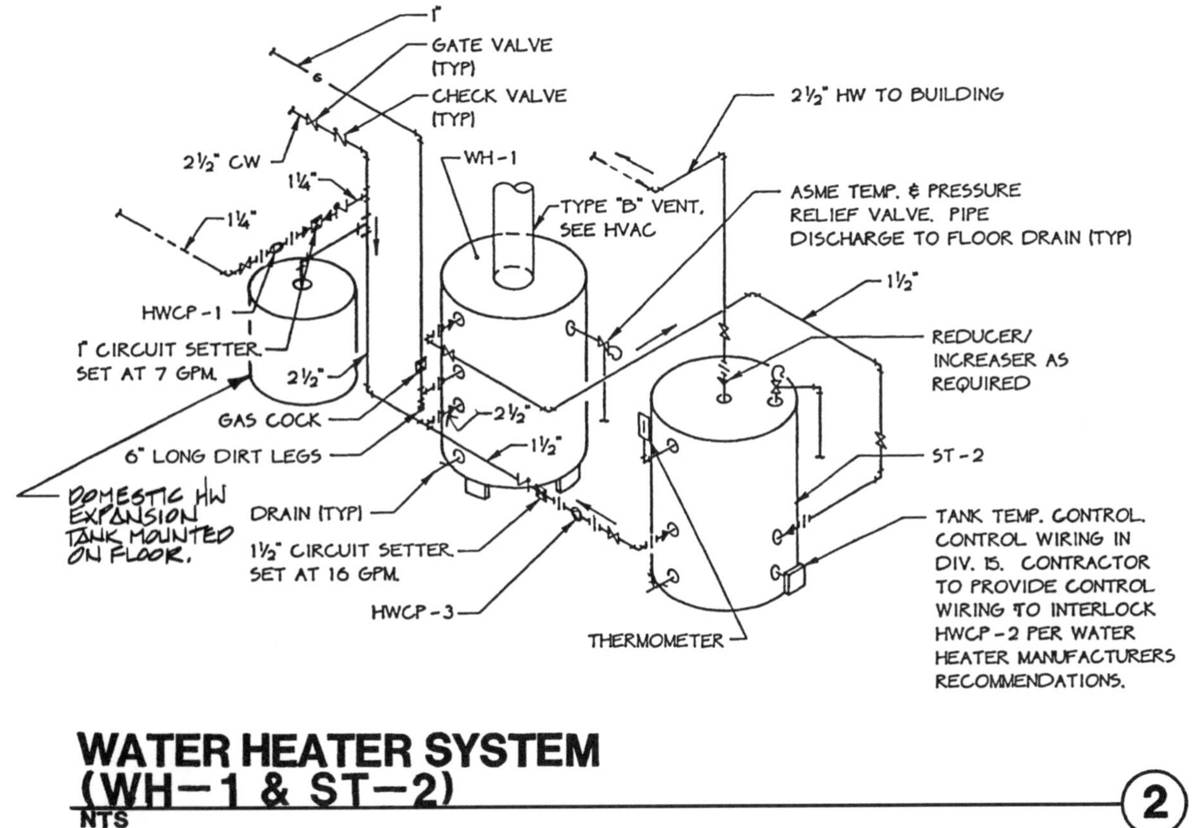

Figure 6-9. Plumbing fixture descriptions are provided with a schedule in mechanical prints. Hot water tanks, connecting piping, and valves are installed according to plumbing detail drawings.

Mechanical prints may contain a schedule of each occupied space for fire protection. See Figure 6-10. The type of system, the sprinkler type, and hazard level may be given on this schedule.

Suppression Systems

Fire protection systems include attachments to water supplies, interior piping, sprinkler systems, and attachments to safety valves and alarms. Mechanical prints indicate locations of pipes, sprinkler head requirements, valve types, alarm box placements, and areas to be protected. See Figure 6-11.

Three types of systems for fire protection are wet, dry, and gaseous. Each of these systems has different applications and requirements for installation. The system used depends on the area requiring protection.

CLASSROOM LEVEL SPRINKLER PROTECTION SCHEDULE					
Room Name	**Occupancy Hazard**	**System**	**Suspended Ceiling**	**Sprinkler Type**	**Temperature Classification**
Elevator Lobby	LH	WP	Yes	Pendant	Ordinary
Elect.	OH-1	WP	Yes	Pendant	Intermediate
Telephone	OH-1	WP	Yes	Pendant	Ordinary
Info. Net. Res. Ctr.	OH-2	WP	Yes	Pendant	Ordinary
Student Lounge	OH-2	WP	Yes	Pendant	Ordinary
Studio	OH-2	WP	Yes	Pendant	Ordinary
Cont. Education	OH-2	WP	Yes	Pendant	Ordinary
Cont. Education	OH-2	WP	Yes	Pendant	Ordinary
Control Room	OH-2	PA	Yes	Pendant	Ordinary
Audio/Visual	OH-2	PA	Yes	Pendant	Ordinary
Tele Seminar	OH-2	WP	Yes	Pendent	Ordinary
TV Seminar	OH-2	WP	Yes	Pendant	Ordinary
Stair	OH-2	WP	Yes	Pendant	Ordinary
Corridor	LH	WP	Yes	Pendant	Ordinary
Corridor	LH	WP	Yes	Pendant	Ordinary
Corridor	LH	WP	Yes	Pendant	Ordinary

Figure 6-10. Building spaces with different occupancy types have varying fire hazard levels.

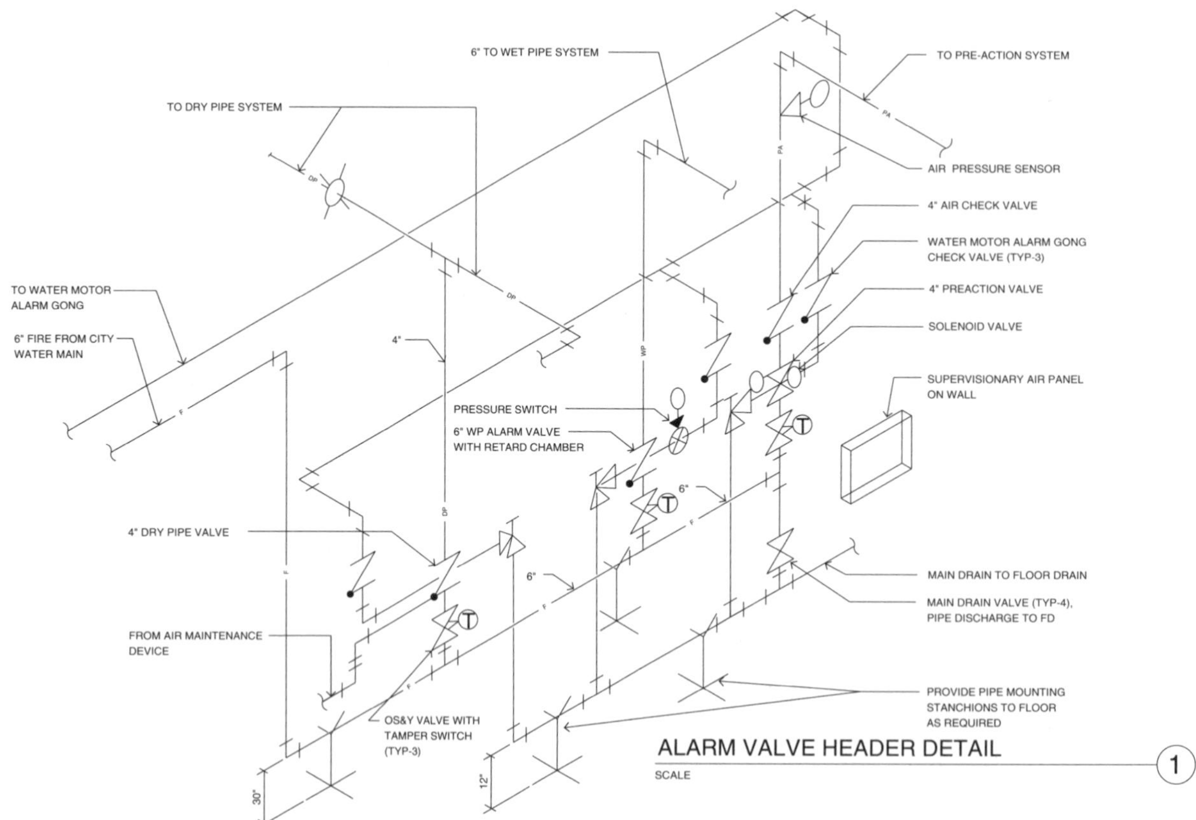

Figure 6-11. Fire protection systems disperse water or chemicals into fire hazard areas. Alarms which are part of a fire protection system notify the fire protection district automatically when the system is activated.

Alarm attachments notify fire protection districts when the system is activated. Wet, dry, and gaseous systems are attached to an alarm valve which initiates notification of the fire department when water, air, or gas begins passing through the system.

Wet Systems. Fire protection pipes are connected to a main water supply source. Exterior fire hydrants are shown on civil prints or mechanical site plans. Sprinkler system piping carries water throughout the structure to various locations where it is necessary to provide fire protection. Sprinkler pipes are shown on plan views with a pipe symbol and abbreviation, such as WP for wet pipe. Isometric drawings of fire protection piping are also provided.

Sprinkler pipes are made of cast iron or any material which does not fail due to heat from a fire. Valves are placed throughout the piping system to allow for periodic testing and to provide for maximum safety. A sprinkler head is installed at the termination point of each pipe. Mechanical plans indicate pipe and sprinkler head locations. See Figure 6-12.

Additional information concerning pipe, sprinkler heads, and valves is found in the specifications. Sprinkler heads in a wet pipe system are designed to open and release water when activated by heat. Sprinkler heads are installed after ceiling tile are in place in areas where suspended ceiling systems are installed.

Dry Systems. In areas which may be exposed to cold temperatures, water in wet system pipes may freeze, resulting in rupture of the pipes. Dry fire protection systems are installed in these areas. Dry system areas are indicated on plan views. See Figure 6-13. Entire structures may also be protected by dry systems. Dry system pipes are noted on plan views with an abbreviation, such as DP for dry pipe. These pipes are connected to the same fire protection water supply as for a wet system. The portion of the system which is dry consists of pipes filled with air. When a fire occurs in an area protected with a dry system, the sprinkler heads release the air and then distribute water from the fire service main.

Preaction systems are systems that are activated by smoke detectors or heat detectors. Fire protection systems are classified as preaction systems based on this activation mechanism, rather than relying on sprinkler head activation.

A fire suppressing gas such as halon may be piped into the area to provide fire protection where electronic equipment such as a computer is installed and cannot be exposed to water. Sprinkler pipes are connected to a tank filled with halon.

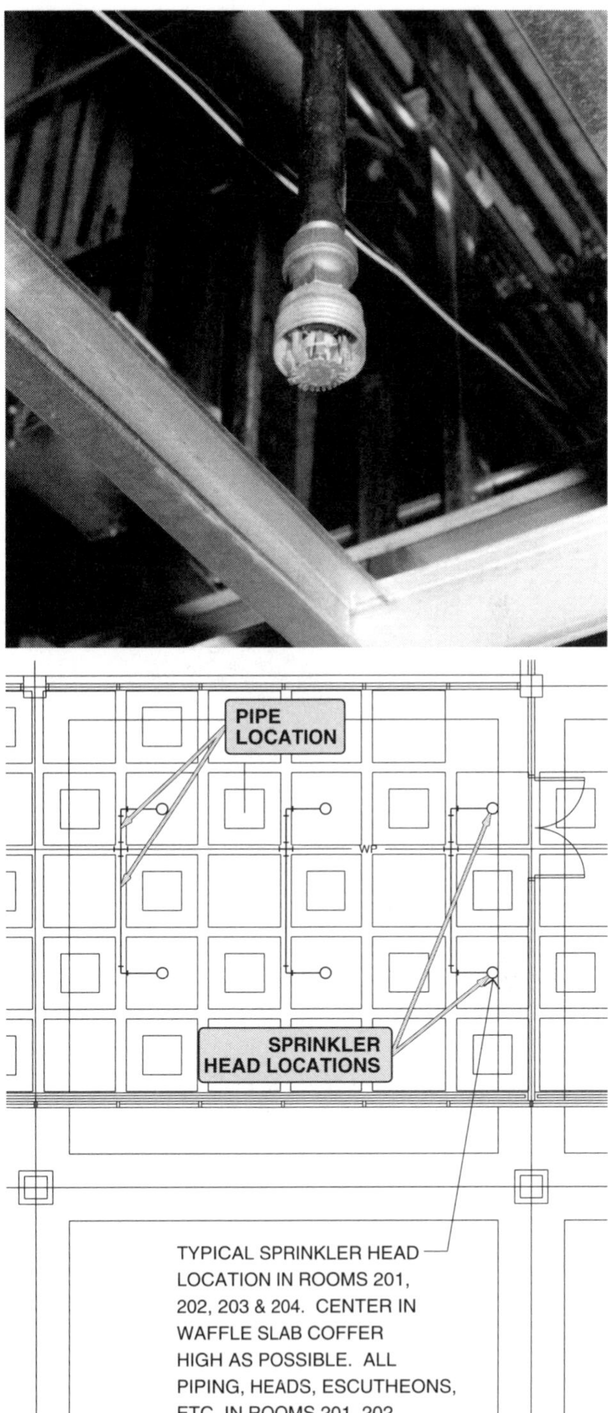

Figure 6-12. Location of sprinkler heads according to the plan view ensure proper dispersion of fire protection materials.

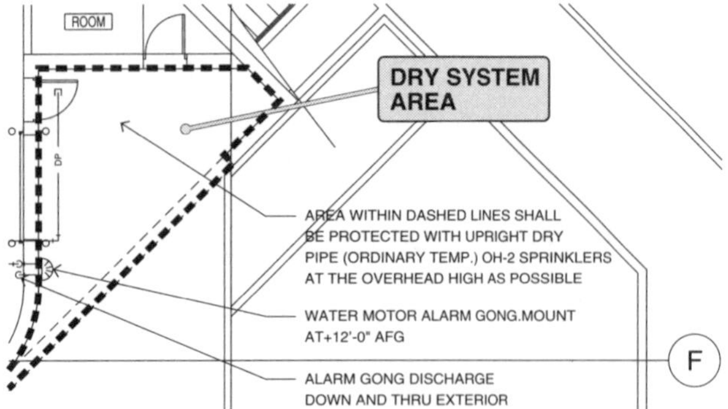

Figure 6-13. Dry fire protection piping systems prevent pipe failures caused by frozen water in the pipes.

The halon gas is released when a fire occurs. The properties of the gas suppress the fire. The piping is not connected to fire protection water mains.

HVAC SYSTEMS

Large commercial buildings have a wide variety of heating, ventilating, and cooling needs. Complex systems are required to provide the temperature control and air circulation required for large public areas, offices, meeting rooms, classrooms, and work areas. Mechanical prints show the heating, cooling, and ventilating systems. Plan and elevation views and detail drawings provide installation and fabrication information.

Specifications, general notes, and schedules contain information concerning the manufacturer's designs and equipment codes. Shop drawings may also be produced by the subcontractor or the supplier to guide in the proper installation of equipment, piping, and ductwork. Mechanical prints are interrelated with architectural, structural, and electrical prints for temperature control systems.

Heating Systems

Two methods used to heat building spaces include forced-air systems and radiant systems. In forced-air systems, air is heated by some heat source, such as natural gas, hot water, or electric coils. The air is then circulated and distributed through a series of ducts. In radiant heat, hot water or steam is circulated through pipes and radiators which heat the surrounding air. Radiant heat may also be produced by electric wires or coils which radiate heat to the surrounding air.

Heat Sources. Heat is generated by the combustion of natural gas. Heat generated by combustion is used in various methods. One method is to raise the temperature of metal plates (heat exchanger). Air is blown across the heat exchanger and heated. The heated air is then moved through ducts and distributed to areas to be heated.

Furnaces with heat exchangers are common in residential applications and for unit heaters in confined areas. Mechanical prints indicate the location of the heaters and piping for natural gas supply. See Figure 6-14. Electric coils may also be energized to generate heat and be used as a heat exchanger. Information concerning electric heat exchange furnaces and unit heaters is contained in the electrical prints.

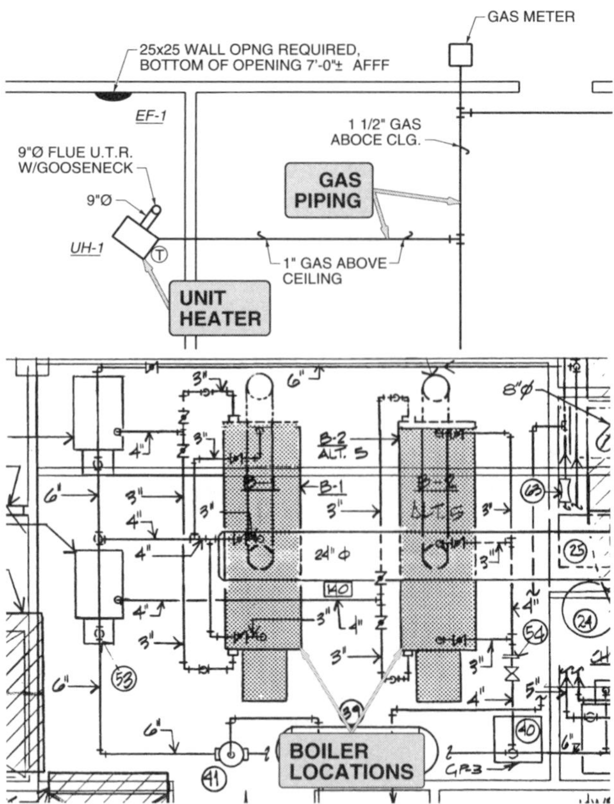

Figure 6-14. Unit heaters are hung from building ceilings at locations noted on plan views. Large boilers are set and anchored in place as shown on mechanical prints.

Natural gas combustion or electric heating elements are used in large commercial applications to heat water or create steam in a boiler. *Hydronic systems* are systems which use hot water to provide heat.

Boiler locations are shown on mechanical plan views and elevation drawings. Specific dimensional locations are not given on the mechanical prints. Dimensions are obtained from the architectural and structural plan views. Information about the boiler type, size, capacity, and heating load are included on a schedule in the mechanical prints or in the specifications. In addition to boiler locations, mechanical and electrical prints show flue piping, water piping, and power and control wiring connections to boilers.

Heat Distribution. In a hydronic system, several steps are necessary to distribute heat. See Figure 6-15. Water to be heated is pumped through the boiler piping. Expansion tanks allow the water to expand as it is heated without causing a dangerous amount of pressure to build up. Heated water is pumped through a series of pipes to the areas to be heated. Heat is radiated from the water at terminal units such as radiators.

Thermostats at each terminal unit indicate the need for heat and may activate valves or fans to bring the temperature to the proper level. The cool water is pumped back to the boiler. The water is reheated and the cycle is repeated. Each portion of the hydronic system is shown on plan views and elevation drawings.

BOILER SCHEDULE (GAS FIRED) MFR: WEIL-McLAIN

#	MODEL	CAPACITY (MBH)		MIN. GAS PRES. ("WC)	HEATING WATER			BLWR. (HP)	OPER. WEIGHT (LBS)	REMARKS
		INPUT (MIN.)	OUTPUT (MIN.) (1)		TEMP. LVG(F)	FLOW GPM	VOL (GAL)			
B-1, 2 (2)	SERIES 88 1488	4474	3550	7"	180	275	339	3	10,675	GAS ONLY GORDON-PIATT BURNER

NOTES
(1) GROSS 1-B-R OUTPUT.
(2) B-1 BASE BID. B-2 IS ALTERNATE NO. 5.

AIR COOLED CONDENSING UNIT SCHEDULE MFR: LIEBERT

#	MODEL	UNIT						COMPR. MOTORS			CONDENSER		OPERATING WEIGHT (LBS)
		CAPACITY (MBH)	AMB. AIR °F	REFRIG. TYPE	COND. TEMP. °F	MIN. CIRCUIT AMPS	V/PH	NO.	AMPS FULL LOAD	AMPS LOCKED ROTOR	NO. OF FANS	TOTAL KW	
CU-1	DMC-027A	23.0	95	R-22	-	-	208/1	1	14.1	-	1	-	180

PUMP SCHEDULE

#	MANUFACTURER	MODEL	TYPE	SERVICE	FLOW (GPM)	HEAD (FT)	MOTOR			NOTES
							HP	RPM	V/Ø	
HWP-1, 2	BELL & GOSSETT	1531-2qf BB	CLOSE-COUPLE	HEATING WATER	240	60	7.5	1750	460/3	(1) (11)
BCP-1, 2	"	1531-3 AB	"	"	275	25	3	1750	460/3	(2) (12)
CHWP-1	"	1531-2qf AB	"	SF-1 HW	150	35	3	1750	460/3	(13)
CHWP-2	"	SERIES 60-1qf A	IN-LINE	SF-4 HW	33	35	eg	1770	460/3	
CHWP-3	"	SERIES 60-1qf A	"	SF-5 HW	30	35	eg	1770	460/3	ALT. NO. 2
CHWP-4	"	SERIES 60-1qf A	"	SF-6 HW	27	25	qg	1750	115/1	ALT. NO. 1
CHP-1	"	1531-3 BB	CLOSE-COUPLE	CHILLED WATER	350	65	10	1750	460/3	(10)
CCHWP-1	"	1531-2qf AB	"	SF-1 CHW	170	35	3	1750	460/3	(9)
CCHWP-2	"	SERIES 60-1qf A	IN-LINE	SF-2 CHW	44	35	1	1770	460/3	
CCHWP-3	"	SERIES 60-2 A	"	SF-3 CHW	88	35	1qf	1750	460/3	
CCHWP-4	"	SERIES 60-2 A	"	SF-4 CHW	64	35	1qf	1750	460/3	
CCHWP-5	"	SERIES 60-1qf A	"	SF-5 CHW	20	35	eg	1750	460/3	ALT. NO. 2

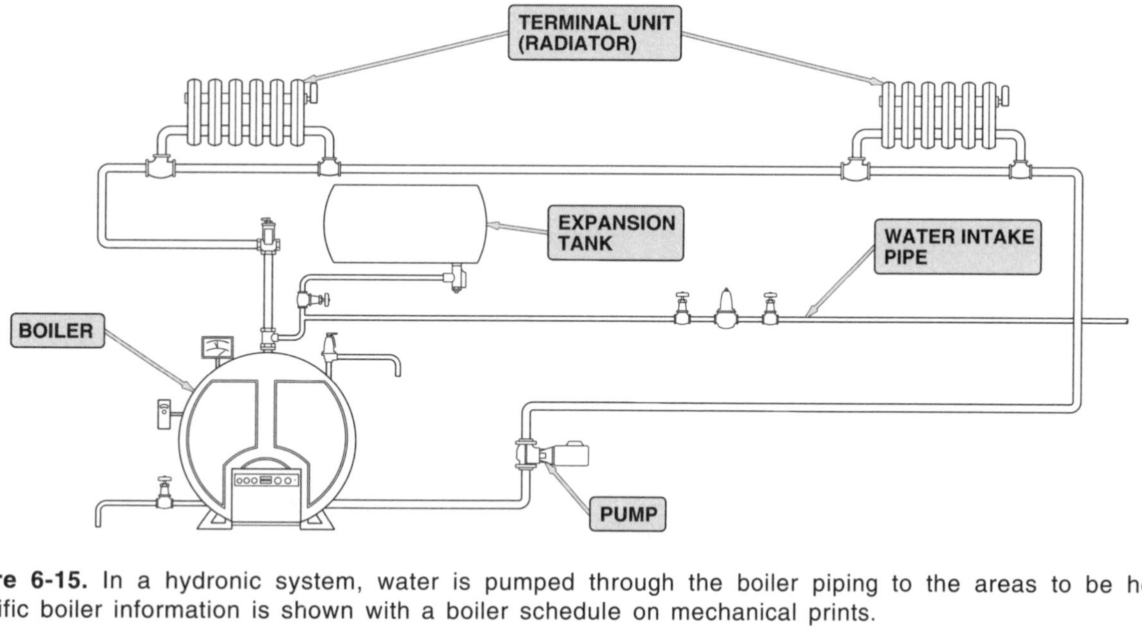

Figure 6-15. In a hydronic system, water is pumped through the boiler piping to the areas to be heated. Specific boiler information is shown with a boiler schedule on mechanical prints.

Locations for pumps for hot water supply and hot water return are shown on mechanical prints. Expansion tanks connected to boilers are also shown. Schedules on mechanical prints provide pump information including the manufacturer's name and model number, flow rate in gallons per minute (gpm), and motor size and speed.

Piping connections between the pumps, expansion tanks, and the boilers are given. Piping information between the boiler, pumps, and expansion tanks includes the inside diameter of the pipes and valve and meter types and locations.

Pipe notations indicate the purpose of the pipe and the direction of water flow. See Figure 6-16. In a one-pipe system, water passes through each terminal unit in a continuous flow back to the boiler. In a two-pipe system, separate pipe systems are installed for supply and return.

In a four-pipe system, separate pipe systems are installed for supply and return for both heating and cooling. Pipes are identified as hot water supply, hot water return, cold water supply, and cold water return. Cold water supply and return pipes are used for cooling operations.

Pipe connections are made to terminal units which transfer heat from the water to the surrounding air. Mechanical plan views show the locations of terminal units. A schedule for terminal units describes the gpm water flow requirements and the cubic feet per minute (cfm) air flow requirements. See Figure 6-17.

Architects use various geometric shapes, such as hexagons, ovals, and circles to allow for easy identification and cross referencing of symbols and numbers to schedules. Detail drawings of terminal units are also provided to indicate water connections and duct connections.

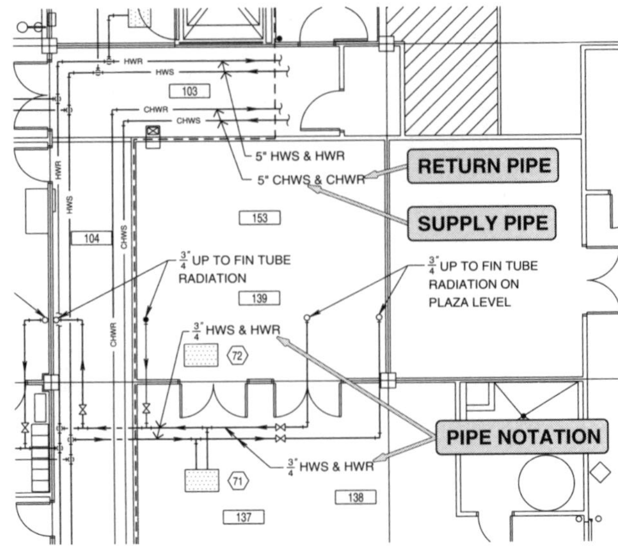

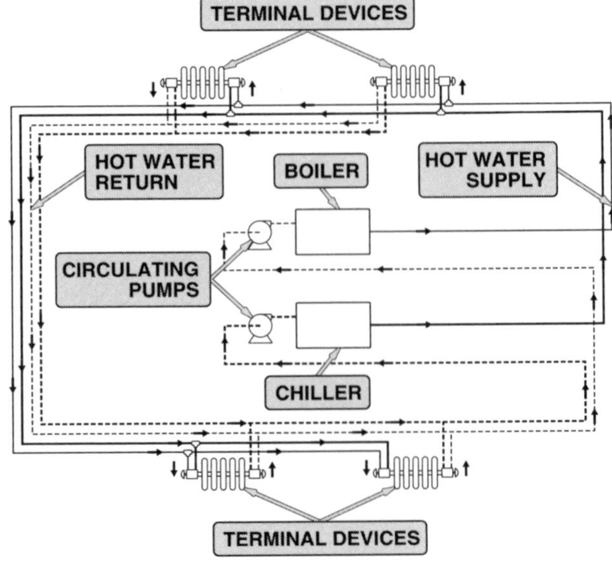

FOUR-PIPE SYSTEM

Figure 6-16. Several series of pipes, including pipes for water supply and return, are used with a boiler heating system.

Cooling Systems

Cooling may be provided by evaporator-type air conditioners acting alone or by chilled water and cooling tower systems. Stand-alone evaporator-type air conditioners are used for all types of cooling loads. Chilled water systems are more commonly used in large buildings.

Evaporator Systems. Electric powered air conditioners are shown on electrical prints. In commercial applications, the electric air conditioners are placed on rooftops or at exterior locations.

Evaporator coils absorb heat from the surrounding air to evaporate refrigerant. The compressor pressurizes the refrigerant and discharges the vapor into a condenser coil. The refrigerant returns to a liquid state and is circulated through an expansion valve. At this point, the pressure and evaporation temperature are reduced. Air is passed over the evaporator coils and distributed to areas to be cooled.

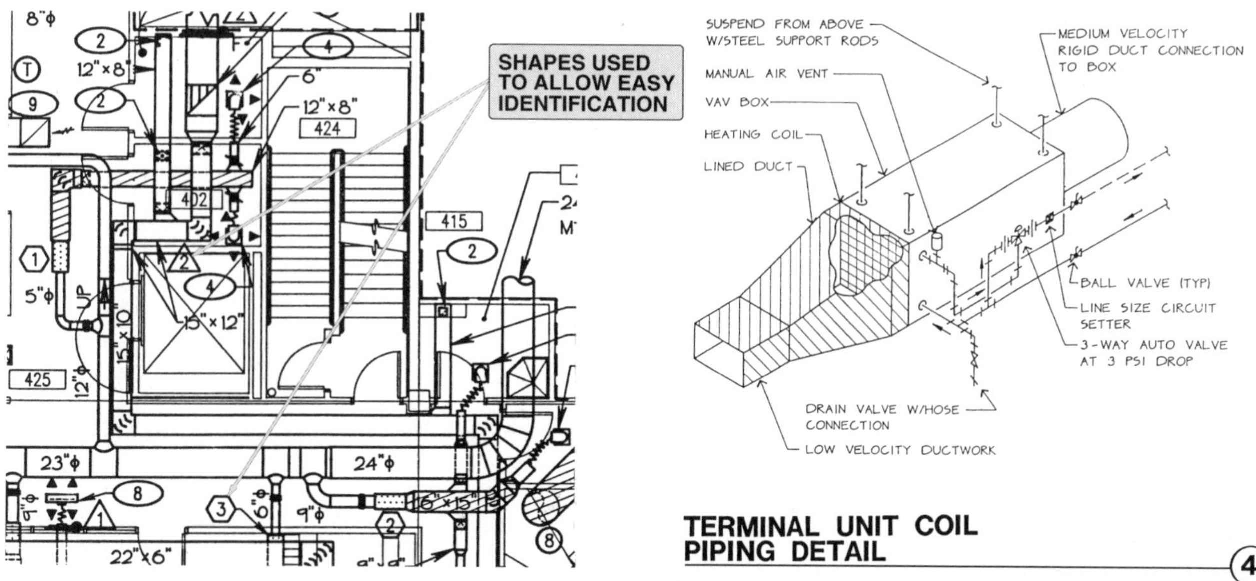

TERMINAL UNIT BOX															
														MFR: TITUS	
#	INLET DIA. (IN)	MAX CFM	MIN CFM	MIN SP (IN)	NOISE CRI AT ROOM(2)	NOISE(1) CRITERIA RADIATED	EAT = 55° HOT WATER COIL EWT = 180°							MODEL NO.	NOTES
							LAT	LWT	GPM	WATER PD (IN)	AIR PD (IN)	# OF ROWS	MBH		
TU-1	5	180	180	0.13	37	27	99	160	0.87	0.63	-	1	-	DESV-3000	SF-4 (6)
2	9	760	760	0.19	39	27	105	158	3.8	1.05	-	2		"	"
3	6	290	110	0.17	33	25	102	159	.54	.20		1		"	" (6)
4	9	700	400	0.16	39	26	115	153	1.9	.31		2		"	"
5	5	215	80	0.11	36	27	109	156	.39	.11		1		"	" (6)
6	6	300	100	0.18	40	27	102	153	.38	.11		1		"	" (6)
7	7	400	200	0.09	35	26	94	157	.79	.53		1		"	" (6)
8	8	750	375	0.23	41	27	117	153	1.7	.25		2		"	"

Figure 6-17. Mechanical plan views are cross-referenced to a terminal unit schedule. Terminal units transfer heat from hot water systems into air which may be circulated through ductwork.

Chilled Water Systems. Water is piped through a chiller, pumped to building areas to be cooled, passed through terminal units through which air is circulated to distribute the cooling, and returned to the chiller to be cooled again. Chillers are added to the evaporation section of the refrigeration cycle.

A cooling tower is added to the condenser coil to remove heat from the chilled water more efficiently. Mechanical prints provide plan views, detail drawings, and schedules of all the components of the system, including chillers, piping, pumps, and terminal units. Cooling tower locations are shown on plan views and site plans.

Air Distribution and Ventilation Systems

Heated and cooled air is moved by fans and air handlers through various ductwork configurations. Ductwork supplies heated and cooled air to diffusers which distribute the conditioned air. Air is then removed from these areas and returned for reheating, recooling, or exhausting.

Air Handlers. *Air handlers* are large fans used in commercial applications. Mechanical prints provide information about air handlers and fans on schedules which are cross referenced to mechanical plan views and elevations. Each air handler and fan is shown by overall diameter of the blades, the size of the motor and rpm, and the cfm which the fan moves. Air handlers are integrated into the ductwork system. See Figure 6-18.

Ductwork. Galvanized sheet metal or plastic is used to form ductwork which distributes air throughout the heating, cooling, and ventilating system. Ductwork for heating and cooling may be insulated to minimize heat transfer.

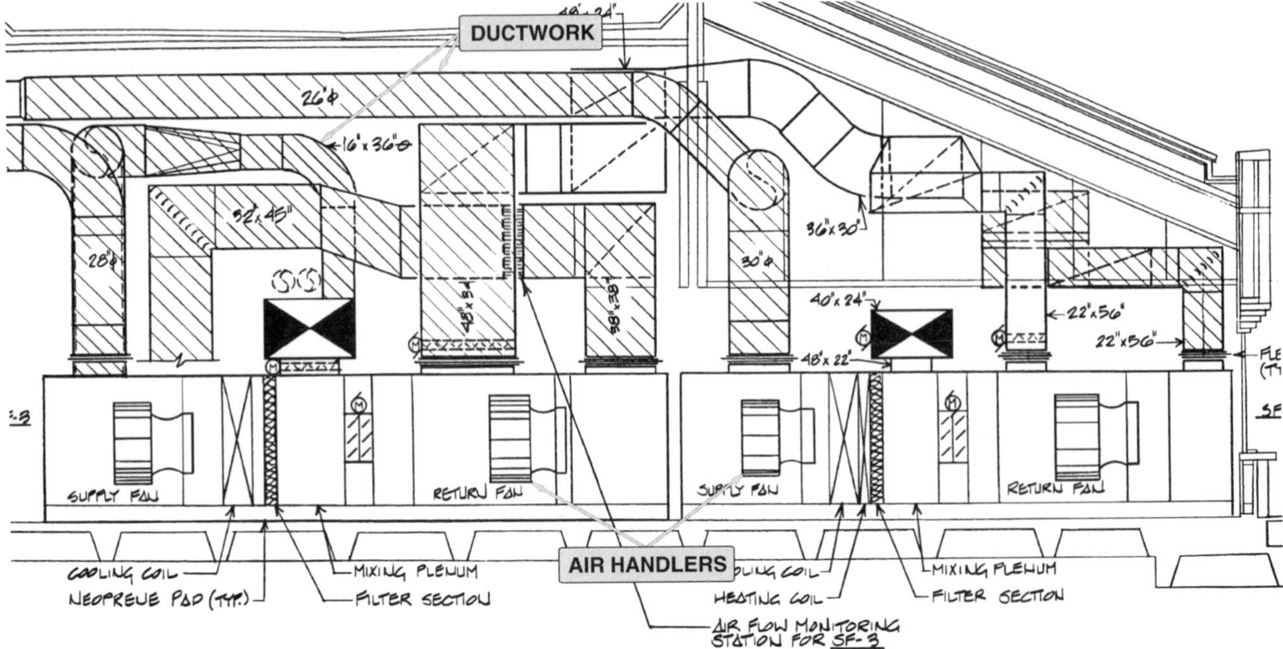

Figure 6-18. Air handlers move large volumes of air through commercial buildings.

Sheet metal ductwork is prefabricated at a shop and transported to the job site for installation. Standard sizes and types of plastic ducts are also available. They are used mostly for applications where flexible ductwork is necessary. Symbols on mechanical prints indicate the types of material used for ductwork. See Figure 6-19.

Ductwork designs are shown with plan views and elevations on mechanical prints. Diameters are indicated for round ducts. Width and height are shown for rectangular or square ducts. Methods for attachment of ductwork to structural members is not shown. Hanging information is included in the specifications or general plan notes.

Different types of diffusers are used at the ends of ductwork. Diffusers deliver widespread flows of air into a room. Standard sizes and types are available from a number of manufacturers. Each diffuser is identified by size and type using symbols on mechanical plan views or on a schedule. See Figure 6-20.

In forced-air systems, return air ductwork is installed to remove air from conditioned areas and return it for reheating or recooling. Air handlers are integrated into the ductwork in a manner similar to air supply ductwork.

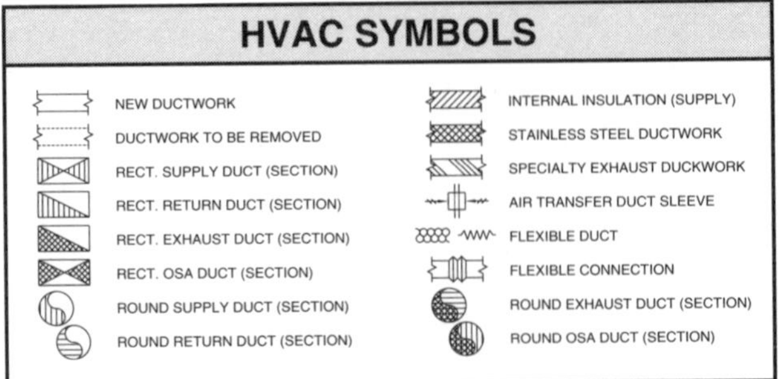

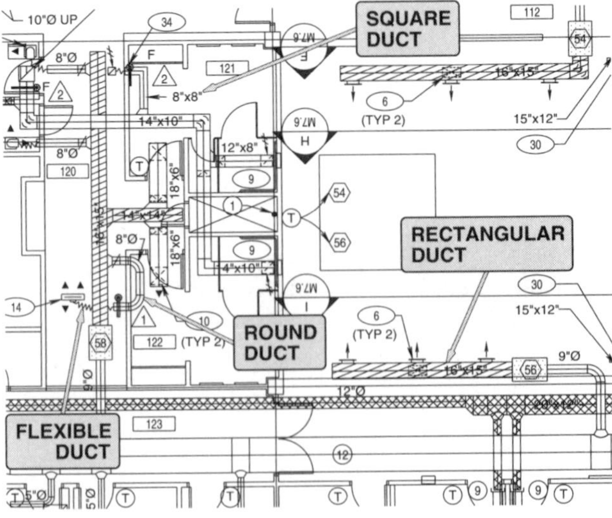

Figure 6-19. Ductwork may be round, rectangular, or square and may be made from a variety of materials.

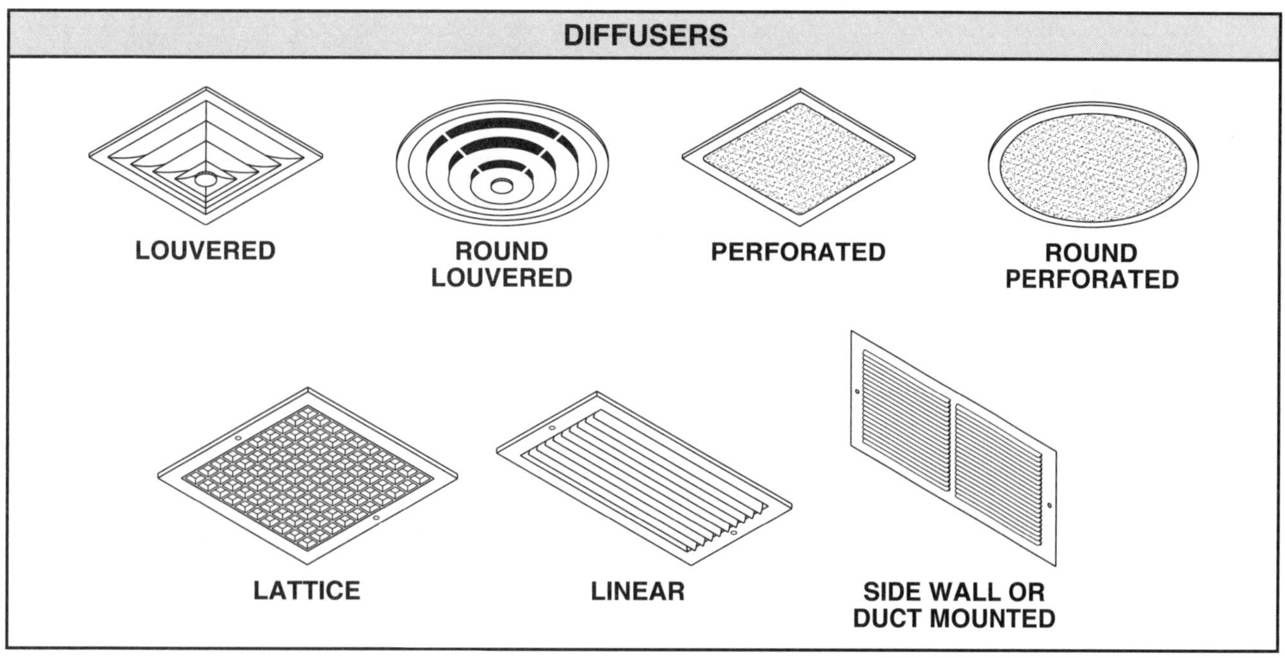

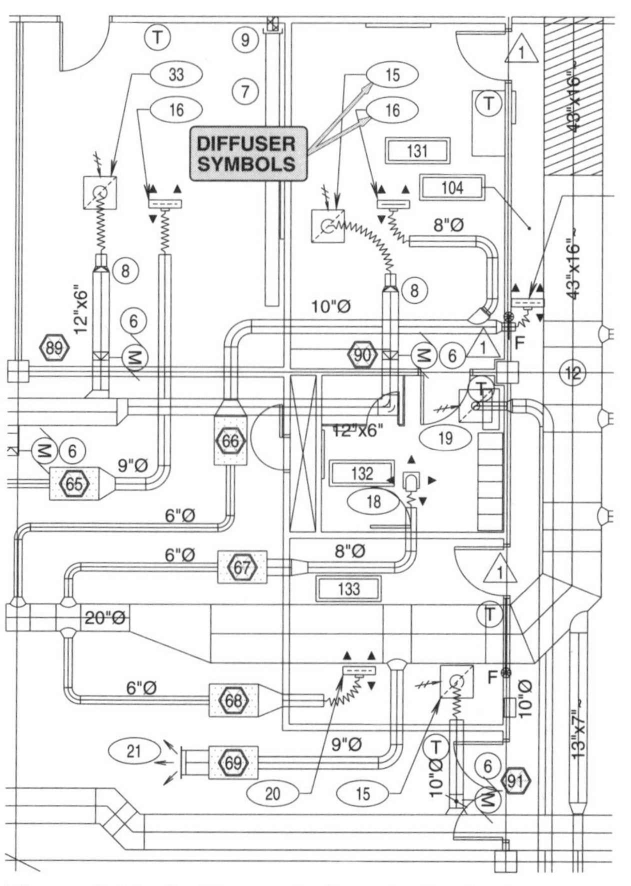

DIFFUSER SCHEDULE

#	DIFFUSER	#	DIFFUSER
1	24" 1 210	18	8"Ø 6 200
2	10"Ø 7 260	19	8"Ø 16 225
3	48" 9 550	20	24" 1 260
4	10"Ø 11	21	16"X12" 14 600
5	9"X6" 12 200	22	8"X6" 13 140
6	14"X8" 13 200	23	12"X10" 2 140
7	8"Ø 6 80	24	12"X8" 2 100
8	6"X6" 2 90	25	6"Ø 3 100
9	18"X18" 2 330	26	10"X4" 2 100
10	18"X18" 17 300	27	6"Ø 6 100
11	24" 4 115	28	48" 4 140
12	6"Ø 15 115	29	24" 4 60
13	24" 4 115	30	21"X10" 2 750
14	24" 1 200	31	10"Ø 16
15	10"Ø 7 260	32	24"X8" 2 550
16	24" 1 240	33	10"Ø 7 300
17	24" 4 100	34	8"Ø 15 200

Figure 6-20. Architects design air distribution systems to use any one of a number of standard air diffusers. Diffuser size and type are shown on plan views and related schedules.

For ventilation systems, ductwork is installed to exhaust air from the building to the outside or to areas to be conditioned and recycled. For food preparation areas of manufacturing operations, large quantities of air may need to be removed quickly and replaced by makeup air systems.

Louvers and vents are installed where ventilation ductwork passes through exterior walls or roofs. Sizes and types of louvers and vents are scheduled or shown on elevation and detail drawings. Ventilation hoods for the collection of fumes or smoke inside buildings are shown with detail drawings. Fans and air handlers are installed in the ventilation ductwork to ensure movement of the air in the proper direction at the required cfm.

Filtration of air within a structure is part of the heating, cooling, and ventilation system. Filtration may be provided by screens and filters through which air flows and particles are blocked. Electronic filter systems use electrostatic energy which attracts particles and removes them as air flows across the energized filters. Locations for filtration within the air circulation system are shown on detail ductwork drawings.

Figure 6-21. Specific dimensions for electrical wiring, equipment, and fixture installation are not given on electrical prints.

ELECTRICAL SYSTEMS

Electrical prints contain information about the wiring to be installed, electrical equipment, and electrical finish materials. See Figure 6-21. As with mechanical prints, specific dimensions for electrical wiring, equipment, and fixture installation are not given. Dimension information is obtained from architectural and structural plan views and elevations. Some electrical information may be shown on an electrical site plan which indicates power sources and exterior lighting.

Wiring

Electrical wiring is located underground, placed in conduit, left as exposed cable, installed in walls, above ceilings, and under floors. Electrical loads vary from low-voltage loads for items such as thermostats, to high-voltage loads for welding equipment or heavy manufacturing machinery. Each wiring condition is shown on the electrical prints.

Electrical prints may be divided into separate sections for lighting, power supply, and signals, such as fire alarms and smoke detectors. Plan views for each application are cross referenced to ensure all electrical needs are met.

The number of conductors in an electrical cable is noted by slash marks along the solid line which indicates the cable run. The number of slash marks is equal to the number of conductors. A cable line on plan views without any slash marks indicates a two-conductor cable. See Figure 6-22.

The cable used and the conduit placement or type are indicated with plan symbols. Conduit is made of galvanized pipes which are installed prior to the placement of poured-in-place concrete or masonry. Ends of conduit are capped to prevent them from filling with concrete or mortar. Conduit is fastened together with a variety of fittings. Conduit is bent on the job site where turns are required.

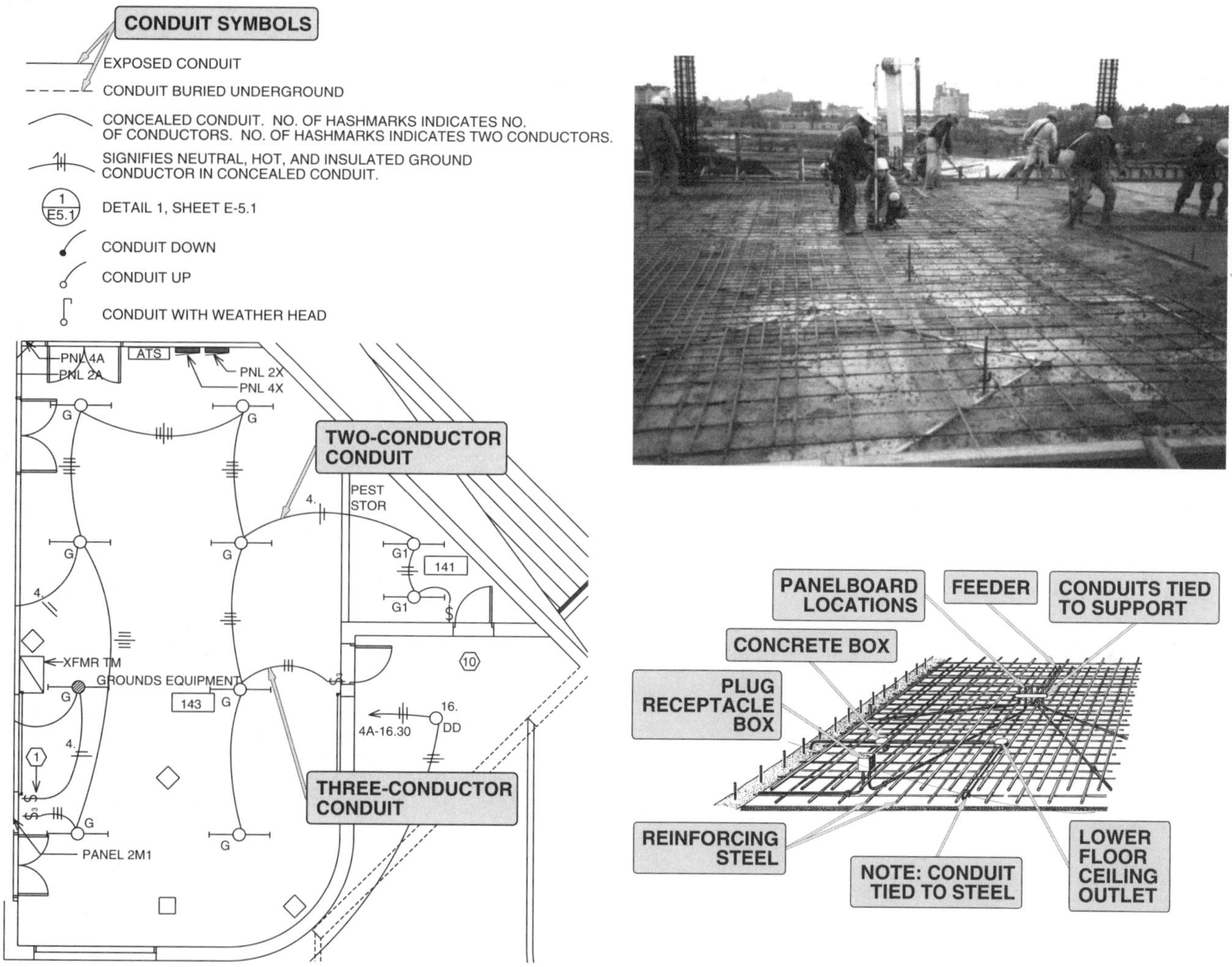

CONDUIT SYMBOLS

EXPOSED CONDUIT

CONDUIT BURIED UNDERGROUND

CONCEALED CONDUIT. NO. OF HASHMARKS INDICATES NO. OF CONDUCTORS. NO. OF HASHMARKS INDICATES TWO CONDUCTORS.

SIGNIFIES NEUTRAL, HOT, AND INSULATED GROUND CONDUCTOR IN CONCEALED CONDUIT.

DETAIL 1, SHEET E-5.1

CONDUIT DOWN

CONDUIT UP

CONDUIT WITH WEATHER HEAD

TWO-CONDUCTOR CONDUIT

THREE-CONDUCTOR CONDUIT

PANELBOARD LOCATIONS

FEEDER

CONDUITS TIED TO SUPPORT

CONCRETE BOX

PLUG RECEPTACLE BOX

REINFORCING STEEL

NOTE: CONDUIT TIED TO STEEL

LOWER FLOOR CEILING OUTLET

Figure 6-22. Electrical cables and conduit are noted on electrical prints with special electrical symbols. Concealed conduit is set in place before concrete slabs are poured or wall finish applied.

After concrete and masonry have reached their set, cables are pulled through the conduit. Exact conduit locations are not given on electrical plan views. Conduit is placed according to architectural and structural plan dimensions and necessary connections at the ends of the conduit.

Heavy cables which carry electrical service from the main power source to panelboards are specified by the wire gauge, number of wires of each gauge, and the diameter of the cable. For example, a notation of 4#4, 1#10 GRD, 1¼″C indicates a cable containing 4 wires of number 4 gauge, one wire of number 10 gauge for use as a ground wire, and an overall cable diameter of 1¼″. See Figure 6-23.

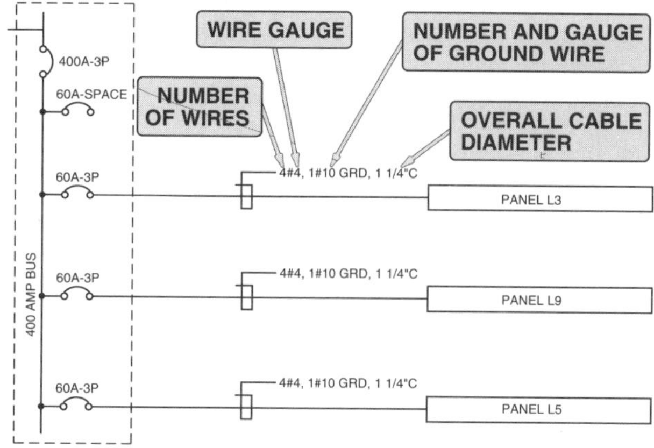

Figure 6-23. Heavy cables are specified by the wire gauge, number of wires of each gauge, and the diameter of the cable.

High wire gauge numbers indicate small diameter wires. Where extremely large electrical loads are carried, the load placed on the wire may be given to size the capacity of wire necessary. Cables are insulated with plastic coating on the wires. A metal sheathed cable consisting of a plastic insulated cable encased in a flexible metal protective covering is used where cables are not installed in conduit.

Supports. Electrical cables are fastened to structural members, suspended behind walls and ceilings, placed in cable trays, buried underground, or placed into poured concrete floors. Clamps are used to fasten conduit and cables to structural steel members. Section views on electrical prints provide information concerning cable trays and sleeves for electrical cable and conduit placed in poured concrete or masonry. See Figure 6-24.

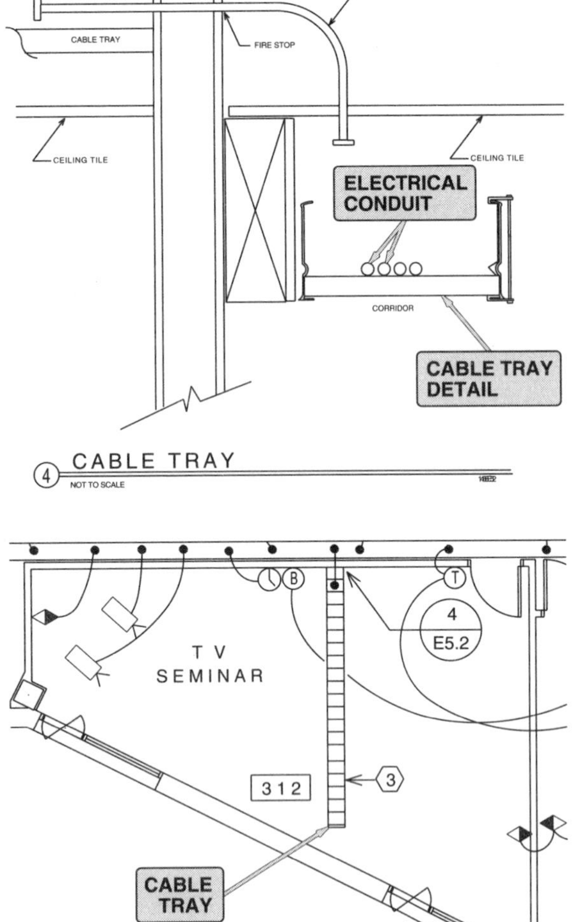

Figure 6-24. Cable trays are installed overhead to support many electrical cables in a confined area.

Cable tray locations are shown on plan views. A *cable tray* is an open grid rack suspended from structural members to allow for a series of cables to be supported. Support and fastening information for cables installed in walls is not commonly provided on electrical prints. The NEC® has established standards for cable and conduit fastening requirements. Cables and conduits must be secured to wall studs or structural members within a certain distance of switches, receptacles, or other electrical fixtures.

Equipment

Electrical prints show the general location of transformers, panelboards, junction boxes, fuses, circuit breakers, bus bars, and switches. Schematic drawings indicate the various electrical loads, circuits, and demands on each leg of the electrical system. See Figure 6-25.

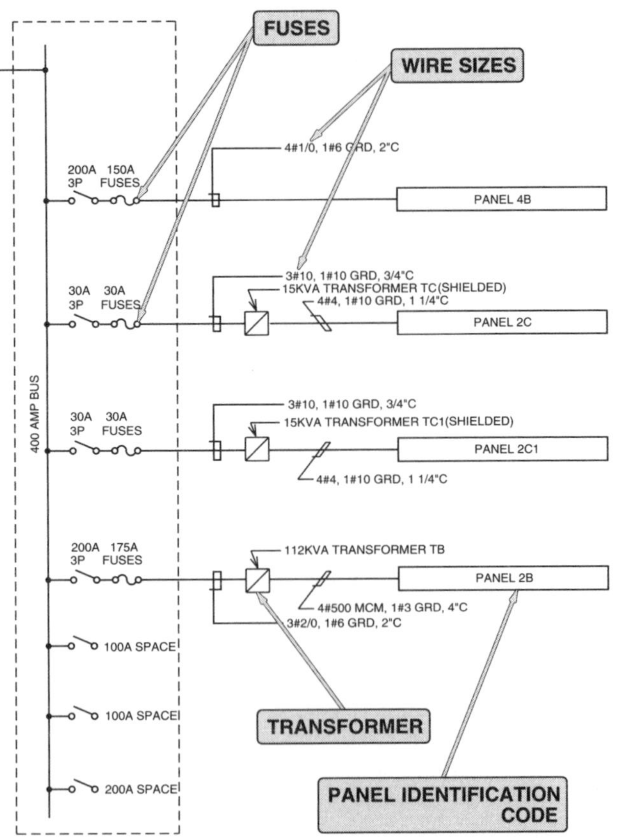

Figure 6-25. Schematic drawings of power systems indicate cable types, wire sizes, transformers, fuses, and circuit breakers.

Transformers are devices which step up or step down alternating voltages. Transformers are sized by the number of kilovolt-amperes (kVA) they can handle. Circuit breakers and fuses open a circuit when an overload condition or short circuit occurs. Circuit breakers and fuses are noted by the number of amps (A) that can flow through safely. Schematic drawings may also be provided for low-voltage control systems for installations such as track lighting.

Panelboards. Locations of panelboards are shown on electrical plan views. The electrical plan views relate to the overall electrical service schematic and to detail drawings. See Figure 6-26. Panelboards are noted by an architectural symbol and may have a letter or number code relating to a schedule. A schedule of panelboards indicates the size of the panelboard, mounting directions, and equipment to be serviced by each circuit.

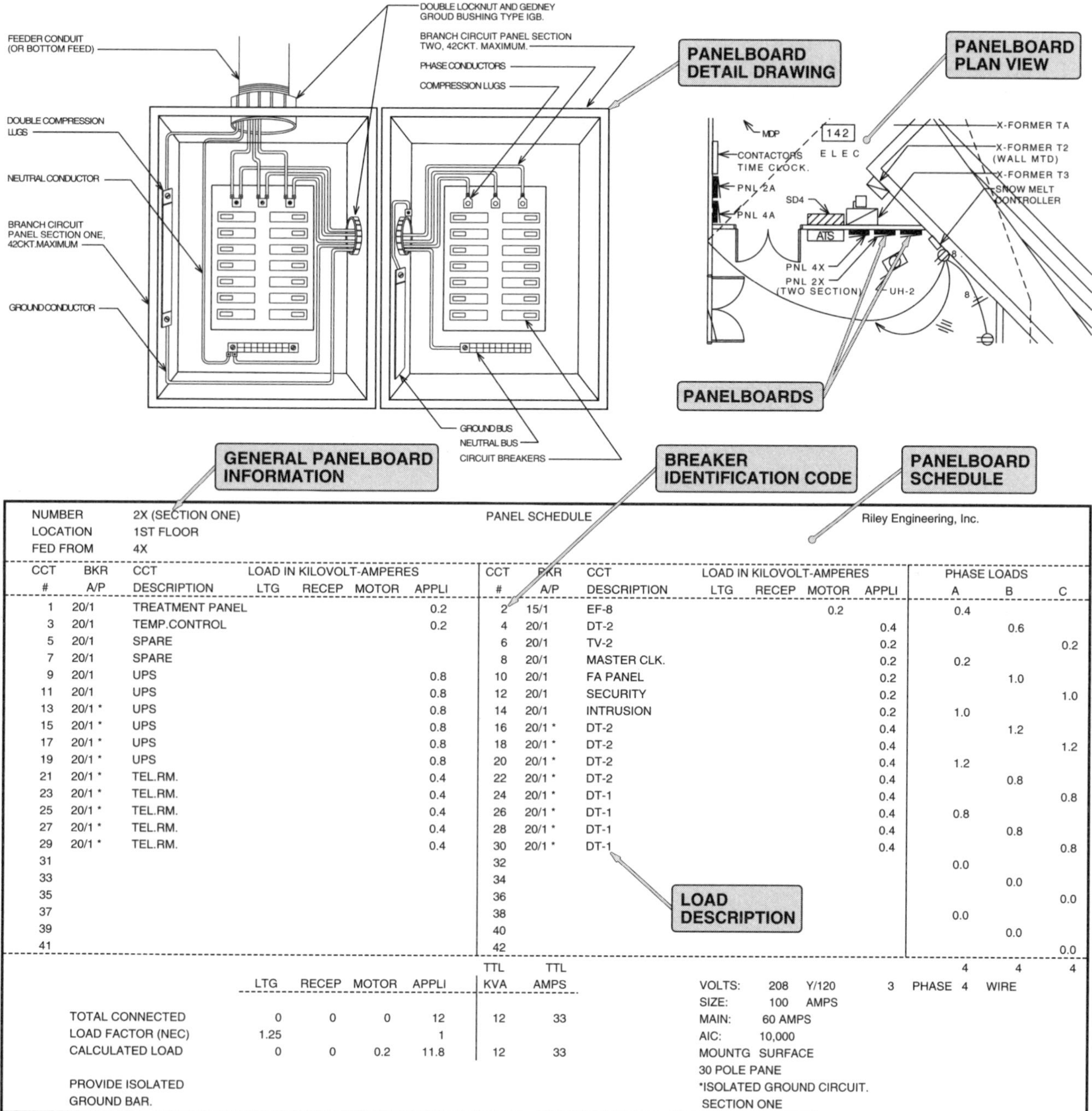

NUMBER 2X (SECTION ONE)
LOCATION 1ST FLOOR
FED FROM 4X

PANEL SCHEDULE

Riley Engineering, Inc.

CCT #	BKR A/P	CCT DESCRIPTION	LTG	RECEP	MOTOR	APPLI	CCT #	BKR A/P	CCT DESCRIPTION	LTG	RECEP	MOTOR	APPLI	PHASE LOADS A	B	C
1	20/1	TREATMENT PANEL				0.2	2	15/1	EF-8			0.2		0.4		
3	20/1	TEMP.CONTROL				0.2	4	20/1	DT-2				0.4		0.6	
5	20/1	SPARE					6	20/1	TV-2				0.2			0.2
7	20/1	SPARE					8	20/1	MASTER CLK.				0.2	0.2		
9	20/1	UPS				0.8	10	20/1	FA PANEL				0.2		1.0	
11	20/1	UPS				0.8	12	20/1	SECURITY				0.2			1.0
13	20/1 *	UPS				0.8	14	20/1	INTRUSION				0.2	1.0		
15	20/1 *	UPS				0.8	16	20/1 *	DT-2				0.4		1.2	
17	20/1 *	UPS				0.8	18	20/1 *	DT-2				0.4			1.2
19	20/1 *	UPS				0.8	20	20/1 *	DT-2				0.4	1.2		
21	20/1 *	TEL.RM.				0.4	22	20/1 *	DT-2				0.4		0.8	
23	20/1 *	TEL.RM.				0.4	24	20/1 *	DT-1				0.4			0.8
25	20/1 *	TEL.RM.				0.4	26	20/1 *	DT-1				0.4	0.8		
27	20/1 *	TEL.RM.				0.4	28	20/1 *	DT-1				0.4		0.8	
29	20/1 *	TEL.RM.				0.4	30	20/1 *	DT-1				0.4			0.8
31							32							0.0		
33							34								0.0	
35							36									0.0
37							38							0.0		
39							40								0.0	
41							42									0.0
														4	4	4

	LTG	RECEP	MOTOR	APPLI	TTL KVA	TTL AMPS
TOTAL CONNECTED	0	0	0	12	12	33
LOAD FACTOR (NEC)	1.25			1		
CALCULATED LOAD	0	0	0.2	11.8	12	33

PROVIDE ISOLATED GROUND BAR.

VOLTS: 208 Y/120 3 PHASE 4 WIRE
SIZE: 100 AMPS
MAIN: 60 AMPS
AIC: 10,000
MOUNTG SURFACE
30 POLE PANE
*ISOLATED GROUND CIRCUIT.
SECTION ONE

Figure 6-26. Panelboard information is given on detail drawings, plan views, and schedules.

Finishes

After panelboards, conduit, and wiring are installed, connections are made to finish electrical fixtures. These include light fixtures, switches, receptacles, communication systems, and alarm systems. Care must be taken in wiring a large panelboard with many circuits and finish fixtures to ensure proper circuits are provided for the finish fixtures.

Lighting. Separate plans and schedules are provided for light fixture installation. See Figure 6-27. Symbols or abbreviations indicate the type of light fixture installed at each location. At the end of each lighting circuit, a notation indicates the panelboard and circuit numbers for attachment to the power source. The types and locations of switches are also shown on electrical plan views.

LIGHT FIXTURE SCHEDULE	
TYPE 'A'	RECESSED MOUNTING 2'X4' FLUORESCENT FIXTURE WITH A 3" DEE PARABOLIC LOUVER. PROVIDE THREE F40T12 ENERGY SAVING LAM FIXTURE. LITHONIA 2PM3-GH-340-18-S-277-ES-GLR, DAYBRITE, METALUX, OR APPROVED SUBSTITUTION.
TYPE 'B'	RECESSED MOUNTING 2'X4' FLUORESCENT FIXTURE WITH REGRESSE ACRYLIC LENS. PROVIDE TWO F40T12 ENERGY SAVING LAMPS PER LITHONIA 2SPGH-240-RN-A12.125-277-ES-GLR, DAYBRITE, COLUM, OR APPROVED SUBSTITUTION.
TYPE 'E'	RECESSED CEILING MOUNTED SINGLE FACE EXIT FIXTURE. PANEL 1/4" PLEXIGLASS WITH ROUTED-IN AND SCREENED LETTERING. G ON WHITE. PROVIDE ONE 8 WATT T-5 FLUORESCENT LAMP PER FI ALKCO RPC-110E, SILTRON, EMERGI-LITE, LITHONIA, OR APPROVE
TYPE 'F'	PENDANT MOUNTING 400 WATT METAL HALIDE LIGHTING FIXTURE W PRISMATIC GLASS REFLECTOR. PROVIDE ONE 400 WATT SUPER ME PER FIXTURE. HOLOPHANE PRSL-400MH-27-QD-E31-F1, GENERAL APPROVED SUBSTITUTION.
TYPE 'G'	CHAIN HUNG SURFACE MOUNTING TWO LAMP OPEN STRIP FIXTURE W GUARD. PROVIDE TWO F40T12 SUPER SAVER LAMPS PER FIXTURE. C240, DAYBRITE, KEYSTONE, METALUX, OR APPROVED SUBSTITUTION.

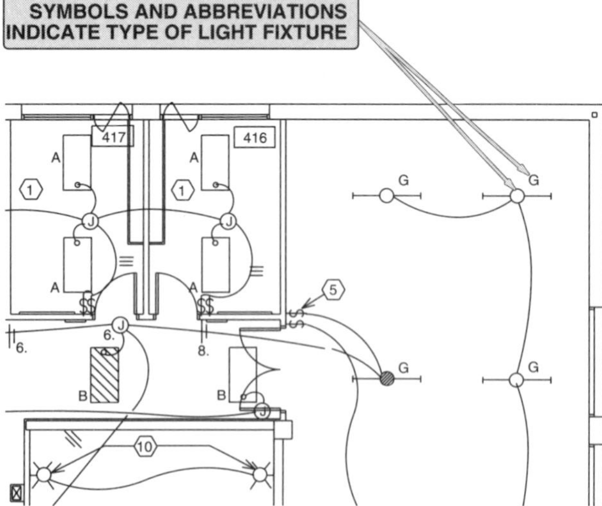

Figure 6-27. Notes on electrical prints and schedules provide detailed light fixture information.

Power. Symbols indicate fan connections, pump connections, motor controls, standard receptacles, switches, and special receptacles for heavy equipment. See Figure 6-28. Electrical prints for power outlet placements show receptacle locations and the type of receptacle at each location. In a manner similar to lighting plans, the panelboard number and circuit numbers are indicated at the end of each wiring run.

$	SINGLE POLE SWITCH- P DENOTES PILOT LIGHT
$₃	THREE-WAY SWITCH
$₄	FOUR-WAY SWITCH
$D	DIMMER SWITCH
$K	KEY OPERATED SWITCH
	DUPLEX RECEPTACLE
	DUPLEX RECEPTACLE W/ GFI
	DUPLEX RECEPTACLE- WEATHERPROOF, GFI
	DOUBLE DUPLEX RECEPTACLE
	SPECIAL RECEPTACLE
	DUPLEX RECEPTACLE – FLOOR MTD.
	SPECIAL RECEPTACLE – FLOOR MTD.
	CLOCK OUTLET
	BELL
	MOTOR CONNECTION
	JUNCTION BOX
	PUSHBUTTON

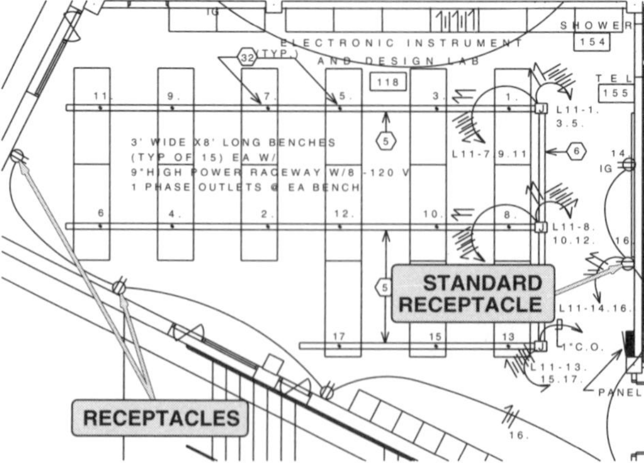

Figure 6-28. Electrical prints for power outlet placements show receptacle locations and the type of receptacle at each location.

Raceways provide a series of fixed placement receptacles and power sources along a continuous strip. Bus bars are installed where heavy power loads are necessary and outlet locations must be flexible and movable. A schedule of all electrical equipment and power requirements may be included in the electrical prints. See Figure 6-29. This schedule names each piece of equipment and shows the amount of electric power necessary, as well as circuit assignments. For example, item CCHWP-1 is a 3 HP pump connected to a 480 V, 3ϕ supply containing a 3-pole, 30 A safety switch that is protected by an 8 A fuse.

Temperature Control, Communications, and Alarms. Locations for thermostats which control the heating, ventilating, and cooling systems are shown on electrical plan views. See Figure 6-30.

Connections from the thermostat to the heating or cooling equipment to be regulated are shown on plan views. Symbols and abbreviations indicate connection locations for electrical systems for televisions, computer networks, speakers, microphones, satellite dishes, and intercom systems. Configurations of wiring for alarm systems for smoke detection, heat detection, and security are also shown on electrical plan views.

It is often required that the fire alarm and security systems be tested prior to the local governmental agency allowing the owner to occupy a large structure. Various types of non-staining smoke may be released in the interior of a building to ensure that all fire warning systems are operable prior to issuance of an occupancy permit.

MECHANICAL EQUIPMENT CIRCUIT SCHEDULE

ITEM	NAME	VOLT/PHASE	HP/AMP	SAFETY SWITCH	FUSE	CIRCUIT	CIRCUIT No.	MAG. STARTER
AC-1	AIR COMP.	480-3Ø	40 HP	3P-100A	80 A	3#4, 1 1/4"C	4M-38.40.42.	DIV.15
	AIR DRYER	480-3Ø	40 HP	3P-30A	50 A	3#6, 1"C	4M-43.45.47.	SIZE 1,FVNR
AS-1	AIR SHOWER	460-1Ø	2 HP	3P-30A	5.6A	3#12,3/4"C	4M-32.34.36.	SIZE 0
B 1	BOILER	480-3Ø	3 HP	3P-30 A	8 A	3#12,3/4"C	4M-1.3.5	DIV 15
B 2	BOILER	480-3Ø	3 HP	3P-30 A	8 A	3#12,3/4"C	4M-7.9.11	DIV 15
BCP-1	CIRC PUMP	480-3Ø	3 HP	3P-30 A *	8 A	3#12,3/4"C	MCC-1A	SIZE 1.FVNR
BCP-2	CIRC PUMP	480-3Ø	3 HP	3P-30 A *	8 A	3#12,3/4"C	MCC-1F	SIZE 1.FVNR
CAB-1	CABINET HEATER	120,1Ø	1/60 HP	DIV.15	N/A	2#12, 3/4"C	2M-9.	N/A
CAB-2	CABINET HEATER	120,1Ø	1/60 HP	DIV.15	N/A	2#12, 3/4"C	2M-9.	N/A
CAB-3	CABINET HEATER	480-3Ø	1/60 HP	3P-30A	N/A	2#12, 3/4"C	4B-22.24.26.	N/A
CAB-4	CABINET HEATER	480-3Ø	1/60 HP	3P-30A	N/A	2#12, 3/4"C	4B-28.30.32.	N/A
CCHWP-1	PUMP	480-3Ø	3 HP	3P-30 A *	8 A	3#12,3/4"C	MCC-1B	SIZE 1,FVNR
CCHWP-2	PUMP	480-3Ø	1 HP	3P-30 A	2.8 A	3#12,3/4"C	MCC-1B	SIZE 1,FVNR
CCHWP-3	PUMP	480-3Ø	1.5 HP	3P-30 A *	4 A	3#12,3/4"C	MCC-2A	SIZE 1,FVNR
CCHWP-4	PUMP	480-3Ø	1.5 HP	3P-30 A *	4 A	3#12,3/4"C	MCC-2A	SIZE 1,FVNR
CCHWP-5	PUMP	480-3Ø	3/4 HP	3P-30 A *	2.25 A	3#12,3/4"C	MCC-1A	SIZE 1,FVNR
CCHWP-6	PUMP	120-1Ø	1/3 HP	1P-30 A	12 A	2#12,3/4"C	2M-2	SIZE 00 FVNR
CH-1	CHILLER	480-3Ø	309 MCA	3P-400 A	400 A	SEE RISER	M.D.P	DIV.15
CH-2	FUTURE CHILLER	480-3Ø	309 MCA			SEE RISER	MDP	
CHP-1	PUMP	480-3Ø	10 HP	3P-30 A *	20 A	3#12,3/4"C	MCC-1F	SIZE 1,FVNR
CHP-2	PUMP	480-3Ø	10 HP	-	-	3/4"C ONLY	MCC-1B	
CHWP-1	PUMP	480-3Ø	3 HP	3P-30 A *	8 A	3#12,3/4"C	MCC-1B	DIV 16
CHWP-2	PUMP	480-3Ø	3/4 HP	3P-30 A *	2.25 A	3#12,3/4"C	MCC-2A	DIV 16
CHWP-3	PUMP	480-3Ø	3/4 HP	3P-30 A *	2.25 A	3#12,3/4"C	MCC-1A	DIV 16
CHWP-4	PUMP	120-1Ø	1/2 HP	3P-30 A *	15A	2#12, 3/4"C	MCC-1E	SIZE 1, FVNR
CT-1	COOLING TOWER	480-3Ø	15 HP	3P-60 A	30 A	3#10,3/4"C	4M-13,15,17	DIV.15
		480-3Ø	10 KW	3P-30 A	N/A	3#12,3/4"C	4M-20,22,24	N/A
CT-2	COOLING TOWER	480-3Ø	15 HP			2)3/4"CO.		
CU-1	CONDENSER	208-1Ø	14.FLA	3P-30A	20A	3#10, 3/4"C	2X1-2.4.	SIZE 1,FVNR
	PAINT BOOTH	120-1Ø	15A	N/A	N/A	2#12, 3/4"C	2A-30.	
	PAINT BOOTH	480-3Ø	3/4 HP	3P-30A	225A	2#12, 3/4"C	4A-23.25.27.	DIV.15
CWP-1	PUMP	480-3Ø	20 HP	3P-60 A	40 A	3#8,1" C	4M-2,4,6	DIV.15
CWP-2	PUMP	480-1Ø	20 HP			1"C ONLY	4M	N/A

Figure 6-29. Electrical schedules give details about each piece of equipment, including switches, fuses, and circuits.

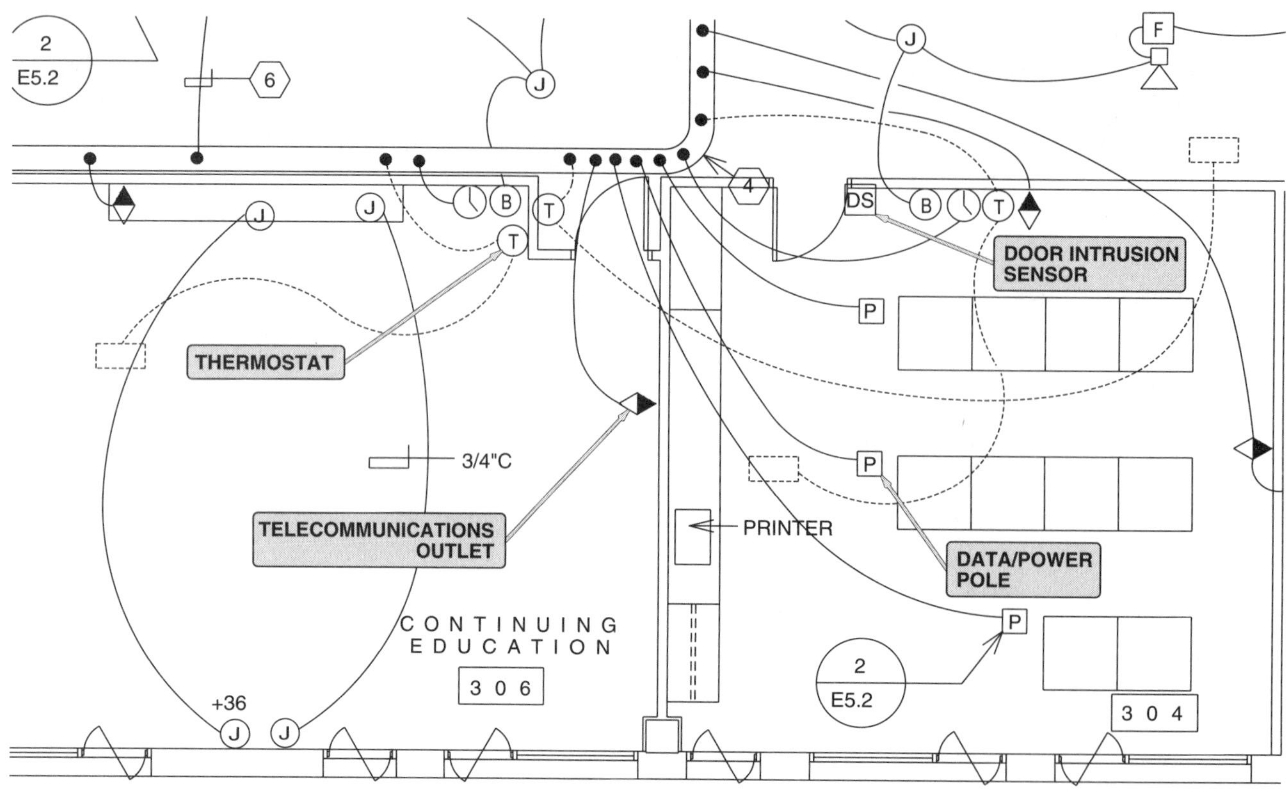

Figure 6-30. Additional electrical installations include connection locations for electrical systems, such as televisions, computer networks, speakers, microphones, satellite dishes, and intercom systems.

CHAPTER 6

MECHANICAL AND ELECTRICAL SYSTEMS

Review Questions

Name ______________________________ Date ______________

Printreading

_________ **1.** A drawing prefix of M indicates _________.

A. machinery drawings
B. mechanical drawings
C. mezzanine level drawings
D. material schedules

T F **2.** Water supply piping sizes shown on plumbing drawings are outside diameters.

_________ **3.** Elevations for plumbing waste pipes are given to the _________ of the pipe.

A. top outside
B. top inside
C. bottom inside
D. bottom outside

T F **4.** Mechanical drawings provide dimensional location information for plumbing fixtures such as sinks.

T F **5.** Electrical drawings provide dimensions to each receptacle location.

_________ **6.** An electrical cable line with no slash marks on a plan view indicates a cable containing _________ conductors.

_________ **7.** In areas prone to freezing, a(n) _________ pipe sprinkler system is required.

T F **8.** Isometric drawings are used to show plumbing pipe installations.

T F **9.** A chase in a concrete above-grade slab floor allows for future placement of plumbing pipe, electrical conduit, or ductwork.

_________ **10.** The best valve for throttling water flow is a _________ valve.

A. gate
B. globe
C. check
D. butterfly

_________ **11.** In a computer room, the best fire protection system is a _________ system.

A. wet pipe
B. dry pipe
C. preaction
D. halon

T F **12.** A #12 gauge wire has a larger diameter than a similar #10 gauge wire.

_________ **13.** A 25′ length run of plumbing waste pipe with a 1% slope changes elevation a total of _________″.

T F **14.** Cable trays are set in place prior to concrete floor slab placement.

_________ **15.** A pipe which carries water from a boiler to a terminal unit is a _________.

A. hot water supply
B. hot water return
C. cold water supply
D. cold water return

T F **16.** Preaction fire protection systems are connected to smoke and heat alarms.

__________ **17.** A ________ is a continuous strip which contains a series of electrical receptacles.

A. panelboard
B. raceway
C. circuit breaker
D. receptacle strip

T F **18.** Two common materials for ductwork are galvanized sheet metal and aluminum.

__________ **19.** The abbreviation CO in relation to plumbing waste piping refers to a(n) ________.

__________ **20.** The abbreviation gpm in relation to boiler pumps indicates ________.

__________ **21.** A drawing abbreviation of FS refers to ________.

A. floor sink
B. front side
C. floor slab
D. finish second

T F **22.** Plumbing prints indicate the size, purpose, type, and elevation of each pipe.

__________ **23.** Vertical pipes on plan views are indicated with a(n) ________ and an architectural note.

T F **24.** Exact dimensions for placement of waste pipes are given on the mechanical prints.

__________ **25.** The three types of systems for fire protection are wet, dry, and ________.

A. foam
B. spray
C. gaseous
D. neither A, B, nor C

__________ **26.** ________ are large fans used in commercial applications.

T F **27.** Electrical prints may be divided into separate sections for lighting, power supply, and signals, such as fire alarms and smoke detectors.

T F **28.** Materials used for waste piping include cast iron and polyvinyl chloride pipe.

__________ **29.** Ductwork may be ________.

A. round
B. square
C. rectangular
D. A, B, and C

T F **30.** Locations for thermostats which control the heating, ventilating, and cooling systems are shown on electrical elevation views.

CHAPTER 6

MECHANICAL AND ELECTRICAL SYSTEMS

Trade Competency Test

Name ______________________________ Date ______________

Trade Competency Test

Refer to Sheets 17, 18, 19, 20, 21, 22, 23, and 24.

T F **1.** There is natural gas service to the hot water storage tank in room 004.

______ **2.** Immediately after entering the building and passing through the main shut off valve, the size of the main water supply pipe is ______″.

A. 3 C. 5
B. 4 D. 6

______ **3.** The 4″ diameter pipe parallel with grid line G inside room 018 is a ______.

A. gas service pipe C. vent pipe
B. roof drain line D. waste stack

T F **4.** Elongated sleeves are installed where plumbing pipes penetrate waffle slab stems.

T F **5.** Air handler 3 has an outside air damper size of 126″ × 36″.

______ **6.** The diameter of the vertical ventilation pipes for the boilers is ______″.

A. 12 C. 20
B. 18 D. 24

T F **7.** Sprinkler piping is placed approximately 8″ to 12″ above the acoustical ceiling.

T F **8.** The contractor installing the sprinkler system is responsible for all piping connected to the system including underground work.

______ **9.** The pipe diameter for condenser supply and return pipes directly at the chiller is ______″.

______ **10.** The electrical chase is located ______.

A. just east of air handler 3 C. just north of the elevators
B. near the cooling tower D. in electrical room 006

______ **11.** Details for gas meter installation and connections are on mechanical drawing sheet number ______.

______ **12.** The size of the gas feed line down to the boiler on the basement floor plan is ______″.

A. 3 C. 5
B. 4 D. 6

______ **13.** The diameter for hot water supply and hot water return pipes for air handler 3 is ______″.

__________ **14.** The note P7 in room 012 refers to ________.

A. a 7″ pipe vent
B. pipe 7
C. the plumbing fixture schedule
D. plumbing sheet 7 for additional details

T F **15.** The main water service enters the basement through the floor in room 018.

T F **16.** Exhaust fan 6 is served by the same panelboard as the temperature control panels in room 018.

T F **17.** Fire alarm system power is provided by panelboard P2-1F4-1.

T F **18.** Water heater detail 1 notes a pressure relief valve discharge to a 2″ floor drain.

T F **19.** Exhaust fan 2 which is south of the chiller in room 007 intakes air from an 18″ square grille.

T F **20.** All sprinkler heads on the basement level are chrome.

__________ **21.** The 48″ × 104″ vertical duct near grid line intersection H5 is connected to ________.

A. outside air intake to air handler 3
B. outside air intake to air handler 3A
C. supply air from air handler 3
D. supply air from air handler 3A

T F **22.** Water supply pipes below the basement floor slab are PVC.

__________ **23.** The diameter of the vent pipe for the sinks in room 010 is ________″.

T F **24.** All cleanouts in the unexcavated area of the basement are 4″ in diameter.

__________ **25.** Showerheads in rooms 009 and 010 are fed with a(n) ________″ diameter mixing pipe.

T F **26.** A hot water heater is located in room 012.

__________ **27.** A 14″ × 8″ air grille accepts 300 cfm which is shown in the southwest corner of room 003 to ________.

A. supply air from air handler 3
B. supply air from air handler 4
C. exhaust air through air handler 3
D. exhaust air through air handler 4

__________ **28.** Circles containing a J on the east side of mechanical room 018 indicate ________.

__________ **29.** The 62″ × 48″ vertical duct between grid lines 4 and 5 and near grid line H is connected to ________.

A. supply air from air handler 3
B. supply air from air handler 3A
C. exhaust air through air handler 3
D. exhaust air through air handler 3A

__________ **30.** The minimum depth of the main service ductbank from the transformer to the main control closet is ________″ below finished grade.

T F **31.** There are two check valves on the water supply for water heater #1.

T F **32.** All three sinks in room 010 are supplied by ½″ cold water and hot water lines.

__________ **33.** The minimum distance between conduits in the main ductbank section is ________″.

__________ **34.** Unit heater 6 is ________.

A. a heat exchanger type furnace powered by natural gas
B. an electric heat exchanger type furnace
C. connected to the boilers
D. supplied by air handler 3

__________ **35.** Elevator 2 control panel is powered by circuit _________ in panelboard P2-BF2-3.

__________ **36.** Air separators are installed _________.

A. on the supply side of the piping
B. on the return side of the piping
C. on both the supply and return sides of the piping
D. detail M9.1 required to determine

__________ **37.** The size of core-drilled holes or sleeve outside diameters through the concrete wall near grid line intersection C2 is _________″.

T F **38.** The height of the gas service line entry into the building is 6″ above grade.

__________ **39.** The slope on roof drain lines is _________%.

T F **40.** Access for the telephone lines is concealed under the floor slab.

T F **41.** The communications panel is located in room 017.

__________ **42.** The abbreviation AFF on basement foundation plan note 29 indicates __________.

T F **43.** Water heater and boiler vent ducts are installed 12″ to 18″ high.

__________ **44.** The supply rate of the water flow valve into the water heater in room 003 is _________ gpm.

T F **45.** The air flowing through the 24″ square duct near grid line intersection H5 is moving in an upward direction.

__________ **46.** The manufacturer's model number for the pipe sleeves installed near grid line intersection F4 is _________.

T F **47.** The overall size of air handler unit 3 is 18′-6″ × 29′-6″.

__________ **48.** The sprinkler system shown is _________.

A. wet pipe
B. dry pipe
C. preaction
D. halon

__________ **49.** The flow rate for the main sprinkler water service is _________ gpm.

__________ **50.** There is a total of _________ sprinkler heads in the two bathrooms on the basement level.

T F **51.** The maintenance office (room 014) has four receptacles.

__________ 52. The diameter of the condensate drain pipe on air handler 4 is _________″.

A. 2
B. 3
C. 4
D. 5

__________ **53.** Air handler 3A is connected to _________.

A. cooling pipes only
B. heating pipes only
C. both heating and cooling pipes
D. detail M9.1 required to determine

T F **54.** A smoke detector and fire alarm pull station are provided in stairway 000A.

T F **55.** Master control closet BF2 houses the controls for both boilers.

T F **56.** The sizes of the vent pipes for the sinks and urinals in room 009 are all 1½″.

T F **57.** There are no manual pull station fire alarms on the roof level.

T F **58.** All receptacles in hallway 002 are powered from panelboard P2-BF2-4.

__________ **59.** The electrical power for air handler 3 in room 018 is provided by panelboard number _________.

A. MCC-BF2
B. P2-BF2-4
C. SF-3
D. BLR-1

__________ **60.** Low-voltage cables serving the chiller have _________.

A. a series of 8¾″ diameter wires
B. 8 wires, each 14 gauge
C. 3 cables, each 4″ in diameter
D. 14 wires, each 8 gauge

T F **61.** The emergency wall switch for the ventilation system is located on the outside of the entry to room 007.

T F **62.** Heat recovery coils are installed in the outside air and exhaust ducts for air handler 3.

__________ **63.** Unit heater 1 in room 015 has a(n) _________-conductor cable and a ground wire.

A. exposed conduit with a 2
B. exposed conduit with a 3
C. concealed conduit with a 2
D. concealed conduit with a 3

__________ **64.** The minimum distance between the top of the electrical busway support and the ceiling above is _________″.

__________ **65.** The main ductbank _________.

A. runs under the concrete slab at at the north end of room 018
B. is in a cable tray through corridor 002
C. drops down from the first floor in service area 018
D. location must be obtained from the site plan

__________ **66.** Electrical service from panelboard P2-BF2-2 serves the _________.

A. alternate bid item #2
B. cooling tower
C. first floor communications room
D. first floor electrical room

__________ **67.** The type of cable used to ground the transformer and the main electrical room is _________.

T F **68.** Pump 1 serves only boiler 1 and pump 2 serves only boiler 2.

T F **69.** Pump 5 serves the heat recovery piping system.

__________ **70.** The cooling tower solenoid valve is powered by circuit _________ in panel P2-BF2-3.

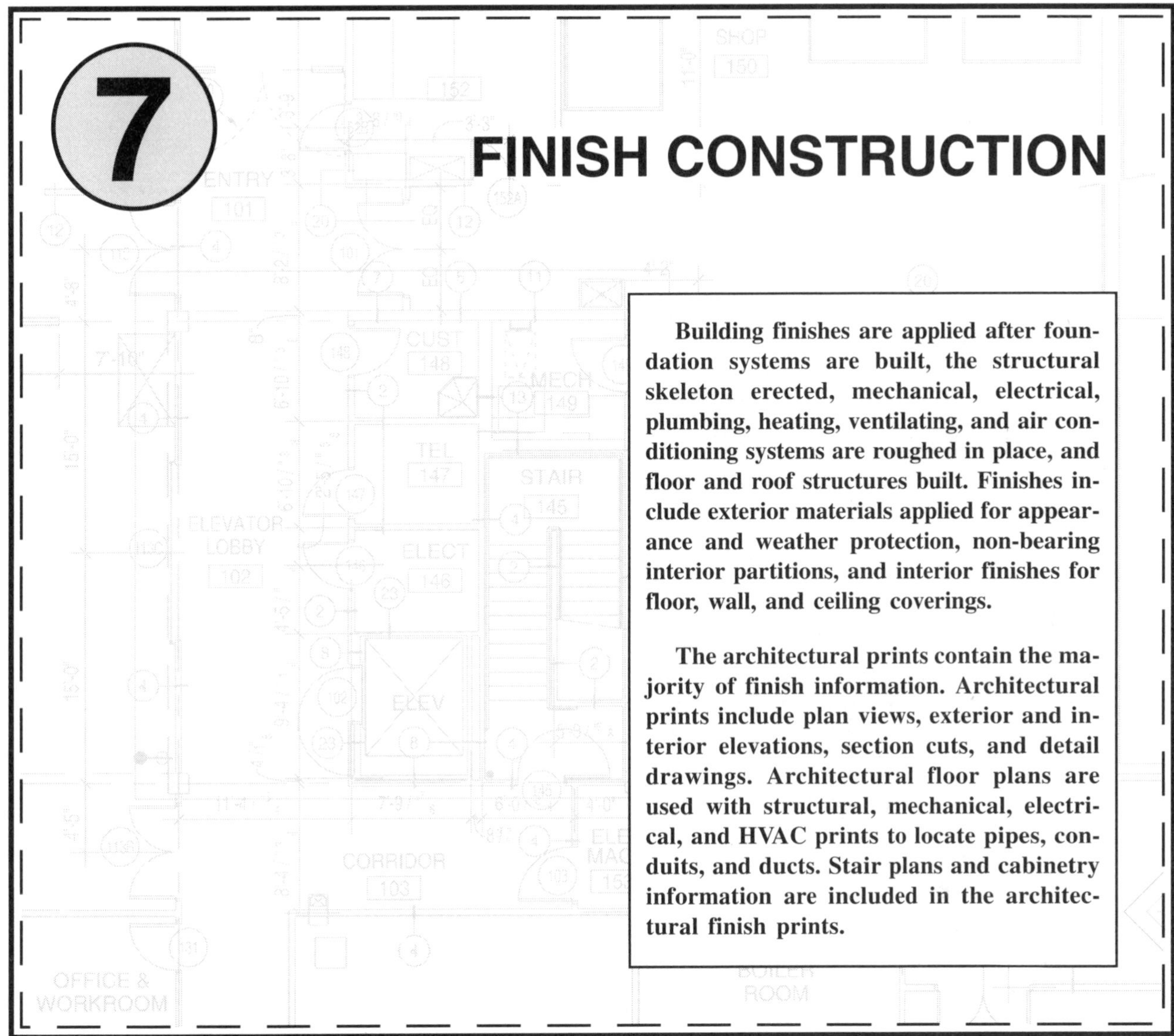

7 FINISH CONSTRUCTION

Building finishes are applied after foundation systems are built, the structural skeleton erected, mechanical, electrical, plumbing, heating, ventilating, and air conditioning systems are roughed in place, and floor and roof structures built. Finishes include exterior materials applied for appearance and weather protection, non-bearing interior partitions, and interior finishes for floor, wall, and ceiling coverings.

The architectural prints contain the majority of finish information. Architectural prints include plan views, exterior and interior elevations, section cuts, and detail drawings. Architectural floor plans are used with structural, mechanical, electrical, and HVAC prints to locate pipes, conduits, and ducts. Stair plans and cabinetry information are included in the architectural finish prints.

EXTERIOR FINISH

Foundation systems and structural members are erected with consideration given to exterior finishes. Structural members may remain exposed to the exterior of a structure. In bridges and road buildings, the structural members are the exterior finish members. Exterior finish members include bearing and non-load bearing walls, roof coverings, and exposed structural members.

Exterior elevation views show the final appearance of the exterior of a building with an orthographic projection drawing. See Figure 7-1.

Masonry, concrete, metal, glass, and all other exterior finishes are shown. Grid lines relate the exterior finish materials to structural elements. Elevations are given for floor levels and roof lines. Typical information is keyed to other prints where details are provided.

Walls

Weather protection, appearance, security, and insulation are some of the factors considered when choosing a commercial exterior wall finish. Commercial exterior wall finishes are designed primarily with low maintenance and high durability in mind.

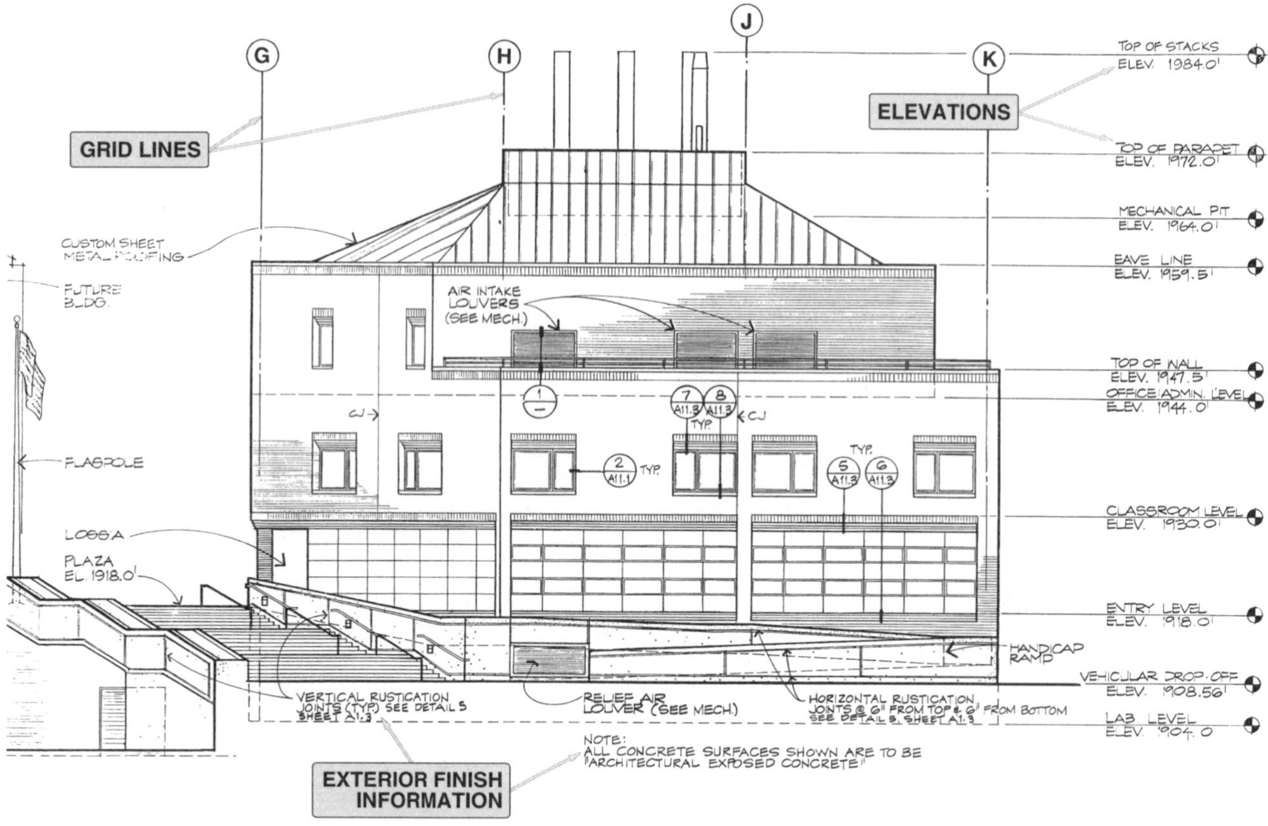

Figure 7-1. Each side of a commercial structure is shown with an exterior elevation view to illustrate exterior finishes and final building appearance.

Wood siding, which is used in residential construction, is uncommon on large commercial structures. Wall finish materials include masonry, concrete, glass, metal, and plaster. Heavy-duty doors and window systems are installed in commercial buildings to give long life with little maintenance.

Section views of exterior walls provide information about exterior finishes. See Figure 7-2. The section views are similar to wall section views on other prints. Brick, plaster, glass, metal, and concrete are used to create an attractive and durable wall system.

Masonry. Exterior masonry walls may be brick, concrete masonry units (CMU), or stone. Masonry walls may be structural bearing walls or built as a veneer around and between structural members. See Figure 7-3.

Masonry units for exterior finish are shown on exterior elevation prints and wall section views. Special masonry units of brick, concrete, or stone may be fabricated specifically for a particular job.

Where masonry units form the structural wall, the exterior finish, including brick bond, face finish of concrete masonry units, mortar color, lintels, and stone patterns and types are given in the specifications and on elevation views. Special brick shapes and coursing information are included in the architectural elevation views. See Figure 7-4.

Locations and types of masonry control and expansion joints are shown on elevation and detail drawings. Wall section views indicate methods for attachment of masonry veneer to structural members and decorative effects. Architects may require that a sample section of masonry wall be laid prior to application to the structure to obtain a view of the finished product.

Masonry veneer walls are commonly built in place. They may also be made of prefabricated panels set in a manner similar to precast concrete panels. Prefabricated masonry panels are laid with steel support frames and inserts, lifted into place, and attached to structural members.

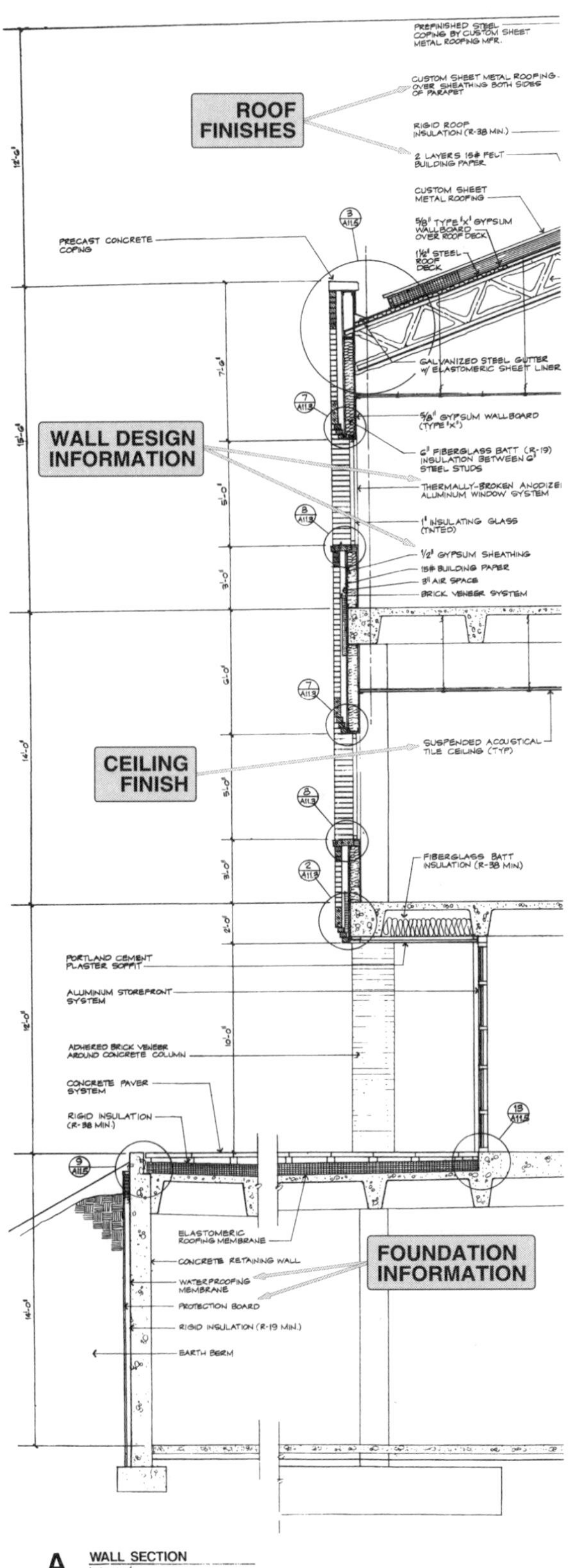

Figure 7-2. Overall foundation, wall, floor, ceiling, and roof finishes are detailed on wall section views.

Figure 7-3. Masonry walls are laid as either structural supporting walls or exterior veneer for structural members.

Concrete. Exterior exposed concrete walls are often architectural concrete. *Architectural concrete* is concrete in which the surface of the concrete is finished to not show exposed form joint marks. Concrete surface finishing information is given by the architect in the specifications or general notes on the architectural prints. Architectural concrete finishes are created by placing form liners inside the concrete forms prior to concrete placement, sandblasting the surface after concrete has set, or rubbing the surface after it has set to smooth it to the required finish. See Figure 7-5. Exterior elevations show exposed concrete wall finishes with architectural notes.

Precast concrete panels are also applied as an exterior finish. Concrete panels are cast in any design the architect specifies and transported to the job site. They are lifted into place with a crane and fastened to the structure. Fastening is done with welding of metal inserts cast into the panels or clips fastened to the structural members.

Glass. Exterior glass finishes are made of glass block or glass panels set in metal or wood frames. Glass blocks are set in mortar similar to brick or concrete masonry units.

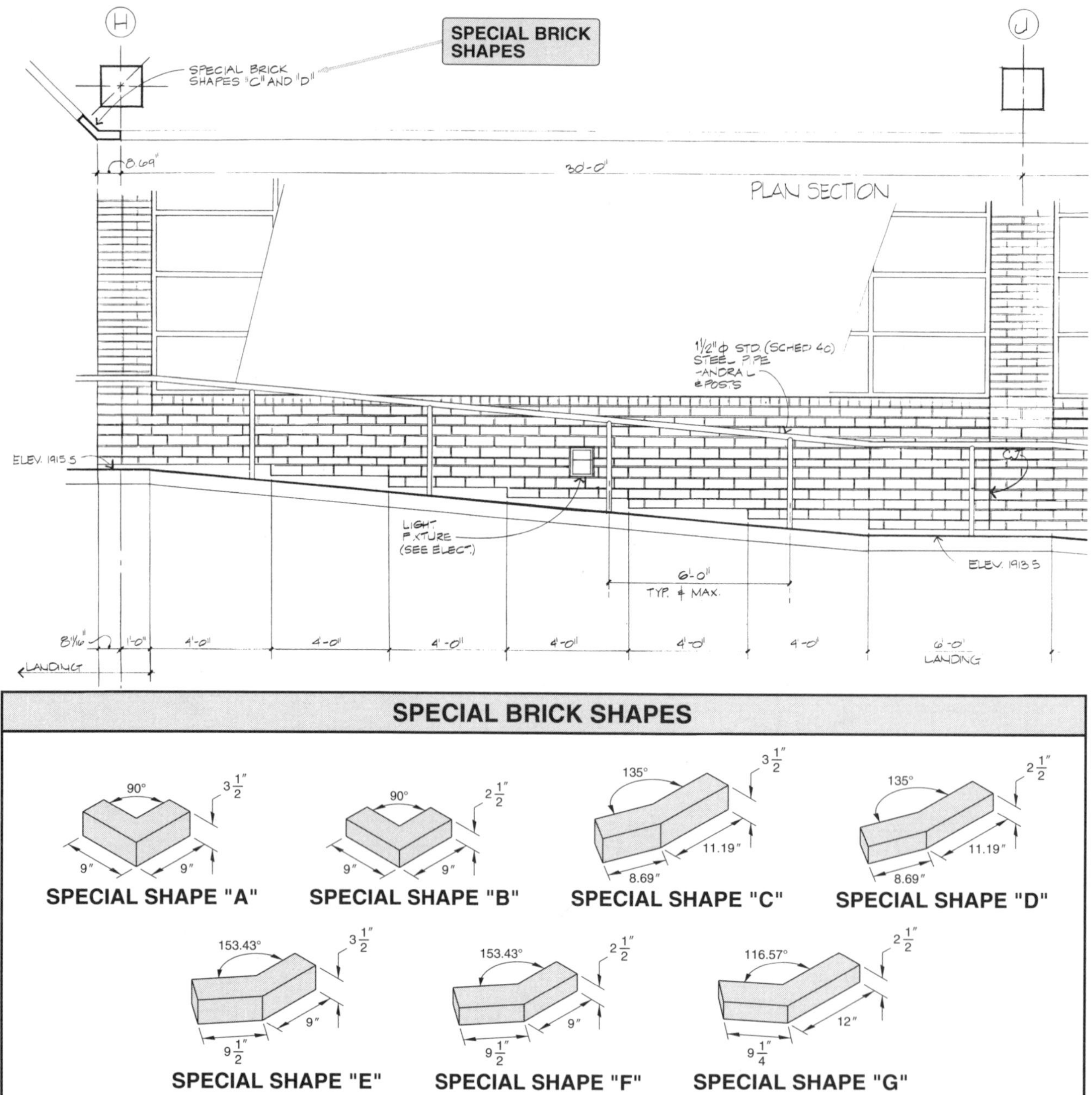

Figure 7-4. Special brick shapes and coursing information are included in the architectural elevation views.

Sections of glass block installation are shown on exterior elevation views and architectural floor plans. Information concerning glass set in metal or wood frames is obtained from both exterior elevations and detail section views. See Figure 7-6. Nonbearing metal or wood frames are attached to structural members in some specified manner. Connections of the frames and glass panels are shown on detail drawings.

Glass sheets are available in many different designs and types. The type of glass installed takes into account such items as wind loads, thermal transmission, privacy, appearance, safety, and security. Clear glass includes window and sheet glass, float glass, and plate glass. Variations of the basic glass types include acoustical, cathedral, heat absorbing tinted, heat strengthened, insulating, obscure, reflective, safety, spandrel, security, tempered, and wire.

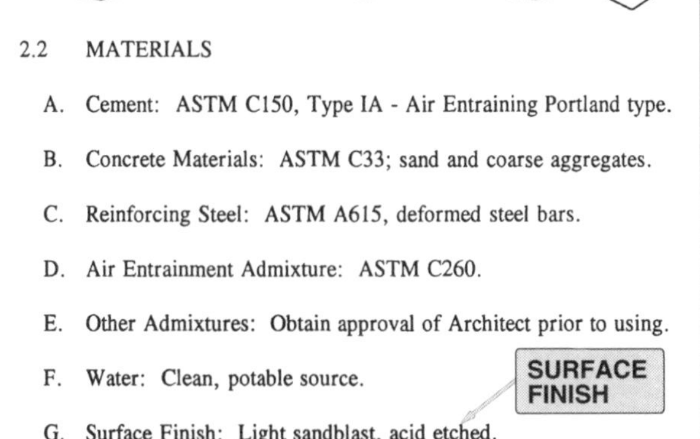

2.2 MATERIALS

A. Cement: ASTM C150, Type IA - Air Entraining Portland type.

B. Concrete Materials: ASTM C33; sand and coarse aggregates.

C. Reinforcing Steel: ASTM A615, deformed steel bars.

D. Air Entrainment Admixture: ASTM C260.

E. Other Admixtures: Obtain approval of Architect prior to using.

F. Water: Clean, potable source.

G. Surface Finish: Light sandblast, acid etched.

H. Grout: Thermo-setting epoxy.

Figure 7-5. Architectural concrete requires additional finishing to create the surface finish noted by the architect.

Mastics, caulks, sealants, rubber or plastic seals, and metal or wood stops secure glass into frames. A majority of the information concerning installed glass is given in the written specifications. Detail drawings may refer to a specific type of glass for an identified area. Exterior elevations and floor plans provide dimensional information for the sizes of glass panels.

Frames for glass panels are installed and attached to the structural members. Suction cups are attached to the face of the glass to lift panels into place. Sealants and frame mullions and stops are applied to secure the glass in the frame.

Metal. Metal panels are used for curtain walls on large commercial buildings. Curtain walls are made up of non-bearing, prefabricated panels which are fastened to structural members. Insulated metal panels and glass are set in a common frame and attached to the structural members as a single unit. Exterior walls made up of glass panels set in metal frames may also be referred to as curtain walls. See Figure 7-7.

The design of curtain wall systems must take into account the expansion and contraction properties of all the materials in the curtain wall panels. Curtain walls are fastened to structural members with welded clips or inserts. Curtain wall panel locations are shown on elevation views. Curtain wall manufacturers may provide shop drawings which identify each panel and location by code letters and numbers.

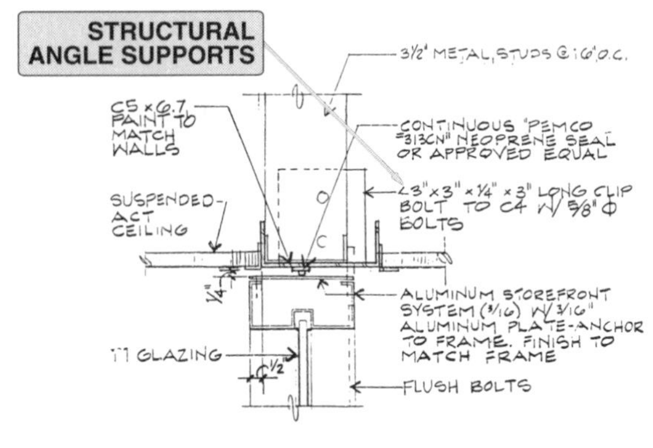

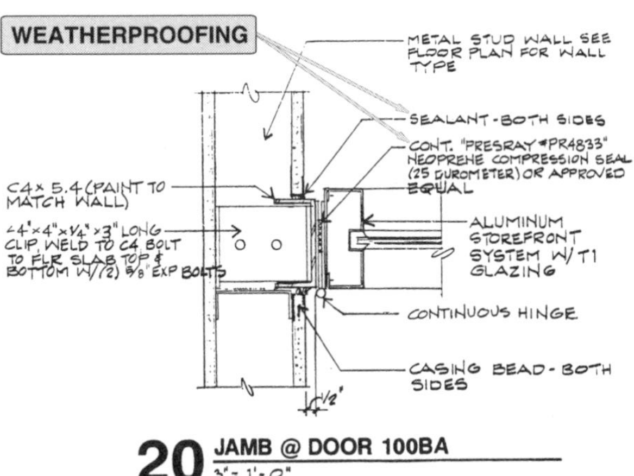

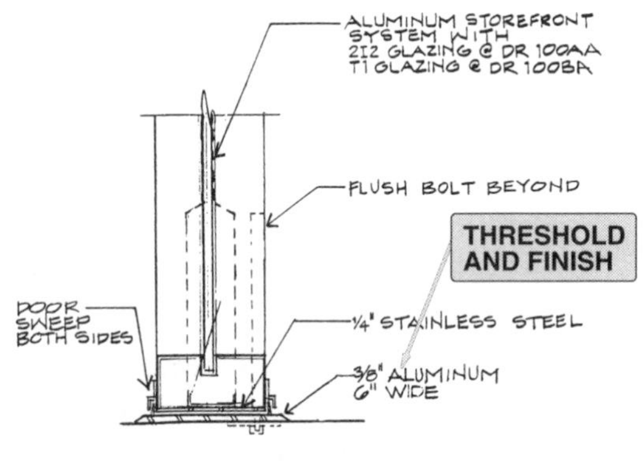

Figure 7-6. Details of head, jamb, and sill attachment and finish show framing members, sealants, frames, and glazing.

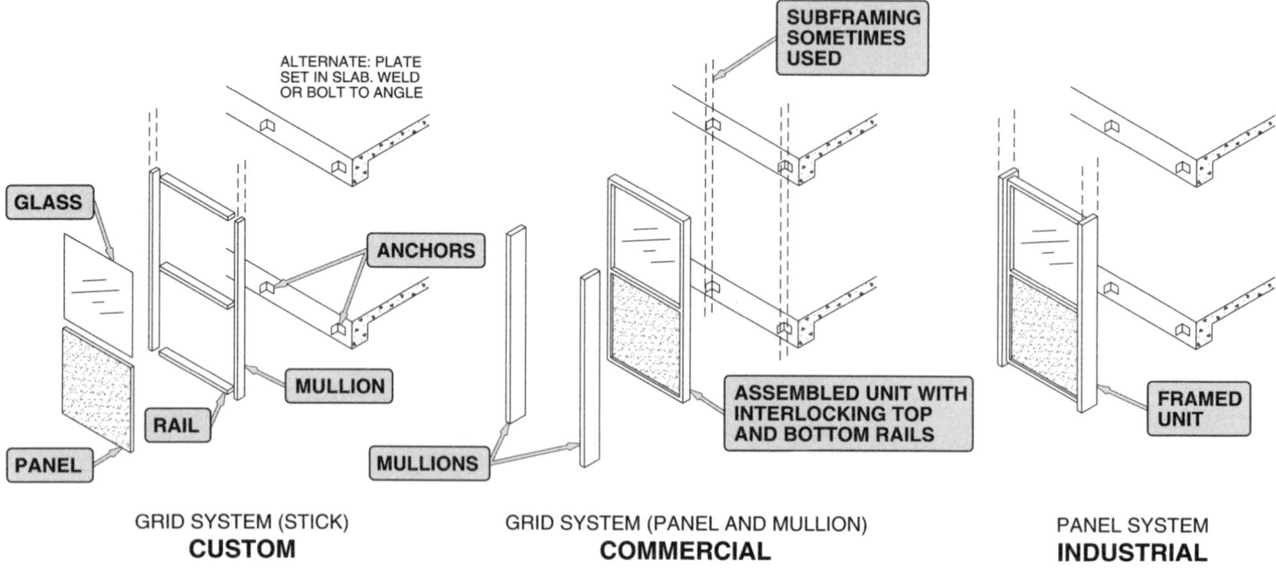

Figure 7-7. Curtain wall systems integrate metal panels and glass into prefabricated units of various designs.

Mullions several stories in length can be installed to cap the joints between curtain wall panels. Mullions and curtain wall frames are made of aluminum or other metals treated to be rust-resistant. Methods for sealing joints between curtain wall panels are shown on detail drawings.

Corrugated metal sheets are used for exterior wall siding on small structural steel buildings. The sheets are prefinished with a baked-on paint finish. Types and colors of metal siding are shown on elevation prints. Wall section views indicate insulation installation.

Plaster. Exterior surfaces are coated with various types of plaster finishes. The surface of the plaster is troweled smooth, swirled, or left with a rough finish as specified by the architect in the specifications or shown on exterior elevation prints.

Portland cement plaster is held in place with lath. Lath is available in sheets of expanded metal or gypsum lath. Expanded metal lath is tied or screwed onto metal furring channels. Gypsum lath is installed in a manner similar to sheets of gypsum drywall. Gypsum lath is screwed onto framing members or metal furring channels. Metal expansion joints and control joints are installed at locations shown on the prints or detailed in the specifications. A base coat of plaster is applied to the lath and left with a rough finish. The finish coat is applied over the surface of the base coat.

Exterior insulation and finish systems (EIFS) are composed of a layer of exterior sheathing, insulation board applied to the exterior of the sheathing, an integrally reinforced base coat spread on the exterior face of the insulation board, and a textured protective finish. See Figure 7-8.

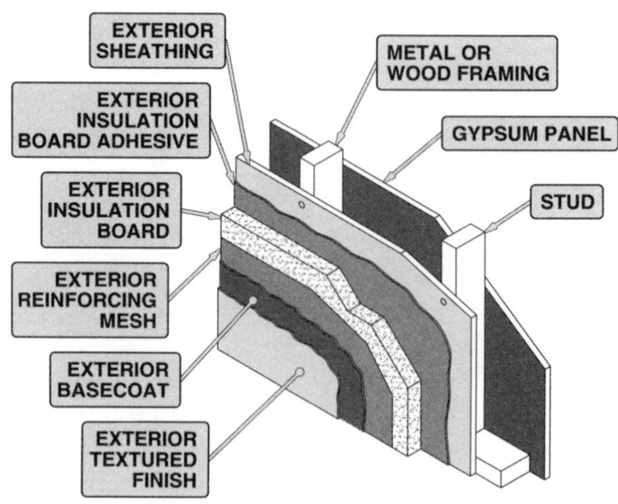

Figure 7-8. Exterior insulation and finish systems (EIFS) incorporate insulation board and polymer-based materials into an exterior finish.

Insulation board is made of extruded or molded expanded polystyrene. Insulation boards provide thermal insulation and flexibility in the plaster structure to minimize cracking. A base coat containing acrylic polymers and portland cement is applied to the surface of the insulation board. The base coat is approximately ¼″ thick. It is troweled onto the surface of the insulation board and reinforced with one or two layers of an open weave glass fiber fabric. After the base coat has set, the surface finish coat of acrylic resins is troweled or sprayed onto the structure to create the desired finish.

Doors and Windows. Schedules for doors and windows in the specifications provide most of the information for the types and styles of exterior doors and windows. Location information is shown on architectural plan views. Detail drawings provide information about the joining of door and window jambs to the various structural and wall finishes. See Figure 7-9.

Roofs

Large commercial building roofs are made of bituminous coatings, such as tar and gravel, elastomeric coatings of various plastics, and galvanized, treated, or decorative metal. Architectural plan views indicate the roof covering, slope, and finish materials. Access doors, skylights, walk pads, and locations for some vent pipes may also appear on roof level plan views. See Figure 7-10.

A system of drains and pipes is installed to collect rain water from the large roof surfaces and channel it to drainage systems. Locations for drains and gutters are shown on roof plan views. Detail drawings show the methods for drain installation and joining roof finish materials to the drains to seal possible leaks. Piping locations are shown on mechanical prints.

Roof detail drawings show methods for joining roof finishes to decking, walls, and parapets. See Figure 7-11. Flashing, gutters, roof covering materials, and sealing materials appear on the detail section views.

Bituminous Coating. Roof decks are covered with a vapor barrier and rigid insulation prior to the application of a bituminous built-up roof. Several plies of felt paper saturated with asphalt or coal tar are rolled across the surface of the roof. Each layer is coated with hot asphalt or coal tar pitch. The entire surface is coated with gravel while the top layer is in a liquid state. The gravel joins to the roof surface. Detail drawings and specifications give information about the bituminous materials to be used and the number of plies.

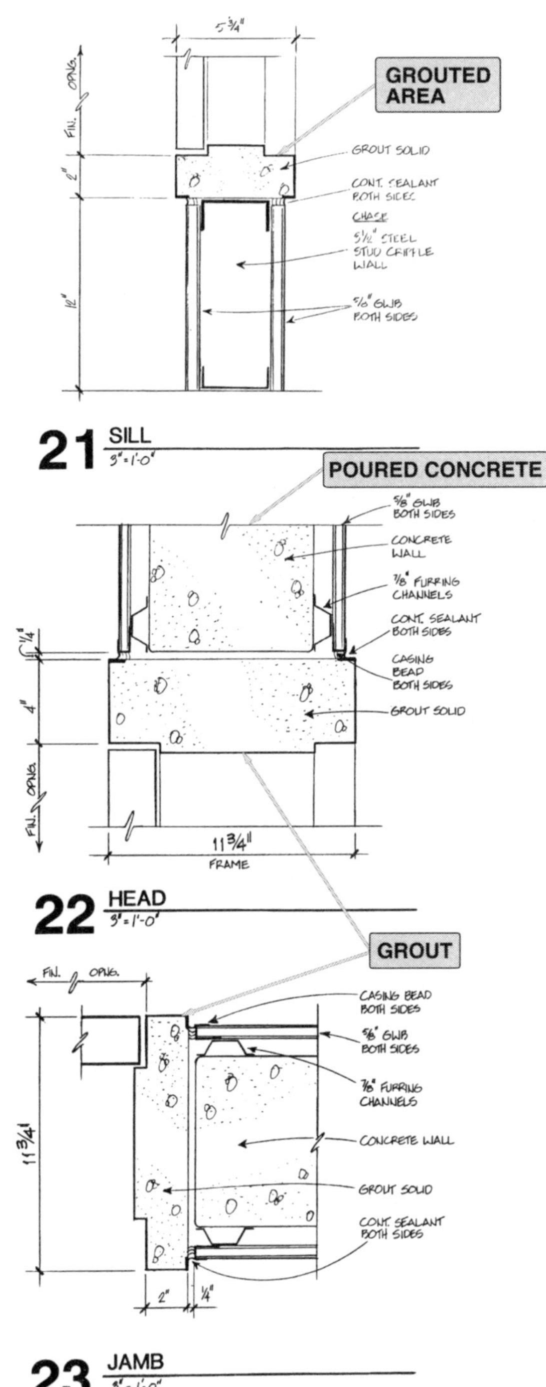

Figure 7-9. The voids behind hollow metal window and door jambs are filled with grout to make them more stable.

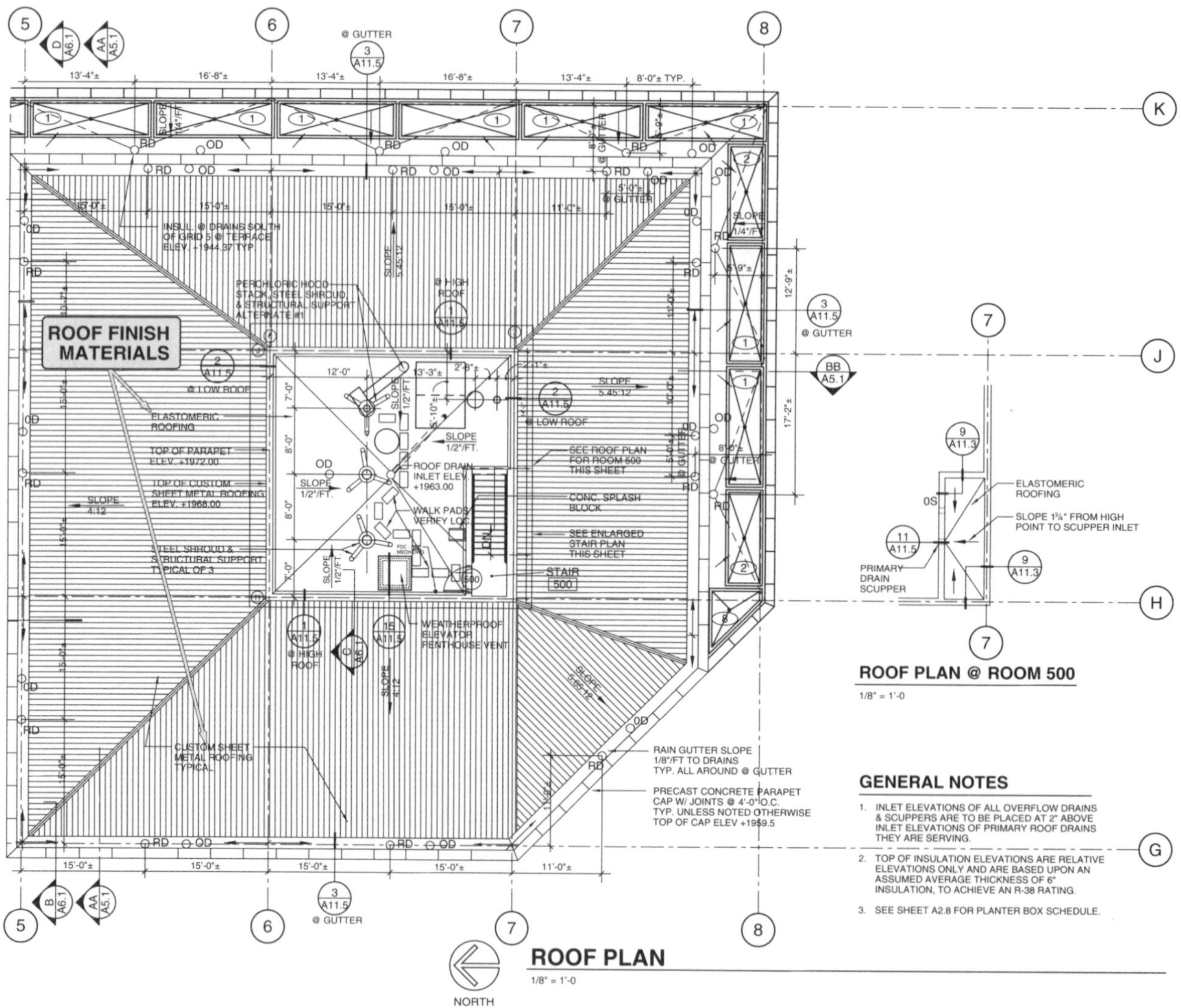

Figure 7-10. Roof finish materials, including metal and elastomeric roofing, are noted on a plan view of the roof.

Elastomeric Coating. Large sheets are laid in place and sealed at the joints to create an elastomeric roofing system. Sheets are made of chlorinated polyethylene (CPE), ethylene propylene diend monomer (EPDM), or polyvinyl chloride (PVC). PVC is the most commonly used material.

Vapor barriers and rigid roof insulation are installed on the surface of the roof deck. Elastomeric sheets are then rolled out across the entire surface of the roof. Joints are sealed with a solvent which joins the sheets into a single unit. The entire surface may be covered with gravel after all joints are sealed. Precast concrete pavers may also be installed on the roofing surface.

Metal. Sloping roofs may be covered with metal roof finishes. Prefinished or decorative metals, such as copper, are used for roof and ornamental coverings. Rigid insulation may be applied to the top of the roof deck and covered with building paper. Sheets of prefinished or ornamental metal are set in place, with the longer dimension placed parallel to rafters running from the bottom of the roof toward the top.

Joints along the sides of the metal sheets are fastened in a variety of designs. They may be flat, ribbed, or standing. See Figure 7-12. Metal roof sheets are fastened to the roof decking with clips or self-tapping screws. Overlapped joints are coated with various waterproof joint sealants.

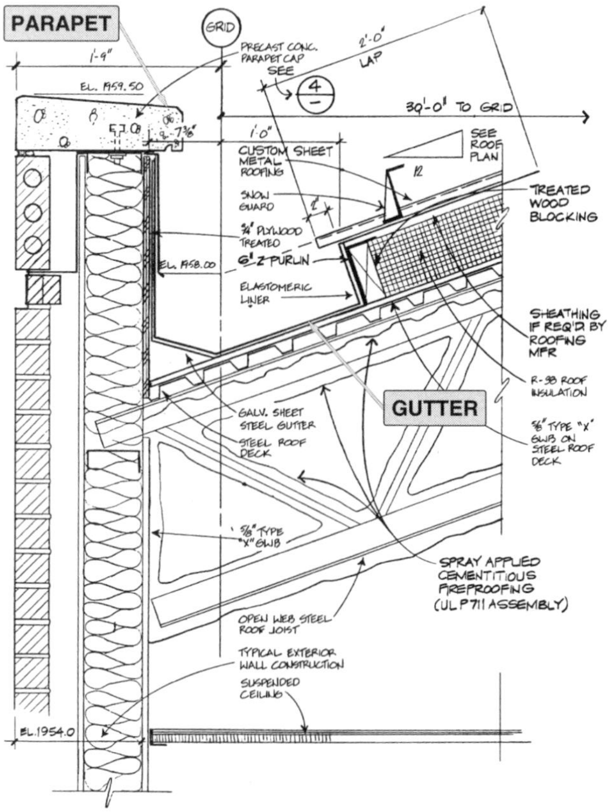

Figure 7-11. Parapet caps and construction, roof decking, gutter construction, and dimensions for overlapping of materials appear on roof detail drawings.

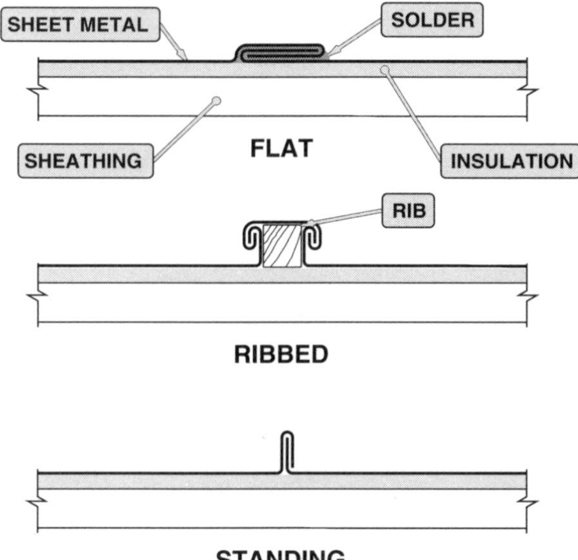

Figure 7-12. Joints along the sides of metal roof sheets may be flat, ribbed, or standing.

Exposed Structural Elements

Architects may design structural members to remain exposed in the finished structure. Examples of such structural members include columns and beams. Elevation prints show the exterior finish of these members. For road and bridge building, structural beams and columns are commonly exposed and finished, as shown on elevation prints. Stairs, landings, and handrails are shown on architectural plan prints, elevation prints, and architectural and structural detail drawings. Due to the nature of stairs as a structural item, they must be exposed and finished as shown.

Columns and Beams. Reinforced concrete and structural steel columns and beams remain exposed in some commercial buildings and all road building. Concrete columns and beams are finished in a manner similar to exposed concrete walls. Chamfer strips are placed in the corners of concrete forms for square or rectangular beams and columns to create beveled edges. Structural steel columns and beams are coated with primer and paint to minimize rust. Structural steel columns, beams, and joists may be sprayed with fireproofing materials as noted on the detail drawings.

Stairs and Ramps. Exterior elevation prints show stair and ramp slopes and locations. See Figure 7-13. Reinforced concrete is the most common material for exterior stairs and ramps on-grade. Dimensions for exterior concrete stairs and ramps are shown on site plans. Surface finishes and reinforcing information are given in the specifications or structural prints.

Structural steel is used for exterior stairs above-grade, such as fire escapes. The stringers and stair carriages are made of structural steel. The treads may be made of perforated or expanded mesh steel or steel pans filled with concrete. See Figure 7-14.

Handrails for exterior stairs and ramps are shown on architectural elevation prints, details, and structural print details. Exterior handrails are most commonly made of steel or a rust-resistant metal. Pipe sections are welded together and finished to create handrails and posts.

Access ladders are shown on architectural plan views and architectural and structural detail drawings. Access ladders are made of welded structural steel members.

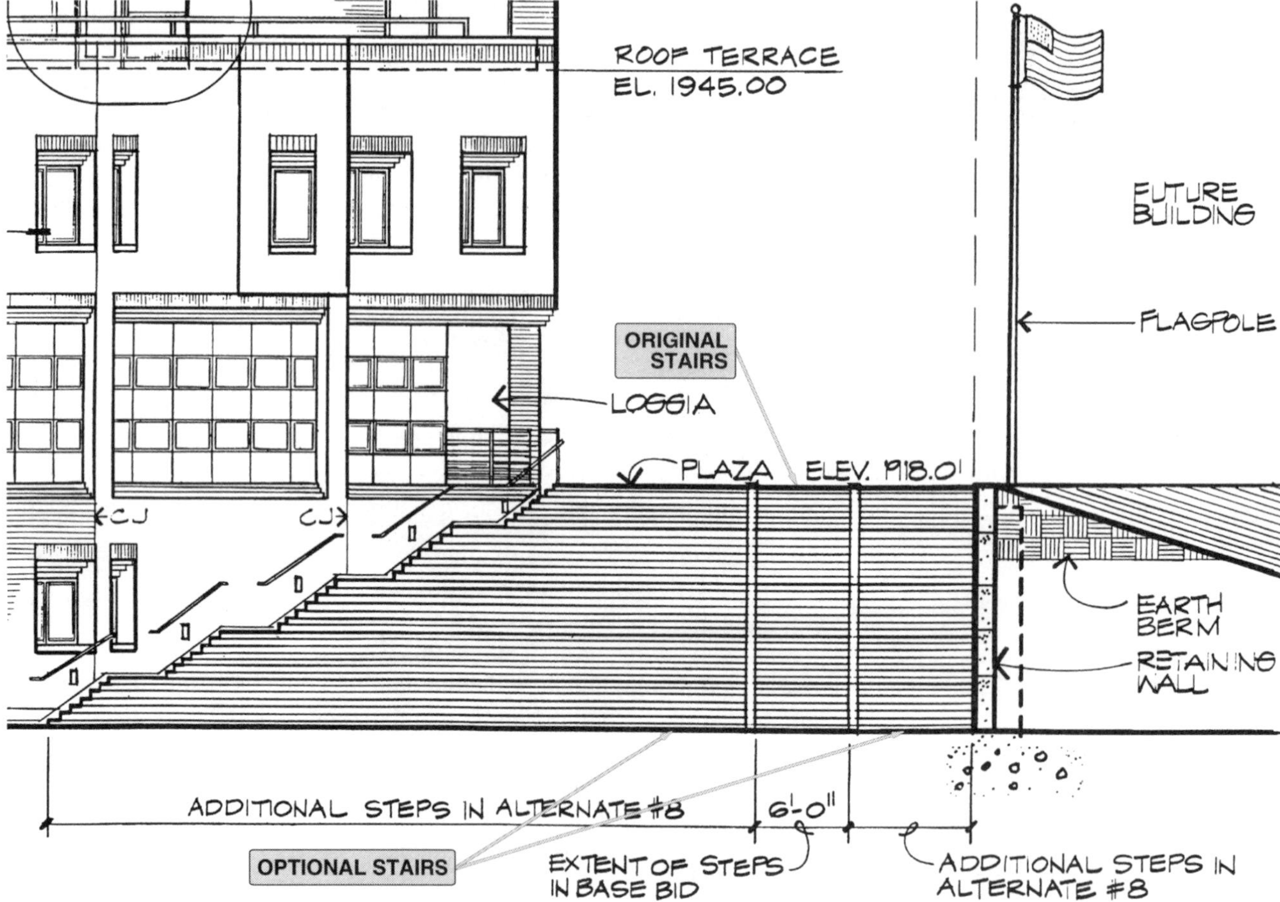

Figure 7-13. Exterior elevation drawings show general stair appearance and alternate additional steps.

INTERIOR FINISH

Walls, floors, and ceilings inside a commercial building have a number of different finish requirements. Public areas are finished with appearance and durability in mind. Manufacturing and mechanical areas are finished with functionality as a primary concern. Office and classroom areas are finished to allow for flexibility of design, comfort, and functionality.

Plan views and interior elevations provide interior finish information. Wall locations and finishes, floor finishes, ceiling heights and finishes, door locations, and window locations are shown on plan views. Interior elevations present orthographic projections of various areas within a structure to show more complex finish treatments and cabinetry and casework installations.

Walls

Interior and exterior walls between structural members are commonly framed with metal studs. Light gauge metal members, including tracks and studs, are fastened to structural members. Batt insulation is placed between the studs as specified on the architectural plan view.

Rough frame openings are created for doors and windows. Architectural plan views and detail drawings give the width of the stud framing, location dimensions, and locations for openings. See Figure 7-15. The surfaces of metal stud framed walls are finished with gypsum drywall, plaster, brick veneer, or other non-bearing finishes. A schedule of wall framing and finishes is cross referenced to the plan view. Interior elevations and a room finish schedule in the specifications indicate the types and locations of wall finishes.

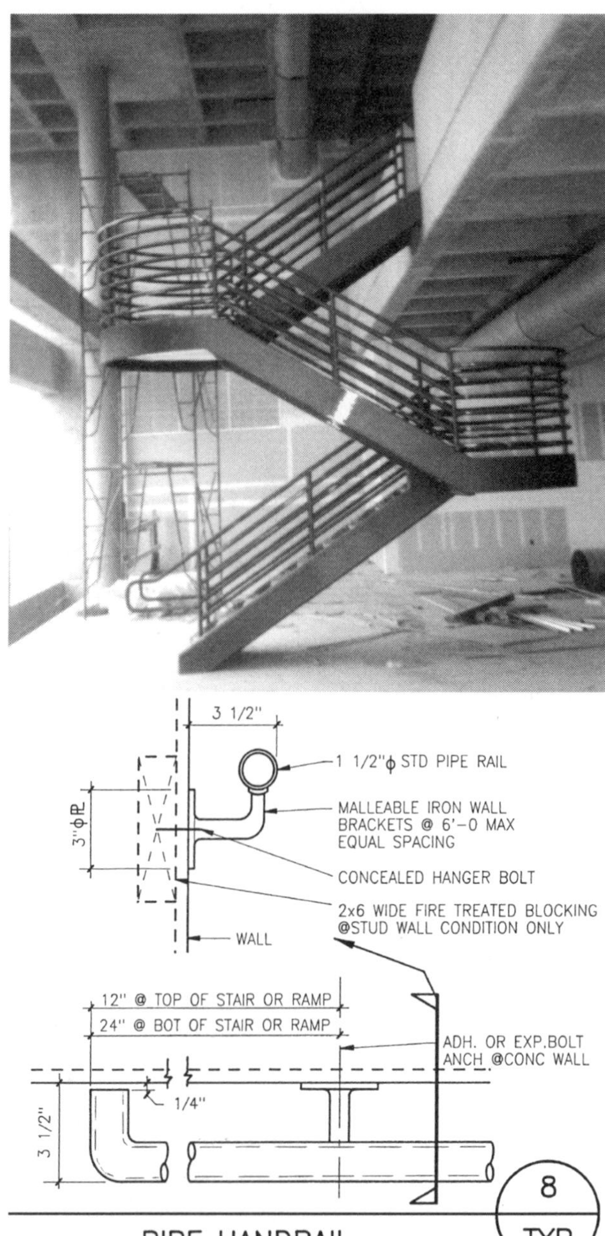

Figure 7-14. Concrete stair treads are supported by structural steel stringers and metal pans. Metal handrails are made of welded pipe and anchored to walls with support brackets.

Gypsum Drywall. A core of gypsum is coated with layers of paper to create gypsum drywall. Sheets are available in 4′ or 5′ widths and lengths from 8′ to 14′ in 2′ increments. Thicknesses vary in ⅛″ increments beginning at ¼″. Gypsum drywall is available in fireproof and waterproof grades.

Gypsum drywall sheets are attached to wood or metal framing members and furring with nails or self-tapping screws. See Figure 7-16. Joints between sheets are finished with a joint compound which is sanded smooth prior to application of surface finishes. Finish materials include paint, wallpaper, wood paneling, or fabric. Gypsum thickness and face finish are shown on detail drawings and room finish schedules.

Plaster. Interior plaster wall finish materials include portland cement plaster on metal lath or gypsum lath and thin coat finishes applied directly to gypsum drywall. Lath, control joints, and trims are installed in a manner similar to exterior plaster applications.

Masonry. Brick, concrete masonry units, and stone are used for interior fire break walls and for exposed interior walls. Finish information for interior masonry walls is similar to exterior exposed masonry, including material, mortar joint color and finish, and bond pattern.

Movable. Large interior spaces designed for division into smaller areas contain operable walls, such as movable and folding partitions or demountable partitions. Large movable wall sections are suspended from an overhead track. See Figure 7-17.

The overhead track is attached to structural members to provide a solid support system for the wall. The bottom edge of the track is flush with or recessed into the ceiling. Rollers which travel in the ceiling track are attached to the top of each wall section.

Suspended movable wall panels may stack against one or several walls, depending on the architect's design. Architectural plan views show the locations of tracks for movable walls. Interior elevation views indicate the method for stacking movable wall panels. Recessed storage closets may be built to conceal movable wall panels when not in use.

Demountable walls are designed to be stationary for longer periods of time than movable walls. Floor and ceiling tracks are fastened in place after ceiling, floor, and wall finishes are installed. The tracks are designed to be installed and removed with a minimal disturbance of finish materials.

Panels are set into the tracks with various designs of intermediate struts or supports. Panels may be prefinished gypsum or metal. Panels are finished with fabric, plastic laminate, prefinished metal cladding, or vinyl coatings. Electrical raceways provide for installation of receptacles for work areas and lighting.

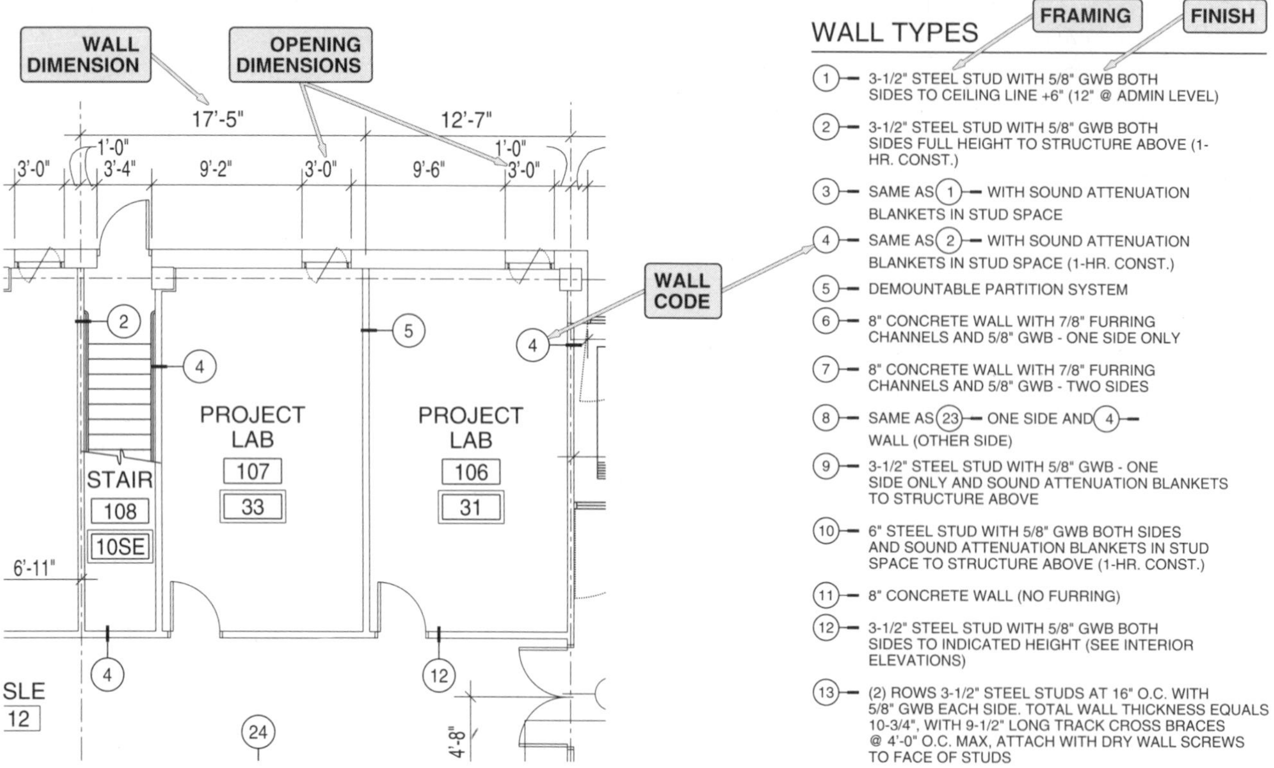

Figure 7-15. Plan views and architectural notes describe wall locations, framing and support members, and finish materials.

Figure 7-16. Sheets of gypsum drywall are hung with nails or self-tapping screws to create a surface for the application of wall finishes.

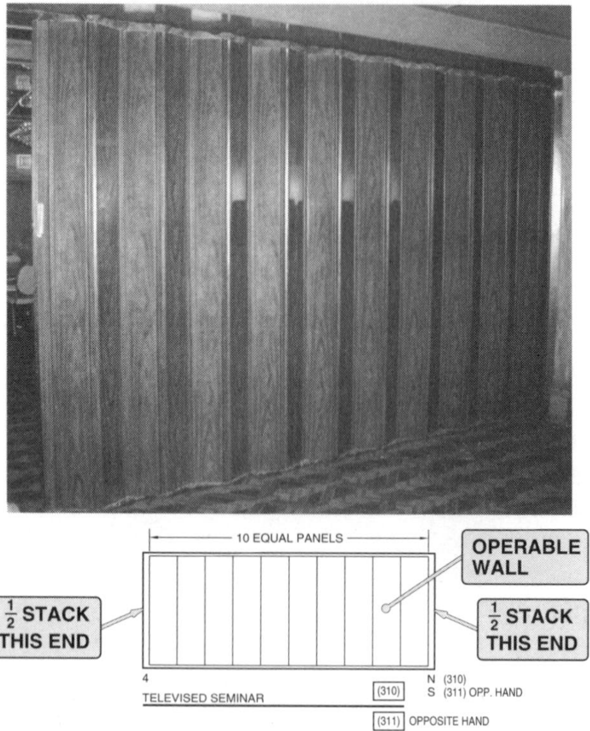

Figure 7-17. Interior elevation views of movable walls show the number of panels and the stacking plans.

Door frames may also be installed in demountable partitions. Demountable partitions may not appear on the architectural prints. Manufacturer's drawings are provided for demountable wall installation. The drawings contain plan views and details giving specific manufacturer's identification codes for panels and framing members.

Doors and Borrowed Light Frames. Interior door and light frame locations are shown on architectural plan views. The swinging direction or hand of each door is indicated along with a schedule number. The door schedule is included in the general plan notes or the written specifications. See Figure 7-18.

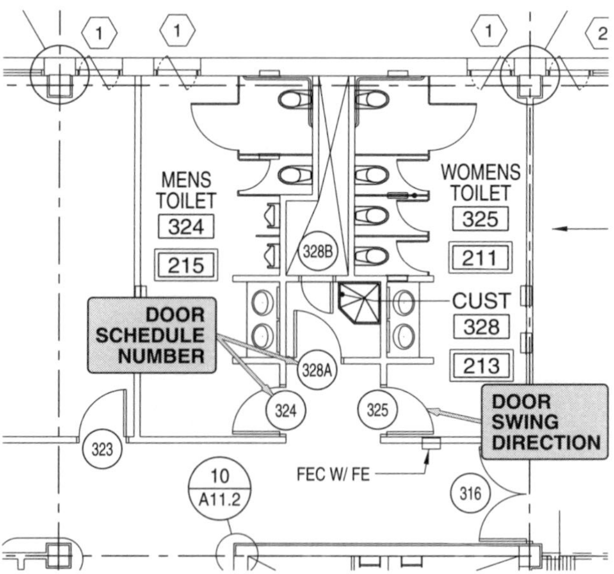

Figure 7-18. Door locations are shown on plan views along with schedule numbers cross referenced to the door schedule.

Borrowed light frames are interior windows. They may be fixed or operable. Information for borrowed light frames is provided on architectural plan views, specifications, and interior elevations in a manner similar to interior doors.

Floors

Commercial floor finishes include concrete, carpet, resilient and ceramic tile, hardwood, and raised floor systems. Each room and area on the architectural floor plan is numbered. The room number referenced in the specifications or general notes finish schedule describes the finish flooring installed. For large areas, the architect may note the floor finish on the architectural plan views. Specific detail drawings may include a note about the floor finish material at a particular location.

Concrete. Manufacturing and mechanical area floors are commonly finished with exposed concrete. Concrete slabs are troweled to a smooth finish as noted in the specifications. Super flat floors may be specified in warehouse applications where forklift or automated material handling traffic requires close floor finish tolerances for optimal operation. See Figure 7-19. Laser screed equipment is used in placing and finishing concrete for super flat floors to ensure minimal surface finish elevation variation.

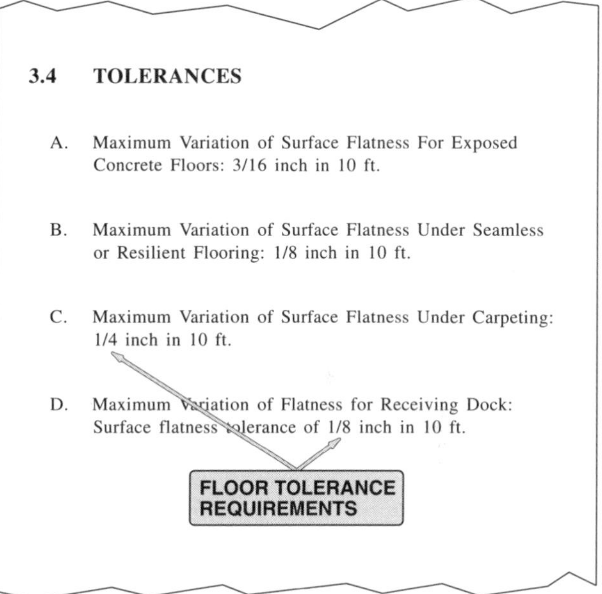

3.4 TOLERANCES

A. Maximum Variation of Surface Flatness For Exposed Concrete Floors: 3/16 inch in 10 ft.

B. Maximum Variation of Surface Flatness Under Seamless or Resilient Flooring: 1/8 inch in 10 ft.

C. Maximum Variation of Surface Flatness Under Carpeting: 1/4 inch in 10 ft.

D. Maximum Variation of Flatness for Receiving Dock: Surface flatness tolerance of 1/8 inch in 10 ft.

Figure 7-19. Exposed concrete finishes are noted in the project specifications.

Carpet. Commercial grade carpets are glued to the supporting floor or stretched across padding and fastened around the perimeter of the area. Seams are sewn or connected with heat tape. Specifications contain the schedule for carpet placement in the room finish schedule. Additional carpet information in the specifications includes the manufacturer's design, weight, backing, and installation instructions.

Tile Products. Ceramic, resilient, or vinyl tiles are installed as floor finish materials. Tile products are attached to the finished surface with mastic. For ceramic tile, grout is applied to fill the voids after mastic has set. For resilient or vinyl tile, the primary installation concern is fitting of the seams between sheets or pieces. In a manner similar to carpet, room finish schedules in the general notes or specifications contain specific tile information. Bathroom elevation prints may show ceramic tile installation dimensions when applied as a wall finish. See Figure 7-20.

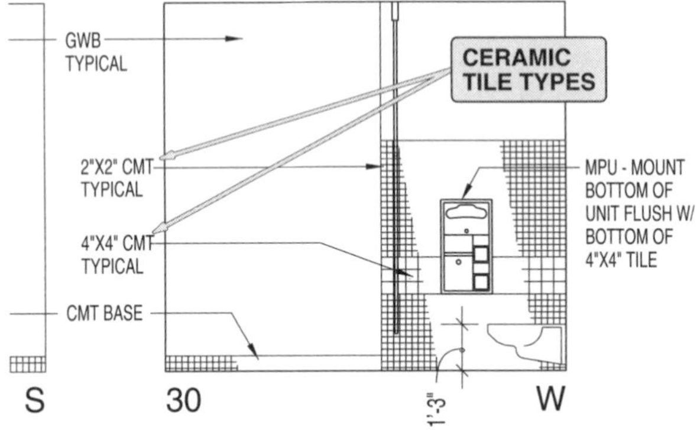

Figure 7-20. Ceramic tile sizes and locations appear on interior wall elevation prints.

Wood. Hardwood flooring of oak, maple, or other decorative woods is shown on architectural plan views. Individual interlocking pieces of hardwood are fastened to concrete with mastic or nailed to wood decking. Wood may be prefinished or sanded, stained, and finished after installation. Enlarged floor plans are provided where specific wood finishes and patterns are designed. In applications without special pattern requirements, hardwood floor information is contained in the room finish schedule.

Raised. A raised floor system is installed in areas where wiring, conduits, and ducts are installed on top of the floor deck. See Figure 7-21. A raised floor system may also be referred to as an access floor or computer floor. A raised floor system consists of base plates set in place in a regular grid layout equal to the dimensions of the raised floor panels. The bottoms of base plates are fastened to the floor deck with mastic or mechanical fasteners.

Threaded pedestals are set into the base plates and adjusted to the proper height with the aid of a rotating laser. Floor panels are then set on pedestal heads at the top of each pedestal or fastened to stringers which span between pedestal heads.

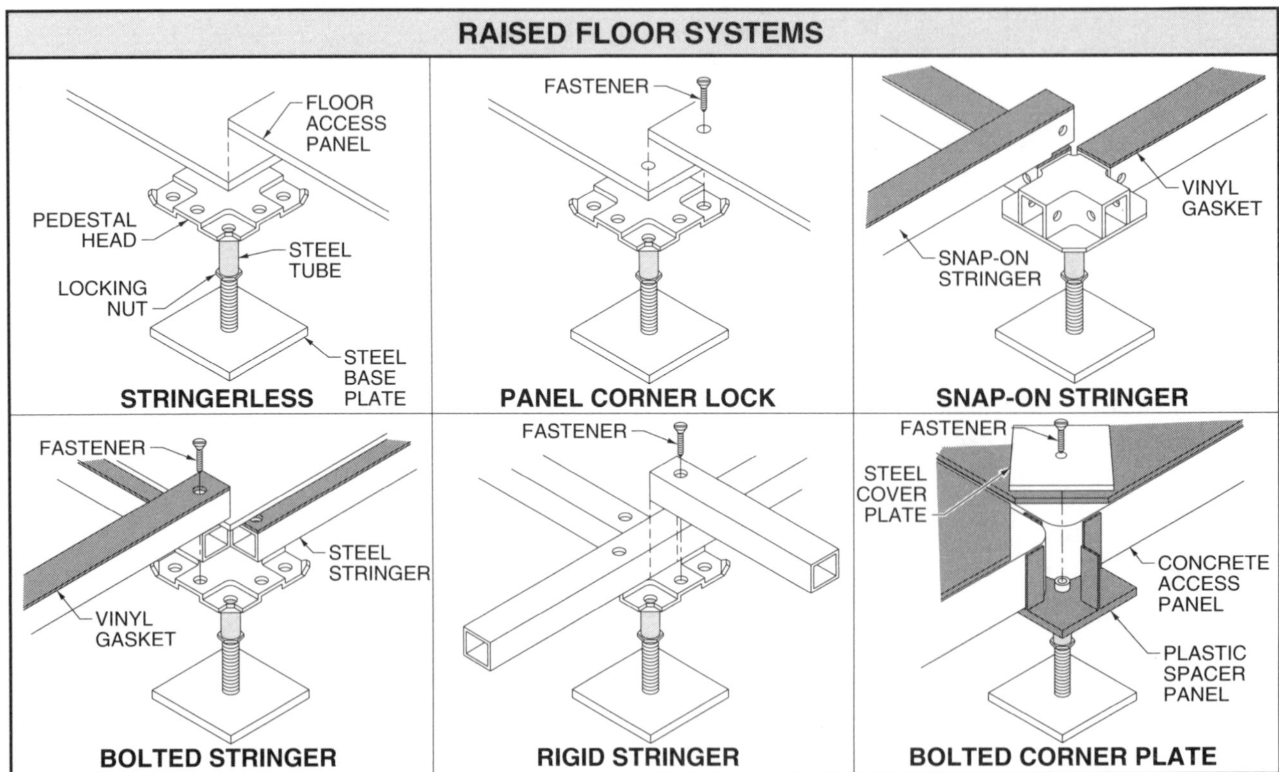

Figure 7-21. Raised floor systems facilitate the placement of and access to electrical wiring and ventilation ducts.

Raised floor panels are prefinished with carpet or tile surfaces. The area below a raised floor system may serve as a plenum for air ventilation.

Ceilings

Ceilings in commercial applications include suspended, furred, and exposed ceilings. Architectural plan views include reflected ceiling plans. See Figure 7-22. Each ceiling finish is shown with ceiling symbols. Symbols also show locations for air diffusers, exhaust fans and intakes, and ceiling-mounted lighting fixtures. Additional information concerning air diffusers and intakes is shown on the mechanical prints. Ceiling-mounted light fixtures are further described in the electrical prints. Fire sprinkler locations may also be shown on reflected ceiling plans.

Suspended Systems. Hanger wires are fastened to structural members above the finished area for suspended ceiling installation. These wires support metal gridwork of various designs.

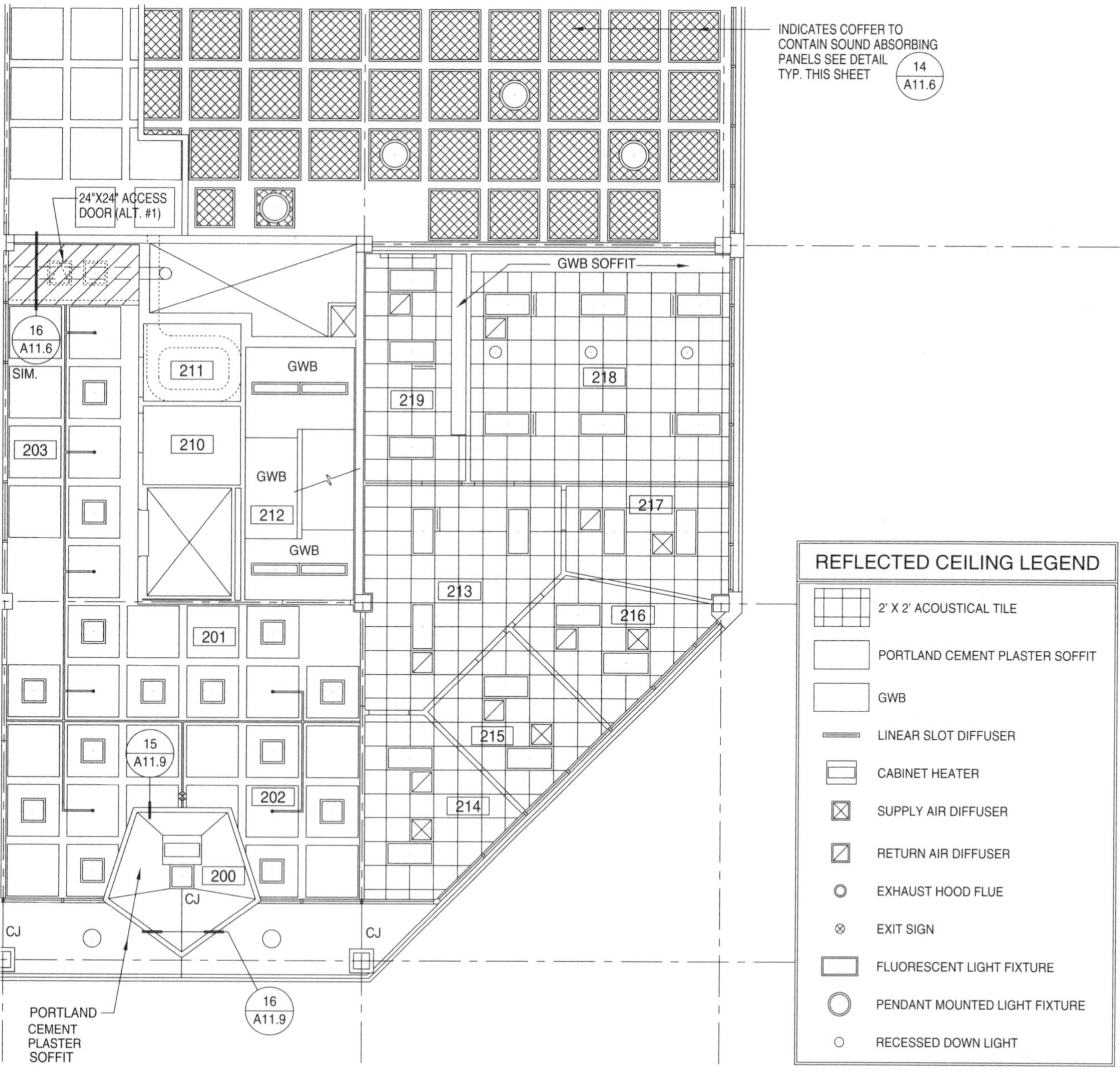

Figure 7-22. Reflected ceiling plans show all ceiling finishes, including exposed ceilings, gypsum drywall ceilings, and suspended ceilings of various designs.

Metal gridwork is designed to support lay-in tiles, concealed grid tiles, metal channels, gypsum drywall, or lath and plaster. The height of the finished ceiling surface above the floor is given on reflected ceiling plan notes or the room finish schedule in the specifications.

The height of the metal gridwork is determined after hanger wires are in place. Suspended ceiling grids are leveled with a rotating laser which projects a level beam of light around the entire space for ceiling installation. Wall channels are fastened to the interior walls around the perimeter of the area to support ceiling finish materials. See Figure 7-23. Light fixtures are set into the gridwork and additional hanger wires are installed as necessary to support the weight of the fixtures.

Figure 7-23. Suspended ceilings use a metal grid system to support tiles or other finishes.

Lay-in tiles are set into the gridwork which remains exposed. Concealed grid tiles are supported at each edge by splines which tie the tile together and hide the gridwork. Metal runners may be designed to allow for prefinished metal channels to be clipped onto the underside of the grid. Gridwork may allow for the attachment of gypsum drywall with self-tapping screws. The gypsum drywall is then finished in a manner similar to wall installations. Metal, expanded wire, or gypsum lath may be attached to the suspended gridwork to support plaster ceilings.

Furred. Ceiling runners are attached directly to structural members, such as steel bar joists or concrete beams and slabs. Runners may be wood furring strips or metal members, such as runners, studs, or hat channels. Prefinished ceiling tiles, gypsum drywall, or lath and plaster are attached to the furring members.

Where soffits and coffered ceilings are shown, framing is built to the dimensions given and attached to structural members. Detail drawings show the framing members installed, finishes applied, and dimensions provided for width and height.

Exposed. Structural steel or reinforced concrete beams, joists, and slabs may remain exposed on the underside to form the ceiling for the space below. Reflected ceiling plans indicate the locations of exposed ceiling areas. The underside of the beams, joists, and floors above may be painted, sprayed with a decorative, acoustical, or fireproofing coating, or may remain untouched. Light fixtures, sprinkler pipes, and ductwork remain open to view.

Stairs

Interior stairwells are shown on section views. Section views show landing elevations and the number of risers in each staircase. See Figure 7-24. Grid lines which relate to the overall structural building grid may be shown on stair sections. Detail drawings give specific information about stair construction, landing finishes, and finish materials for the top surface and underside of the stairs. Structural prints may provide additional stair information.

Special shop drawings are developed for areas where spiral or curving metal or wood stairs are installed. For spiral or curving wood stairs, assemblies may be prefabricated by a stair manufacturer and delivered unassembled to the job site. The stringers, treads, risers, and handrails are installed according to the manufacturer's shop drawings. Structural steel stairs may be made up at a fabrication shop and delivered to the job site as a single unit or in sections ready for assembly. Stair detail drawings show the radius of the stair curves, overall height, and number of risers when these types of finish stairs are built on the job site.

Cabinetry and Casework

Architectural symbols drawn on room plan views provide orientation for the interior elevations. Arrows or some other symbols indicate the interior walls shown on elevation prints. For example, an arrow pointing toward an interior wall with a number 19 refers to the interior elevation drawing 19. See Figure 7-25.

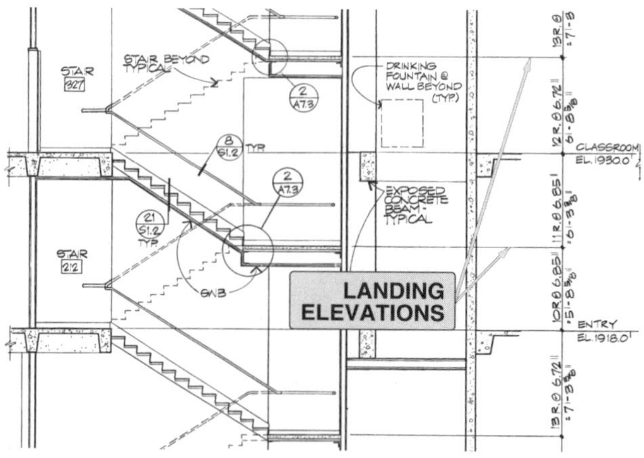

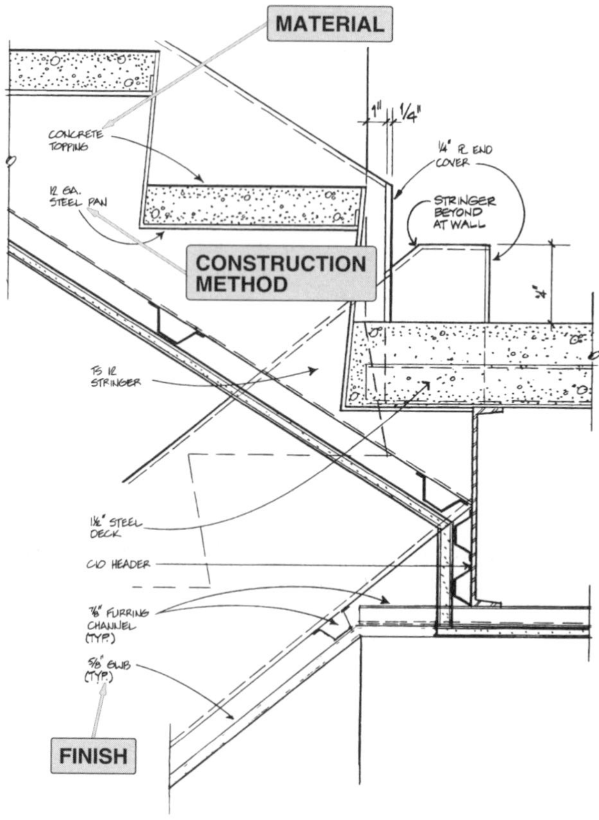

Figure 7-24. Stair elevation and section views show elevations, construction methods, materials, and finishes.

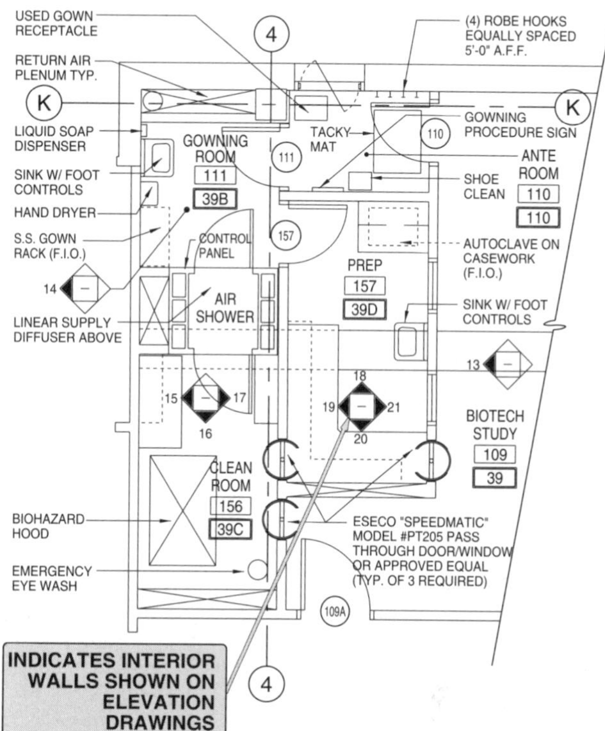

Figure 7-25. Architectural symbols drawn on room plan views provide orientation for the interior elevations.

Interior elevations and schedules provide location, dimension, and finish information for cabinetry, casework, and other interior specialties, such as chalkboards and projection screens. Architectural notes and codes on interior elevations relate to a schedule for cabinetry and casework. The schedule shows width, height, and depth of each cabinet and countertop treatment. Cabinetry may be metal, finished wood, or plastic laminate. See Figure 7-26.

Cabinet units are commonly prefabricated at a cabinet shop and delivered to the job site ready for installation. Some custom built cabinetry may be built in place. Countertops are built of particle board covered with plastic laminate or ceramic tile or made of solid surface materials. Additional interior elevation information is provided to show chalkboards, projection screens, lockers, marker boards, and miscellaneous fixtures. The size and manufacturer's code for many of these fixtures is noted in the specifications and the room finish schedule.

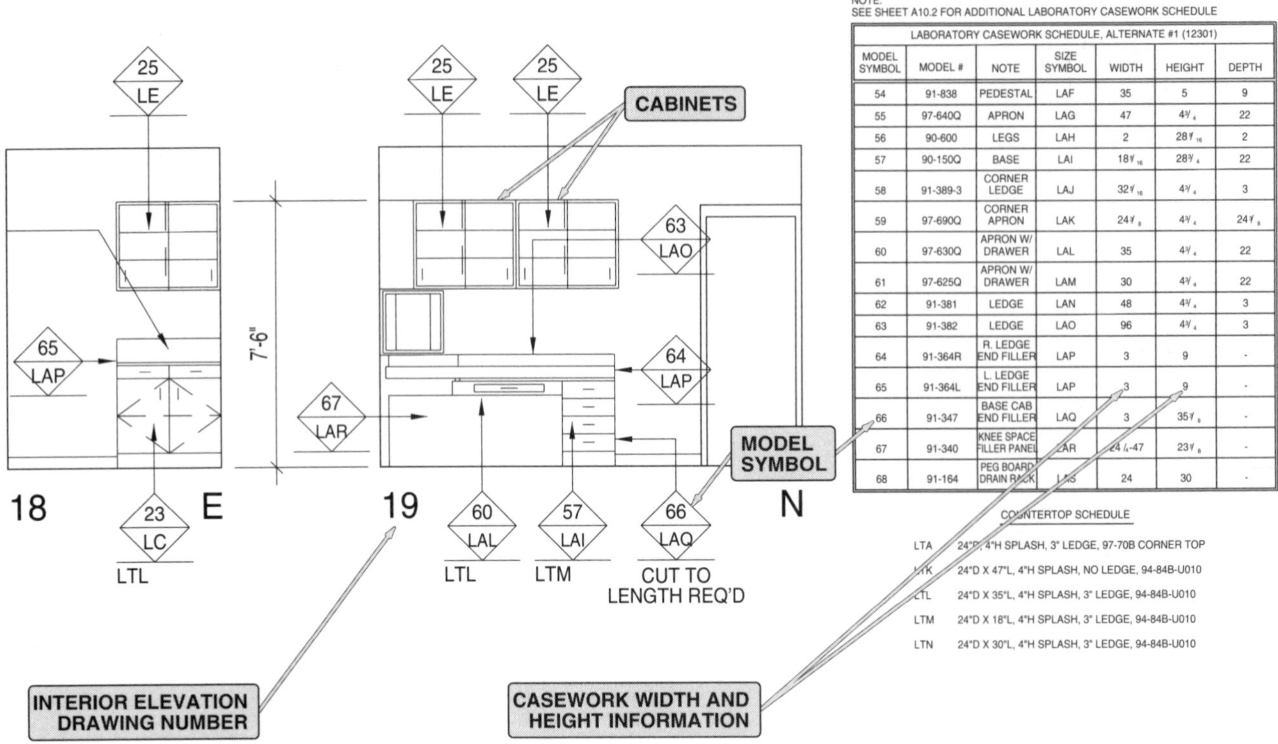

Figure 7-26. Elevation prints and schedules give cabinet and casework information, including placement, sizes, and finishes.

Review Questions

Name ____________________ Date ____________________

Printreading

T F **1.** Orthographic projections are used for exterior elevation drawings.

_______ **2.** Metal roof seams may be flat, ribbed, and _________.

T F **3.** Masonry control joints are shown on elevation drawings.

_______ **4.** A borrowed light frame is similar to an _________.

A. interior window
B. electric light fixture
C. access panel
D. exhaust grille

T F **5.** Elastomeric roofs are created by seaming together large sheets of PVC.

T F **6.** Structural steel stringers with concrete filled pan treads are used for above-grade stairs.

_______ **7.** Portland cement plaster is supported by _________.

T F **8.** A raised floor system is also referred to as a computer floor system.

_______ **9.** Glass panels are lifted and set into place with _________.

A. adhesive hangers
B. suction cups
C. padded lifters
D. padded vertical clamps

_______ **10.** Curtain walls _________.

A. integrate glass and metal panels to a single unit
B. divide large interior areas into smaller rooms
C. are similar to coiling partitions
D. are recessed above suspended ceilings

T F **11.** Metal grid members are exposed in a lay-in tile suspended ceiling.

T F **12.** Gypsum drywall may not be suspended below structural members but must be attached to furring for fire code reasons.

_______ **13.** The material to which the base coat is applied for exterior insulation and finish systems (EIFS) is _________.

A. wire mesh
B. gypsum board
C. masonry
D. expanded polystyrene

T F **14.** Light gauge metal framing members do not allow for the placement of insulation batts.

T F **15.** Demountable wall sections are installed after all other wall, floor, and ceiling finishes are in place.

_______ **16.** Bituminous materials are used on _________ roofs.

A. built-up
B. elastomeric
C. decorative metal
D. sheet metal

__________ **17.** A sheet which is placed inside a concrete form to create a decorative finish is a(n) _________.

__________ **18.** Movable wall sections are supported by _________.

A. structural columns
B. a track at the ceiling line
C. rollers at the floor level
D. wall hinges

T F **19.** Architectural plan views note the material for each door, e.g., wood or metal.

__________ **20.** Floor finish information, such as types of carpet and tile, are most likely found _________.

A. on elevation views
B. on architectural plan views
C. in the specifications
D. on enlarged plan views

__________ **21.** Raised floor system tiles are supported by _________.

A. pedestals
B. mastic
C. metal furring channel
D. precast concrete

__________ **22.** Concrete members which remain exposed and are rubbed or finished to a specific surface texture are _________ concrete.

T F **23.** Portland cement plaster is applied in a single coat, one-step operation.

T F **24.** Masonry veneer walls are not anchored to structural members.

__________ **25.** A concrete floor installed in a warehouse with automated mechanical material handling equipment must meet close tolerances and is referred to as a(n) _________.

__________ **26.** Ceilings in commercial applications may be _________.

A. suspended
B. furred
C. exposed
D. A, B, and C

T F **27.** Exterior insulation and finish systems incorporate insulation board and polymer-based materials into an exterior finish.

__________ **28.** Large commercial building roofs may be made of _________.

A. bituminous coatings
B. metal
C. elastomeric coatings
D. A, B, and C

T F **29.** The surfaces of metal stud framed walls may be finished with gypsum drywall, plaster, or brick veneer.

T F **30.** Commercial floor finishes include concrete, carpet, resilient and ceramic tile, hardwood, and raised floor systems.

Trade Competency Test

Name____ Date ________________

Riverpoint

Refer to Sheet 25. Note: *Cross-referencing between sheets is required to answer several questions.*

T F **1.** Door 248A connects the slide resource room and the men's toilet.

T F **2.** The roof on the circular classroom slopes from a high point on the north to a low point on the south.

__________ **3.** The second floor plan north shows _________ roof drains.

__________ **4.** The abbreviation C.G. to the south of grid line 3 between grid lines F and G indicates _________.

A. cleanout grids
B. corner guards
C. ceramic glazed tile
D. compressed gas

T F **5.** There is a sink in the janitor's closet room 247.

__________ **6.** Additional information about stair 5 is found on drawing sheet _________.

A. A7.1
B. A8.7
C. A9.4
D. A11.7 drawing 110

T F **7.** There are two liquid marker boards in room 254.

__________ **8.** When checking the interior room finish schedule, the room number for the design studio is _________.

T F **9.** The sizes of the tackboard and the liquid marker board on the north wall of room 254 are equal.

__________ **10.** Detail information concerning the shelving in room 260 is located on _________.

A. typical wall detail drawing 2H
B. typical wall detail drawing 3H
C. detail 50 sheet A12.5
D. detail 28 sheet 12.8

T F **11.** There are no exterior windows in conference room 262.

__________ **12.** The abbreviation DF in hall 252 indicates a(n) _________.

__________ **13.** The dashed line with the notation 3/A9.3 at stair 1 indicates _________.

A. a recessed floor area
B. hidden fire sprinkler piping
C. a fire wall
D. an enlarged drawing view

T F **14.** Office 266 is the only office on the second floor without built-in shelving.

__________ **15.** There are _________ tackable wall panels between doors 253 and 254.

Refer to Sheet 26.

T F **1.** Room 127 has exposed ducts.

T F **2.** Room 126 has a drywall ceiling.

__________ **3.** Dashed lines around the perimeter of room 152 indicate a(n) _________.

__________ **4.** The ceiling in room 149 is _________.

A. exposed concrete dome pan slab
B. suspended acoustical ceiling tile
C. GWB ceiling
D. hardwood panels

T F **5.** Room 122 has both fluorescent and recessed incandescent light fixtures.

__________ **6.** There is/are _________ sprinkler head(s) in room 136.

__________ **7.** There are _________ supply air diffusers in the ceiling of room 147.

T F **8.** The metal partition between rooms 132 and 133 is full height and fastened directly to the waffle slab above.

T F **9.** The circle at the intersection of grid lines 4 and G on the ceiling plan denotes a concrete column.

__________ **10.** The abbreviation AFF in the ceiling plan of room 125 indicates _________.

T F **11.** Light fixtures in room 100A are recessed above the suspended ceiling.

__________ **12.** The height of the soffit in room 136 above the finished floor is _________.

Refer to Sheet 27.

T F **1.** There are four horizontal control joints in the brick veneer on the south elevation.

__________ **2.** The difference in elevations between the floors are all equal at _________.

T F **3.** There are exposed concrete beams and columns on the north elevation.

__________ **4.** The predominant second floor exterior finish material is _________ on the south exterior elevation.

A. architectural concrete
B. portland cement plaster
C. precast concrete
D. brick veneer

__________ **5.** The typical center-to-center spacing for concrete form snap ties is _________.

T F **6.** There are seven doors shown on the south elevation.

__________ **7.** The exterior finish of the wall between grid lines C and D is _________ on the north exterior elevation.

A. architectural concrete
B. portland cement plaster
C. precast concrete
D. brick veneer

__________ **8.** The elevation of the penthouse floor level is _________′.

T F **9.** Control joints on the south exterior elevation brick veneer are placed at the concrete columns.

T F **10.** Lintels above windows on the brick veneer walls are precast concrete.

__________ **11.** The difference in elevation between the finished first floor level and the top of the brick veneer service yard screen wall is ________.

T F **12.** Section cut M on sheet A8.8 is used to see the exterior elevation of the circular portion of the building hidden from view on the north elevation.

Refer to Sheet 28.

T F **1.** The exterior soffit system at the first floor level is a suspended soffit.

__________ **2.** The roof finish is ________.

A. bituminous built-up roofing
B. elastomeric roofing
C. metal roofing
D. unsure without roof plan

__________ **3.** The thickness of the drywall on the inside of the first floor north wall is ________″.

T F **4.** The exterior of the first floor north wall between columns D and E is portland cement plaster.

__________ **5.** According to the wall section drawings of the north wall, spacing for metal studs in exterior walls is ________″ on center.

T F **6.** Interior window sills for the windows on the first floor between columns D and E are made of treated 2 × 4s.

__________ **7.** Curtain wall frames in the north wall are made of ________.

__________ **8.** The first floor brick veneer north wall is backed up by ________.

A. poured concrete
B. wood framing
C. metal studs
D. rigid insulation

__________ **9.** The height of the parapet wall above the concrete roof deck is ________.

T F **10.** The depth of the exterior architectural concrete reveal joints is given on structural sheet 1.2 detail 7.

__________ **11.** The offset between the face of the brick veneer north wall first floor and the concrete caps covering the exterior floor rigid insulation is ________″.

Refer to Sheet 29.

T F **1.** The height of the built-in desktop in room 254 is 2′-6″.

T F **2.** There are no exposed ducts in the design studio.

__________ **3.** The distance between the top of the base cabinets and the bottom of the wall cabinets on the south wall of the design studio is ________.

__________ **4.** The wall finish for the gypsum drywall walls in room 257 is ________.

A. painted
B. wood veneer paneling
C. thin coat plaster
D. brick veneer

T F 5. Maple is used for veneer work on the third floor corridors.

__________ 6. Countertops in the design resource room are finished with _________.

T F 7. The opening frame to the right of grid line F on interior elevation 105 in room 257 is an outside window frame.

__________ 8. The height to the top of the tackboard in room 254 is _________.

__________ 9. The interior of the outside wall on the west side of hallway 252 is _________.

A. gypsum drywall
B. wood veneer paneling
C. thin coat plaster
D. brick veneer

__________ 10. The door at the far right of the drawing is the entry door for room _________ on interior elevation 105 in room 257.

T F 11. The height of the handrails above the landing in the design studio stair is 3′-0″.

__________ 12. On interior elevation 106 in room 257, the door at the far right of the drawing is the entry door for _________.

Refer to Sheet 30.

T F 1. Airspace distances between brick veneer walls and backing structures are not all equal.

T F 2. A layer of building paper is applied between brick veneer and exterior metal stud framed walls.

__________ 3. Nominal thickness of the curtain wall metal framing which attaches to the underside of the overhanging roof deck on the north wall is _________″.

T F 4. The windows on the first floor of the north wall between grid lines G and H are recessed from the face of the concrete foundation wall 9⅝″.

T F 5. The thickness of the insulation above the exterior brick veneer wall on the first floor of the north elevation is 12″.

__________ 6. The dimensions of the chamfer installed around window openings is _________ on exterior architectural concrete.

A. ⅜″ × ⅜″
B. ⅜″ × ½″
C. ⅜″ × ¾″
D. ¾″ × ¾″

__________ 7. The thickness of the reinforced concrete member covering the exterior floor slab insulation is _________″.

T F 8. Where interior gypsum wall covering meet exposed concrete columns, they are finished with a casing bead and sealant.

T F 9. Where window openings are formed in the first floor north concrete wall, the outside sill of the opening is sloped away from the window ¼″.

T F 10. Brick veneer walls are finished with brick coming to within ½″ of concrete columns.

__________ 11. Batt insulation in exterior walls has an R rating of _________.

CHAPTER 8

Final Test

Name ______________________________ Date ______________

Riverpoint

Refer to Sheets 2, 31, 32, 33, 34, 35, 36, 37, 38, 39, 40, 41, and 42.

T F **1.** The two storm drain pipes which flow into catch basin 10 are of equal diameter.

T F **2.** The distance between the project northern building wall and the main storm drain line on the project northern side of the building is 8″.

_________ **3.** The closest grid point to the second floor drinking fountain is _________.

_________ **4.** The thickness of the roof insulation on the second floor plan south between grid lines G and H and south of grid line 8 is _________″.

T F **5.** The building lot generally slopes downward towards the north.

_________ **6.** The small squares throughout the vestibule area indicate _________.

A. square suspended ceiling tiles
B. ceramic square tiles
C. slate paving tiles
D. construction joints

_________ **7.** The parapet cap on the circular classroom is _________.

A. limestone
B. precast concrete
C. CMU
D. shown on the partial West elevation section at the courtyard

T F **8.** The connection of the storm drains to the city sewer system is made at catch basin #1.

_________ **9.** The dimension from the floor to the bottom of the tackboard in room 207 is _________.

_________ **10.** There are _________ equal sized base cabinets on the east wall of the teaching computer lab room 209.

_________ **11.** The height of the countertop in room 209 at grid point K6 is _________.

T F **12.** The reinforced concrete column shown on the partial West elevation is outside of the doors and windows shown.

T F **13.** All windows on the North and West courtyard elevations have precast concrete sills.

T F **14.** There is no basement under the first floor circular classroom.

_________ **15.** The height to the bottom of the soffit at the north wall of room 229 is _________.

T F **16.** On the North elevation, the column at building line E is offset at the third floor elevation.

_________ **17.** The two squares with Xs to the north of the seminar room 225 indicate _________.

A. elevators
B. air ducts
C. service drain tubs
D. electrical conduit chases

T F **18.** The width of each of the nine louvers on the north elevation is 8′-0″.

_________ **19.** There are _________ shelf standards on the east wall of the chair's office room 238.

_________ **20.** The shelves in the chair's office room 238 require _________ shelf brackets.

_________ **21.** The wall finish on the east wall of the chair's office room 238 is _________.

A. exposed concrete
B. brick veneer
C. painted gypsum drywall
D. fabric covered gypsum drywall

_________ **22.** Column B6 in the chair's office room 238 is _________.

A. left exposed
B. wrapped with metal studs and gypsum drywall
C. covered with gypsum wallboard and fabric
D. shown on wall detail 1A

_________ **23.** On sheet A11.6, the door on interior elevation 76 enters a(n) _________.

A. office
B. closet
C. hallway
D. stairwell

T F **24.** There is a construction joint in exterior concrete walls at each column grid line.

T F **25.** The concrete snap tie locations are commonly 2′-0″ on center.

_________ **26.** The wall between the open computer lab 207 and the teaching computer lab 209 on which the liquid marker board is mounted is built of _________.

A. metal studs and drywall
B. materials which are only shown on detail 6A
C. wood studs and drywall
D. demountable partition sections

T F **27.** There is no basement below the first floor at wall section I.

_________ **28.** On interior elevation sheet A11.6 drawing 76, the cabinetry is finished with _________.

A. varnished wood veneer
B. painted particle board
C. painted wood veneer
D. plastic laminate

_________ **29.** On sheet A11.6 interior elevation 77, the irregular wall line on the right side wall indicates _________.

A. shelving
B. recessed cabinetry
C. a window
D. a marker board

T F **30.** On wall section J, the interior wall finish at elevation 1950′ is exposed masonry.

_________ **31.** On sheet A11.6, the concrete column on interior elevation 74 is located at the intersection of grid line 6 and grid line _________.

T F **32.** On wall section J, batt insulation is placed between the cast-in-place concrete wall sections and the interior brick wall finish.

T F **33.** On wall section J, all ceilings are exposed concrete.

_________ **34.** Detail information concerning the guardrails around the openings in the second floor lobby is found on sheet _________.

________ **35.** The note 1A SB in corridor 203 notes ________.

A. wall type 1A with a sound batten
B. wall type 1A with solid brick
C. receptacle type 1A with a safety barrier
D. switch type 1A with single bypass

________ **36.** The width of the marker board in student room 210 is ________′.

A. 3
B. 4
C. 5
D. 6

T F **37.** There are three waterproof receptacles on the third floor outside wall along grid line K.

T F **38.** Isolated ground receptacles on the third floor are powered by panel P2-3F7-1.

T F **39.** Details of the construction of the seismic joint are found on sheet A12.1.

________ **40.** The outside of the first floor circular classroom is finished with ________.

A. architectural concrete
B. brick veneer
C. stone veneer
D. plaster

T F **41.** The South elevation/section drawing indicates an open web structural steel joist construction.

________ **42.** Where the top level roof slab joins the exterior poured concrete south and east walls, steel reinforcing bars are overlapped a distance of ________.

________ **43.** The distance from the top of the parapet wall to the top of the third floor projecting balcony roof on the south and east walls is ________.

T F **44.** There are two isolated ground receptacles in conference room 316.

T F **45.** The receptacles in the chair's office room 362 are on two separate circuits.

T F **46.** There are five receptacles in corridor 304.

________ **47.** The existing grade on Riverpoint Boulevard at the northern entrance drive is ________′.

________ **48.** The radius of the curve shown on C2.1 for Trent Avenue is ________′.

A. 190.52
B. 584.25
C. 650.00
D. not shown

T F **49.** Fluorescent light fixtures in AV storage room 314 are recessed above the ceiling.

________ **50.** The three concentric ovals with the numbers 1918, 1919, and 1920 on the southwest side of the building on C2.1 indicate ________.

A. storm drains
B. catch basins
C. a depressed area in the grade
D. a small mound

T F **51.** The light fixtures in room 328 have 3″ deep 32-cell louvers.

T F **52.** The main circuit breaker on panelboard P2-3F7-1 has a higher circuit rating than the main circuit breaker on panelboard P2-3F7-2.

________ **53.** The slab shown on the project east side of the building on C2.1 has a total downward slope at the north and south corners of ________″.

________ **54.** On the project south side of the building, the difference in elevation between the first floor finish floor and the finish grade is ________″.

T F **55.** The lights in room 346 are controlled by 3-way switches.

_________ **56.** Storm water from the south side of the building flows into catch basin _________.

A. 2A
B. 4
C. 7
D. 10

_________ **57.** The total area of each louver on the south elevation/section – courtyard is _________sq ft.

T F **58.** There are 10 light fixtures in the faculty lounge room 364.

T F **59.** There are six exterior windows in teaching computer lab 209.

T F **60.** On A3.10, the elevation of the drain inlets for the small south roof sections is equal to the finish floor elevation.

_________ **61.** On S4.2 section 1, the outside dimension of the tubular steel which reinforces the third floor exterior metal framed wall between the columns is _________″.

_________ **62.** The diameter of the water supply pipe to the toilet in room 344 is _________″.

T F **63.** Office 232 is the only office on the second floor plan south with a closet.

_________ **64.** Brick veneer walls are capped with _________.

A. precast concrete
B. stone
C. brick soldier course
D. poured-in-place concrete

T F **65.** The walls between offices 212/213 and 220/221 are identical.

T F **66.** Office 234 has no exterior window.

T F **67.** There is no concrete column at grid point D5.

_________ **68.** The finish of the second floor at wall section I is _________.

A. exposed concrete
B. vinyl tile
C. carpet
D. ceramic tile

_________ **69.** On the South elevation/section – courtyard, the distance from the rustication joint at elevation 1933.75′ to the top of the concrete wall supporting the second story windows is _________.

T F **70.** The liquid marker board on the west wall of room 209 is centered between door 209C and the adjacent south wall.

_________ **71.** The percent of slope of all roof drain piping is _________%.

T F **72.** Door 209B has a glass panel at the west side.

T F **73.** There is a gypsum wallboard soffit on the south wall of room 229.

_________ **74.** On M2.9, the abbreviation VTR in room 316 means _________.

T F **75.** The four marker boards in rooms 225, 226, 227, and 228 are all of equal sizes.

_________ **76.** At wall section I, the first floor ceiling is _________.

A. exposed concrete
B. gypsum drywall
C. suspended acoustical tiles
D. plaster

_________ **77.** The height of the wall-mounted fixture on the north wall of the southeast stairwell near grid line intersection K7 is _________′.

T F **78.** The tackboard sizes are equal in student lounge 227 and 240.

_________ **79.** The interior of the basement wall at wall section J is covered with _________.

A. ½″ gypsum wall board
B. ⅝″ gypsum wall board
C. exposed masonry
D. exposed concrete

_________ **80.** Detail information concerning the depth of the rustication joints is obtained on sheet _________.

_________ **81.** The slope on the small roof deck on sheet A3.10 between grid lines H and J and south of grid line 8 is _________″ per foot.

_________ **82.** On the roof section on A3.10 between grid lines B and C and south of grid line 8, the difference in elevation between the overflow drain and the roof drain is _________″.

_________ **83.** On the partial West elevation/section–courtyard, the material used for window frames on the nine small windows at the left of the elevation is _________.

A. brick
B. precast concrete
C. aluminum
D. wood

T F **84.** The concrete columns shown on interior elevations 85 and 87 are actually the same column from two different views.

T F **85.** Hooked steel reinforcing bars which tie the third floor south concrete wall into the top level roof concrete slab are held back from the face of the wall a minimum of ¾″.

_________ **86.** The difference in height between a standard water closet and a handicapped water closet is _________″.

_________ **87.** On M2.9, in room 342 the abbreviation COIW indicates a(n) _________.

T F **88.** Brick veneer is tied to the concrete slabs at each floor level with a 4″ × 3″ × ¼″ steel angle.

_________ **89.** The maximum heating air supply to box 106 is _________ cfm.

T F **90.** The spacing of metal framing angle braces above the third floor south windows is 4′-0″ on center.

T F **91.** There is no first floor balcony on the east side of the building at grid line K.

_________ **92.** The main circuit breaker for panel P4-3F7 has a capacity of _________ A.

_________ **93.** The home run wiring for lighting from the junction box in room 313 has _________ conductors.

T F **94.** For poured-in-place concrete stair landings, the diameter and spacing of the lower reinforcing bars is ½″, 12″ on center.

T F **95.** Where reinforcing bars are hooked to tie foundation walls and footings together, all hooks are turned towards the outside of the building.

T F **96.** In hallway 304, the drinking fountain is supplied with a 1¼″ cold water supply line.

_________ **97.** The maximum cooling of the terminal unit located in room 112 is _________ cfm.

T F **98.** On the east wall at grid line K, brick veneer is anchored to the concrete slab at the second floor slab level with 4″ × 3″ × ¼″ angle fillet welded to 4″ × 5″ steel plate shims welded to Type C embeds.

T F **99.** The sink in room 364 has a garbage disposal unit installed.

T F **100.** The water closet in room 315 is mounted on the floor.

T F **101.** Plumbing hookups for a refrigerator-installed ice maker are provided in room 364.

_________ **102.** On M3.4, the note AHU-4 in the circular classroom refers to _________.

T F **103.** The sinks in rooms 315 and 316A share a common set of shut-off valves.

T F **104.** At wall section J, the parapet wall is constructed of metal framing with brick veneer.

T F **105.** At the top of stair landings, steel stringers are supported by a $\frac{3}{16}''$ steel plate cast into the concrete stair landing.

_________ **106.** The maximum heating cfm supplied by the terminal unit in room 106 is _________ cfm.

_________ **107.** The ceiling light fixture in room 310 receives _________ fluorescent light bulbs.

_________ **108.** On S4.2 section 4, the distance from the face of the brick veneer to the face of the raised floor slab is _________″.

_________ **109.** On sheet E2.6, the notation to the right of the circular classroom which reads $\frac{3}{4}''$, 2 #10, 1#10G is interpreted as a(n) _________.

_________ **110.** The diameter of the roof drain lines in the southeast stairwell is _________″.

_________ **111.** The sink in room 316A is _________.

A. stainless steel
B. vitreous china
C. terrazzo with a stainless steel cap
D. polished brass

_________ **112.** Circuit 1 of panel P2-3F7-2 has _________ receptacles.

T F **113.** Corridor lighting and emergency lighting for the third floor south is provided on panel P4-3F7 on circuits 7, 9, and 11.

T F **114.** All roof drain lines are routed to drain down through the chase in the southwest stairwell.

T F **115.** The sink in room 315 is provided with a vandal-proof faucet.

_________ **116.** The diameter of the floor drain in room 310 is _________″.

A. 3
B. 4
C. 6
D. there is no floor drain in room 310

_________ **117.** The 1″ diameter pipe in hallway 302 to the south of room 357 is for _________.

A. cold water
B. hot water
C. waste vent
D. waste pipe

_________ **118.** The minimum throat dimension for concrete stairs on structural fill is _________″.

_________ **119.** The diameter of the waste pipes down from the water closet in room 344 is _________″.

_________ **120.** The line in the west side of room 349 with a notation of 2″ indicates a _________ pipe.

A. cold water
B. hot water
C. waste vent
D. waste

_________ **121.** On sheet E2.6, the abbreviation GFI in alcove 316A refers to a(n) _________.

_________ **122.** There are _________ smoke dampers on the third floor.

T F **123.** All water closets on the third floor are handicapped accessible.

T F **124.** The east and west stairwells along grid line 7 have no air returns at the first floor level.

_________ **125.** The vent pipe for the sink in room 346 is _________.

A. 1¼″
B. 1½″
C. 3″
D. manufacturer type #8714

_________ **126.** The diameter of the air supply duct to stairwell 100A is _________″.

_________ **127.** The weld symbol on detail 25 on sheet S1.4 is read as _________.

_________ **128.** The distance from the exterior face of the east second floor stairwell to grid line J is _________.

_________ **129.** The piping in hallway 102 indicates a hydronic system with a _________-pipe system.

A. one
B. two
C. three
D. four

T F **130.** The thermostat for room 108 is located near the north entry door into the room.

T F **131.** Room 107 has no direct air supply duct but relies on flow through return air for temperature control.

_________ **132.** The second floor concrete slab elevation at the intersection of grid lines E.4 and 6 is _________′.

_________ **133.** The air flowing into the 18″ × 18″ return air duct in the south of room 109 is circulated _________.

A. to room 108 through 56″ × 2″ insulated duct
B. to terminal unit 66
C. upward through the chase at the north of room 113
D. downward through the chase at the north of room 113

_________ **134.** There are _________ electrical receptacles in storage room 314.

_________ **135.** The receptacles on the north walls of offices 319 through 322 are served at panel number P2-3F7-2 on circuit number _________.

_________ **136.** Supply air for room 112 is circulated through the chase at the _________.

A. south of hallway 103
B. north of room 111
C. north of room 113
D. north of room 115

T F **137.** Terminal unit 64 is controlled by a thermostat in room 121/123.

T F **138.** Terminal unit 103 in room 116 has a 16″ × 16″ air inflow pipe and two air outflow pipes of 10″ in diameter and 12″ in diameter.

_________ **139.** The width of each balcony section on the south wall of the second floor framing plan is _________.

_________ **140.** The center-to-center spacing for the steel bar joists on the circular classroom roof is _________.

_________ **141.** Heating and cooling for room 119 is supplied by terminal unit _________.

_________ **142.** On sheet M3.4, the triangle with the number 3 in east stairwell 103A indicates the type of _________.

A. diffuser
B. smoke damper
C. fan
D. thermostat

_________ **143.** The distance from the face of the second floor exterior wall parallel to grid line E between grid lines 5 and 6 to the center of column E.4-5.7 is _________.

T F **144.** The 40″ × 4″ type 9 supply air diffuser for room 123 is supplied by the 14″ × 12″ supply pipe at the north side of hallway 103.

_________ **145.** The three third floor electrical panels are located in room _________.

_________ **146.** The thickness of the parapet wall along the south wall of the building is _________″.

_________ **147.** Detail drawings concerning the second floor slab reinforcing steel are found on sheet _________.

_________ **148.** The type of cable used for motorized screen switches on the third floor is _________.

A. two conductor with ground wire
B. three conductor with ground wire
C. four conductor with ground wire
D. not shown

_________ **149.** Electrical power is provided to the third floor by conduit through the floor near the intersection of grid lines _________.

A. C7
B. F6
C. F7
D. G7

T F **150.** The smoke damper in the ductwork of corridor 303 is powered from panel P2-3F7-2 on circuit number 40.

_________ **151.** On S4.2 section 1, the projection of the poured-in-place concrete shade screen above the third floor balconies slopes _________″ at the top to drain water away from the building.

_________ **152.** The abbreviation PDF at the third floor ceiling line on S4.2 section 1 means _________.

_________ **153.** On sheet E3.6, light fixtures which are shaded half light and half dark on an angle denote _________.

A. switching configuration
B. four lamps
C. dimmer switches
D. battery backup

T F **154.** Office 319 has the same lighting installation as office 309.

T F **155.** Room 108 and room 121 are both served by the same air handler.

_________ **156.** The most typical fixture used in third floor corridors is F _________.

_________ **157.** In reference to catch basin #2A, the abbreviation IE stands for _________.

_________ **158.** The overall drop in elevation in the storm drain pipe between catch basin #2A and catch basin #2 is _________′.

_________ **159.** Panelboard P4-3F7 is located in room _________.

T F **160.** The lights in conference room 342 are all incandescent.

T F **161.** The vertical dashed line through the center of wall section J indicates concrete reinforcing.

T F **162.** Steel stair stringers are fastened to concrete slabs with ¾″ expansion bolts.

_________ **163.** In the dean's office room 311, there is a switching arrangement which allows for _________.

A. dimming of the fluorescent fixtures
B. turning ON half of the fixtures in banks of north or south from the south door
C. turning ON half of the fixtures in banks of north or south from the west door
D. turning ON half of the fixtures in banks of north or south from either the south or west doors

_________ **164.** The notation 17 LF 12″ SD between catch basin #7 and catch basin #8 is read as _________.

_________ **165.** The highest amount of parking lot slope shown on C2.1 is _________%.

_________ **166.** Lowercase letters such as a, b, c are used on sheet E3.6 to denote _________.

A. type of light fixtures
B. switching arrangements
C. number of bulbs per fixture
D. type of connecting cables

_________ **167.** Based on C2.1, the elevation to the top of the curb at the southeast corner of the parking lot on the north side of the building is _________′.

T F **168.** Where steel open web joists are supported by the masonry walls for the circular classroom, they are fastened to ¾″ steel plates with ¼″ fillet welds which are 4″ long.

T F **169.** The overall height of the steel open web joists for the penthouse is 12″.

_________ **170.** The third floor finish elevation is _________′.

_________ **171.** Where top tracks for metal stud walls must be spliced, the length of the splice piece is _________″.

T F **172.** Where non-bearing stud walls are not built full height to the floor above and are braced to the structure above, braces are placed 4′-0″ on center and made of 3″ × 3″ × ¼″ angle.

_________ **173.** The horizontal distance between control joints on the partial west elevation is _________.

_________ **174.** Steel joists in the central portion of the circular classroom are supported on the north end by a _________.

A. concrete beam
B. steel girder
C. masonry wall
D. concrete slab

_________ **175.** The depth of the corrugations for the roof deck on the circular classroom is _________″.

A. ½
B. 1
C. 1½
D. 2

_________ **176.** The height of the exterior handrail along the ramp on the north side of room 105 is _________.

_________ **177.** The elevation of the highest point of the building walls on the north elevation is _________′.

_________ **178.** The outside diameter of the circular classroom is _________.

T F **179.** No. 6 wafer-head screws are used for metal stud framing attachments.

T F **180.** The typical spacing of intermediate fasteners for the exterior ½″ gypsum sheathing applied to structural studs on wall section J is 16″.

__________ **181.** The thickness of the concrete sunscreens on the windows on the South elevation/section – courtyard at grid line E is _________″.

__________ **182.** From grid line 5 to grid line 6, the circular classroom roof has a total slope of _________″.

A. $11\frac{1}{4}$
B. $12\frac{7}{8}$
C. 18
D. $39\frac{1}{2}$

T F **183.** At column C8, the notation 8#4×128H means an 8′ by 4′ mat of reinforcing bars 128″ long of high strength steel.

T F **184.** The parapet wall along grid line K is exposed poured concrete.

T F **185.** The third floor exterior balcony wall on S4.2 section 1 is secured to the slab with a $2\frac{1}{2}$″ × $2\frac{1}{2}$″ piece of welded tubular steel to a Type F embed.

__________ **186.** The thickness of the foundation wall at grid line K is _________″.

__________ **187.** At wall section I, the perimeter slab insulation extends in from the inside face of the foundation wall a minimum of _________.

__________ **188.** On the south elevation/section – courtyard, the distance from the first floor window sills to the bottom of the sunscreen is _________.

T F **189.** The seismic joint is located at grid line 5.

__________ **190.** At wall section J, the amount of slope on the first floor concrete sills is _________″.

__________ **191.** The thickness of the concrete walls at elevation 1935′ on wall section J is _________″.

T F **192.** The second floor windows on either side of the stairwell at grid line intersection K and 7 are of equal width.

T F **193.** The notation E3 on the second floor framing plan indicates that two 1″ diameter reinforcing bars are placed in two joists in each strip noted.

__________ **194.** The steel gauge for the pans on steel stair bases is #_________.

__________ **195.** Handrail posts are embedded in concrete curbs to a depth of _________.

__________ **196.** The typical projection from the face of a wall to the outside of a pipe handrail fastened to the wall is _________″.

T F **197.** There are no domes placed in the second floor slab adjacent to concrete columns.

T F **198.** The second floor slab surrounding columns B8 and J6 have similar steel reinforcing bar patterns.

__________ **199.** The overall length of the steel lintel at a 5′-0″ wide opening is _________.

__________ **200.** The gauge of the 6″ wall studs shown on the second floor framing plan is #_________.

Appendix

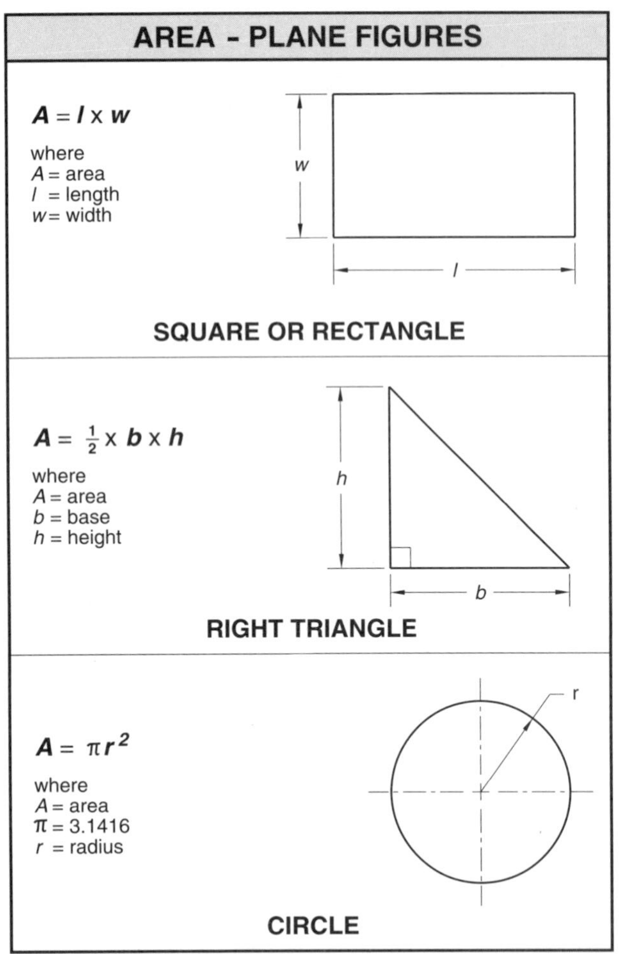

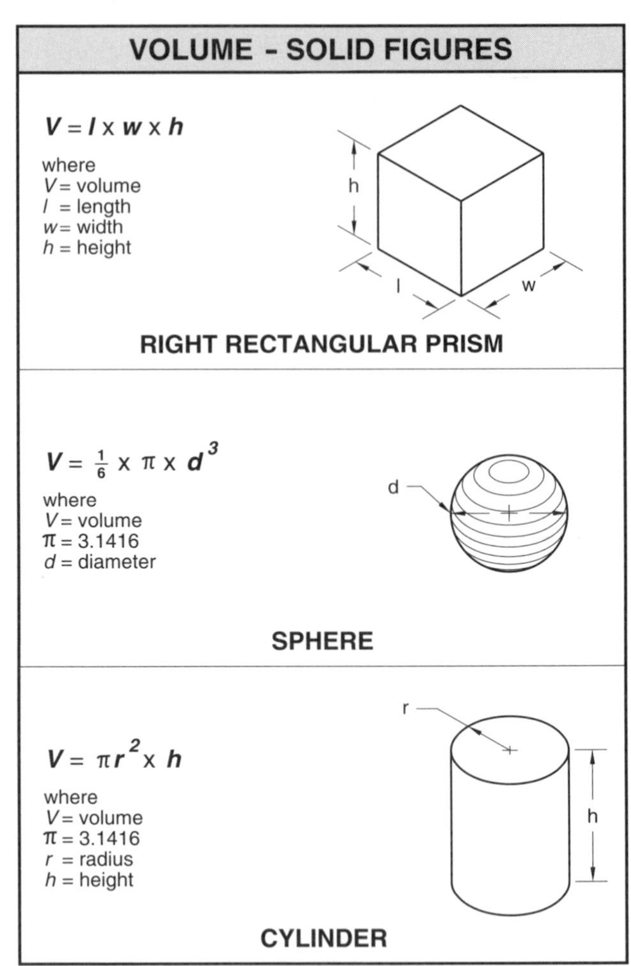

DECIMAL EQUIVALENTS OF AN INCH

Fraction	Decimal	Fraction	Decimal	Fraction	Decimal	Fraction	Decimal
1/64	0.015625	17/64	0.265625	33/64	0.515625	49/64	0.765625
1/32	0.03125	9/32	0.28125	17/32	0.53125	25/32	0.78125
3/64	0.046875	19/64	0.296875	35/64	0.546875	51/64	0.796875
1/16	0.0625	5/16	0.3125	9/16	0.5625	13/16	0.8125
5/64	0.078125	21/64	0.328125	37/64	0.578125	53/64	0.828125
3/32	0.09375	11/32	0.34375	19/32	0.59375	27/32	0.84375
7/64	0.109375	23/64	0.359375	39/64	0.609375	55/64	0.859375
1/8	0.125	3/8	0.375	5/8	0.625	7/8	0.875
9/64	0.140625	25/64	0.390625	41/64	0.640625	57/64	0.890625
5/32	0.15625	13/32	0.40625	21/32	0.65625	29/32	0.90625
11/64	0.171875	27/64	0.421875	43/64	0.671875	59/64	0.921875
3/16	0.1875	7/16	0.4375	11/16	0.6875	15/16	0.9375
13/64	0.203125	29/64	0.453125	45/64	0.703125	61/64	0.953125
7/32	0.21875	15/32	0.46875	23/32	0.71875	31/32	0.96875
15/64	0.234375	31/64	0.484375	47/64	0.734375	63/64	0.984375
1/4	0.250	1/2	0.500	3/4	0.750	1	1.000

ENGLISH SYSTEM

Quantity	Measure	Unit	Abbr	Equivalents
LENGTH		mile	mi	5280′, 320 rd, 1760 yd
		rod	rd	5.50 yd, 16.5′
		yard	yd	3′, 36″
		foot	ft *or* ′	12″, .333 yd
		inch	in. *or* ″	.083′, .028 yd
AREA A = l x w		square mile	sq mi *or* mi^2	640 A, 102,400 sq rd
		acre	A	4840 sq yd, 43,560 sq ft
		square rod	sq rd *or* rd^2	30.25 sq yd, .00625 A
		square yard	sq yd *or* yd^2	1296 sq in., 9 sq ft
		square foot	sq ft *or* ft^2	144 sq in., .111 sq yd
		square inch	sq in. *or* in^2	.0069 sq ft, .00077 sq yd
VOLUME V = l x w x t		cubic yard	cu yd *or* yd^3	27 cu ft, 46,656 cu in.
		cubic foot	cu ft *or* ft^3	1728 cu in., .0370 cu yd
		cubic inch	cu in. *or* in^3	.00058 cu ft, .000021 cu yd
CAPACITY WATER, FUEL, ETC.	*U.S. liquid measure*	gallon	gal.	4 qt (231 cu in.)
		quart	qt	2 pt (57.75 cu in.)
		pint	pt	4 gi (28.875 cu in.)
		gill	gi	4 fl oz (7.219 cu in.)
		fluidounce	fl oz	8 fl dr (1.805 cu in.)
		fluidram	fl dr	60 min (.226 cu in.)
		minim	min	1/6 fl dr (.003760 cu in.)
VEGETABLES, GRAIN, ETC.	*U.S. dry measure*	bushel	bu	4 pk (2150.42 cu in.)
		peck	pk	8 qt (537.605 cu in.)
		quart	qt	2 pt (67.201 cu in.)
		pint	pt	1/2 qt (33.600 cu in.)
DRUGS	*British imperial liquid and dry measure*	bushel	bu	4 pk (2219.36 cu in.)
		peck	pk	2 gal. (554.84 cu in.)
		gallon	gal.	4 qt (277.420 cu in.)
		quart	qt	2 pt (69.355 cu in.)
		pint	pt	4 gi (34.678 cu in.)
		gill	gi	5 fl oz (8.669 cu in.)
		fluidounce	fl oz	8 fl dr (1.7339 cu in.)
		fluidram	fl dr	60 min (.216734 cu in.)
		minim	min	1/60 fl dr (.003612 cu in.)
MASS AND WEIGHT COAL, GRAIN, ETC.	*avoirdupois*	ton	t	2000 lb
		short ton		2000 lb
		long ton		2240 lb
		pound	lb *or* #	16 oz, 7000 gr
		ounce	oz	16 dr, 437.5 gr
		dram	dr	27.344 gr, .0625 oz
		grain	gr	.037 dr, .002286 oz
GOLD, SILVER, ETC.	*troy*	pound	lb	12 oz, 240 dwt, 5760 gr
		ounce	oz	20 dwt, 480 gr
		pennyweight	dwt *or* pwt	24 gr, .05 oz
		grain	gr	.042 dwt, .002083 oz
DRUGS	*apothecaries'*	pound	lb ap	12 oz, 5760 gr
		ounce	oz ap	8 dr ap, 480 gr
		dram	dr ap	3 s ap, 60 gr
		scruple	s ap	20 gr, .333 dr ap
		grain	gr	.05 s, .002083 oz, .0166 dr ap

METRIC SYSTEM			
	Unit	**Abbr**	**Number of Base Units**
LENGTH	kilometer	km	1000
	hectometer	hm	100
	dekameter	dam	10
	***meter**	m	1
	decimeter	dm	.1
	centimeter	cm	.01
	millimeter	mm	.001
AREA	square kilometer	sq km *or* km^2	1,000,000
	hectare	ha	10,000
	are	a	100
	square centimeter	sq cm *or* cm^2	.0001
VOLUME	cubic centimeter	cu cm, cm^3, *or* cc	.000001
	cubic decimeter	dm^3	.001
	***cubic meter**	m^3	1
CAPACITY	kiloliter	kl	1000
	hectoliter	hl	100
	dekaliter	dal	10
	***liter**	l	1
	cubic decimeter	dm^3	1
	deciliter	dl	.10
	centiliter	cl	.01
	milliliter	ml	.001
MASS AND WEIGHT	metric ton	t	1,000,000
	kilogram	kg	1000
	hectogram	hg	100
	dekagram	dag	10
	***gram**	g	1
	decigram	dg	.10
	centigram	cg	.01
	milligram	mg	.001

* base units

METRIC TO ENGLISH EQUIVALENTS

	Unit	British Equivalent		
LENGTH	kilometer	.62 mi		
	hectometer	109.36 yd		
	dekameter	32.81′		
	meter	39.37″		
	decimeter	3.94″		
	centimeter	.39″		
	millimeter	.039″		
AREA	square kilometer	.3861 sq mi		
	hectacre	2.47 A		
	are	119.60 sq yd		
	square centimeter	.155 sq in.		
VOLUME	cubic centimeter	.061 cu in.		
	cubic decimeter	61.023 cu in.		
	cubic meter	1.307 cu yd		
CAPACITY		***cubic***	***dry***	***liquid***
	kiloliter	1.31 cu yd		
	hectoliter	3.53 cu ft	2.84 bu	
	dekaliter	.35 cu ft	1.14 pk	2.64 gal.
	liter	61.02 cu in.	.908 qt	1.057 qt
	cubic decimeter	61.02 cu in.	.908 qt	1.057 qt
	deciliter	6.1 cu in.	.18 pt	.21 pt
	centiliter	.61 cu in.		338 fl oz
	milliliter	.061 cu in.		.27 fl dr
MASS AND WEIGHT	metric ton	1.102 t		
	kilogram	2.2046 lb		
	hectogram	3.527 oz		
	dekagram	.353 oz		
	gram	.035 oz		
	decigram	1.543 gr		
	centigram	.154 gr		
	milligram	.015 gr		

ENGLISH TO METRIC EQUIVALENTS

		Unit	Metric Equivalent
LENGTH		mile	1.609 km
		rod	5.029 m
		yard	.9144 m
		foot	30.48 cm
		inch	2.54 cm
AREA		square mile	2.590 k^2
		acre	.405 hectacre, 4047 m^2
		square rod	25.293 m^2
		square yard	.836 m^2
		square foot	.093 m^2
		square inch	6.452 cm^2
VOLUME		cubic yard	.765 m^3
		cubic foot	.028 m^3
		cubic inch	16.387 cm^3
CAPACITY	*U.S. liquid measure*	gallon	3.785 l
		quart	.946 l
		pint	.473 l
		gill	118.294 ml
		fluidounce	29.573 ml
		fluidram	3.697 ml
		minim	.061610 ml
	U.S. dry measure	bushel	35.239 l
		peck	8.810 l
		quart	1.101 l
		pint	.551 l
	British imperial liquid and dry measure	bushel	.036 m^3
		peck	.0091 m^3
		gallon	4.546 l
		quart	1.136 l
		pint	568.26 cm^3
		gill	142.066 cm^3
		fluidounce	28.412 cm^3
		fluidram	3.5516 cm^3
		minim	.059194 cm^3
MASS AND WEIGHT	*avoirdupois*	short ton	.907 t
		long ton	1.016 t
		pound	.454 kg
		ounce	28.350 g
		dram	1.772 g
		grain	.0648 g
	troy	pound	.373 kg
		ounce	31.103 g
		pennyweight	1.555 g
		grain	.0648 g
	apothecaries'	pound	.373 kg
		ounce	31.103 g
		dram	3.888 g
		scruple	1.296 g
		grain	.0648 g

ALPHABET OF LINES

NAME AND USE	CONVENTIONAL REPRESENTATION	EXAMPLE
OBJECT LINE Define shape. Outline and detail objects.	THICK	OBJECT LINE
HIDDEN LINE Show hidden features.	$\frac{1}{8}$″ (3 mm) THIN $\frac{1}{32}$″ (0.75 mm)	HIDDEN LINE
CENTER LINE Locate centerpoints of arcs and circles.	$\frac{1}{16}$″ (1.5 mm) THIN $\frac{1}{8}$″ (3 mm) $\frac{3}{4}$″ (18 mm) TO $1\frac{1}{2}$″ (36 mm)	CENTER LINE CENTERPOINT
DIMENSION LINE Show size or location. EXTENSION LINE Define size or location.	DIMENSION LINE DIMENSION THIN 2′-6″ EXTENSION LINE	DIMENSION LINE $1\frac{3}{4}$ EXTENSION LINE
LEADER Call out specific features.	OPEN ARROWHEAD THIN X CLOSED ARROWHEAD 3X	$1\frac{1}{2}$ DRILL LEADER
CUTTING PLANE Show internal features.	THICK $\frac{1}{8}$″ (3 mm) $\frac{1}{16}$″ (1.5 mm) A A $\frac{3}{4}$″ (18 mm) TO $1\frac{1}{2}$″ (36 mm)	A A LETTER IDENTIFIES SECTION VIEW CUTTING PLANE LINE
SECTION LINE Identify internal features.	$\frac{1}{16}$″ (1.5 mm) THIN	SECTION LINES
BREAK LINE Show long breaks. BREAK LINE Show short breaks.	$\frac{3}{4}$″ (18 mm) TO $1\frac{1}{2}$″ (36 mm) THIN FREEHAND THICK	LONG BREAK LINE SHORT BREAK LINE

TRANSVERSAL SPACING (″)
LONGITUDINAL SPACING (″)
W = SMOOTH WIRE
D = DEFORMED WIRE

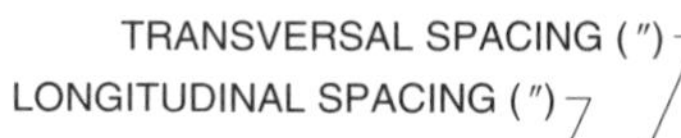

LONGITUDINAL WIRE SIZE (CROSS-SECTIONAL AREA)
TRANSVERSAL WIRE SIZE (CROSS-SECTIONAL AREA)

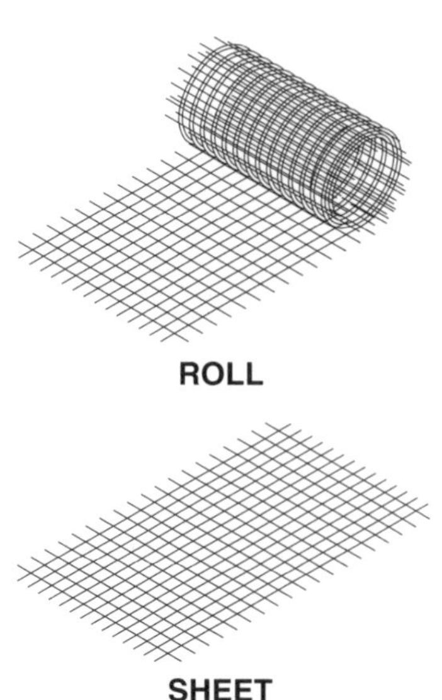

ROLL

SHEET

COMMON STOCK SIZES FOR WELDED WIRE FABRIC				
Style Designation		Steel Area (sq in. per ft)		Weight Approx lb per 100 sq ft
New Designation (By W-Number)	Old Designation (By Steel Wire Gauge)	Longitude	Transverse	
Rolls				
6 × 6 – W1.4 × W1.4	6 × 6 – 10 × 10	.028	.028	21
6 × 6 – W2.0 × W2.0	6 × 6 – 8 × 8	.040	.040	29
6 × 6 – W2.9 × W2.9	6 × 6 – 6 × 6	.058	.058	42
6 × 6 – W4.0 × W4.0	6 × 6 – 4 × 4	.080	.080	58
4 × 4 – W1.4 × W1.4	4 × 4 – 10 × 10	.042	.042	31
4 × 4 – W2.0 × W2.0	4 × 4 – 8 × 8	.060	.060	43
4 × 4 – W2.9 × W2.9	4 × 4 – 6 × 6	.087	.087	62
4 × 4 – W4.0 × W4.0	4 × 4 – 4 × 4	.120	.120	85
Sheets				
6 × 6 – W2.9 × W2.9	6 × 6 – 6 × 6	.058	.058	42
6 × 6 – W4.0 × W4.0	6 × 6 – 4 × 4	.080	.080	58
6 × 6 – W5.5 × W5.5	6 × 6 – 2 × 2	.110	.110	80
4 × 4 – W4.0 × W4.0	4 × 4 – 4 × 4	.120	.120	85

Wire Reinforcement Institute

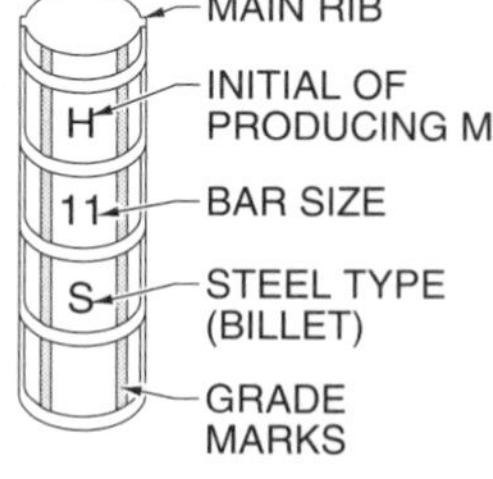

LINE SYSTEM GRADE MARKS

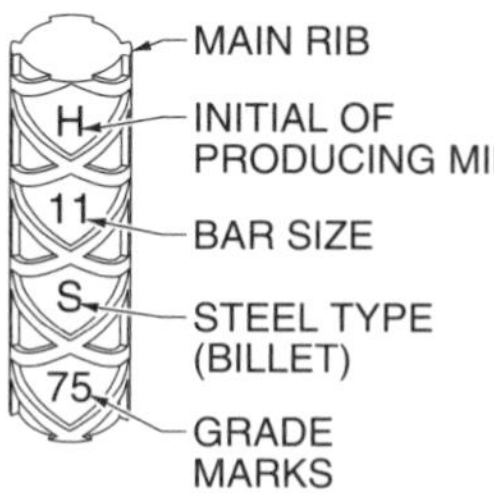

NUMBER SYSTEM GRADE MARKS

STANDARD REBAR SIZES						
Bar Size Designation	Weight per Foot		Diameter		Cross-Sectional Area[2]	
	lb	kg	in.	cm	in.	cm
#3	0.376	0.171	0.375	0.953	0.11	0.71
#4	0.668	0.303	0.500	1.270	0.20	1.29
#5	1.043	0.473	0.625	1.588	0.31	2.00
#6	1.502	0.681	0.750	1.905	0.44	2.84
#7	2.044	0.927	0.875	2.223	0.60	3.87
#8	2.670	1.211	1.000	2.540	0.79	5.10
#9	3.400	1.542	1.128	2.865	1.00	6.45
#10	4.303	1.952	1.270	3.226	1.27	8.19
#11	5.313	2.410	1.410	3.581	1.56	10.07
#14	7.650	3.470	1.693	4.300	2.25	14.52
#18	13.600	6.169	2.257	5.733	4.00	25.81

ASTM

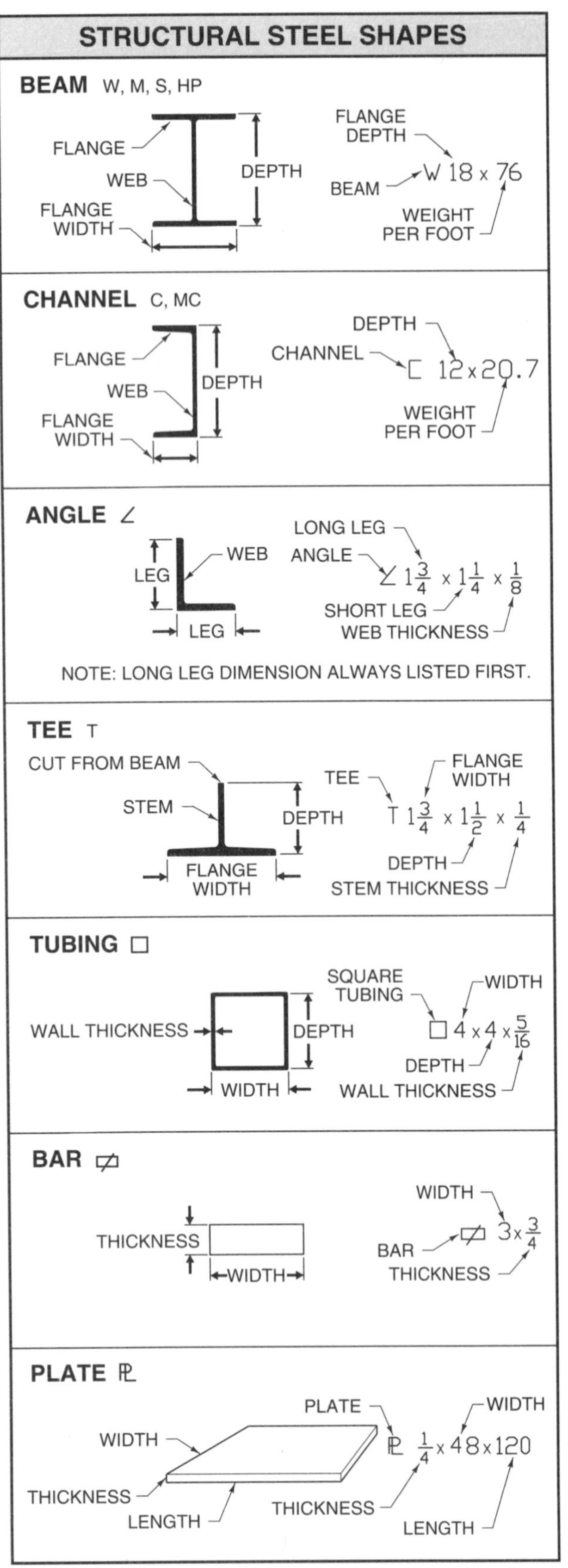

AMERICAN STANDARD CHANNELS

Designation	Depth d*	Flange		Web Thickness t_w*
		Width b_f*	Average Thickness t_f*	
C15 × 50	15	3 3/4	5/8	11/16
× 40	15	3 1/2	5/8	1/2
× 33.9	15	3 3/8	5/8	3/8
C12 × 30	12	3 1/8	1/2	1/2
× 25	12	3	1/2	3/8
× 20.7	12	3	1/2	5/16
C10 × 30	10	3	7/16	11/16
× 25	10	2 7/8	7/16	1/2
× 20	10	2 3/4	7/16	3/8
× 15.3	10	2 5/8	7/16	1/4
C 9 × 20	9	2 5/8	7/16	7/16
× 15	9	2 1/2	7/16	5/16
× 13.4	9	2 3/8	7/16	1/4
C 8 × 18.75	8	2 1/2	3/8	1/2
× 13.75	8	2 3/8	3/8	5/16
× 11.5	8	2 1/4	3/8	1/4
C 7 × 14.75	7	2 1/4	3/8	7/16
× 12.25	7	2 1/4	3/8	5/16
× 9.8	7	2 1/8	3/8	3/16
C 6 × 13	6	2 1/8	5/16	7/16
× 10.5	6	2	5/16	5/16
× 8.2	6	1 7/8	5/16	3/16
C 5 × 9	5	1 7/8	5/16	5/16
× 6.7	5	1 3/4	5/16	3/16
C 4 × 7.25	4	1 3/4	5/16	5/16
× 5.4	4	1 5/8	5/16	3/16
C 3 × 6	3	1 5/8	1/4	3/8
× 5	3	1 1/2	1/4	1/4
× 4.1	3	1 3/8	1/4	3/16

* in in.

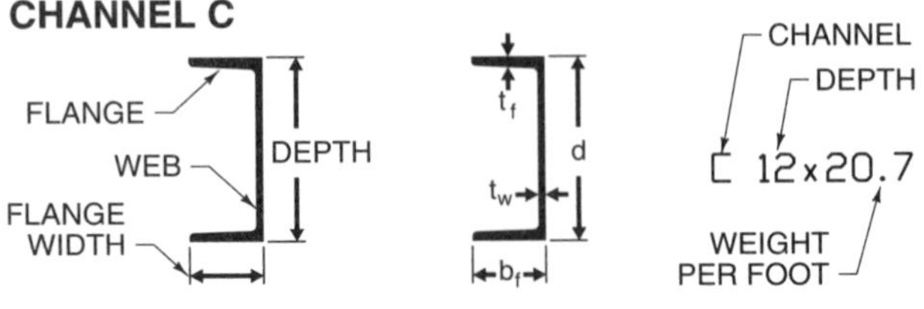

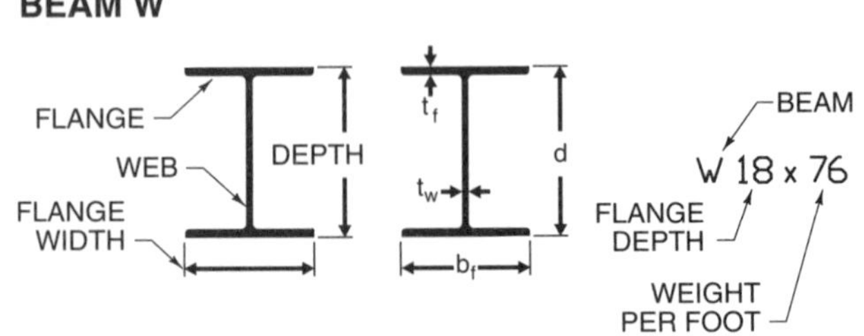

Note: See W Shapes – Dimensions for Detailing.

W SHAPES – DIMENSIONS FOR DETAILING

Designation	Depth d*	Flange		Web
		Width b_f*	Thickness t_f*	Thickness t_w*
W18 × 119	19	11 1/4	1 1/16	5/8
× 106	18 3/4	11 1/4	15/16	9/16
× 97	18 5/8	11 1/8	7/8	9/16
× 86	18 3/8	11 1/8	3/4	1/2
× 76	18 1/4	11	11/16	7/16
W18 × 71	18 1/2	7 5/8	13/16	1/2
× 65	18 3/8	7 5/8	3/4	7/16
× 60	18 1/4	7 1/2	11/16	7/16
× 55	18 1/8	7 1/2	5/8	3/8
× 50	18	7 1/2	9/16	3/8
W18 × 46	18	6	5/8	3/8
× 40	17 7/8	6	1/2	5/16
× 35	17 3/4	6	7/16	5/16
W16 × 100	17	10 3/8	1	9/16
× 89	16 3/4	10 3/8	7/8	1/2
× 77	16 1/2	10 1/4	3/4	7/16
× 67	16 3/8	10 1/4	11/16	3/8
W16 × 57	16 3/8	7 1/8	11/16	7/16
× 50	15 1/4	7 1/8	5/8	3/8
× 45	16 1/8	7	9/16	3/8
× 40	16	7	1/2	5/16
× 36	15 7/8	7	7/16	5/16
W16 × 31	15 7/8	5 1/2	7/16	1/4
× 26	15 3/4	5 1/2	3/8	1/4
W14 × 730	22 3/8	17 7/8	4 15/16	3 1/16
× 665	21 5/8	17 5/8	4 1/2	2 13/16
× 605	20 7/8	17 3/8	4 3/16	2 5/8
× 550	20 1/4	17 1/4	3 13/16	2 3/8
× 500	19 5/8	17	3 1/2	2 3/16
× 455	19	16 7/8	3 3/16	2
W14 × 426	18 5/8	16 3/4	3 1/16	1 7/8
× 398	18 1/4	16 5/8	2 7/8	1 3/4
× 370	17 7/8	16 1/2	2 11/16	1 5/8
× 342	17 1/2	16 3/8	2 1/2	1 9/16
× 311	17 1/8	16 1/4	2 1/4	1 7/16
× 283	16 3/4	16 1/8	2 1/16	1 5/16
× 257	16 3/8	16	8 7/8	1 3/16
× 233	16	15 7/8	1 3/4	1 1/16
× 211	15 3/4	15 3/4	1 9/16	1
× 193	15 1/2	15 3/4	1 7/16	7/8
× 176	15 1/4	15 5/8	1 5/16	13/16
× 159	15	15 5/8	1 3/16	3/4
× 145	14 3/4	15 1/2	1 1/16	11/16
W14 × 132	14 5/8	14 3/4	1	5/8
× 120	14 1/2	14 5/8	15/16	9/16
× 109	14 3/8	14 5/8	7/8	1/2
× 99	14 1/8	14 5/8	3/4	1/2
× 90	14	14 1/2	11/16	7/16
W14 × 82	14 1/4	10 1/8	7/8	1/2
× 74	14 1/8	10 1/8	13/16	7/16
× 68	14	10	3/4	7/16
× 61	13 7/8	10	5/8	3/8
W14 × 53	13 7/8	8	11/16	3/8
× 48	13 3/4	8	5/8	5/16
× 43	13 5/8	8	1/2	5/16
W14 × 38	14 1/8	6 3/4	1/2	5/16
× 34	14	6 3/4	7/16	5/16
× 30	13 7/8	6 3/4	3/8	1/4
W14 × 26	13 7/8	5	7/16	1/4
× 22	13 3/4	5	5/16	1/4

Designation	Depth d*	Flange		Web
		Width b_f*	Thickness t_f*	Thickness t_w*
W12 × 336	16 7/8	13 3/8	2 15/16	1 3/4
× 305	16 3/8	13 1/4	2 11/16	1 5/8
× 279	15 7/8	13 1/8	2 1/2	1 1/2
× 252	15 3/8	13	2 1/4	1 3/8
× 230	15	12 7/8	2 1/16	1 5/16
× 210	14 3/4	12 3/4	1 7/8	1 3/16
W12 × 190	14 3/8	12 5/8	1 3/4	1 1/16
× 170	14	12 5/8	1 9/16	15/16
× 152	13 3/4	12 1/2	1 3/8	7/8
× 136	13 3/8	12 3/8	1 1/4	13/16
× 120	13 1/8	12 3/8	1 1/8	11/16
× 106	12 7/8	12 1/4	1	5/8
× 96	12 3/4	12 1/8	7/8	9/16
× 87	12 1/2	12 1/8	13/16	1/2
× 79	12 3/8	12 1/8	3/4	1/2
× 72	12 1/4	12	11/16	7/16
× 65	12 1/8	12	5/8	3/8
W12 × 58	12 1/4	10	5/8	3/8
× 53	12	10	9/16	3/8
W12 × 50	12 1/4	8 1/8	3/8	5/8
× 45	12	8	5/16	9/16
× 40	12	8	5/16	1/2
W12 × 35	12 1/2	6 1/2	5/16	1/2
× 30	12 3/8	6 1/2	1/4	7/16
× 26	12 1/4	6 1/2	1/4	3/8
W12 × 22	12 1/4	4	1/4	7/16
× 19	12 1/8	4	1/4	3/8
× 16	12	4	1/4	1/4
× 14	11 7/8	4	3/16	1/4
W10 × 112	11 3/8	10 3/8	1 1/4	3/4
× 100	11 1/8	10 3/8	1 1/8	11/16
× 88	10 7/8	10 1/4	1	5/8
× 77	10 5/8	10 1/4	7/8	1/2
× 68	10 3/8	10 1/8	3/4	1/2
× 60	10 1/4	10 1/8	11/16	7/16
× 54	10 1/8	10	5/8	3/8
× 49	10	10	9/16	5/16
W10 × 45	10 1/8	8	5/8	3/8
× 39	9 7/8	8	1/2	5/16
× 33	9 3/4	8	7/16	5/16
W10 × 30	10 1/2	5 3/4	1/2	5/16
× 26	10 3/8	5 3/4	7/16	1/4
× 22	10 1/8	5 3/4	3/8	1/4
W10 × 19	10 1/4	4	3/8	1/4
× 17	10 1/8	4	5/16	1/4
× 15	10	4	1/4	1/4
× 12	9 7/8	4	3/16	3/16
W8 × 67	9	8 1/4	15/16	9/16
× 58	8 3/4	8 1/4	13/16	1/2
× 48	8 1/2	8 1/8	11/16	3/8
× 40	8 1/4	8 1/8	9/16	3/8
× 35	8 1/8	8	1/2	5/16
× 31	8	8	7/16	5/16
W8 × 28	8	6 1/2	7/16	5/16
× 24	7 7/8	6 1/2	3/8	1/4
W8 × 21	8 1/4	5 1/4	3/8	1/4
× 18	8 1/8	5 1/4	5/16	1/4
W8 × 15	8 1/8	4	5/16	1/4
× 13	8	4	1/4	1/4
× 10	7 7/8	4	3/16	3/16

* in in.

ANGLES (EQUAL LEGS) – DIMENSIONS FOR DETAILING

Size and Thickness*	Size and Thickness*	Size and Thickness*
L 8 × 8 × 1 1/8	L 4 × 4 × 3/4	L 2 × 2 × 3/8
1	5/8	5/16
7/8	1/2	1/4
3/4	7/16	3/16
5/8	3/8	1/8
9/16	5/16	L 1 3/4 × 1 3/4 × 1/4
1/2	1/4	3/16
L 6 × 6 × 1	L 3 1/2 × 3 1/2 × 1/2	1/8
7/8	7/16	L 1 1/2 × 1 1/2 × 1/4
3/4	3/8	3/16
5/8	5/16	5/32
9/16	1/4	1/8
1/2	L 3 × 3 × 1/2	L 1 1/4 × 1 1/4 × 1/4
7/16	7/16	3/16
3/8	3/8	1/8
5/16	5/16	L 1 × 1 × 1/4
L 5 × 5 × 7/8	1/4	3/16
3/4	3/16	1/8
5/8	L 2 1/2 × 2 1/2 × 1/2	
1/2	3/8	
7/16	5/16	
3/8	1/4	
5/16	3/16	

* in in.

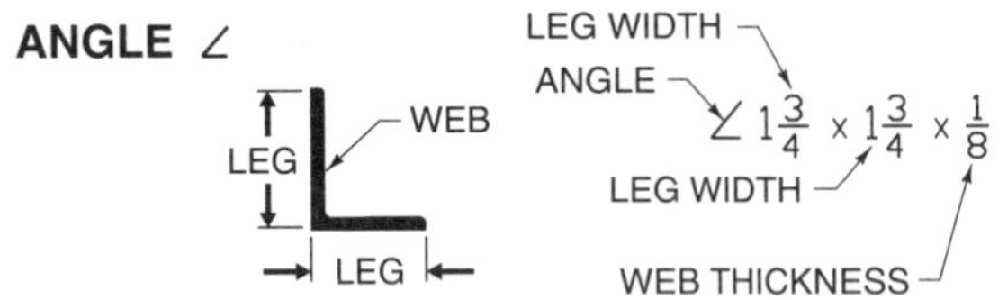

ANGLES (UNEQUAL LEGS) – DIMENSIONS FOR DETAILING

Size and Thickness*	Size and Thickness*	Size and Thickness*
L 9 × 4 × 1	L 6 × 3 1/2 × 1/2	L 3 1/2 × 2 1/2 × 1/2
7/8	3/8	7/16
3/4	5/16	3/8
5/8	1/4	5/16
9/16	L 5 × 3 1/2 × 3/4	1/4
1/2	5/8	L 3 × 2 1/2 × 1/2
L 8 × 6 × 1	1/2	7/16
7/8	7/16	3/8
3/4	3/8	5/16
5/8	5/16	1/4
9/16	1/4	3/16
1/2	L 5 × 3 × 1/2	L 3 × 2 × 1/2
7/16	7/16	7/16
L 8 × 4 × 1	3/8	3/8
7/8	5/16	5/16
3/4	1/4	1/4
5/8	L 4 × 3 1/2 × 5/8	3/16
9/16	1/2	L 2 1/2 × 2 × 3/8
1/2	7/16	5/16
7/16	3/8	1/4
L 7 × 4 × 7/8	5/16	3/16
3/4	1/4	L 2 1/2 × 1 1/2 × 5/16
5/8	L 4 × 3 × 5/8	1/4
9/16	1/2	3/16
1/2	7/16	L 2 × 1 1/2 × 1/4
7/16	3/8	3/16
3/8	5/16	1/8
L 6 × 4 × 7/8	1/4	L 2 × 1 1/4 × 1/4
3/4	L 3 1/2 × 3 × 1/2	3/16
5/8	7/16	1/8
9/16	3/8	L 1 3/4 × 1 1/4 × 1/4
1/2	5/16	3/16
7/16	1/4	1/8
3/8		
5/16		
1/4		

* in in.

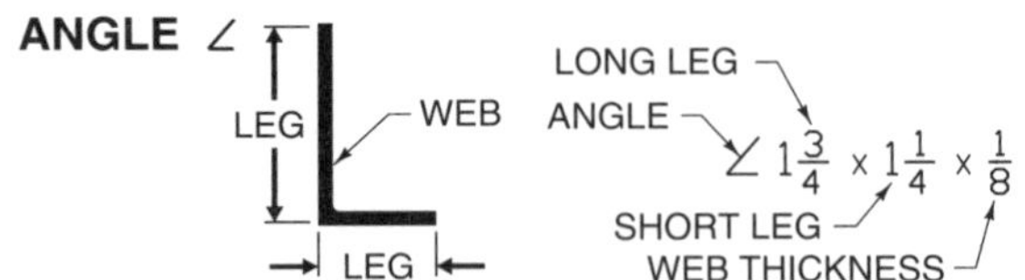

PIPE							
NOMINAL ID (IN.)	OD (BW GAUGE)	INSIDE DIAMETER (BW GAUGE)			NOMINAL WALL THICKNESS		
		STD	XS	XXS	SCHEDULE40	SCHEDULE60	SCHEDULE80
1/8	0.405	0.269	0.215		0.068	0.095	
1/4	0.540	0.364	0.302		0.088	0.119	
3/8	0.675	0.493	0.423		0.091	0.126	
1/2	0.840	0.622	0.546	0.252	0.109	0.147	0.294
3/4	1.050	0.824	0.742	0.434	0.113	0.154	0.308
1	1.315	1.049	0.957	0.599	0.133	0.179	0.358
1 1/4	1.660	1.380	1.278	0.896	0.140	0.191	0.382
1 1/2	1.900	1.610	1.500	1.100	0.145	0.200	0.400
2	2.375	2.067	1.939	1.503	0.154	0.218	0.436
2 1/2	2.875	2.469	2.323	1.771	0.203	0.276	0.552
3	3.500	3.068	2.900	2.300	0.216	0.300	0.600
3 1/2	4.000	3.548	3.364	2.728	0.226	0.318	
4	4.500	4.026	3.826	3.152	0.237	0.337	0.674
5	5.563	5.047	4.813	4.063	0.258	0.375	0.750
6	6.625	6.065	5.761	4.897	0.280	0.432	0.864
8	8.625	7.981	7.625	6.875	0.322	0.500	0.875
10	10.750	10.020	9.750	8.750	0.365	0.500	
12	12.750	12.000	11.750	10.750	0.406	0.500	

STANDARD SERIES THREADS – GRADED PITCHES						
NOMINAL DIAMETER	UNC		UNF		UNEF	
	TPI	TAP DRILL	TPI	TAP DRILL	TPI	TAP DRILL
0 (.0600)			80	3/64		
1 (.0730)	64	No. 53	72	No. 53		
2 (.0860)	56	No. 50	64	No. 50		
3 (.0990)	48	No. 47	56	No. 45		
4 (.1120)	40	No. 43	48	No. 42		
5 (.1250)	40	No. 38	44	No. 37		
6 (.1380)	32	No. 36	40	No. 33		
8 (.1640)	32	No. 29	36	No. 29		
10 (.1900)	24	No. 25	32	No. 21		
12 (.2160)	24	No. 16	28	No. 14	32	No.13
1/4 (.2500)	20	No. 7	28	No. 3	32	7/32
5/16 (.3125)	18	F	24	I	32	9/32
3/8 (.3750)	16	5/16				
7/16 (.4375)	14	U	20	25/64		
1/2 (.5000)	13	27/64				
9/16 (.5625)	12	31/64				
5/8 (.6250)	11	17/32				
11/16 (.6875)					24	41/64
3/4 (.7500)	10	21/32				
13/16 (.8125)					20	49/64
7/8 (.8750)	9	49/64				
15/16 (.9375)					20	57/64
1 (1.000)	8	7/8	12	59/64		

TWIST DRILL FRACTIONAL, NUMBER, AND LETTER SIZES

Drill No.	Frac	Deci	Drill No.	Frac	Deci	Drill No.	Frac	Deci	Drill No.	Frac	Deci
80	—	.0135	42	—	.0935	7	—	.201	X	—	.397
79	—	.0145	—	3/32	.0938	—	13/64	.203	Y	—	.404
—	1/64	.0156				6	—	.204			
78	—	.0160	41	—	.0960	5	—	.206	—	13/32	.406
77	—	.0180	40	—	.0980	4	—	.209	Z	—	.413
			39	—	.0995				—	27/64	.422
76	—	.0200	38	—	.1015	3	—	.213	—	7/16	.438
75	—	.0210	37	—	.1040	—	7/32	.219	—	29/64	.453
74	—	.0225				2	—	.221			
73	—	.0240	36	—	.1065	1	—	.228	—	15/32	.469
72	—	.0250	—	7/64	.1094	A	—	.234	—	31/64	.484
			35	—	.1100				—	1/2	.500
71	—	.0260	34	—	.1110	—	15/64	.234	—	33/64	.516
70	—	.0280	33	—	.1130	B	—	.238	—	17/32	.531
69	—	.0292				C	—	.242			
68	—	.0310	32	—	.116	D	—	.246	—	35/64	.547
—	1/32	.0313	31	—	.120	—	1/4	.250	—	9/16	.562
			—	1/8	.125				—	37/64	.578
67	—	.0320	30	—	.129	E	—	.250	—	19/32	.594
66	—	.0330	29	—	.136	F	—	.257	—	39/64	.609
65	—	.0350				G	—	.261			
64	—	.0360	—	9/64	.140	—	17/64	.266	—	5/8	.625
63	—	.0370	28	—	.141	H	—	.266	—	41/64	.641
			27	—	.144				—	21/32	.656
62	—	.0380	26	—	.147	I	—	.272	—	43/64	.672
61	—	.0390	25	—	.150	J	—	.277	—	11/16	.688
60	—	.0400				—	9/32	.281			
59	—	.0410	24	—	.152	K	—	.281	—	45/64	.703
58	—	.0420	23	—	.154	L	—	.290	—	23/32	.719
			—	5/32	.156				—	47/64	.734
57	—	.0430	22	—	.157	M	—	.295	—	3/4	.750
56	—	.0465	21	—	.159	—	19/64	.2297	—	49/64	.766
—	3/64	.0469				N	—	.302			
55	—	.0520	20	—	.161	—	5/16	.313	—	25/32	.781
54	—	.0550	19	—	.166	O	—	.316	—	51/64	.797
			18	—	.170				—	13/16	.813
53	—	.0595	—	11/64	.172	P	—	.323	—	53/64	.828
—	1/16	.0625	17	—	.173	—	21/64	.328	—	27/32	.844
52	—	.0635				Q	—	.332			
51	—	.0670				R	—	.339			
50	—	.0700	16	—	.177	—	11/32	.344	—	55/64	.859
			15	—	.180				—	7/8	.875
49	—	.0730	14	—	.182	S	—	.348	—	57/64	.891
48	—	.0760	13	—	.185	T	—	.358	—	29/32	.906
—	5/64	.0781	—	3/16	.188	—	23/64	.359	—	59/64	.922
47	—	.0785				U	—	.368			
46	—	.0810	12	—	.189	—	3/8	.375	—	15/16	.938
			11	—	.191				—	61/64	.953
45	—	.0820	10	—	.194	V	—	.377	—	31/32	.969
44	—	.0860	9	—	.196	W	—	.386	—	63/64	.984
43	—	.0890	8	—	.199	—	25/64	.391	—	1	1.000

METRIC SCREW THREADS

Coarse (general purpose)		Fine	
Nom Size & Thd Pitch	Tap Drill Dia (mm)	Nom Size & Thd Pitch	Tap Drill Dia (mm)
M1.6 × 0.35	1.25	—	—
M1.8 × 0.35	1.45	—	—
M2 × 0.4	1.6	—	—
M2.2 × 0.45	1.75	—	—
M2.5 × 0.45	2.05	—	—
M3 × 0.5	2.50	—	—
M3.5 × 0.6	2.90	—	—
M4 × 0.7	3.30	—	—
M4.5 × 0.75	3.75	—	—
M5 × .8	4.20	—	—
M6.3 × 1	5.30	—	—
M7 × 1	6.00	—	—
M8 × 1.25	6.80	M8 × 1	7.00
M9 × 1.25	7.75		
M10 × 1.5	8.50	M10 × 1.25	8.75
M11 × 1.5	9.50		
M12 × 1.75	10.30	M12 × 1.25	10.50
M14 × 2	12.00	M14 × 1.5	12.50
M16 × 2	14.00	M16 × 1.5	14.50
M18 × 2.5	15.50	M18 × 1.5	16.50
M20 × 2.5	17.50	M20 × 1.5	18.50
M22 × 2.5	19.50	M22 × 1.5	20.50
M24 × 3	21.00	M24 × 2	22.00
M27 × 3	24.00	M27 × 2	25.00
M30 × 3.5	26.50	M30 × 2	28.00
M33 × 3.5	29.50	M30 × 2	31.00
M36 × 4	32.00	M36 × 3	33.00
M39 × 4	35.00	M39 × 3	36.00
M42 × 4.5	37.50	M42 × 3	39.00
M45 × 4.5	40.50	M45 × 3	42.00
M48 × 5	43.00	M48 × 3	45.00
M52 × 5	47.00	M52 × 3	49.00
M56 × 5.5	50.50	M56 × 4	52.00
M60 × 5.5	54.50	M60 × 4	56.00
M64 × 6	58.00	M64 × 4	60.00
M68 × 6	62.00	M68 × 4	64.00
M72 × 6	66.00	—	—
M80 × 6	74.00	—	—
M90 × 6	84.00	—	—
M100 × 6	94.00	—	—

CHAIRS			
Symbol	**Bar Support Illustration**	**Support**	**Standard Sizes**
SB	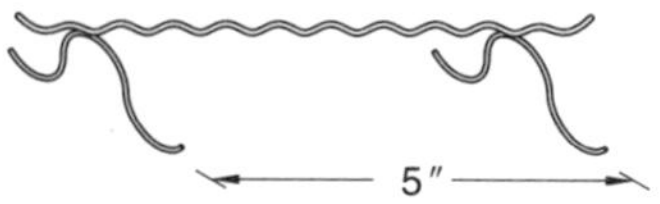 5″	Slab Bolster	$\frac{3}{4}$″, 1″, $1\frac{1}{2}$″, and 2″ heights in 5′ and 10′ lengths
SBU*	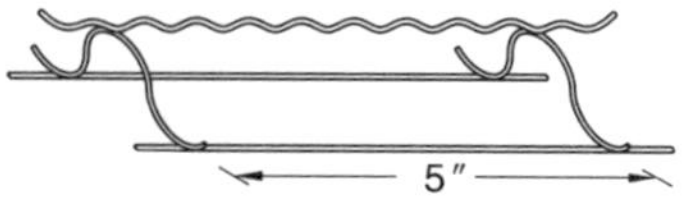 5″	Slab Bolster Upper	Same as SB
BB	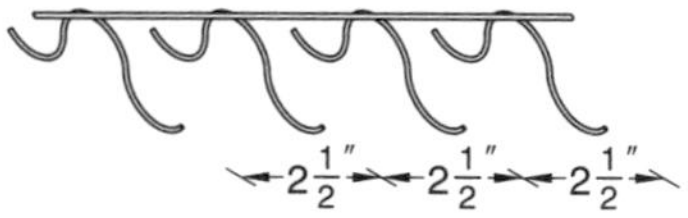 $2\frac{1}{2}$″ $2\frac{1}{2}$″ $2\frac{1}{2}$″	Beam Bolster	1″, $1\frac{1}{2}$″, 2″, over 2″ to 5″ heights in $\frac{1}{4}$″ increments in 5′ lengths
BBU*	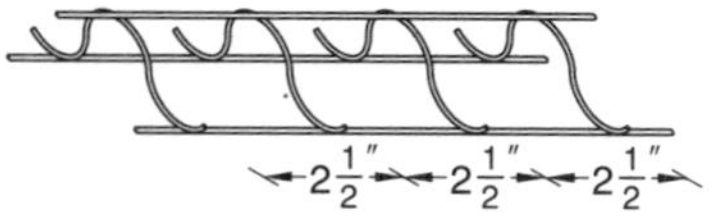 $2\frac{1}{2}$″ $2\frac{1}{2}$″ $2\frac{1}{2}$″	Beam Bolster Upper	Same as BB
BC		Individual Bar Chair	$\frac{3}{4}$″, 1″, $1\frac{1}{2}$″, and $1\frac{3}{4}$″ heights
JC	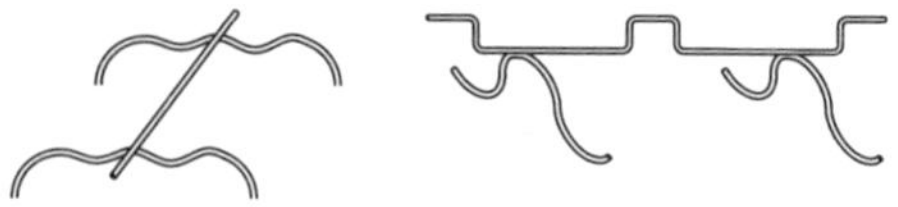	Joist Chair	4″, 5″, 6″ widths and $\frac{3}{4}$″, 1″, and $1\frac{1}{2}$″ heights
HC		Individual High Chair	2″ to 15″ heights in $\frac{1}{4}$″ increments
HCM*		High Chair for Metal Deck	2″ to 15″ heights in $\frac{1}{4}$″ increments
CHC	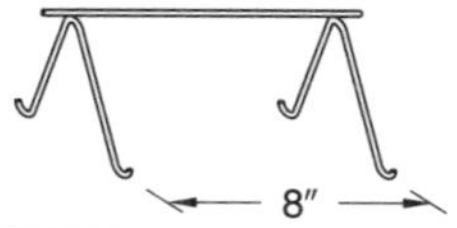 8″	Continuous High Chair	Same as HC in 5′ and 10′ lengths
CHCU*	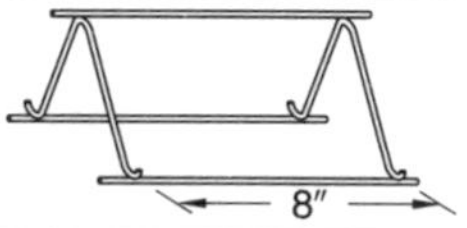 8″	Continuous High Chair Upper	Same as CHC
CHCM*	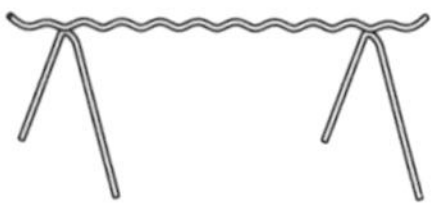	Continuous High Chair for Metal Deck	Up to 5″ heights in $\frac{1}{4}$″ increments
JCU**	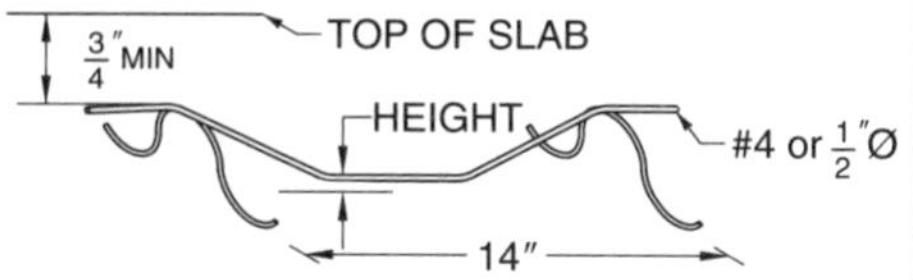 $\frac{3}{4}$″ MIN; TOP OF SLAB; HEIGHT; #4 or $\frac{1}{2}$″Ø; 14″	Joist Chair Upper	14″ Span. 1″ through 3″ heights in $\frac{1}{4}$″ increments

* Available in Class 3 only, except on special order.
** Available in Class 3 only, with upturned or end bearing legs.

LIFT ANCHORS AND BRACE INSERTS

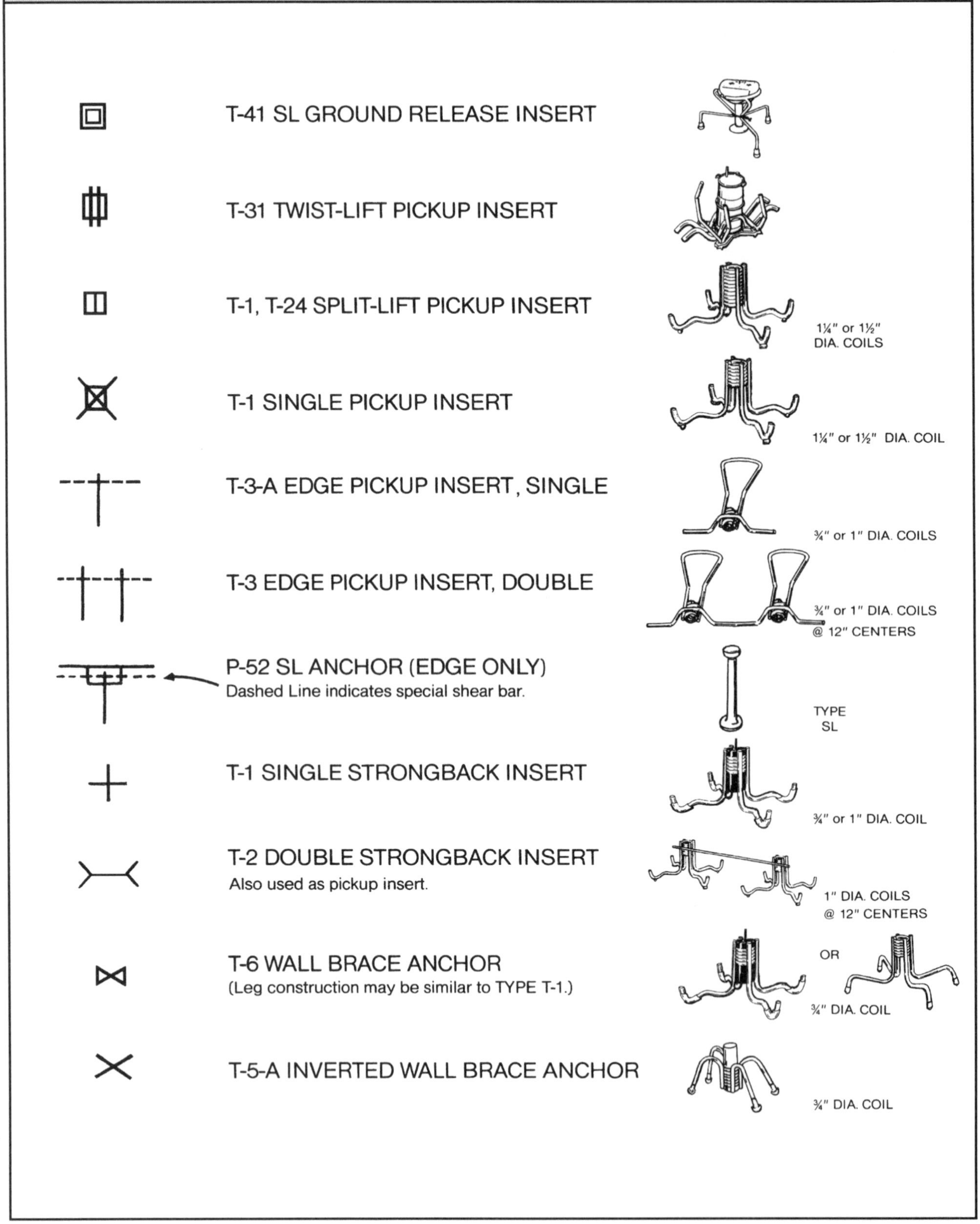

T-41 SL GROUND RELEASE INSERT

T-31 TWIST-LIFT PICKUP INSERT

T-1, T-24 SPLIT-LIFT PICKUP INSERT

1¼" or 1½" DIA. COILS

T-1 SINGLE PICKUP INSERT

1¼" or 1½" DIA. COIL

T-3-A EDGE PICKUP INSERT, SINGLE

¾" or 1" DIA. COILS

T-3 EDGE PICKUP INSERT, DOUBLE

¾" or 1" DIA. COILS @ 12" CENTERS

P-52 SL ANCHOR (EDGE ONLY)
Dashed Line indicates special shear bar.

TYPE SL

T-1 SINGLE STRONGBACK INSERT

¾" or 1" DIA. COIL

T-2 DOUBLE STRONGBACK INSERT
Also used as pickup insert.

1" DIA. COILS @ 12" CENTERS

T-6 WALL BRACE ANCHOR
(Leg construction may be similar to TYPE T-1.)

OR

¾" DIA. COIL

T-5-A INVERTED WALL BRACE ANCHOR

¾" DIA. COIL

Dayton Superior Corporation

PRECAST CONCRETE SLABS

Flat Slabs (4′ width)	Designation	Topping Thickness*	Thickness*
	FS4	NONE	4
	FS4+2	2	
	FS6	NONE	6
	FS6+2	2	
	FS8	NONE	8
	FS8+2	2	
Hollow Core Slabs (4′ width)			
	4HC6	NONE	6
	4HC6+2	2	
	4HC8	NONE	8
	4HC8+2	2	
	4HC10	NONE	10
	4HC10+2	2	
	4HC12	NONE	12
	4HC12+2	2	

Hollow Core Slab Types

Type	Thickness*	Width
A	6, 8, 12, 15	4′ - 0″
B	4, 6, 8, 10	4′ - 0″
C	6, 8, 10, 12	8′ - 0″
D	6, 8, 10, 12	1′ - 4″, 1′ - 8″, 2′ - 0″
E	4, 6, 8, 10, 12	3′ - 4″
F	8, 12	4′ - 0″
G	8, 12	8′ - 0″
H	4, 6, 8, 10, 12	4′ - 0″

* in in.
** available in Class 3 only, with upturned or end bearing legs

ARCHITECTURAL SYMBOLS. . .			
Material	**Elevation**	**Plan**	**Section**
EARTH			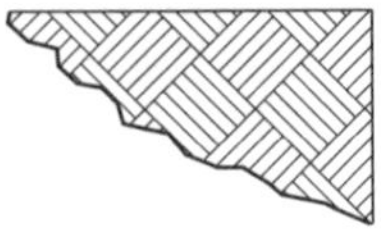
BRICK	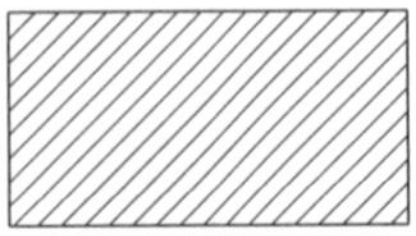 WITH NOTE INDICATING TYPE OF BRICK (COMMON, FACE, ETC.)	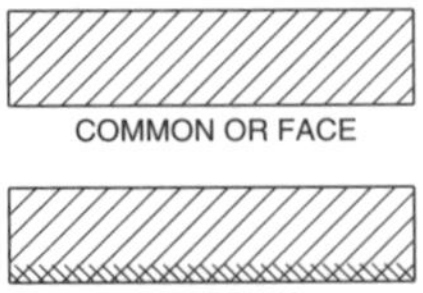 COMMON OR FACE FIREBRICK	SAME AS PLAN VIEWS
CONCRETE	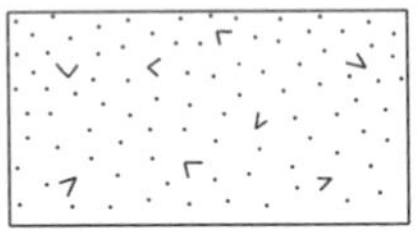	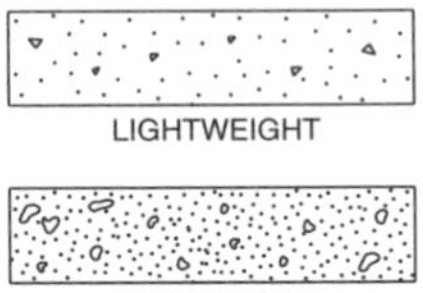 LIGHTWEIGHT STRUCTURAL	SAME AS PLAN VIEWS
CONCRETE BLOCK	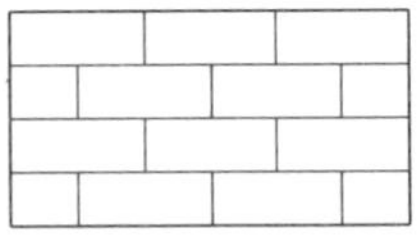	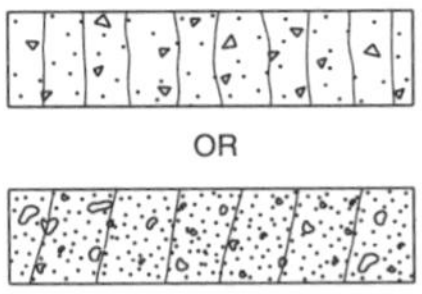 OR	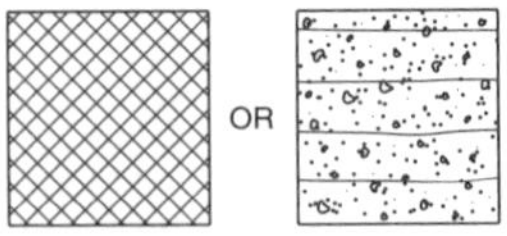 OR
STONE	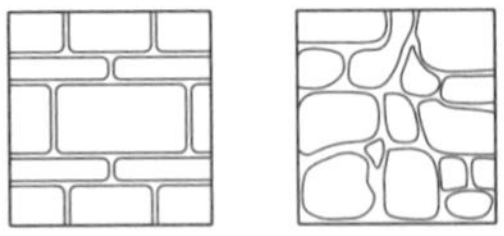 CUT STONE RUBBLE	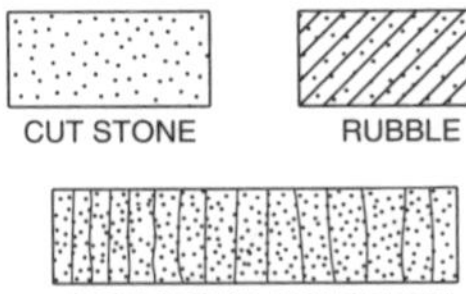 CUT STONE RUBBLE CAST STONE (CONCRETE)	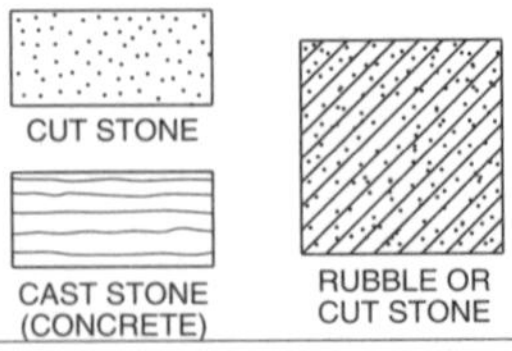 CUT STONE CAST STONE (CONCRETE) RUBBLE OR CUT STONE
WOOD	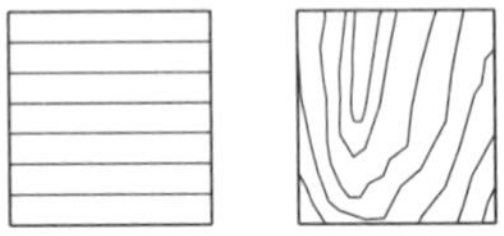 SIDING PANEL	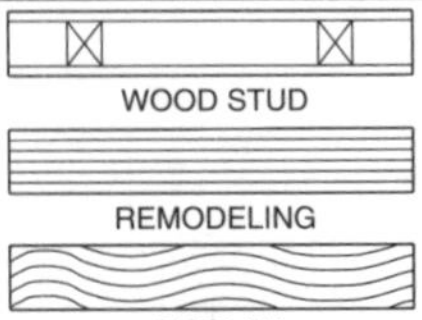 WOOD STUD REMODELING DISPLAY	 ROUGH MEMBERS FINISHED MEMBERS PLYWOOD
PLASTER	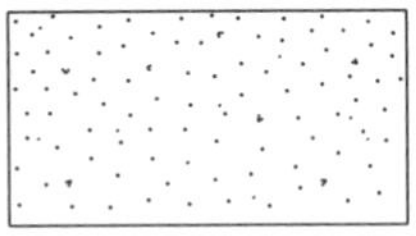	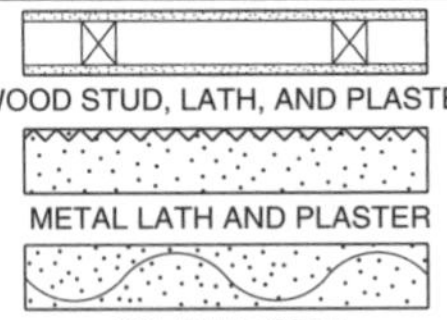 WOOD STUD, LATH, AND PLASTER METAL LATH AND PLASTER SOLID PLASTER	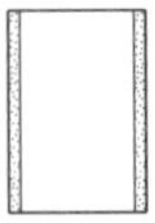 LATH AND PLASTER
ROOFING	 SHINGLES	SAME AS ELEVATION VIEW	
GLASS	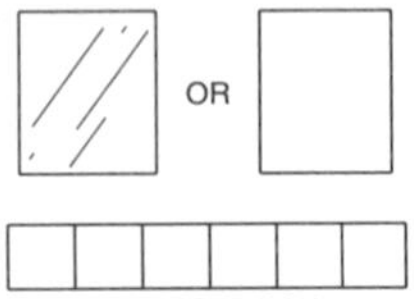 OR GLASS BLOCK	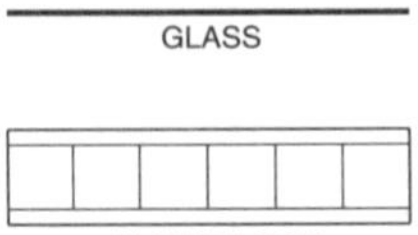 GLASS GLASS BLOCK	SMALL SCALE LARGE SCALE

. . .ARCHITECTURAL SYMBOLS

Material	Elevation	Plan	Section
FACING TILE	CERAMIC TILE	FLOOR TILE	CERAMIC TILE LARGE SCALE CERAMIC TILE SMALL SCALE
STRUCTURAL CLAY TILE			SAME AS PLAN VIEW
INSULATION		LOOSE FILL OR BATTS RIGID SPRAY FOAM	SAME AS PLAN VIEWS
SHEET METAL FLASHING		OCCASIONALLY INDICATED BY NOTE	
METALS OTHER THAN FLASHING	INDICATED BY NOTE OR DRAWN TO SCALE	SAME AS ELEVATION	SMALL SCALE STEEL CAST IRON ALUMINUM BRONZE OR BRASS
STRUCTURAL STEEL	INDICATED BY NOTE OR DRAWN TO SCALE	OR	REBARS SMALL SCALE LARGE SCALE L-ANGLES, S-BEAMS, ETC.

PLOT PLAN SYMBOLS

N — NORTH	FIRE HYDRANT	WALK	E OR — ELECTRIC SERVICE
POINT OF BEGINNING (POB)	MAILBOX	IMPROVED ROAD	G OR — NATURAL GAS LINE
UTILITY METER OR VALVE	MANHOLE	UNIMPROVED ROAD	W OR — WATER LINE
POWER POLE AND GUY	TREE	BUILDING LINE	T OR — TELEPHONE LINE
LIGHT STANDARD	BUSH	PROPERTY LINE	NATURAL GRADE
TRAFFIC SIGNAL	HEDGE ROW	PROPERTY LINE	FINISH GRADE
STREET SIGN	FENCE	TOWNSHIP LINE	+ XX.00′ — EXISTING ELEVATION

ELECTRICAL SYMBOLS. . .

LIGHTING OUTLETS

- OUTLET BOX AND INCANDESCENT LIGHTING FIXTURE — CEILING, WALL
- INCANDESCENT TRACK LIGHTING
- BLANKED OUTLET — B
- DROP CORD — D
- EXIT LIGHT AND OUTLET BOX. SHADED AREAS DENOTE FACES.
- OUTDOOR POLE-MOUNTED FIXTURES
- JUNCTION BOX — J
- LAMPHOLDER WITH PULL SWITCH — L PS
- MULTIPLE FLOODLIGHT ASSEMBLY
- EMERGENCY BATTERY PACK WITH CHARGER — B
- INDIVIDUAL FLUORESCENT FIXTURE
- OUTLET BOX AND FLUORESCENT LIGHTING TRACK FIXTURE
- CONTINUOUS FLUORESCENT FIXTURE
- SURFACE-MOUNTED FLUORESCENT FIXTURE

PANELBOARDS

- FLUSH-MOUNTED PANELBOARD AND CABINET
- SURFACE-MOUNTED PANELBOARD AND CABINET

CONVENIENCE OUTLETS

- SINGLE RECEPTACLE OUTLET
- DUPLEX RECEPTACLE OUTLET
- TRIPLEX RECEPTACLE OUTLET
- SPLIT-WIRED DUPLEX RECEPTACLE OUTLET
- SPLIT-WIRED TRIPLEX RECEPTACLE OUTLET
- SINGLE SPECIAL-PURPOSE RECEPTACLE OUTLET
- DUPLEX SPECIAL-PURPOSE RECEPTACLE OUTLET
- RANGE OUTLET — R
- SPECIAL-PURPOSE CONNECTION — DW
- CLOSED-CIRCUIT TELEVISION CAMERA
- CLOCK HANGER RECEPTACLE — C
- FAN HANGER RECEPTACLE — F
- FLOOR SINGLE RECEPTACLE OUTLET
- FLOOR DUPLEX RECEPTACLE OUTLET
- FLOOR SPECIAL-PURPOSE OUTLET
- UNDERFLOOR DUCT AND JUNCTION BOX FOR TRIPLE, DOUBLE, OR SINGLE DUCT SYSTEM AS INDICATED BY NUMBER OF PARALLEL LINES

BUSDUCTS AND WIREWAYS

- SERVICE, FEEDER, OR PLUG-IN BUSWAY — B B B
- CABLE THROUGH LADDER OR CHANNEL — C C C
- WIREWAY — W W W

SWITCH OUTLETS

- SINGLE-POLE SWITCH — S
- DOUBLE-POLE SWITCH — S_2
- THREE-WAY SWITCH — S_3
- FOUR-WAY SWITCH — S_4
- AUTOMATIC DOOR SWITCH — S_D
- KEY-OPERATED SWITCH — S_K
- CIRCUIT BREAKER — S_{CB}
- WEATHERPROOF CIRCUIT BREAKER — S_{WCB}
- DIMMER — S_{DM}
- REMOTE CONTROL SWITCH — S_{RC}
- WEATHERPROOF SWITCH — S_{WP}
- FUSED SWITCH — S_F
- WEATHERPROOF FUSED SWITCH — S_{WF}
- TIME SWITCH — S_T
- CEILING PULL SWITCH — S
- SWITCH AND SINGLE RECEPTACLE — S
- SWITCH AND DOUBLE RECEPTACLE — S
- A STANDARD SYMBOL WITH AN ADDED LOWERCASE SUBSCRIPT LETTER IS USED TO DESIGNATE A VARIATION IN STANDARD EQUIPMENT — a.b, a.b, $S_{a.b}$

. . .ELECTRICAL SYMBOLS

COMMERCIAL AND INDUSTRIAL SYSTEMS

PAGING SYSTEM DEVICE

FIRE ALARM SYSTEM DEVICE

COMPUTER DATA SYSTEM DEVICE

PRIVATE TELEPHONE SYSTEM DEVICE

SOUND SYSTEM

FIRE ALARM CONTROL PANEL — FACP

SIGNALING SYSTEM OUTLETS FOR RESIDENTIAL SYSTEMS

PUSHBUTTON

BUZZER

BELL

BELL AND BUZZER COMBINATION

COMPUTER DATA OUTLET

BELL RINGING TRANSFORMER — BT

ELECTRIC DOOR OPENER — D

CHIME — CH

TELEVISION OUTLET — TV

THERMOSTAT — T

UNDERGROUND ELECTRICAL DISTRIBUTION OR ELECTRICAL LIGHTING SYSTEMS

MANHOLE — M

HANDHOLE — H

TRANSFORMER-MANHOLE OR VAULT — TM

TRANSFORMER PAD — TP

UNDERGROUND DIRECT BURIAL CABLE

UNDERGROUND DUCT LINE

STREET LIGHT STANDARD FED FROM UNDERGROUND CIRCUIT

ABOVE-GROUND ELECTRICAL DISTRIBUTION OR LIGHTING SYSTEMS

POLE

STREET LIGHT AND BRACKET

PRIMARY CIRCUIT

SECONDARY CIRCUIT

DOWN GUY

HEAD GUY

SIDEWALK GUY

SERVICE WEATHERHEAD

PANEL CIRCUITS AND MISCELLANEOUS

LIGHTING PANEL

POWER PANEL

WIRING – CONCEALED IN CEILING OR WALL

WIRING – CONCEALED IN FLOOR

WIRING EXPOSED

HOME RUN TO PANEL BOARD
Indicate number of circuits by number of arrows. Any circuit without such designation indicates a two-wire circuit. For a greater number of wires indicate as follows: (3 wires)
(4 wires), etc.

FEEDERS
Use heavy lines and designate by number corresponding to listing in feeder schedule

WIRING TURNED UP

WIRING TURNED DOWN

GENERATOR — G

MOTOR — M

INSTRUMENT (SPECIFY) — I

TRANSFORMER — T

CONTROLLER

EXTERNALLY-OPERATED DISCONNECT SWITCH

PULL BOX

PLUMBING SYMBOLS. . .

FIXTURES...

Fixture	Symbol
STANDARD BATHTUB	
OVAL BATHTUB	
WHIRLPOOL BATH	
SHOWER STALL	
SHOWER HEAD	
TANK-TYPE WATER CLOSET	
WALL-MOUNTED WATER CLOSET	
FLOOR-MOUNTED WATER CLOSET	
LOW-PROFILE WATER CLOSET	
BIDET	
WALL-MOUNTED URINAL	
FLOOR-MOUNTED URINAL	
TROUGH-TYPE URINAL	
WALL-MOUNTED LAVATORY	
PEDESTAL LAVATORY	
BUILT-IN LAVATORY	
WHEELCHAIR LAVATORY	
CORNER LAVATORY	
FLOOR DRAIN	
FLOOR SINK	

...FIXTURES

Fixture	Symbol
LAUNDRY TRAY	
BUILT-IN SINK	
DOUBLE OR TRIPLE BUILT-IN SINK	
COMMERCIAL KITCHEN SINK	
SERVICE SINK	SS
CLINIC SERVICE SINK	
FLOOR-MOUNTED SERVICE SINK	
DRINKING FOUNTAIN	DF
WATER COOLER	
HOT WATER TANK	HW T
WATER HEATER	WH
METER	M
HOSE BIBB	HB
GAS OUTLET	G
GREASE SEPARATOR	G
GARAGE DRAIN	
FLOOR DRAIN WITH BACKWATER VALVE	

PIPING...

Piping	Symbol
SOIL, WASTE, OR LEADER – ABOVE GRADE	
SOIL, WASTE, OR LEADER – BELOW GRADE	
VENT	
COMBINATION WASTE AND VENT	SV
STORM DRAIN	SD
COLD WATER	

...PIPING

Piping	Symbol
CHILLED DRINKING WATER SUPPLY	DWS
CHILLED DRINKING WATER RETURN	DWR
HOT WATER	
HOT WATER RETURN	
SANITIZING HOT WATER SUPPLY (180°F)	
SANITIZING HOT WATER RETURN (180°F)	
DRY STANDPIPE	DSP
COMBINATION STANDPIPE	CSP
MAIN SUPPLIES SPRINKLER	S
BRANCH AND HEAD SPRINKLER	
GAS – LOW PRESSURE	G G
GAS – MEDIUM PRESSURE	MG
GAS – HIGH PRESSURE	HG
COMPRESSED AIR	A
OXYGEN	O
NITROGEN	N
HYDROGEN	H
HELIUM	HE
ARGON	AR
LIQUID PETROLEUM GAS	LPG
INDUSTRIAL WASTE	INW
CAST IRON	CI
CULVERT PIPE	CP
CLAY TILE	CT
DUCTILE IRON	DI
REINFORCED CONCRETE	RCP
DRAIN – OPEN TILE OR AGRICULTURAL TILE	

. . .PLUMBING SYMBOLS

PIPE FITTING AND VALVE SYMBOLS

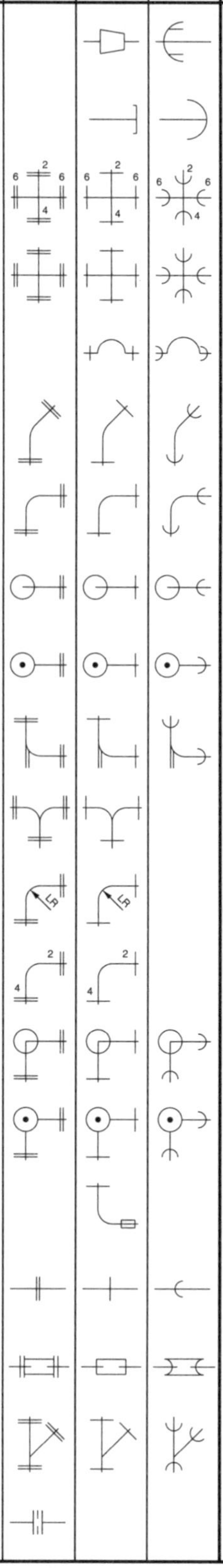

	FLANGED	SCREWED	BELL & SPIGOT
BUSHING			
CAP			
REDUCING CROSS			
STRAIGHT-SIZE CROSS			
CROSSOVER			
45° ELBOW			
90° ELBOW			
ELBOW – TURNED DOWN			
ELBOW – TURNED UP			
BASE ELBOW			
DOUBLE-BRANCH ELBOW			
LONG-RADIUS ELBOW			
REDUCING ELBOW			
SIDE OUTLET ELBOW – OUTLET DOWN			
SIDE OUTLET ELBOW – OUTLET UP			
STREET ELBOW			
CONNECTING PIPE JOINT			
EXPANSION JOINT			
LATERAL			
ORIFICE FLANGE			

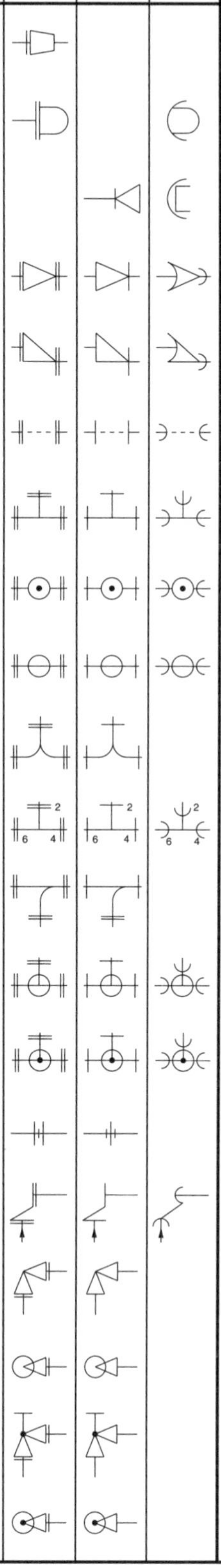

	FLANGED	SCREWED	BELL & SPIGOT
REDUCING FLANGE			
BULL PLUG			
PIPE PLUG			
CONCENTRIC REDUCER			
ECCENTRIC REDUCER			
SLEEVE			
STRAIGHT-SIZE TEE			
TEE – OUTLET UP			
TEE – OUTLET DOWN			
DOUBLE-SWEEP TEE			
REDUCING TEE			
SINGLE-SWEEP TEE			
SIDE OUTLET TEE – OUTLET DOWN			
SIDE OUTLET TEE – OUTLET UP			
UNION			
ANGLE CHECK VALVE			
ANGLE GATE VALVE – ELEVATION			
ANGLE GATE VALVE – PLAN			
ANGLE GLOBE VALVE – ELEVATION			
ANGLE GLOBE VALVE – PLAN			

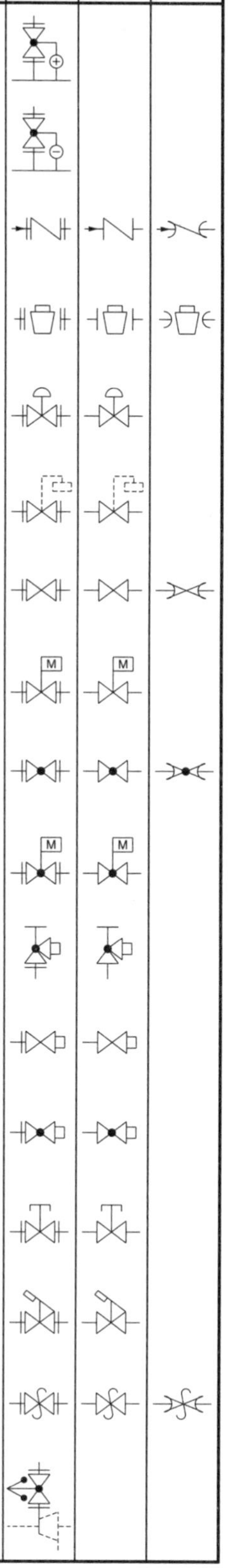

	FLANGED	SCREWED	BELL & SPIGOT
AUTOMATIC BY-PASS VALVE			
AUTOMATIC REDUCING VALVE			
STRAIGHT CHECK VALVE			
COCK			
DIAPHRAGM VALVE			
FLOAT VALVE			
GATE VALVE			
MOTOR-OPERATED GATE VALVE			
GLOBE VALVE			
MOTOR-OPERATED GLOBE VALVE			
ANGLE HOSE VALVE			
GATE VALVE			
GLOBE VALVE			
LOCKSHIELD VALVE			
QUICK-OPENING VALVE			
SAFETY VALVE			
GOVERNOR-OPERATED AUTOMATIC VALVE			

HVAC SYMBOLS

EQUIPMENT SYMBOLS

- EXPOSED RADIATOR
- RECESSED RADIATOR
- FLUSH ENCLOSED RADIATOR
- PROJECTING ENCLOSED RADIATOR
- UNIT HEATER (PROPELLER) – PLAN
- UNIT HEATER (CENTRIFUGAL) – PLAN
- UNIT VENTILATOR – PLAN
- STEAM
- DUPLEX STRAINER
- PRESSURE-REDUCING VALVE
- AIR LINE VALVE
- STRAINER
- THERMOMETER
- PRESSURE GAUGE AND COCK
- RELIEF VALVE
- AUTOMATIC 3-WAY VALVE
- AUTOMATIC 2-WAY VALVE
- SOLENOID VALVE (S)

DUCTWORK

- DUCT (1ST FIGURE, WIDTH; 2ND FIGURE, DEPTH) — 12 X 20
- DIRECTION OF FLOW
- FLEXIBLE CONNECTION
- DUCTWORK WITH ACOUSTICAL LINING
- FIRE DAMPER WITH ACCESS DOOR — FD | AD
- MANUAL VOLUME DAMPER — VD
- AUTOMATIC VOLUME DAMPER
- EXHAUST, RETURN OR OUTSIDE AIR DUCT – SECTION — 20 X 12
- SUPPLY DUCT – SECTION — 20 X 12
- CEILING DIFFUSER SUPPLY OUTLET — 20" DIA CD 1000 CFM
- CEILING DIFFUSER SUPPLY OUTLET — 20 X 12 CD 700 CFM
- LINEAR DIFFUSER — 96 X 6-LD 400 CFM
- FLOOR REGISTER — 20 X 12 FR 700 CFM
- TURNING VANES
- FAN AND MOTOR WITH BELT GUARD
- LOUVER OPENING — 20 X 12-L 700 CFM

HEATING PIPING

HIGH-PRESSURE STEAM	HPS
MEDIUM-PRESSURE STEAM	MPS
LOW-PRESSURE STEAM	LPS
HIGH-PRESSURE RETURN	HPR
MEDIUM-PRESSURE RETURN	MPR
LOW-PRESSURE RETURN	LPR
BOILER BLOW OFF	BD
CONDENSATE OR VACUUM PUMP DISCHARGE	VPD
FEEDWATER PUMP DISCHARGE	PPD
MAKEUP WATER	MU
AIR RELIEF LINE	V
FUEL OIL SUCTION	FOS
FUEL OIL RETURN	FOR
FUEL OIL VENT	FOV
COMPRESSED AIR	A
HOT WATER HEATING SUPPLY	HW
HOT WATER HEATING RETURN	HWR

AIR CONDITIONING PIPING

REFRIGERANT LIQUID	RL
REFRIGERANT DISCHARGE	RD
REFRIGERANT SUCTION	RS
CONDENSER WATER SUPPLY	CWS
CONDENSER WATER RETURN	CWR
CHILLED WATER SUPPLY	CHWS
CHILLED WATER RETURN	CHWR
MAKEUP WATER	MU
HUMIDIFICATION LINE	H
DRAIN	D

REFRIGERATION SYMBOLS

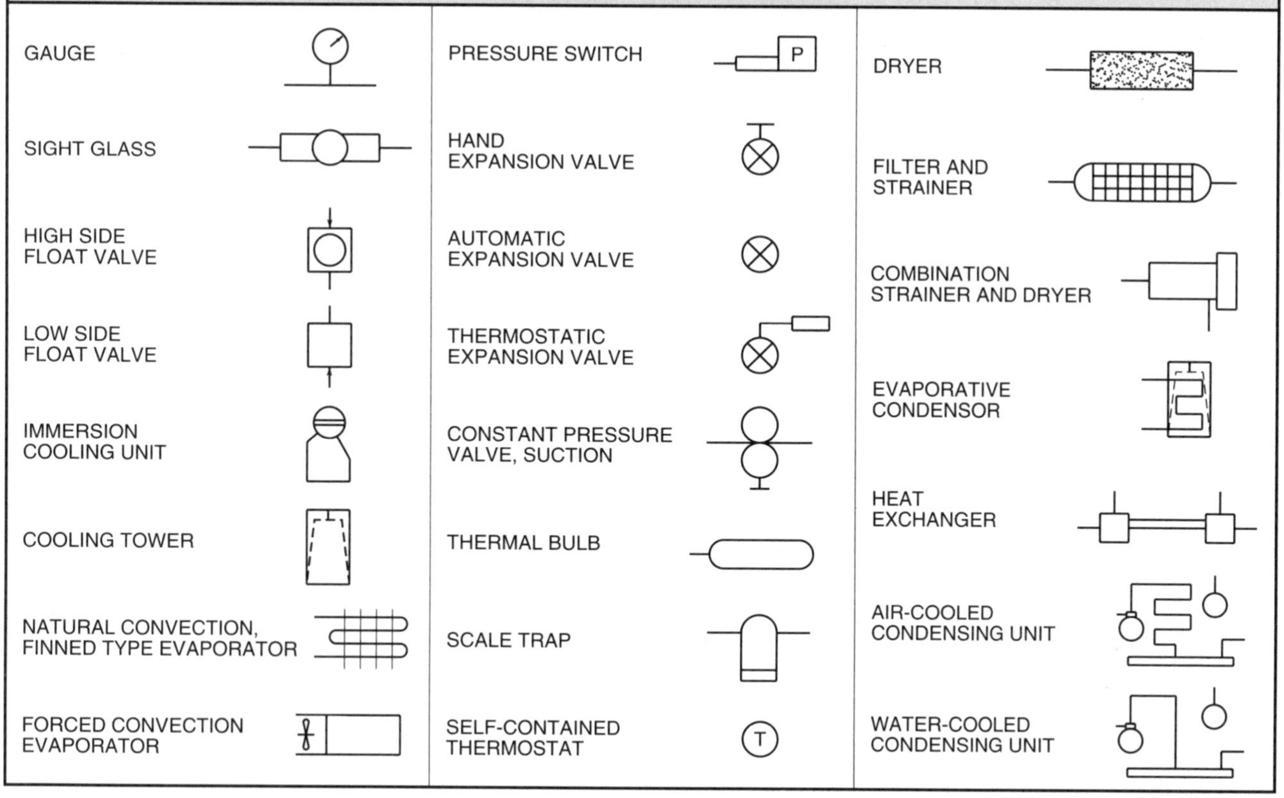

GAUGE	PRESSURE SWITCH	DRYER
SIGHT GLASS	HAND EXPANSION VALVE	FILTER AND STRAINER
HIGH SIDE FLOAT VALVE	AUTOMATIC EXPANSION VALVE	COMBINATION STRAINER AND DRYER
LOW SIDE FLOAT VALVE	THERMOSTATIC EXPANSION VALVE	EVAPORATIVE CONDENSOR
IMMERSION COOLING UNIT	CONSTANT PRESSURE VALVE, SUCTION	HEAT EXCHANGER
COOLING TOWER	THERMAL BULB	AIR-COOLED CONDENSING UNIT
NATURAL CONVECTION, FINNED TYPE EVAPORATOR	SCALE TRAP	WATER-COOLED CONDENSING UNIT
FORCED CONVECTION EVAPORATOR	SELF-CONTAINED THERMOSTAT	

WELD JOINTS AND POSITIONS

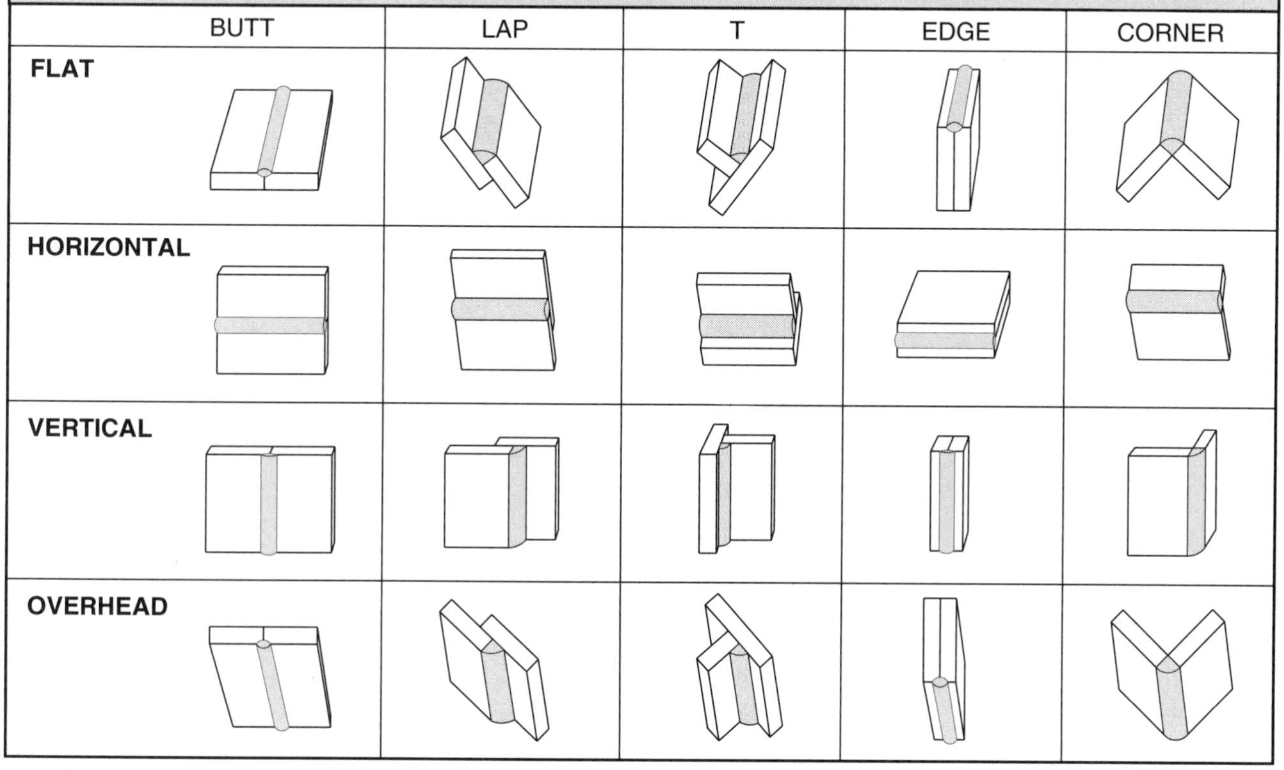

	BUTT	LAP	T	EDGE	CORNER
FLAT					
HORIZONTAL					
VERTICAL					
OVERHEAD					

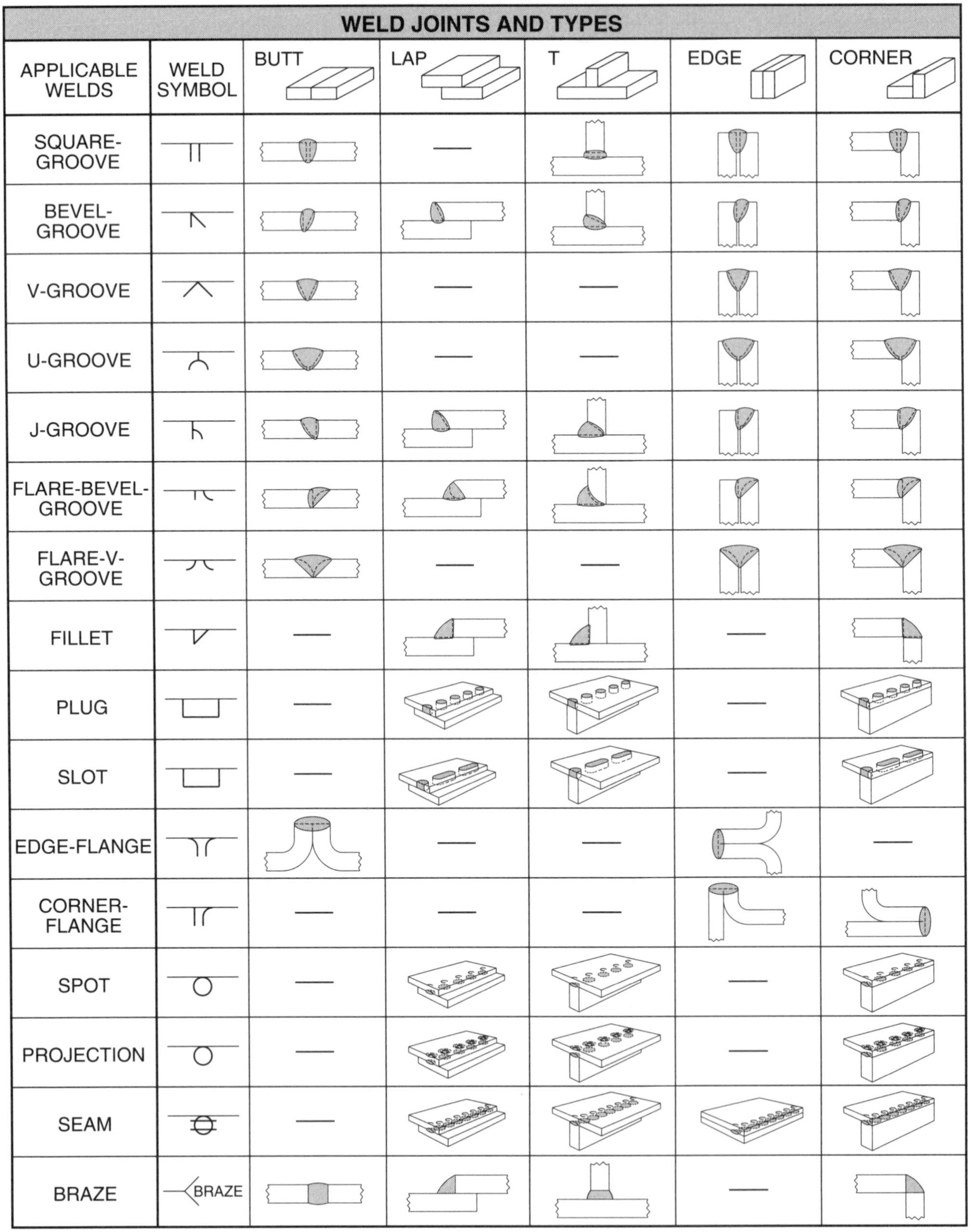

WELD JOINTS AND TYPES						
APPLICABLE WELDS	WELD SYMBOL	BUTT	LAP	T	EDGE	CORNER
SQUARE-GROOVE			—			
BEVEL-GROOVE						
V-GROOVE			—	—		
U-GROOVE			—	—		
J-GROOVE						
FLARE-BEVEL-GROOVE						
FLARE-V-GROOVE			—	—		
FILLET		—			—	
PLUG		—			—	
SLOT		—			—	
EDGE-FLANGE			—	—		—
CORNER-FLANGE		—	—	—		
SPOT		—			—	
PROJECTION		—			—	
SEAM		—				
BRAZE	BRAZE				—	

WELDING SYMBOL

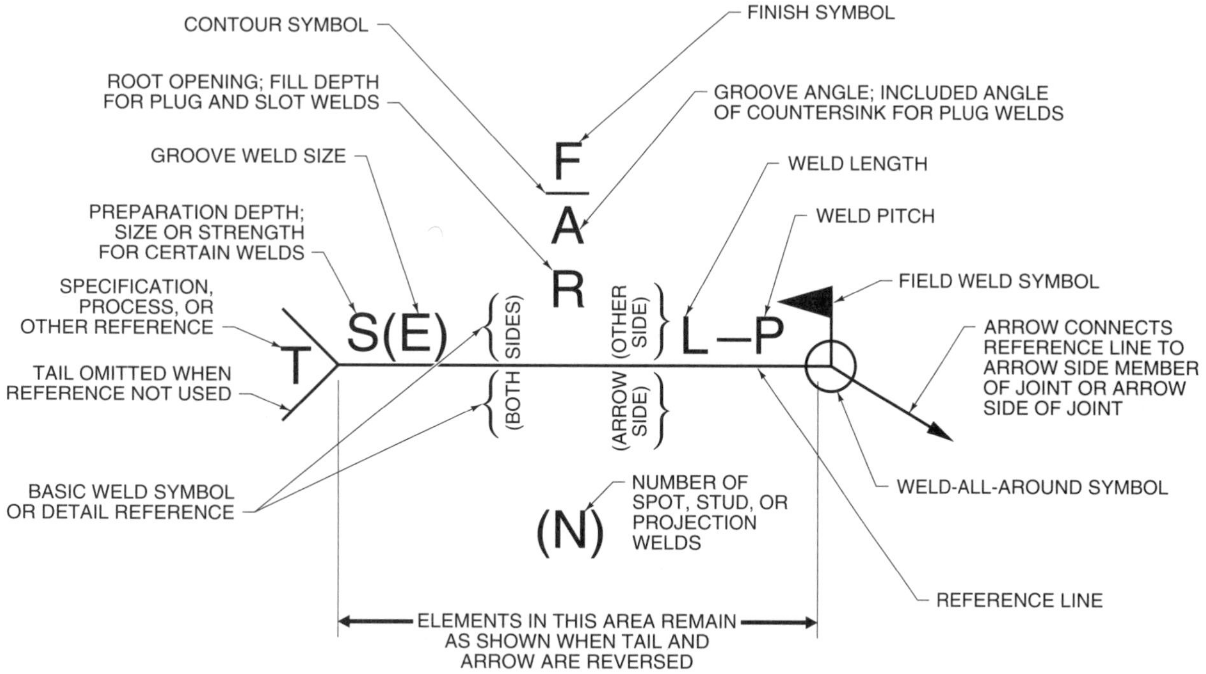

CONTOUR SYMBOL
FINISH SYMBOL
ROOT OPENING; FILL DEPTH FOR PLUG AND SLOT WELDS
GROOVE ANGLE; INCLUDED ANGLE OF COUNTERSINK FOR PLUG WELDS
GROOVE WELD SIZE
F
A
R
WELD LENGTH
WELD PITCH
PREPARATION DEPTH; SIZE OR STRENGTH FOR CERTAIN WELDS
FIELD WELD SYMBOL
SPECIFICATION, PROCESS, OR OTHER REFERENCE
S(E)
(BOTH SIDES)
(OTHER SIDE)
L–P
ARROW CONNECTS REFERENCE LINE TO ARROW SIDE MEMBER OF JOINT OR ARROW SIDE OF JOINT
T
TAIL OMITTED WHEN REFERENCE NOT USED
(ARROW SIDE)
BASIC WELD SYMBOL OR DETAIL REFERENCE
NUMBER OF SPOT, STUD, OR PROJECTION WELDS
(N)
WELD-ALL-AROUND SYMBOL
REFERENCE LINE
ELEMENTS IN THIS AREA REMAIN AS SHOWN WHEN TAIL AND ARROW ARE REVERSED

NONDESTRUCTIVE EXAMINATION SYMBOL

NUMBER OF EXAMINATIONS
(N)
EXAMINE IN FIELD
SPECIFICATION OR OTHER REFERENCES
(BOTH SIDES)
(OTHER SIDE)
L
EXAMINE-ALL-AROUND
T
TAIL
ARROW
(ARROW SIDE)
BASIC EXAMINATION SYMBOL
BASIC EXAMINATION SYMBOL
EXAMINE-ALL-AROUND
FIELD EXAMINATION
RADIATION DIRECTION
EXAMINE IN FIELD
VISUAL EXAMINATION
VT
RADIATION DIRECTION SYMBOL
RT
RADIOGRAPHIC EXAMINATION
FILLET WELD COMPLETED FIRST

SEPARATE NONDESTRUCTIVE EXAMINATION SYMBOL

SEPARATE REFERENCE LINE ON WELDING SYMBOL

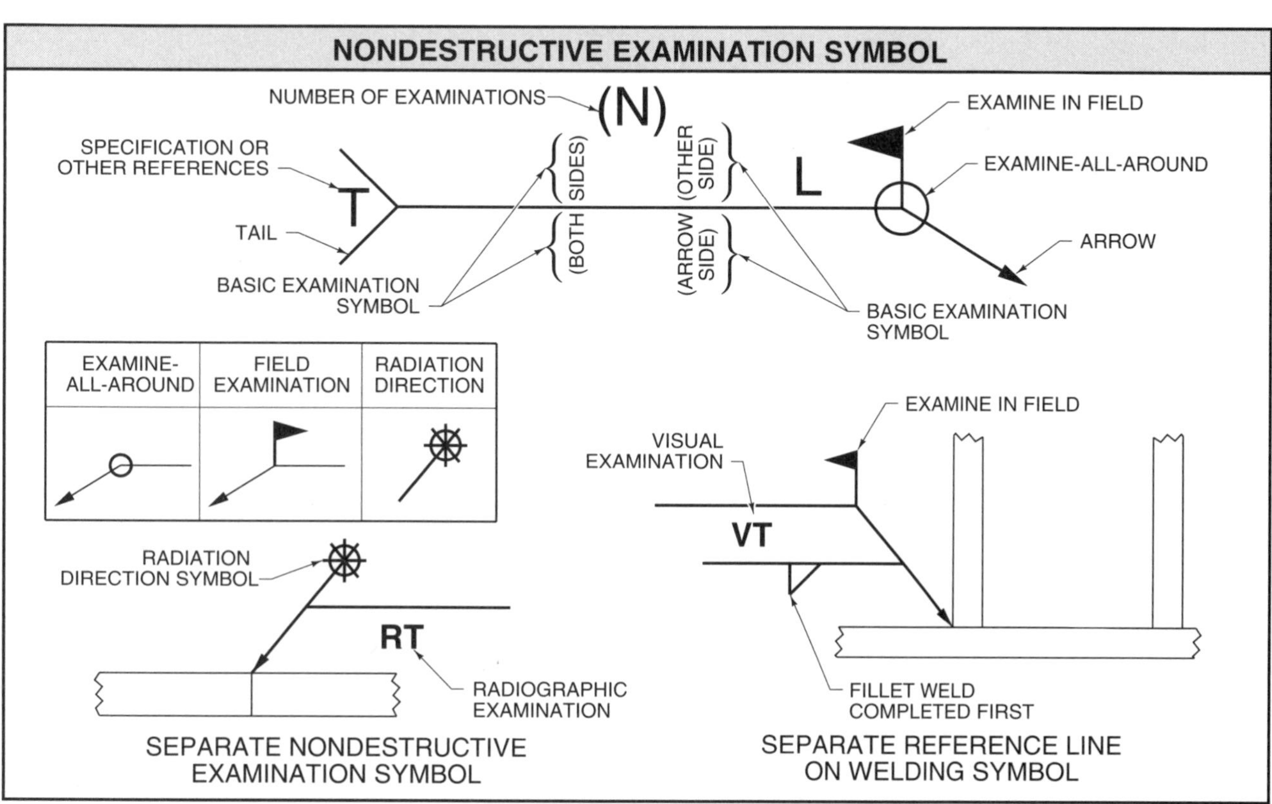

CSI MASTERFORMAT™

The MasterFormat™ is a master list of numbers and titles for organizing information about construction requirements, products, and activities into a standard sequence. MasterFormat™ is a uniform system for organizing information in project manuals, for organizing cost data, for filing product information and other technical data, for identifying drawing objects, and for presenting construction market data. The latest edition of the MasterFormat™ was produced jointly by the Construction Specifications Institute (CSI) and Construction Specifications Canada (CSC) with extensive public review and coordination with industry users.

Groupings

The numbers and titles in MasterFormat™ are grouped under the general headings:

Introductory Information (numbered 00001 to 00099)

Bidding Requirements (numbered 00100 to 00499)

Contracting Requirements (numbered 00500 to 00999)

Facilities and Spaces (no numbering)

Systems and Assemblies (no numbering)

Construction Products and Activities (Divisions 1-16)

Divisions

MasterFormat™ arranges related construction products and activities into 16 level one titles, called Divisions. The numbers and titles of the Divisions are:

Division 1 General Requirements

Division 2 Site Construction

Division 3 Concrete

Division 4 Masonry

Division 5 Metals

Division 6 Wood and Plastics

Division 7 Thermal and Moisture Protection

Division 8 Doors and Windows

Division 9 Finishes

Division 10 Specialties

Division 11 Equipment

Division 12 Furnishings

Division 13 Special Construction

Division 14 Conveying Systems

Division 15 Mechanical

Division 16 Electrical

The level two titles (formerly called "broadscope titles") identify clusters of products and activities having an identifying characteristic in common. Level two titles are the highest level generally used in titling and arranging units of construction information. In MasterFormat™, level two titles are presented as all uppercase letters and bold typeface.

MasterFormat™ shows both numbers and titles at level three. Level three titles are presented as first letter uppercase and bold typeface. Level three numbers are presented as the last three digits of the five-digit designation in bold typeface.

MasterFormat™ suggests titles at level four, but does not indicate numbers. Users should create numbers by interpolating between assigned numbers when using level four titles or creating new titles. Level four titles are presented alphabetically in regular typeface.

For example, Division 16 Electrical includes basic information about products and activities related to wiring, electrical power, transmission and distribution, low-voltage distribution, lighting, and communications.

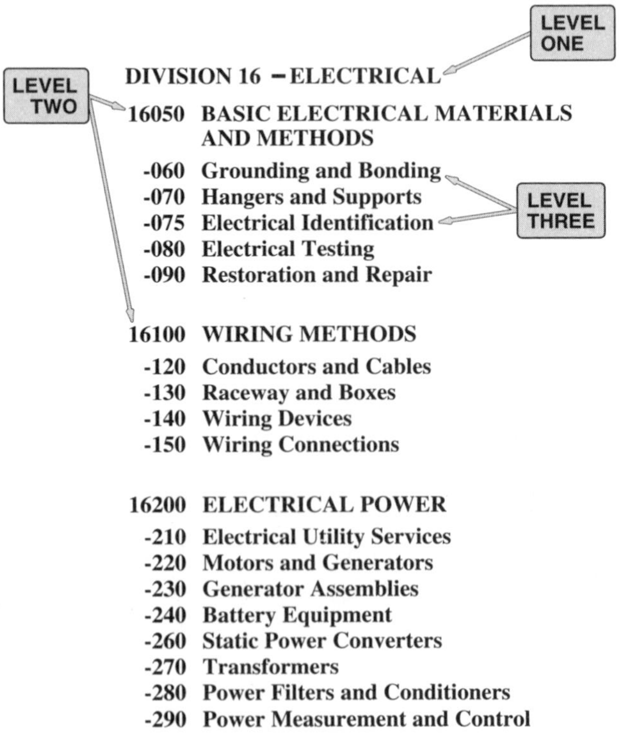

LEVEL ONE

LEVEL TWO

LEVEL THREE

DIVISION 16 – ELECTRICAL

16050 BASIC ELECTRICAL MATERIALS AND METHODS
- **-060 Grounding and Bonding**
- **-070 Hangers and Supports**
- **-075 Electrical Identification**
- **-080 Electrical Testing**
- **-090 Restoration and Repair**

16100 WIRING METHODS
- **-120 Conductors and Cables**
- **-130 Raceway and Boxes**
- **-140 Wiring Devices**
- **-150 Wiring Connections**

16200 ELECTRICAL POWER
- **-210 Electrical Utility Services**
- **-220 Motors and Generators**
- **-230 Generator Assemblies**
- **-240 Battery Equipment**
- **-260 Static Power Converters**
- **-270 Transformers**
- **-280 Power Filters and Conditioners**
- **-290 Power Measurement and Control**

Reprinted from the Construction Specifications Institute and Construction Specifications Canada *MasterFormat™ 1995 Edition* with permission from Construction Specifications Institute, 1997.

ABBREVIATIONS OF TERMS. . .

A

acoustic	ACST
acoustical tile	AT or ACT
adhesive	ADH
aileron	AIL
air conditioner	AIR COND
alloy	ALY
alternating current	AC
ambient	AMB
American Wire Gauge	AWG
ampere	AMP
anchor bolt	AB
architecture	ARCH
area	A
area drain	AD
asphalt	ASPH
asphalt tile	AT
as required	AR
astragal	A
automatic	AUTO
automatic sprinkler	AS
auxiliary	AUX
azimuth	AZ

B

bathroom	B
beam	BM
bearing	BRG
bearing plate	BPL or BRG PL
bench mark	BM
board	BD
board foot	BF
brick	BRK
bridge	BRDG
building	BLDG
building line	BL
built-up roofing	BUR

C

cased opening	CO
casement	CSMT
cast iron	CI
cast-iron pipe	CIP
cast steel	CS
Celsius	°C
cement	CEM
cement floor	CF
center	CTR
centerline	CL
center-to-center	C to C
ceramic	CER
ceramic tile	CT
ceramic-tile floor	CTF
circuit breaker	CB
circuit interrupter	CI
cleanout	CO
coarse	CRS
coaxial	COAX
cold air	CA
cold water	CW
column	COL
compacted	COMP
composition	CMPSN
compressed air	COMPA
concrete	CONC
concrete block	CCB
concrete floor	CCF
concrete pipe	CP
condenser	COND
conductor	CNDCT
conduit	CND
construction joint	CJ
contour	CTR
control joint	CLJ
cubic	CU
cubic foot per minute	CFM
cubic foot per second	CFS
cubic inch	CU IN
cubic yard	CU YD
culvert	CULV
cutoff valve	COV
cutout valve	COV
cylinder lock	CYLL

D

dead load	DL
decibel	DB
deck	DK
demolition	DML
diagonal	DIAG
dimension	DIM
direct current	DC
discharge	DISCH
disconnect switch	DS
dishwater	DW
distribution panel	DPNL
division	DIV
double-acting	DBL ACT
double-pole double-throw	DPDT
double-pole double-throw switch	DPDT SW
double-pole single-throw	DPST
double-pole single-throw switch	DPST SW
double-pole switch	DP SW
downspout	DS
drain	DR
drain tile	DT
drinking fountain	DF
drywall	DW
duplex	DX
duty cycle	DTY CY

E

each	EA
east	E
electric panel	EP
electromechanical	ELMCH
electronic	ELEK
elevation	EL
elevator	ELEV
entrance	ENTR
equipment	EQPT
equivalent	EQUIV
estimate	EST
expanded metal	EM
exterior	EXT
exterior grade	EXT GR

F

face brick	FB
Fahrenheit	°F
fastener	FSTNR
fiberboard	FBRBD
fiberboard, corrugated	FBDC
fiberboard, double wall	FDWL
fiberboard, solid	FBDS
figure	FIG
finish	FNSH
finish all over	FAO
finished floor	FNSH FL
finish grade	FG
finish one side	F1S
finish two sides	F2S
firebrick	FBCK
fire door	FDR
fire extinguisher	FEXT
fire hydrant	FHY
fireproof	FPRF
fire wall	FW
fixed window	FX WDW
flagstone	FLGSTN
flammable	FLMB
flashing	FL
floor	FL
floor drain	FD
fluorescent	FLUOR
footing	FTG
foot per minute	FPM
foot per second	FPS
foundation	FDN
four-pole	4P
four-pole double-throw switch	4PDT SW
four-pole single-throw switch	4PST SW
four-pole switch	4PSW
front view	FV
furring	FUR
fuse	FU
fuse block	FB
fuse box	FUBX
fuse holder	FUHLR
fusible	FSBL

G

gauge	GA
gallon per hour	GPH
gallon per minute	GPM
garage	GAR
glass	GL
glass block	GLB
glaze	GLZ
grade	GR
gravel	GVL
gross vehicle weight	GVW
ground	GND
grounded (outlet)	G
ground-fault circuit interrupter	GFCI
gypsum	GYP

H

hazardous	HAZ
heating, ventilating, and air conditioning	HVAC
heavy-duty	HD
hertz	Hz
highway	HWY
horizontal	HOR
hot water	HW
hydraulic	HYDR

I

inch	IN
inch per second	IPS
inch-pound	IN LB
infrared	IR
interior	INTR
iron pipe	IP

J

jamb	JB or JMB
joist	J
junction	JCT

K

keyway	KWY
kiln-dried	KD
knife switch	KN SW
knockout	KO

L

lavatory	LAV
left	L
left hand	LH
lighting	LTG
linoleum	LINOL
lintel	LNTL
live load	LL

M

main	MN
manhole	MH
masonry	MSNRY
maximum working pressure	MWP
medicine cabinet	MC
metal anchor	MA
metal door	METD
metal flashing	METF
metal lath and plaster	MLP
metal threshold	MT
mezzanine	MEZZ
mile per gallon	MPG
mile per hour	MPH
miscellaneous	MISC
monolithic	ML
mortar	MOR

. . .ABBREVIATIONS OF TERMS

N

nameplate	NPL
National Electrical Code	NEC
net weight	NTWT
north	N
nosing	NOS

O

on center	OC
opaque	OPA
open web joist	OJ or OWJ
outlet	OUT

P

panel	PNL
parallel	PRL
peak-to-peak	P-P
perpendicular	PERP
phase	PH
piling	PLG
pitch	P
plank	PLK
plate glass	PLGL
plumbing	PLMB
plywood	PLYWD
pneumatic	PNEU
point of beginning	POB
pole	P
porcelain	PORC
pound	LB
pound-foot	LB FT
precast	PRCST
prefabricated	PREFAB
prefinished	PFN
property line	PL
pull box	PB
pull switch	PS

Q

quadrant	QDRNT
quarry tile	QT
quart	QT
quick-acting	QA

R

recess	REC
reference	REF
reinforced concrete	RC
reinforcing steel	RST
reverse-acting	RACT
revolution per minute	RPM
revolution per second	RPS
ribbed	RIB
right	R
right hand	RH
rigid	RGD
riser	R
roll roofing	RR
roofing	RFG
rotor	RTR
rough sawn	RS

S

sanitary	SAN
schedule	SCHED
section	SECT
sheet	SH
sheet metal	SM
sill cock	SC
single-phase	1PH
single-pole	SP
single-pole double-throw	SPDT
single-pole double-throw switch	SPDT SW
single-pole single-throw	SPST
single-pole single-throw switch	SPST SW
single-pole switch	SP SW
skylight	SLT
sliding door	SLD
slope	SLP
solenoid	SOL
south	S
specification	SPEC
square	SQ
square foot	SQ FT
square inch	SQ IN
square yard	SQ YD
stainless steel	SST
structural glass	SG
surfaced or dress four sides	S4S
surfaced or dressed one side	S1S
switch	SW

T

telephone	TEL
temperature	TEMP
three-phase	3PH
three-pole	3P
three-pole double-throw	3PDT
three-pole single-throw	3PST
three-way	3WAY
three-wire	3W
threshold	TH
timber	TMBR
total	TOT
triple-pole double-throw	3PDT
triple-pole double-throw switch	3PDT SW
triple-pole single-throw	3PST
triple-pole single-throw switch	3PST SW
triple-pole switch	3P SW
truss	TR
two-phase	2PH
two-pole	DP
two-pole double-throw	DPDT
two-pole single-throw	DPST

V

valley	VAL
valve	V
vent	V
vertical	VERT
voltage	V
voltage drop	VD
volume	VOL

W

walk in closet	WIC
waste pipe	WP
waste stack	WS
water	WTR
water closet	WC
water heater	WH
water meter	WM
watt	W
weatherproof	WTHPRF
welded wire fabric	WWF
west	W
without	W/O
wood	WD

Glossary

A

abutment: **1.** Structure that supports the end of a bridge or arch. **2.** Anchorage for bridge suspension or prestressing cables. **3.** Side of an earth bank that supports a dam.

acetylene: Colorless gas formed from a mixture of calcium carbide and water, commonly combined with air or oxygen to form a combustible gas. Stable under low pressure; unstable if compressed to more than 15 psi.

acoustical material: Material used to absorb sound waves and prevent passage of sound. Includes tile, expanded foam, plastic, or material primarily composed of mineral, wood, cork, metal, or vegetable fibers.

addendum: Written document or drawing issued before the execution of a contract. It modifies the original drawing and/or specifications.

admixture: Material other than water, aggregate, fiber reinforcement, and cement. It is used as an ingredient in a batch of concrete or mortar to add color, control strength, shorten or lengthen setting time, or modify the temperature range of the mix. It may be incorporated into the mix before or during mixing.

aerator: Mechanical device used to introduce air into water, soil, or sewage.

aggregate: Granular material such as gravel, sand, vermiculite, or perlite that is added to cement paste to form concrete, mortar, or plaster. Graded as fine coarse, lightweight, and heavyweight. Comprises 60% to 80% of the volume of concrete.

air entrainment: Process in which minute air bubbles, ranging in size from .01″ to .001″, are mixed in a concrete or mortar mix. Improves workability and frost resistance of the mix. In specifications, designated by the letter A following the concrete type designation.

air handlers: Large fans used in commercial applications.

allowable load: Maximum load an object or assembly can support within specified safety tolerances.

allowable span: Maximum distance a structural member can be unsupported and maintain structural integrity.

allowable stress: Maximum stress an object or assembly can withstand within specified safety tolerances.

anticipator: Fixed or adjustable thermostat component used to regulate a heating and/or AC unit. It prevents overheating or overcooling of an area beyond a predetermined temperature.

architectural concrete: Concrete in which the surface is finished to not show exposed form joint marks.

areaway: Open, below-grade area around a basement window or door. Provides light, ventilation, and means of access.

B

backing board: Gypsum drywall installed in a suspended ceiling. Serves as an attachment surface for acoustical tile.

backing brick: Lower-quality brick used for constructing the inner part of a brick wall.

bar joist: An open web joist with steel angles at the top and bottom of the joist and bars for the intermediate members.

baseline: Established reference axis from which measurements are taken when laying out building lines, property lines, street lines, or other working lines.

beam: Horizontal structural member made of a single member of concrete, timber, stone, iron, or other structural material and installed horizontally to support loads over an opening.

beam and column construction: Construction consisting of bays framed of structural steel which are repeated to create large structures.

bearing plate: Flat piece of steel placed under a heavily loaded truss, beam, girder, or column to distribute the load so pressure will not exceed bearing strength of the supporting member.

bid bond: Form of security executed by the bidder. It is designed to guarantee that the bidder will actually sign a contact for the project and provide other required bonding.

blueprint: Set of drawings with dimensions and materials for a structure or building project. The term is derived from the old reproduction process, which produced a drawing copy sheet with a blue black-ground and white lines. The term *print* is preferred today.

box beam: Hollow horizontal member formed like a long box. Either a structural or ornamental member, depending on materials and design.

box column: Built-up, hollow, usually square, vertical support member used in porch construction.

box girder: Horizontal support member of steel or cast iron with a hollow square or rectangular design.

box pile: Foundation support formed by welding two steel channels or other structural steel shapes along their long axis, forming a void in the middle.

building area: Total ground space covered by each building and accessory building, not including uncovered entrances, terraces, and steps.

building code: Regulations adopted by a federal, state, county, or city government for the structure of buildings in a safe and structurally-sound manner to protect the heath, safety, and general welfare of those within or near the buildings.

building line: Boundary on a building site within which walls of the building must be confined.

built-up roofing: Covering normally used on flat roofs composed of several layers of bituminous materials applied in an overlapping manner and sealed to provide a waterproof covering. Commonly covered with a thin layer of gravel.

C

cable tray: An open grid rack suspended from structural members to allow for a series of cables to be supported.

caisson: A poured-in-place concrete piling of large diameter.

catch basin: Reservoir used to retain surface water.

ceramic: Material made from clay or similar materials that are baked in an oven at high temperatures.

chair: Device used to support rebars in the proper position during concrete placement.

circuit breaker: Device that opens and closes a circuit by nonautomatic means, and automatically opens a circuit when a predetermined current overload is reached without damage to itself.

civil engineer: Person who designs and assists in the construction of static structures such as roads, bridges, etc.

climbing tower crane: Crane used in the erection of high-rises. Consists of a vertical mast fastened to structural members and moved up as construction reaches higher levels. Horizontal boom is rotated atop the mast to facilitate lifting.

composite joist: Intermediate horizontal structural member composed of different types of building materials; e.g., concrete with reinforcing steel.

concrete masonry unit: Precast hollow or solid masonry unit made of cement and fine aggregate, with or without admixtures or pigments. It is formed into modular or non-modular dimensions to be laid with other similar units.

contour line: Dashed or solid line on a plot plan used to show elevations of the surface. A dashed line indicates the existing elevation and a solid line indicates the finished elevation. The actual elevation may be written on each contour line.

contract documents: All written and graphic materials used for design and construction of a project, including the agreement, general conditions, prints, specifications, addenda, etc.

contractor: Individual or company responsible for performance of construction work, including labor and materials, according to plans and specifications.

curtain wall: Non-bearing exterior panel suspended on or supported by the primary structure.

D

dampproofing: Treatment of mortar or concrete to prevent passage of water or water vapor. Available as a coating for exposed surfaces, admixture to concrete or mortar, or plastic film.

datum: Reference point to which other elevations, angles, or measurements are related.

demand: Electrical load over a specified interval of time. Expressed as kilowatts, kilovolt-amperes, kilovars, and/or amperes.

differential hammer: Pile hammer that uses steam, compressed air, or high-pressure hydraulic fluid to raise the ram and accelerate the fall.

disconnecting means: Device or group of devices used to disconnect conductors of an electrical circuit from the energy source.

distribution panelboard: Electrical panel or group of electrical panels assembled into a single unit that is installed in a cabinet or cutout box accessible from the front only. Includes buses with or without switches and/or automatic overcurrent protection devices.

dressed lumber: Wood in which one or more surfaces have been surfaced at a mill.

drive cap: Cushion between a pile hammer and a pile. Used to prevent damage to the pile while being driven.

drop hammer: Heavy weight that moves freely between two vertical guide rails to exert force to the top of a pile. Used to drive piles for small projects and in remote locations.

E

earthwork: Digging and excavating operations.

easements: Areas of property set aside for the use of utility companies which allow for placement and maintenance of utility services.

effective voltage: Working voltage in alternating current equal to .707 times the peak voltage.

elastomeric: Made of a pliable synthetic polymer.

electrical plan: Print showing placement of electrical fixtures, appliances, and circuits. Exact placement of conductors is not specified. Commonly noted with a capital E preceding the sheet number.

embankment: Raised surface of rock, fill material, or earth used to retain water or support a roadway.

erection: To build with structural steel.

evaporator: Portion of a cooling system used to vaporize liquid refrigerant.

exothermic: Chemical reaction that releases heat.

F

faced wall: Masonry wall in which one or both sides are finished with material different from the body of the wall. Exterior surfaces and body are tied together to form a single load-bearing unit.

fixture: 1. Device that holds an electric lamp and is secured to a wall or ceiling. **2.** Part of a plumbing system that provides access for water or waste disposal; e.g., lavatories, water closets, sinks. **3.** Device that secures components or members while they are machined, welded, or drilled. Does not guide the tool during the operation.

float glass: High quality, smooth-surfaced sheet glass manufactured by applying molten glass to a bed of metal.

form lines: Contour lines drawn from visual observation and without accurate elevation information.

freestanding: Not fastened or attached to a support.

full-load current: Electric current that rotating equipment draws from a power source while operating at the rated voltage, speed, and torque.

G

gang form: Prefabricated form panels used to construct a lager form to retain concrete during placement and until it sets and used to facilitate erection and stripping of forms.

gas shielded arc welding: Process used to join metal by heating with an electric arc produced between a consumable electrode and base metal.

general contractor: Person or company that agrees to fulfill an entire building agreement with various items or types of work to be completed such as carpentry, electrical, and plumbing work. Subcontractors may be hired to do some work of the actual building.

glass block: Hollow, opaque, or transparent block made of glass. Used in non-bearing walls and partitions.

gluelam (glued-and-laminated): A structural member constructed by bonding several layers of lumber with adhesive. Commonly used for large curved structural members.

grade beam: Reinforced concrete beam placed at ground level. Member is supported by piles or piers at the end and intermediate positions.

grounded conductor: Intentionally grounded electrical system.

ground-fault circuit-interrupter (GFCI): Device that automatically de-energizes a circuit or a portion of a circuit when the grounded current exceeds a predetermined value that is less than required to operate the overcurrent protection device. Used to protect personnel.

ground-fault protection of equipment (GFPE): Electrical equipment protection provided by disconnecting the equipment from the power source when a predetermined current-to-ground value is obtained.

H

hand signal: Hand and/or arm movement and position used to indicate specific operation to be performed. Commonly used in rigging or surveying where verbal commands cannot be used.

hazardous location: Area containing highly flammable or combustible products, vapors, or fumes.

heavy timber construction: Structure in which fire resistance is achieved with wood structural members, floors, and roofs of a specified dimension and composition.

hydration: Chemical reaction of water with another material, such as cement, that bonds the molecules, resulting in hardening of the mixture.

hydronic system: A system which uses hot water to provide heat.

I

I beam: Structural steel member with cross-sectional area resembling the capital letter I.

impedance: Total resistance and reactance in an alternating current circuit. Expressed in ohms.

impermeable: Not permitting passage of liquid; e.g., asphalt shingles.

impregnate: To thoroughly saturate a material, such as timber, under pressure.

incombustible: Unable to ignite into flame or support fire at 1200°F over a period of 5 minutes.

insulating concrete: Concrete that decreases thermal and sound transmission.

intermittent duty: Operation of electrical circuit or device for alternate intervals of load and no load; load and rest; or load, no load, and rest.

L

laser level: Leveling device in which a concentrated beam of light is projected horizontally or vertically from the source and used as a reference for leveling or verifying horizontal or vertical alignment.

lateral: **1.** Positioned at 90° to another line or object. **2.** Diagonal brace. **3.** Small irrigation ditch or pipe. **4.** Underground electrical service.

leaching: **1.** Separating liquid from solid material by percolating them into soil. **2.** Movement of liquid through rock or porous soil while seeking the path of least resistance.

lift slab: Method of concrete construction in which horizontal slabs are cast on top of each other, jacked into position, and secured to columns at the desired elevation. Successive slabs are separated by a chemical-release agent.

long span construction: Construction consisting of large horizontal steel members, such as girders and trusses, that are fastened together to create large girders and trusses.

M

magazine: Storage facility for explosives.

magnetic switch: Electrical switch in which the contacts are controlled by an electromagnet. Commonly used in motors.

material safety data sheet (MSDS): Document that describes the components of various substances on a construction site including their dangers, proper personal protective equipment worn during exposure, disposal procedures, and necessary actions in case of an emergency.

metal stud: C-shaped, corrosion-resistant member used as a non-bearing structural component of interior partitions. Fastened between flanges or U-shaped metal track with screws or crimpers. Commonly prepunched for installation of electrical conductors and plumbing pipes.

model code: Building code developed by a regional committee of building officials. Recognized building codes in the United States are the *National Building Code*, published by Building Officials and Code Administrators International; *Standard Building Code*, published by the Southern Building Code Congress International; *Uniform Building Code*, published by the International Conference of Building Officials; and *CABO One and Two Family Dwelling Code*, published jointly by these organizations.

monolithic concrete: Concrete formed as a single, continuous member. Only construction joins are used.

N

National Electrical Code®: Nationally-accepted electrical code designed to protect persons and property from hazards arising from the use of electricity. Sponsored and published by the National Fire Protection Association.

natural aggregate: Material such as crushed stone, gravel, and sand that is quarried or mined from the earth.

network: Electrical conductors that are interconnected.

non-bearing: To support no load other than its own.

notice to bidders: Written portion of the bidding documents that gives the bidders the proper procedures for bidding submission.

O

Occupational Safety and Health Administration (OSHA): Federally-funded agency created with the Department of Labor to encourage employers and employees to reduce job site hazards, implement new or revise existing safety programs, monitor job-related injuries and illnesses, and develop job safety and health standards.

open web studs: Light-gauge, non-bearing steel framing member constructed of diagonal wire rods welded to double rod flanges. Used for backing lath.

optical fiber: Thin, flexible glass or plastic fiber used to transmit light for control, signal, and communication applications. Consists of a core, cladding, and protective jacket. Three types of optical fiber are nonconductive (no metallic parts), conductive (noncurrent-carrying metallic parts), and hybrid (containing optical fibers and current-carrying metallic conductors).

orifice: Small opening.

outlet: Point in an electrical system where current is taken to supply utilization equipment.

P

pilaster: Projection from the face of a wall that extends the full height of the wall to provide lateral support.

pile: A structural member installed in the ground to provide vertical and/or horizontal support.

pile cap: A large unit of concrete placed on top of a pile or group of piles.

plat: A drawing of a parcel of land giving its legal description.

plate glass: Polished glass manufactured in large sheets. Thicker and of higher quality than ordinary glass.

plate steel: Flat steel with a thickness of 3/16" or greater. Sheared plate steel is trimmed on all edges during the manufacturing process.

polyvinyl chloride (PVC): 1. Rigid plastic material used for water stops and plumbing pipes and fittings. **2.** Rigid nonmetallic conduit, either thin-walled (Schedule 40) or thick-walled (Schedule 80), approved by the National Electrical Code® as a raceway system for conductors.

post-tensioned concrete: Concrete with steel reinforcing tenons pulled tight and placed in tension after the concrete hardens.

preaction systems: Systems that are activated by smoke detectors or heat detectors.

precast concrete: Large sections of walls, floors, beams, or other structures formed and poured in other than their final position.

pretensioned concrete: Concrete with steel reinforcing tenons pulled tight and placed in tension before the concrete hardens. After the concrete hardens, the steel remains in tension.

project manager: Person or company managing administrative and technical responsibilities of a construction project.

R

raceway: Enclosed channel for routing and placing electrical conductors and cables.

record drawings: Prints that are marked to indicate changes to a project and provide a historical record of the changes.

reinforced concrete: Concrete with embedded reinforcing bars or fibrous material to provide additional tensile strength.

revetment: 1. Facing put on wall or sloping surface to protect against erosion. **2.** Wall with severe slope away from the base.

roadbed: Portion of highway construction over which pavement is laid.

R value: Measure of the effectiveness of a material to provide thermal insulation. Higher R values indicate greater insulating capabilities.

S

service: Conductors and equipment used to deliver electrical energy from the secondary distribution or street main to the wiring system of the location served.

service conductors: Electrical conductors extending from the street main or transformer to the service equipment at the location served.

service equipment: Complete electrical assembly used for main control and as a means for cutoff of the supply. Includes circuit breaker or switch and fuses and accessories. Located near the entrance of service-entrance conductors into a structure.

shaking out: The process of unloading steel members in a planned manner to minimize the amount of moving of pieces during the erection process.

sheet glass: Clear or opaque material manufactured in continuous, long flat pieces and cut to desired sizes and shapes.

slump: Measure of consistency of freshly mixed concrete expressed as inches of fall to the nearest ¼″ of the fresh mix.

solar photovoltaic system: System and components that convert radiant energy into electrical energy.

spandrel beams: Beams bolted to the columns around the perimeter of a building.

structural steel: Load-bearing steel members in a structure.

structural steel joists: Lightweight beams spaced less than 4′ on center.

subcontractor: Person or party that performs part of the work on a construction project under an agreement with the general contractor.

superintendent: Contractor's field representative responsible for supervision of an entire project.

T

tempered glass: Glass that is prestressed by heating and rapidly cooling. Used to increase strength of the glass.

tempered hardboard: Pressed wood panel in which the surface is impregnated with a compound of oil and resin and baked to form a water-resistant finish.

terrazzo: Mixture of cement and water with colored stone, marble chips, or other decorative aggregate embedded in the surface. Surface is ground and polished when hardened to produce a hard, durable surface.

tilt-up panels: Panels which are precast and lifted into place at the job site.

tower crane: Crane consisting of a fixed vertical mast with a pivoting boom at the top. A winch moves along the length of the boom to provide access to any point within the diameter of the boom. Crane lines are attached to the winch for hoisting loads.

U

uncased pile: Pile formed by drilling a hole into the ground and filling the hole with concrete without using a liner or tube. May be reinforced.

Underwriters' Laboratories, Inc.: Not-for-profit organization that examines and evaluates devices, systems, and materials to determine their degree of safety.

uniform load: Load such as stress or pressure that is distributed equally over an area.

utilization equipment: Equipment that uses electricity to produce motion, heat, light, or perform similar functions.

W

wall bearing construction: Construction integrating horizontal steel beams and joists into other construction methods such as masonry and reinforced concrete.

water cement ratio: Comparison of the weight of water to cement in a concrete or mortar mix. Expressed as a decimal.

watertight: Of tight construction so as to prevent entry of water into an enclosed area.

weatherproof: Constructed or protected so that exposure to the weather does not affect operation or planned use.

welded wire fabric: Heavy gauge wires joined in a grid used to reinforce and increase tensile strength of concrete.

5
A7.3

Index

H

I

J

L

M

O

P

Q

R

S

T

U

V

W